Strategic Human Resources in the Modern Service Economy

Varinder Singh Rana
https://orcid.org/0000-0001-6158-9195
City University, Ajman, UAE

Aisha Khan
https://orcid.org/0009-0009-7679-3661
Bath Spa University, UAE

IGI Global
Scientific Publishing
Publishing Tomorrow's Research Today

Vice President of Editorial	Melissa Wagner
Director of Acquisitions	Mikaela Felty
Director of Book Development	Jocelynn Hessler
Production Manager	Mike Brehm
Cover Design	Jose Rosado

Published in the United States of America by
IGI Global Scientific Publishing
701 East Chocolate Avenue
Hershey, PA, 17033, USA
Tel: 717-533-8845 | Fax: 717-533-7115
Website: https://www.igi-global.com E-mail: cust@igi-global.com

Library of Congress Cataloging-in-Publication Data

Names: Rana, Varinder Singh editor | Khan, Aisha, 1989- editor
Title: Strategic human resources in the modern service economy / edited by Varinder Singh Rana, Aisha Khan.
Description: Hershey, PA : IGI Global Scientific Publishing, [2026] | Includes bibliographical references and index. | Summary: "This book provides a focused understanding of how strategic human resource management can drive performance and innovation within service-based industries. It bridges the gap between academic research and real-world application by offering insights that are both evidence-based and industry relevant"-- Provided by publisher.
Identifiers: LCCN 2025038293 (print) | LCCN 2025038294 (ebook) | ISBN 9798337363950 hardcover | ISBN 9798337363967 paperback | ISBN 9798337363974 ebook
Subjects: LCSH: Service industries--Personnel management | Personnel management
Classification: LCC HD9980.5 .S763 2026 (print) | LCC HD9980.5 (ebook)
LC record available at https://lccn.loc.gov/2025038293
LC ebook record available at https://lccn.loc.gov/2025038294

British Cataloguing in Publication Data
A Cataloguing in Publication record for this book is available from the British Library.

Table of Contents

Detailed Table of Contents

The hospitality industry has shifted from product-centered models to service-oriented paradigms, where human capital is the central driver of organizational success. Grounded in the Resource-Based View (RBV), employees are positioned as valuable, rare, inimitable, and non-substitutable (VRIN) resources capable of sustaining long-term competitive advantage. A review of the literature highlights that High-Performance Work Systems (HPWS)—including selective hiring, comprehensive training, performance appraisal, and employee engagement—enhance service quality, guest satisfaction, and overall performance. Emotional intelligence that remain the most critical sources of value creation. Consequently, Human Resource Management (HRM) is redefined from an administrative function into a strategic role, emphasizing talent development, employer branding, and HR analytics. The study concludes that future competitiveness in hospitality depends on harmonizing digital transformation with emotionally intelligent and adaptable workforces to deliver unique, personalized, and memorable guest experiences

Drawing on social exchange theory and street-level bureaucracy perspectives, this study explores how Indian public banks strategically manage frontline staff to sustain performance amid economic instability. Using semi-structured interviews with 28 employees across four banks and analysing data through the Gioia methodology, the research identifies three factor categories: job-related (staff discretion, role nature and recruitment of qualified talent), learning-related (continuous development, rise of MBA programs, workforce resilience) and context-related (career advancement opportunities, enhanced incentives during turbulence). Together, these factors explain how employees maintain stable performance despite national challenges. The study recommends continued investment in training particularly in crisis management, customer relations, well-being and urges other public sector bodies to replicate banking best practices.

The study assesses the role of Service Economy in supporting diversity, inclusion, and equity in employee mental health in the Service Economy based on through an analysis of current literature it recreates the importance of well-being standards to effectively attract, support and upload a diverse workforce. Leadership is identified as a key driver in shaping organizational culture, with effective leaders serving as role models who promote values of respect, fairness, and inclusion. We have the opportunity human spirit, creativity, and a collective belief in a better future as powerful drivers of innovation. To create truly equitable Service Economy, it is critical to address the systems and processes that shape employee experiences. Trust in the process, transparency, and a commitment to the principles of equity are key to recovery and growth. Employers play a dual role they can either perpetuate or alleviate inequities, depending on how they respond to the unique experiences of individuals based on intersecting social identities such as gender, age. Ensure clear standards for workplace counsellors, and a commitment to employee mental health these are essential in diverse work progress, diversity alone does not guarantee positive outcomes it must be ensure all employees feel valued and supported. Moreover, equity ensuring fair treatment, access, and opportunity is essential in addressing systemic and achieving meaningful representation across all levels of a Service Economy. Real transformation starts with understanding our own mental health tuning into self-awareness and aligning behaviour with intentional growth. When individuals show up with clarity, teams thrive through deeper connection, stronger collaboration, and shared purpose. This same mindset should drive how organisation craft their policies and shape decisions rooted in awareness, built on empathy, and designed for new impact. They contribute diverse, valuable and competitively relevant insights into how work truly gets done shaping how processes are designed,

This chapter explores the positioning of education within the contemporary service economy, proposing a cross-disciplinary framework that integrates self-regulation, emotional labour and resilient engagement. Education increasingly conceptualised as a service, demands that educators navigate complex interpersonal and emotional dynamics while fostering meaningly learner outcomes. The chapter examines how adherence to display rules and the strategic management of emotions through surface and deep acting shape professional experiences, engagement and well-being. Self-regulation emerges as a central mechanism enabling educators to manage emotional dissonance, and sustain resilient engagement. Drawing on a combination of theoretical perspectives, empirical evidence, and illustrative case studies, the chapter highlights the interconnections between emotional labour, and educator resilience. The chapter provides a nuanced framework for enhancing educational service quality, teacher well-being and sustainable professional engagement in complex learning environments.

In today's fast-paced service-driven economy, technical expertise alone no longer guarantees success. Increasingly, it is the human side of work—our ability to understand emotions, communicate effectively, adapt, and build meaningful relationships—that drives real value within organizations. This chapter explores how emotional intelligence, and soft skills have become essential elements of strategic human resource development, especially in industries where service quality and customer experience are paramount. Rather than viewing soft skills as secondary or innate traits, the chapter highlights their growing significance as learnable, measurable competencies that contribute directly to employee performance, leadership effectiveness, and organizational resilience. Drawing from psychological theories and contemporary HR frameworks, the discussion examines how these capabilities can be purposefully cultivated through recruitment strategies, staff training, coaching programs, and performance evaluations.

Preface

The global service economy is undergoing an unprecedented transformation shaped by digitalization, artificial intelligence, global mobility, sustainability imperatives, and human-centered management philosophies. As service organizations evolve into technology-enabled, customer-centric ecosystems, the role of strategic human resource management (SHRM) has moved far beyond traditional administrative functions. HR is now positioned at the heart of organizational strategy—shaping talent capabilities, enabling innovation, driving sustainability, and building resilient workplaces.

This edited volume, Strategic Human Resources in the Modern Service Economy, brings together diverse international perspectives, empirical studies, conceptual models, and sector-specific insights that collectively redefine the strategic importance of human resources in today's dynamic service landscape. The chapters illuminate how HR leaders, scholars, and practitioners can navigate complexity, adopt emerging technologies, and advance sustainable growth while ensuring employee well-being and organizational excellence.

The book is structured to offer a broad yet coherent understanding of the future of HRM across hospitality, aviation, education, tourism, gig work, public service, and platform-based economies. The authors present research that explores intersections between technology, sustainability, emotional intelligence, DEI, leadership development, and organizational performance—thereby strengthening the theoretical and practical foundations of SHRM in the service economy.

CHAPTER OVERVIEWS

Chapter 1 analyzes human capital as a strategic asset in the hotel industry, highlighting the HR practices that drive service excellence.

Chapter 2 discusses strategic HRM as a tool to safeguard employee well-being during economic crises and uncertainty.

Chapter 3 addresses DEI frameworks as essential strategic drivers for equitable and inclusive service organizations.

Chapter 4 examines succession planning as a strategic imperative for leadership continuity and capability building.

Chapter 5 demonstrates how employee satisfaction influences hotel performance, drawing insights from the J&K hotel industry.

Chapter 6 offers a cross-disciplinary framework linking emotional labour, self-regulation, and resilient engagement in service-oriented education.

Chapter 7 highlights the strategic importance of emotional intelligence and soft skills development in contemporary service industries.

Chapter 8 examines emotional intelligence among gig workers and its role in achieving sustainable work–life balance.

Chapter 9 investigates the combined influence of employee engagement, emotional intelligence, and well-being on service-sector performance.

Chapter 10 provides insights into employee retention strategies in Tunisia's private sector through a comparative case study. Romania's Ministry of Internal Affairs as a case.

Chapter 11 introduces a faith-inspired approach to human capital development within the modern service sector from an Islamic perspective.

Together, these chapters provide a rich, multidimensional exploration of how strategic human resource management continues to evolve at the intersection of technology, sustainability, well-being, and organizational performance. This volume is designed to support academic researchers, industry leaders, HR practitioners, and policymakers seeking evidence-based insights and forward-thinking strategies for navigating the service economy of the future.

We extend our deepest appreciation to all contributing authors for their scholarly commitment and intellectual contributions, to the reviewers for their valuable feedback, and to IGI Global for supporting this initiative. Their collective effort has shaped a volume that meaningfully advances global HR scholarship and practice.

Varinder Rana
City University Ajman, UAE

Aisha Khan
Bath Spa University, UAE

Chapter 1
Human Capital as a Strategic Asset:
Redefining HR in the Modern Hotel Service Economy

Rameez Ahmad Mir
http://orcid.org/0009-0005-1442-4909
Central University of Kashmir, India

Shabir Ahmad Dar
Central University of Kashmir, India

Qazi Ruban
http://orcid.org/0000-0001-9463-3594
Central University of Kashmir, India

ABSTRACT

The hospitality industry has shifted from product-centered models to service-oriented paradigms, where human capital is the central driver of organizational success. Grounded in the Resource-Based View (RBV), employees are positioned as valuable, rare, inimitable, and non-substitutable (VRIN) resources capable of sustaining long-term competitive advantage. A review of the literature highlights that High-Performance Work Systems (HPWS)—including selective hiring, comprehensive training, performance appraisal, and employee engagement—enhance service quality, guest satisfaction, and overall performance. Emotional intelligence that remain the most critical sources of value creation. Consequently, Human Resource Management (HRM) is redefined from an administrative function into a strategic role, emphasizing talent development, employer branding, and HR analytics. The

DOI: 10.4018/979-8-3373-6395-0.ch001

study concludes that future competitiveness in hospitality depends on harmonizing digital transformation with emotionally intelligent and adaptable workforces to deliver unique, personalized, and memorable guest experiences

INTRODUCTION

For the past decade, the hospitality industry has grown consistently and transformed vertically, shifting decisively from a product-centric model to a service-oriented model. This transition has identified human capitals key role in organizational success, while, employees play on driving seat to satisfy guests during stay, brand differentiation, and long-term competitive advantage (Kandampully et al., 2018). Within the wider economic spectrum (Pine & Gilmore, 1998), this service-enabled sector is continuously challenged by increasing demand of guest's demand authentic, memorable, and personalized experiences rather than routine transactions. In this context, hotel employees play more advanced role far beyond their orthodox roles as service producers to become co-producers of value and architects of the overall and standard guest experience (Chathoth et al., 2016).

Due to the active role of human capital in hospitality originated from industry's dynamic characteristics. Such as; intangible, perishable, inseparable, simultaneity, variability and ownership nature of services, though the daily operational capability solely depends upon employee competency, performance, behavior, and emotional intelligence (Hochschild, 1983). In the era of automation where many physical elements of a hotel stay can be interfered by technology, the integration of knowledge, kills, creativity and commitment of the workforce thus plays a foundation for value preposition. So, the human element remains the most inimitable and enduring differentiator (Kandampully et al., 2018).

Theoretically grounded·on the Resource-Based View (RBV) of the firm (Barney, 1991), that suggests that sustained competitive advantage can be achieved by possessing resources that are Valuable, Rare, Inimitable, and Non-substitutable (VRIN). When human resource development of the hospitality is done through unique corporate culture and committed HR approach, definitely fulfills the VRIN criteria. Rivals can always imitate the physical facilities, menu, and services, but not the deeply rooted culture of genuine hospitality, employee engagement, and tacit knowledge (Lado & Wilson, 1994).

This statement is supported by empirical evidence. Outcome has suggested positive relationship between High Performance Work Systems (HPWS) based on selective hiring and recruitment, training and performance management activities and compensation and key outcomes such as revenue per available room (RevPAR), customer satisfaction, and profitability for hotels (Combs et al., 2006; Machado &

de Castro Junior, 2019). Employees are also identified as a key source for service innovation that allows hotels to modify and create new and unique service experiences based on customer demands (Nieves & Quintana, 2018).

Such factors require a new paradigm for the role of HR in the hospitality industry. The role of HR profession is no longer as administrative specific only but, have extended to roles like, strategic partner, change manager, and employee advocate (Ulrich & Dulebohn, 2015). Organisations can change the approach of being reactive to predictive by using HR analytics, leveraging data related to employee turnover, engagement, and performance to proactively address issues (Marler & Boudreau, 2017). Simultaneously, different approaches can be utilized to manage talent, including company branding, soft skills development, and retention strategies to offer psychological thrust, inclusive leadership, and cultural intelligence (Karatepe & Olugbade, 2016; Madera et al., 2019; Theurer et al., 2018).

In competition to the emerging trends, the technology is also gaining the significant place in transforming the management of human capital in the hospitality industry. Artificial intelligence plays a role in recruitment by assistance, workforce predictions, training modules using virtual reality, and mobile app learning (Garcia et al., 2019; Tambe et al., 2019) creates world full of scope for improvement in terms of increased efficiency and effective performance. The need is to integrate these technologies in a manner that augments human capabilities rather than replacing them.

The study supports the existing literature and suggest human capital as a strategic resource in the hospitality service industry. Further, the study analyses the impact of human capital on organizational performance using the RBV paradigm with in the changing nature of the strategic role of HR, because its focuses remains on the innovations and technologies needed for the effective exploitation of this key resource particularly in the hotel industry where quality service has been the fundamental determinant of success.

LITERATURE REVIEW

The hospitality sector is known as people-centric, and its dependence on human interaction makes it a primary model through which value is webbed. This defining character positions human capital the collective knowledge, skills, abilities, and attributes embedded within the workforce as a valuable and inimitable resource that drives service quality, guest experience, and customer loyalty (Kandampully et al., 2018). Since, previous studies have significantly highlighted that the human capital should not be regarded merely as an operational expense but rather as a foundational stone for the sustainable and competitive advantages (Barney & Wright, 1998; Lado & Wilson, 1994).

The Resource-Based View (RBV) of the firm (Barney, 1991) provides a strong theoretical foundation for this approach. Under RBV, a firm can sustain a competitive advantage only if its resources are characterized by the criteria of being Valuable, Rare, Inimitable, and Non-substitutable (VRIN). In the context of the hospitality industry, human capital that is developed through high-commitment HR and a unique organizational culture satisfies these criteria. Replication of other types of assets such as a hotel facility and marketing approach by a competitor may be easy and straightforward, but replicating the tacit knowledge and hard work of a competent and engaged employee is extremely difficult (Lado & Wilson, 1994). Indeed, as argued by Ferrary (2015), investment by a firm in a valuable and transferable asset such as human capital, especially within luxury hotels, increases firm performance by allowing organizations to capitalize on employee capabilities within networks and partnerships that can create value outside the firm as well.

The value of human capital as a strategic asset is best understood through the efficient implementation of Human Resource Management (HRM) systems. A rigors literature scan has empirically confirmed that High-Performance Work Systems (HPWS), which combine comprehensive training, selective staffing, compensation, performance-based and decision-making participation, positively impact key performance measures. Machado and de Castro Junior (2019) link these practices with strong occupancy levels and desired revenue per available room (RevPAR), while Combs et al. (2006) emphasize their contributions to increased employee productivity and decreases turnover ratio. Moreover, HRM systems are significant promotors for innovation. Nieves and Quintana (2018) argues human capital as the mediator between HR practices and innovation outcomes for hotels, thus emphasizing the value-adding co-creative capabilities of employees (Chathoth et al., 2016). The capability to innovate indicates a significant paradigm shift from considering only HR as an administrative function towards becoming a strategic partner as well. Never the less this strategic engagement is important for HR, because it promotes workforce capabilities with longer-term organizational goals, as further emphasized by Madera, Dawson, and Guchait (2017). Further it was supported by Gannon, Roper, and Doherty (2015), their study claimed that big brand multinational hotels acquire better market positioning likely due to integrating HR strategy with overall corporate planning. The difficulty of balancing standardized service delivery and local responsiveness. Rossidis, Belias, and Vasiliadis (2021) said in their study that brand consistency across international hotel brands can be achieved by strategizing the HR practices, flexibility can be achieved to address cultural variations, diverse labor market, and country-specific regulatory contexts. All the said changes are necessary for effective talent management particularly in the field of hospitality.

Abdullah et al. (2013) highlight the role of knowledge management systems in enhancing human capital by facilitating knowledge sharing, thereby enhancing service innovation and guest satisfaction. Digital platforms that regulate and portray best practices and tacit knowledge play a pivotal role in this process.

Integration of digitization in HRM, together ignite new dynamics in the human capital management in the hospitality industry. The extensive use of technology in the HR, such as virtual training, predictive workforce analytics, recruitment software's, and mobile app learning mediums is rewriting the definition and concept of talent management practices in the contemporary field of hospitality (Marler & Boudreau, 2017; Tambe et al., 2019). These digital advancements have proved long term benefits in terms of accuracy, effectiveness, and efficiency (Garcia et al., 2019).

CHALLENGES AND OPPORTUNITIES IN LEVERAGING HUMAN CAPITAL

This section explores the critical issues faced by the hotel industry in fully utilizing human capital resources. We also explore the innovation opportunities in human capital management. In addition to the typical issues in the hotel industry like seasonality and high turnover rates, there are many more complex issues arising in this industry. The gig economy is both an innovation in human resource management in terms of staffing adaptability and an issue in maintaining the hotel's culture. The integration of gig economy resources into the hotel team without undermining the hotel brand is an innovative human resource management issue (Spreitzer et al., 2017). Moreover, the high level of emotional work done in the hotel industry results in high risks of burnout. The innovative human resource management is now understanding the importance of employee mental health. They are now focusing on mental health programs in organizations (Krasnik et al., 2021). The scope remains in the leveraging diversity, inclusion, and equity (DEI) as a strategic asset. A diverse team of employees may better understand and deliver to a global clientele, promoting innovation and enhancing the brand's appeal as a socially responsible employer (Yang & Konrad, 2011).

The Impact of the COVID-19 Pandemic on Human Capital and HR Strategies

The COVID-19 pandemic leaves with visible level stress test for all humans epically for capital management in the hotel industry, acting as a catalyst for elevated change and creating a demand for re-evaluation of long-held practices. The crisis resulted in the immediate and massive layoffs, expected furloughs, and unprecedented operational disruptions, resulting in the degrading the quality and quantity of workforce (Baum et al., 2020). However, the after crisis period revealed deeper and lasting implications for HR.

1) COVID-19 crisis compliments and compounds in the problem already existing skilled labor shortages and elevates employee expectations such as; flexible working hours, job security, and compensation. This major shuffling compelled many skilled workers to take the decision of skip, switch or retain for comfortable, stable or flexible sectors. Among all who chose to stay with the hospitality industry preferred flexible working hours against long and break shift, higher wages and over time, advanced and improved safety majors, and a significant concern for well-being (Gursoy & Chi, 2020). This transaction had shifted power dynamics in the hospitalities labor market, forcing employers to offer more competitive and holistic employment value propositions.

2) The role of HR from strategic partner to crisis manager and chief empathy officer has been significantly transformed, earlier HR was kept to be responsible for develop, communicate and look after health and safety related policies and mitigate the work related stress, and navigate government and society related complex programs. Thus the critical importance of transparent communication and compassionate leadership was indicated (Wong et al., 2021).

3) The COVID-19 pandemic speeds up the need of adoption of technology like, new work models. Contactless check-ins, mobile keys, and room service robots reduced frontline interactions, changing the nature of service roles. Administrative staff working remotely, hotels were compelled to adopt cloud-based HR systems and digital workflows, the concept of remote work was considered obsolete in the past but seems much possible with the current trends (Ivanov et al., 2020).

4) The pandemic highlights the vital importance of employer branding and organizational trust. Hotels with policies to support their employees through the crisis with transparency, financial support where possible, and clear rehiring protocols are now better positioned to hunt for the talent. The pandemic evolves with clear understanding that a reputation for valuing people is not just an ethical stance but a critical strategic asset in the war for talent in the post-pandemic world.

OBJECTIVES

After reviewing the relevant literature, this study aims to answer the following objectives:

1. Analyze the changing landscape of the hospitality industry and its implications for human capital management.

2. Examine the strategic importance of human capital in creating sustainable competitive advantage in the hotel sector.
3. Explore the evolving role of HR in aligning human capital strategies with organizational goals.
4. Discuss best practices for developing, managing, and retaining talent in the modern hotel service economy.
5. Investigate the impact of technology and innovation on human capital management in hospitality.

METHODOLOGY: A SYSTEMATIC NARRATIVE REVIEW

The study employee's systematic literature review, using comprehensive search of peer reviewed research articles across all major research data bases such as, Scopus, Web of Science, and ProQuest, by using key words like, "HR, Human Resource, Human Capital, Service Economy, Hotel, Hotel Employees, Hospitality, and Technology."

The studies focused on human capital as an asset in hotel sector, was included for the screening in the current studies quality and applicability, Findings were evaluated using narrative synthesis technique, The new systematic review was developed and consolidated by identifying and organizing key topics and areas:

1. Formulation of the Research Question and Scope:

The review conducted was guided by the five primary objectives of the study, which collectively address the central question: "How can human capital be effectively leveraged as a strategic asset through HRM in the modern hotel service economy to achieve sustainable competitive advantage?" The scope was limited to the hospitality industry, with a specific focus on the hotel sector, and to literature published within the last 15 years (2009-2024) to ensure contemporary relevance.

2. Literature Search and Identification:

Systematic search was conducted across all the major academic databases covering, Scopus, Web of Science, EBSCOhost (e.g., Business Source Complete, Hospitality & Tourism Index), and Google Scholar. To capture the multidisciplinary nature of the topic, search terms were combined from three clusters:

- Context: "hospitality*", "hotel", "lodging", "service economy".

- Concept: “human capital”, “strategic asset”, “talent management”, “HRM”, “human resource management”.
- Outcome: “competitive advantage”, “organizational performance”, “innovation”, “customer satisfaction”, “employee retention”, “turnover”.

Boolean operators (AND, OR) were used to combine these terms (e.g., “strategic HRM” AND “hotel” AND “performance”). The search was initially conducted for article titles, keywords, and abstracts.

3. Screening and Selection Criteria:

The initial search yielded a large number of results. To maintain focus and quality, the following inclusion and exclusion criteria were applied:

- Inclusion Criteria:
  Inclusion criteria included peer reviewed journal articles, book chapters and conference proceedings, selected literature was explicitly focused on the hospitality or hotel sector, further it was refined with the criterion of published in the English language from 2009 to 2024. Further studies that empirically examined the link between HRM practices, human capital and organizational outcomes.
- Exclusion Criteria:
  Literature that was not as per above inclusion criteria was excluded from the current study, such as articles focused on other industries without specific hospitality implications. Publications not written in English. Non-peer-reviewed commentaries, editorials, or magazine articles

The screening process involved reviewing titles and abstracts against the criteria, followed by a full-text review of the remaining articles. This process ensured the final corpus of literature was both relevant and of high academic standard.

4. Analysis and Synthesis:

Thematic analysis approach the most appropriate such studies, was used to analyze the selected literature (Braun & Clarke, 2006). An initial scanning and reading guided to identify key themes and patterns and then coded. These codes were then grouped into the major thematic sections that lead the structure for this study:

- The Strategic Value of Human Capital
- The Evolution of HR as a Strategic Partner

- Talent Management Strategies
- Technology and Innovation in HRM
- The Impact of the COVID-19 Pandemic
- Future Trends and Challenges

To reach the conclusion and gaps from the literature, results from the various studies were examined, contrasted, and synthesized within each subject. After summarizing, the synthesis was sought to insight fresh interpretative narrative that focuses on the body of knowledge present and lays down foundation for future studies and applications.

Limitation: Even a through was made still, some pertinent research could have been missed unintentionally. Additionally, a geographic bias may exist due to dependence on English language. However, these risks are reduced and a representative picture of the topic is guaranteed by the methodical procedure.

RESULTS AND FINDINGS

The analysis of previous available literature indicates a critical evidence of emotional intelligence acts catalyst to integrate artificial intelligence and technology in the hospitality sector (R.A., & Rastogi, E. 2025), (Garcia & Lee, 2022). The findings depict a clear contrast: While AI can be best used for jobs requiring data analytics, computational accuracy, and automated efficiency, due to less need of socioemotional aspects that value service experiences. (Ivanov & Webster, 2019). This study suggests emotional intelligence is the significant antidote to technology integration (Prentice, 2020).

The results are listed into four primary thematic findings:

1. The Primacy of EI in Guest Experience and Satisfaction

The study demonstrates that the attributes underpinned by EI such as empathetic engagement, authentic trust-building, and the intricate regulation of emotions during service recovery are very difficult to replace by AI (Kim et al., 2021). While, AI can personalize on certain areas such AI can personalize room's temperature, recommend a restaurant based on past behavior, but, it cannot perceive a guest's unspoken disappointment that can be judged from gestures only and need human intelligence to handle or respond with genuine compassion to a service failure (Tung & Law, 2022). It is evident from studies done over customer satisfaction and indicates that interactions staffed by high-EI employees consistently result in higher guest loyalty, positive reviews, and a stronger perception of brand value, highlighting a direct correlation between EI competencies and superior experiential outcomes (Majeed et al., 2023).

2. EI as a Critical Moderator in AI Implementation and Acceptance

A significant finding of this study is that the efficacy of AI-enabled tools is not absolute but is instead moderated by the emotional intelligence of the employees who manage and implement them (Gursoy et al., 2019). For example, an AI based platform such as a chatbot may handle a routine booking efficiently, but a complex or emotionally issue needs an EI-equipped employee to simmer the hot situation, interpret subtleties, and provide a satisfactory resolution (Li et al., 2021).

3. Organizational Impact:

Long term employment and leadership skills for organizations, this study reveals a significant positive relationship between investment in emotional intelligence development and key human resource metrics (Kotsou et al., 2019). Employers must reduce employee turnover intentions when they implement organized EI training programs and incorporate these abilities into leadership development frameworks. (Miao et al., 2022, Karim & Weisz, 2021). Furthermore, leaders demonstrating high EI are better equipped to manage diverse teams, drive change management initiatives involving new technology, and inspire a customer-centric culture, thereby creating a sustainable competitive advantage (Salovey & Grewal, 2020).

4. The Strategic Imperative: Synthesizing Technological and Human Capital

Adoption of new technologies and human services alone cannot determine long-term competitiveness. (Ivanov et al., 2023). Instead, it depends upon the ability of organization to architect between AI-enabled efficiency and EI-enabled empathy (Prentice & Nguyen, 2021). Strategical application of AI manages volumetric, data-intensive tasks with the most success because they free up human resources to concentrate on high-value, emotionally complicated interactions. (Tussyadiah, 2020). This strategic harmonization is identified as the new cornerstone for building resilience, ensuring customer loyalty, and achieving market differentiation (Kandampully et al., 2021).

PRACTICAL IMPLICATIONS

The results of this study validates human capital been a foundation for competitive advantage in the modern hospitality service economy. Advancement of technologies and changing work dynamics with evolving social norms have changed industry evolution, scoping both for enormous difficulties and previously unknown possibilities. Hence, three key practice related implications and a well-defined future research directions are brought from this endeavor.

First, hotels should target broad area of focus and strategic integration of the HR function. Human resource management must think out of box beyond the conventional administrative focus and concentrate on the key role as a strategic motivator of business objectives if it is to be competitive. The key area of focus should be the coordination between strategic goals and workforce capabilities, preparedness for operations and man power development for service enhancement (Madera et al., 2017; Ulrich & Dulebohn, 2015). Such integration plays a vital role in mitigating the sensitivity and dynamics landscape.

Second, in the high demanding sector of hospitality it is very difficult to retain talent for long time hence it increases turn over ration to mitigate globally HR professionals are in race to find and retain talent it further demands holistic developmental programmes and consistent commitment because in this sector irregular training initiatives seems inadequate. Instead, sector should invest in sustained, multi-dimensional development programs. (Sharma et al., 2021). Increasingly, the upgradation of skill enabled organizations requires a paradigm shift, moving beyond traditional job description to flexible task and project allocation based on individual competencies. This likely foster inter-departmental mobility and organizational resilience (World Economic Forum, 2020).

Third, the integration of technologies may be done in a steady and guided way of human centric philosophy. The adaptation of Artificial Intelligence (AI), automation, and digitization promises substantial efficiency gains and strategic insights, yet it should play a role of augment human potential rather than replace it (Raisch & Krakowski, 2021). However, the USP of hospitality lies in empathy, interpersonal service areas where technology should play a supporting hand, rather than replace, human services (Larivière et al., 2017). The optimal model is a collaborative effort of human and technology(AI) by which predictive analytics are integrated with the creativity and emotional intelligence of employees.

Above implications highlights areas for future researches. Examining on the impact of gig-based employment models on employee loyalty and service quality in hotels if explored in future may provide valuable guidance and future (Tambe et al., 2019). One of the interesting area would be return on investment of ESG-focused HR practices. longitudinal study design may result in different dimensions by comparing the effectiveness of skills-based organizational models with traditional hierarchical structures in hospitality, may provide more valuable guidance for researchers and practitioners.

In conclusion, the guidance for hotel leaders and HR professionals is clear: human capital is the golden strategic asset. Its thoughtful, future-oriented management strategically integrated, continuously developed, and technologically augmented without sacrificing the human essence constitutes the essential prerequisite for achieving sustainable competitive advantage in the experience-driven hospitality economy of the future.

DISCUSSION

The screening of the literature evident human capital as a fundamental for competitive advantage in hospitality, may be due to industry's service dependency, labor-intensive in nature. In addition to physical or financial assets, the skills, knowledge, and emotional intelligence of workface directly plays in shaping the service experience and customer loyalty.

First, integration of human resource is necessary and hotel administration no longer view HR as purely administrative concern but keeps central to organizational strategy, shaping culture, employee behavior, and service upgradation. Hoque (2013) argues that integrating of HR into strategic decision-making allows firms to better align human capital with market needs, improving adaptability in dynamic environments.

Second, it still remains difficult to retain and manage talent in the hospitality industry. High turnover, seasonal fluctuations, and labor shortages over rates by the COVID-19 pandemic make it difficult for hotels to retain professional and skilled employees. However, research suggests that ventures investing in employee engagement programs, training, leadership and adaptability helps achieve higher retention and innovation capacity (Nieves & Quintana, 2018).

Third, Technology is applied in HRM to transform workforce management. Predictive analytics may be used to to analyze and understand employee needs and motivation, for recruitment and selection Artificial Intelligence can be proved helping hand. One side these developments increase efficiency, but same time they also raise questions about containing the human centric values that foster hospitality operations (Madera et al., 2017).

Fourth, the globalization of hotel brands requires complete balance between standardization and localization in HR policies and practices. While global policies concentrate on brand consistency, local adaptation is essential to reflect cultural norms and labor market conditions (Rossidis et al., 2021).

Finally, this study proposes sustainability as a critical theme. Literature suggests that investing in sustainable HR practices such as green HRM, diversity initiatives, and fair labor policies, not only helps in corporate reputation but also contributes to long-term resilience (Machado & de Castro Junior, 2019).

CONCLUSION

Emotional intelligence appears with a key role in the process of AI integration in the field of hospitality in the current study. While artificial intelligence supports to increases operational efficiency during hospitality operation, enhances personalization, and emotional intelligence plays in creating the radius by utilizing the employee capabilities of personalization by encompassing trust, empathy, relationships. The amalgamation of EI and AI demonstrates crucial potential for improvement in organizational performance, elevates level of employee well-being, and enhances guest satisfaction.

To stay in the competition, it requires implementation of multi layered strategical precession such as, integration of artificial intelligence to increase efficiency and fostering emotional intelligence to support and enrich human interactions. Implementation of Such balanced approach may help not only in sustainable growth and competitive advantage but also in ethical considerations and long-term value creation. Ultimately, the technology dependence may create a dim in future of the hospitality in order to avoid certain possibilities it is necessary to harmonize digital innovation with emotional intelligence. Development of emotionally intelligent leadership and conducive workplace cultures, may help the sector to gain the upper hand in ethical challenges, empower its workforce, and deliver service experiences that are technologically advanced and authentically human.

REFERENCES

Abdullah, Z., Ahsan, N., & Alam, S. S. (2013). The effect of human capital and knowledge management on organizational performance. *Proceedings of the International Conference on Social Science Research.*

Barney, J. (1991). Firm resources and sustained competitive advantage. *Journal of Management, 17*(1), 99–120. DOI: 10.1177/014920639101700108

Barney, J. B., & Wright, P. M. (1998). On becoming a strategic partner: The role of human resources in gaining competitive advantage. *Human Resource Management, 37*(1), 31–46. DOI: 10.1002/(SICI)1099-050X(199821)37:1<31::AID-HRM4>3.0.CO;2-W

Baum, T., Mooney, S. K., Robinson, R. N., & Solnet, D. (2020). COVID-19's impact on the hospitality workforce–new crisis or amplification of the norm? *International Journal of Contemporary Hospitality Management, 32*(9), 2813–2829. DOI: 10.1108/IJCHM-04-2020-0314

Chathoth, P., Altinay, L., Harrington, R. J., Okumus, F., & Chan, E. S. (2016). Co-production versus co-creation: A process based continuum in the hotel service context. *International Journal of Hospitality Management, 32*, 11–20. DOI: 10.1016/j.ijhm.2012.03.009

Combs, J., Liu, Y., Hall, A., & Ketchen, D. (2006). How much do high-performance work practices matter? A meta-analysis of their effects on organizational performance. *Personnel Psychology, 59*(3), 501–528. DOI: 10.1111/j.1744-6570.2006.00045.x

Ferrary, M. (2015). Investing in transferable strategic human capital through alliances in the luxury hotel industry. *Journal of Knowledge Management, 19*(5), 1006–1023. DOI: 10.1108/JKM-01-2015-0045

Gannon, J. M., Roper, A., & Doherty, L. (2015). Strategic human resource management: Insights from the international hotel industry. *International Journal of Hospitality Management, 47*, 65–75. DOI: 10.1016/j.ijhm.2015.03.003

Garcia, M. B., Revano, T. F., & Contreras, G. S. (2019). Microlearning as a learning tool for hospitality training. *Journal of Human Resources in Hospitality & Tourism, 18*(4), 516–533.

Garcia, R., & Lee, C. (2022). Beyond automation: The role of emotional intelligence in the digitalized hospitality sector. *Journal of Hospitality and Tourism Technology, 13*(1), 45–62.

Gursoy, D., & Chi, C. G. (2020). Effects of COVID-19 pandemic on hospitality industry: A review of the current situations and a research agenda. *Journal of Hospitality Marketing & Management, 29*(5), 527–529. DOI: 10.1080/19368623.2020.1788231

Gursoy, D., Chi, O. H., Lu, L., & Nunkoo, R. (2019). Consumers' acceptance of artificially intelligent (AI) device use in service delivery. *International Journal of Information Management, 49*, 157–169. DOI: 10.1016/j.ijinfomgt.2019.03.008

Hoque, K. (2013). *Human resource management in the hotel industry: Strategy, innovation and performance*. Routledge., DOI: 10.4324/9780203020869

Ivanov, S., Gretzel, U., Berezina, K., Sigala, M., & Webster, C. (2023). Progress on robotics in hospitality and tourism: A review of the literature. *Journal of Hospitality and Tourism Technology, 14*(2), 145–183.

Ivanov, S., & Webster, C. (2019). Conceptual framework of the use of robots, artificial intelligence and service automation in travel, tourism, and hospitality companies. In S. Ivanov & C. Webster (Eds.), *Robots, Artificial Intelligence, and Service Automation in Travel, Tourism and Hospitality*. Emerald Publishing Limited. DOI: 10.1108/978-1-78756-687-320191001

Ivanov, S., Webster, C., & Stoilova, E. (2020). The impact of automation and AI on the hospitality workforce. In *Robots, artificial intelligence, and service automation in travel, tourism and hospitality*. Emerald Publishing Limited.

Kandampully, J., Zhang, T., & Bilgihan, A. (2018). Customer loyalty: A review and future directions with a special focus on the hospitality industry. *International Journal of Contemporary Hospitality Management, 30*(4), 2194–2214.

Kandampully, J., Zhang, T., & Bilgihan, A. (2021). Emotional intelligence: The essential ingredient for success in the hospitality industry. *Journal of Hospitality and Tourism Insights, 4*(4), 400–416.

Karatepe, O. M., & Olugbade, O. A. (2016). The mediating role of work engagement in the relationship between high-performance work practices and job outcomes of employees in Nigeria. *International Journal of Contemporary Hospitality Management, 28*(10), 2350–2371. DOI: 10.1108/IJCHM-03-2015-0145

Karim, J., & Weisz, R. (2021). Emotional intelligence as a moderator of stressor–strain relationships: A study of managers in a developing country. *Journal of Managerial Psychology, 36*(3), 234–247.

Kim, M., Kim, J., & Wong, A. K. F. (2021). The impact of artificial intelligence and emotional intelligence on customer satisfaction in the hotel industry. *Journal of Hospitality Marketing & Management, 30*(6), 677–702.

Kotsou, I., Mikolajczak, M., Heeren, A., Grégoire, J., & Leys, C. (2019). Improving emotional intelligence: A systematic review of existing work and future challenges. *Emotion Review, 11*(2), 151–165. DOI: 10.1177/1754073917735902

Krasnik, M. S., Verma, R., & Andersson, T. D. (2021). Employee well-being and burnout in the hospitality industry: A systematic review. *International Journal of Hospitality Management, 94*, 102824.

Lado, A. A., & Wilson, M. C. (1994). Human resource systems and sustained competitive advantage: A competency-based perspective. *Academy of Management Review, 19*(4), 699–727. DOI: 10.2307/258742

Larivière, B., Bowen, D. A., Andreassen, T. W., Kunz, W., Sirianni, N. J., Voss, C., Wünderlich, N. V., & De Keyser, A. (2017). Service Encounter 2.0: An investigation into the roles of technology, employees and customers. *Journal of Business Research, 79*, 238–246. DOI: 10.1016/j.jbusres.2017.03.008

Li, J., Bonn, M. A., & Ye, B. H. (2021). The effect of emotional intelligence on turnover intention in the hospitality industry: The mediating role of job satisfaction. *International Journal of Contemporary Hospitality Management, 33*(4), 1259–1278.

Machado, C., & de Castro, P. J. Junior. (2019). Strategic human resource management and hotel performance: A systematic literature review. *Journal of Human Resources in Hospitality & Tourism, 18*(4), 434–460.

Machado, L. A. N., & de Castro, D. F. L., Junior. (2019). Strategic human resources management and hotel performance. *European Journal of Tourism, Hospitality and Recreation, 9*(2), 117–130. https://tmstudies.net/index.php/ectms/article/view/1065

Madera, J. M., Dawson, M., & Guchait, P. (2017). The role of HR in promoting ethical leadership and psychological safety in the hospitality industry. *Cornell Hospitality Quarterly, 58*(3), 239–249.

Madera, J. M., Dawson, M., Guchait, P., & Belarmino, A. M. (2017). Strategic human resources management research in hospitality and tourism: A review of current literature and suggestions for the future. *International Journal of Contemporary Hospitality Management, 29*(1), 48–67. DOI: 10.1108/IJCHM-02-2016-0051

Madera, J. M., Dawson, M., Guchait, P., & Belarmino, A. M. (2019). Strategic human resources management research in hospitality and tourism: A review of current literature and suggestions for the future. *International Journal of Contemporary Hospitality Management, 31*(1), 439–462.

Majeed, S., Kim, W. G., & Kim, H. (2023). The role of emotional intelligence in frontline employees' customer-oriented behaviors. *Journal of Services Marketing*, *37*(1), 78–92.

Marler, J. H., & Boudreau, J. W. (2017). An evidence-based review of HR Analytics. *International Journal of Human Resource Management*, *28*(1), 3–26. DOI: 10.1080/09585192.2016.1244699

Miao, C., Humphrey, R. H., & Qian, S. (2022). A meta-analysis of emotional intelligence and work attitudes. *Journal of Occupational and Organizational Psychology*, *95*(1), 1–27.

Mir, R. A., & Rastogi, E.R.A. (2025). Mitigating employee turnover in hospitality industry through emotional intelligence: Evidence from Kashmir India. *Geo Journal of Tourism and Geosites*, *58*(1), 250–270. DOI: 10.30892/gtg.58144-1429

Nieves, J., & Quintana, A. (2018). Human resource practices and innovation in the hotel industry: The mediating role of human capital. *Tourism and Hospitality Research*, *18*(1), 72–83. DOI: 10.1177/1467358415624137

Pine, B. J., & Gilmore, J. H. (1998). Welcome to the experience economy. *Harvard Business Review*, *76*, 97–105. PMID: 10181589

Prentice, C. (2020). Emotional intelligence and the hospitality workforce: A systematic review. *Anatolia*, *31*(2), 331–342.

Prentice, C., & Nguyen, M. (2021). The role of emotional intelligence in the service encounter: A systematic review. *Journal of Service Theory and Practice*, *31*(1), 1–24.

Raisch, S., & Krakowski, S. (2021). Artificial intelligence and management: The automation–augmentation paradox. *Academy of Management Review*, *46*(1), 192–210. DOI: 10.5465/amr.2018.0072

Rossidis, I., Belias, D., & Vasiliadis, L. (2021). Strategic human resource management in the international hospitality industry: An extensive literature review. In Kavoura, A., Kefallonitis, E., & Theodoridis, P. (Eds.), *Strategic innovative marketing and tourism* (pp. 173–182). Springer., DOI: 10.1007/978-3-030-72469-6_22

Rossidis, I., Belias, D., & Vasiliadis, L. (2021). Standardization vs. adaptation of HRM practices in the hospitality industry: A systematic literature review. *Tourism and Hospitality*, *2*(4), 365–379.

Rossidis, I., Belias, D., & Vasiliadis, L. (2021). Standardization vs. localization in HRM: A review of the literature in the hospitality context. *Journal of Tourism. Heritage & Services Marketing*, *7*(1), 3–10.

Salovey, P., & Grewal, D. (2020). The science of emotional intelligence. *Current Directions in Psychological Science*, *29*(6), 531–535.

Sharma, A., Shin, H., Santa-María, M. J., & Nicolau, J. L. (2021). The role of emotional intelligence in the service recovery performance of hospitality employees. *International Journal of Hospitality Management*, *94*, 102837.

Sharma, P., Kong, T. T. C., & Kingshott, R. P. (2021). Internal service quality as a driver of employee satisfaction, commitment and performance: Exploring the role of employee readiness for change. *Journal of Service Management*, *32*(1), 118–140.

Spreitzer, G. M., Cameron, L., & Garrett, L. (2017). Alternative work arrangements: Two images of the new world of work. *Annual Review of Organizational Psychology and Organizational Behavior*, *4*(1), 473–499. DOI: 10.1146/annurev-orgpsych-032516-113332

Tambe, P., Cappelli, P., & Yakubovich, V. (2019). Artificial intelligence in human resources management: Challenges and a path forward. *California Management Review*, *61*(4), 15–42. DOI: 10.1177/0008125619867910

Theurer, C. P., Tumasjan, A., Welpe, I. M., & Lievens, F. (2018). Employer branding: A brand equity-based literature review and research agenda. *International Journal of Management Reviews*, *20*(1), 155–179. DOI: 10.1111/ijmr.12121

Tung, V. W. S., & Law, R. (2022). The potential for tourism and hospitality experience research using artificial intelligence. *Journal of Travel Research*, *61*(4), 735–739.

Tussyadiah, I. P. (2020). A review of research into automation in tourism: Launching the Annals of Tourism Research Curated Collection on Artificial Intelligence and Robotics in Tourism. *Annals of Tourism Research*, *81*, 102883. DOI: 10.1016/j.annals.2020.102883

Ulrich, D., & Dulebohn, J. H. (2015). Are we there yet? What's next for HR? *Human Resource Management Review*, *25*(2), 188–204. DOI: 10.1016/j.hrmr.2015.01.004

Wong, A. K. F., Kim, S., Kim, J., & Han, H. (2021). How the COVID-19 pandemic affected hotel employee stress: The moderating role of emotional intelligence. *International Journal of Hospitality Management*, *93*, 102798. DOI: 10.1016/j.ijhm.2020.102798 PMID: 36919180

World Economic Forum. (2020). *The future of jobs report 2020*. World Economic Forum.

Yang, Y., & Konrad, A. M. (2011). Understanding diversity management practices: Implications of institutional theory and resource-based theory. *Group & Organization Management*, *36*(1), 6–38. DOI: 10.1177/1059601110390997

Chapter 2
Navigating Economic Uncertainty Through Strategic Human Resource Management:
Safeguarding Employee Well-Being

Navneet Ranjan
http://orcid.org/0009-0000-2048-0513
Medhavi Skills University, India

Atanu Bhattacharya
http://orcid.org/0000-0003-2856-031X
ITM Vocational University, Vadodara, India

Uday Pratap Singh
http://orcid.org/0000-0003-0632-9934
Amity University, Jaipur, India

Manidipa Mukherjee
http://orcid.org/0009-0009-5182-2390
International School of Hospitality Management, Kolkata, India

Sanjit Cletus Gomes
http://orcid.org/0009-0000-3180-953X
International School of Hospitality Management, Kolkata, India

DOI: 10.4018/979-8-3373-6395-0.ch002

ABSTRACT

Drawing on social exchange theory and street-level bureaucracy perspectives, this study explores how Indian public banks strategically manage frontline staff to sustain performance amid economic instability. Using semi-structured interviews with 28 employees across four banks and analysing data through the Gioia methodology, the research identifies three factor categories: job-related (staff discretion, role nature and recruitment of qualified talent), learning-related (continuous development, rise of MBA programs, workforce resilience) and context-related (career advancement opportunities, enhanced incentives during turbulence). Together, these factors explain how employees maintain stable performance despite national challenges. The study recommends continued investment in training particularly in crisis management, customer relations, well-being and urges other public sector bodies to replicate banking best practices.

INTRODUCTION

In the contemporary world, societies are facing a continuous series of unpredictable challenges, ranging from climate change and global health crises to political turmoil in developing regions, escalating terrorist threats and violent armed conflicts (Kwong et al., 2021; Mousa & Abdelgaffar, 2023). These issues have contributed significantly to economic instability across nations (Arslan et al., 2022). Scholars widely agree that for organizations of all kinds, establishing a strategic human resource management (SHRM) framework is crucial for ensuring a reliable workforce, maintaining adaptability in volatile circumstances and sustaining competitive advantage (Kabalina et al., 2019; Wright & Snell, 1998). SHRM was described as "the pattern of planned human resource deployment and activities intended to enable an organization to achieve its goals" (Wright & McMahan, 1992). SHRM involves examining HRM systems and their connections with broader organizational structures, both internal and external, as well as recognizing the diverse actors who shape HR practices and the stakeholders who assess organizational performance and long-term viability (Jackson et al., 2014).

Strategic human resource management emphasizes aligning HR systems—such as employee competencies, knowledge, and behaviour—with the organizational environment in which they operate (Cooke et al., 2021; Delery & Gupta, 2016; Sikora et al., 2016). This alignment explains why HR frameworks created in Western contexts may not always be suitable for developing countries (Mousa & Samara, 2022). From the perspective of neo-institutional theory (DiMaggio & Powell, 1991), organizations must adapt to their external environment and address the diverse expectations of stakeholders, which requires organizational members to demonstrate flexibility and adaptability (Zucker, 1991). Since organizations fundamentally depend on their workforce for survival (Kwong et al., 2021), resilience during turbulent times or extreme events becomes essential (Mousa, 2024a; Mousa, 2024b). Nonetheless, many employees struggle to perform effectively in uncertain conditions (Reade, 2009), often due to elevated stress and burnout (Ererdi et al., 2022). In some cases, staff even resort to sick leave during crises (Howie, 2007). Conversely, employees who are strategically trained to navigate complexity and withstand challenging circumstances are more likely to sustain consistent performance (Mousa, 2024a; Mousa, 2024b).

The relationship between strategic human resource management and both individual and organizational performance has long been established (Collins, 2021; Larsson et al., 2022). Empirical evidence from earlier studies (Bowen & Ostroff, 2004; Jiang et al., 2012; Paauwe, 2009; Paauwe et al., 2013) confirms that specific HR practices are positively linked to firm performance. Yet, most of this research has been conducted in Western contexts and under stable conditions, predating recent disruptions such as the COVID-19 pandemic, the Russia–Ukraine conflict and the war in Gaza (Akwei & Nwachukwu, 2023). Scholars have also highlighted the scarcity and limited development of conceptual and empirical work on SHRM (Akwei & Nwachukwu, 2023; Ogunyomi & Bruning, 2016). In particular, researchers (Akwei & Nwachukwu, 2023; Anibaba & Adeleye, 2014; Dibben et al., 2017) emphasize the need for examining SHRM practices within African nations in the post-colonial period. Along similar lines, researchers call for investigating the role of SHRM in helping employees adjust to extreme workplace demands (Mousa, 2024a; Mousa, 2024b). More than a decade earlier, research had already questioned the applicability of Western-developed SHRM models to Asian contexts (Adeleye, 2011), while others encouraged further exploration of how religious beliefs may shape HR strategies (Okpilike, 2012).

Asian nations vary considerably in terms of political stability, bureaucratic structures and levels of economic development, with differences evident in factors such as population size, corruption levels, youth demographics, fertility rates and the volatility of business environments (Gok & Gok, 2016; Pandit et al., 2018). Despite this diversity, there remains a scarcity of qualitative research on strategic human resource management (SHRM) (Larsson et al., 2022), particularly within Asian contexts (Akwei & Nwachukwu, 2023) and even fewer studies examining SHRM during periods of uncertainty (Mousa, 2024a; Mousa, 2024b). To address this gap, the present study investigates an underexplored setting by examining how public banks in India—a South-East Asian country grappling with prolonged economic instability—strategically manage their frontline employees. Specifically, the study seeks to answer the question: How do Indian public banks sustain frontline employee performance in the face of economic uncertainty through SHRM practices?

Unlike earlier research, the contribution of this paper lies in pinpointing the key factor influencing SHRM under conditions of economic instability, specifically within the Indian context – a South-East Asian nation currently challenged by foreign currency shortages and rising public debt. The study further illustrates that employee resilience plays a central role in driving SHRM and in turn, organizational performance during times of economic volatility. In addition, it demonstrates how continuous skill development through training and the prudent exercise of discretionary power by public bank employees enhance SHRM practices in such environments. Accordingly, this research offers valuable insights for public sector institutions across the Global South that operate under conditions of heightened economic uncertainty.

LITERATURE REVIEW

Strategic Human Resource Management (SHRM) is a long-term approach to managing employees, emphasizing factors such as commitment, organizational culture and quality, all of which support an organization's long-term goals (Chartered Institute of Personnel and Development, 2017). This approach aims to ensure that employees possess the skills, motivation and competencies required to adapt to changes both within the organization and in the external market (Haque & Khan, 2023; Mousa, 2024a; Mousa, 2024b; Mousa, 2025; Storey et al., 2019). SHRM highlights how an organization's strategic priorities can influence traditional HR functions, including recruitment, placement, training, motivation and compensation (Dello Russo et al., 2018). Research suggests that HR systems impact strategic organizational outcomes through employee-related variables, such as attitudes and behaviours (Cooke et al., 2021). These systems typically operate along three dimensions: enhancing skills, fostering motivation and providing opportunities (Jiang et al., 2012). Decisions regarding HR system improvements are shaped by both internal factors, such as organizational size, budget, structure, and strategy and external factors, including national culture, economic conditions, political stability, competitive pressures and regulatory frameworks (Jackson & Schuler, 1995; King, 2017; Li et al., 2015; Wallo & Coetzer, 2023). The key distinction between traditional HRM and SHRM is that the latter explicitly considers organizational and environmental influences on employee performance (Delery & Roumpi, 2017), demonstrating how business strategy can guide HR practices to affect overall organizational performance.

SHRM reflects the link between HRM practices and organizational performance (Haddock-Millar et al., 2016; Roumpi & Delery, 2019; Roumpi et al., 2020). It takes into account various contextual factors, such as labour market fluctuations, economic stability, and market conditions (Jiang & Messersmith, 2018). SHRM is essential for organizations to effectively navigate extreme events, geopolitical tensions, and uncertain environments (Lakshman et al., 2022). To equip HR personnel to address the negative impacts of major challenges or crises, several scholars (Chang et al., 2013; Delery & Doty, 1996; King et al., 2016; Lakshman et al., 2022; Lepak & Shaw, 2008; Wright & Snell, 1998) emphasize the relevance of dynamic capability theory (Mousa & Samara, 2022). This theory highlights the need for organizations to continuously monitor their environment and update employees' skills and competencies to manage transformations or market shifts effectively. In particular, dynamic capability theory enables organizational members to maintain flexibility and continuously adapt their skills and behaviours to meet the demands of an ever-changing environment (Chang et al., 2013; Jiang & Messersmith, 2018; Roumpi, 2023; Zahoor et al., 2024).

Employees are able to navigate difficulties and uncertainties effectively only when the organizational culture promotes openness, risk-taking and a willingness to embrace change (Cooke et al., 2019). The uncertainties faced by employers can stem from both isolated incidents and routine, unpredictable events (Branicki et al., 2019; Delery & Roumpi, 2017; Murphy et al., 2017). To address this, organizations should implement uncertainty preparedness programs that focus on building resilience and enabling employees to respond swiftly to unforeseen major events (Arslan et al., 2022; Britt et al., 2016; Coutu, 2002). A primary benefit of applying SHRM and fostering employee adaptability is the development of individual resilience, defined as the capacity of employees to leverage resources to continually adjust and thrive at work, even under challenging conditions (Kuntz et al., 2016). Employee resilience reflects the ability to overcome obstacles, recover from setbacks and endure work-related challenges (Cooper et al., 2014; Williams & Shepherd, 2016), making it a valuable outcome of HR investments. Supporting resilience involves providing flexible work arrangements, ongoing organizational support, continuous learning opportunities, reasonable workloads, appropriate work hours and motivational mechanisms (Bardoel et al., 2014; Frankl, 2017; Mousa & Samara, 2022; Pollard, 2001). Importantly, individual resilience serves as a foundation for organizational resilience, which refers to an organization's ability to adapt its processes under difficult conditions, recover from adverse events and sustain desired functions and outcomes despite pressures (Gittell et al., 2006).

The employee–employer relationship can be understood as a form of mutual exchange, where employers provide salaries, promotion prospects and developmental opportunities, such as training and learning programs, in return for employees' high performance, commitment, loyalty and organizational citizenship behaviour (Shaw et al., 2009; Sun et al., 2007; Wang et al., 2003). The nature of this exchange is strongly influenced by the socio-cultural context in which employment occurs (Kim & Wright, 2011; Schalk, 2004). For example, in India, public sector employees often accept demanding job responsibilities despite low salaries, primarily due to limited employment alternatives (Mousa et al., 2023a; Mousa et al., 2023b). More broadly, social interactions operate on the principle of reciprocity, as emphasized in social exchange theory (Blau, 1964), which posits that employees tend to perform well when they perceive fair compensation and equitable treatment (Prendergast & Topel, 1996). Nevertheless, these exchanges are shaped by power dynamics and social networks (Blau, 1964), meaning that employer–employee exchanges are not always balanced or equitable (Gouldner, 1960; Turhan, 2014).

Frontline employees in public organizations, such as banks, hospitals and police departments, who regularly interact with citizens to deliver public services, are referred to as street-level bureaucrats (Lipsky, 1980). According to street-level bureaucracy theory, the primary role of these employees—specifically, frontline staff in public banks—is to maintain smooth and effective interactions between the government and citizens (Brodkin, 2011; Lipsky, 1980). These employees often face challenges such as limited resources and continuously high citizen expectations (Mousa, 2024a; Mousa, 2024b; Mousa et al., 2023a; Mousa et al., 2023b). Additionally, street-level bureaucrats exercise discretionary power granted by the government, allowing them to make decisions about whom to serve, when and how (Farr-Wharton et al., 2021). This study focuses on frontline employees in public banks because they regularly engage with citizens and must use their discretionary authority to manage relationships between clients, who are experiencing severe economic hardship and the government, which is often blamed for economic instability in India. Therefore, the primary objective of these public employees is to allocate scarce public resources effectively to meet the growing demands of the citizens they serve (Pedersen et al., 2020).

Economic uncertainty refers, in part, to the unpredictability of government economic policies and serves as an indicator of a country's political stability (Farooq et al., 2024; Ozdemir et al., 2022). Such uncertainty can lead organizations to delay or even cancel hiring decisions and expansion plans (Ren et al., 2019) and it often heightens distrust between investors and capital market regulators (Chen et al., 2019). Generally, economic uncertainty has adverse effects on investment levels and employment rates (Baker et al., 2016; Brogaard & Detzel, 2015), while ordinary citizens tend to reduce spending and increase cash holdings during uncertain periods (Lee et al., 2019). Factors contributing to economic uncertainty include political dynamics, government policies, macroeconomic conditions, social issues and national-level influences, all of which can negatively impact industries, businesses, purchasing power and employment (Miller, 1991). This type of uncertainty often stems from state fragility and an inability to implement economic decisions effectively (Feng, 2001; Feng et al., 2019) or from frequent and abrupt reversals in government policies (Sahinoz & Cosar, 2018). In response, governments frequently seek assistance from supranational organizations and financial institutions, such as the World Bank and the International Monetary Fund, to stabilize their financial markets and economy (Kwong et al., 2021).

Following two political revolutions in 2011 and 2013, along with the Russian plane crash over Sinai, a key tourist region, Egypt experienced a sharp economic slowdown and a severe shortage of foreign currency (Mousa & Abdelgaffar, 2023). The decline in incoming revenues, primarily from Suez Canal traffic (accounting for approximately 8% of government revenue), remittances from Egyptians abroad (23–30% of revenue) and tourism (10–15% of revenue), combined with the adverse impacts of the COVID-19 pandemic and the Russia–Ukraine war, led the Central Bank of Egypt to announce a partial devaluation of the Egyptian pound (Al Helou, 2024; Español, 2023; Flynn, 2022). This measure was part of an agreement with the International Monetary Fund (IMF), under which Egypt secured a three-billion-dollar rescue loan to cover public sector salaries and subsidies for low-income citizens (Flynn, 2022). The partial devaluation allowed market forces of supply and demand to influence the exchange rate, which stood at 31 EGP per 1 USD in 2022 (Al Helou, 2024).

The IMF's rescue loan to Egypt in December 2022 aimed to stabilize the country's macroeconomic situation and promote inclusive, private-sector-led growth (Mohnblatt, 2023). However, the IMF has expressed concerns about Egypt's economic policies, particularly in 2023, due to the economy's strong reliance on short-term foreign investments, often referred to as "hot money" (The Statesman, 2023). The situation is further complicated by tensions in the Gaza Strip along Egypt's eastern border, which have intensified economic uncertainty and led to the cancellation of tourism bookings at Sinai resorts located near the conflict zone. These developments have raised doubts about the Egyptian economy's capacity to withstand additional negative shocks.

A 2023 report by BNP Paribas indicates that the Egyptian government is essentially postponing an inevitable further devaluation of the Egyptian pound (Devaux, 2023). The report highlights that Egypt continues to face severe inflationary pressures, a balance of payments crisis, and a shortage of foreign currency, conditions expected to persist until 2025 (Devaux, 2023). This scarcity has given rise to a parallel foreign exchange market, where 1 USD trades for more than 60 EGP, despite the official bank rate being 31 EGP per USD (Al Helou, 2024). In response, the International Monetary Fund has recommended an additional devaluation of the national currency and suggested that the military reduce its involvement in the economy (Mohnblatt, 2023).

It is notable that, according to a 2019 World Bank report, nearly 60% of Indians were living below the poverty line (World Bank, 2023). The situation deteriorated further in 2022 and 2023, as inflation surpassed 33%, causing daily increases in the prices of basic goods (Michaelson & Farouk, 2023). Al Jazeera Staff (2023) reported a 72% rise in food prices in 2023, resulting in approximately two-thirds of Indians being unable to afford meat or meet the current cost of living (Al Jazeera Staff, 2023). The unemployment rate reached 7.1% in 2023 (Trading Economics, 2023), while economic growth slowed to 4% (World Bank, 2023). This economic crisis has been described as the most severe since the 2011 revolution. In light of these pressing economic challenges, examining the dynamics of SHRM in this context is likely to provide valuable insights for both theory and practice, particularly in countries of the Global South.

RESEARCH METHODOLOGY

Out of the 28 banks operating in India, 10 are publicly owned (Ghoneim, 2023). Notably, the Reserve Bank of India's regulations allow both Indians and foreigners to hold bank capital without restrictions (Ghoneim, 2023). As of June 2023, the total workforce in the Indian banking sector was 17,68,794, up from 14,97,259 in December 2022 (Ghoneim, 2023). In 2017, the Reserve Bank of India identified that only 68.2% of Indians had a bank account, prompting the launch of a financial inclusion initiative aimed at expanding access to affordable financial services for both individuals and institutions. This program has achieved measurable progress, with the proportion of Indians holding bank accounts rising to 79.7% by June 2023 (Ghoneim, 2023).

Considering the relative novelty of SHRM practices in non-western contexts, especially during periods of economic uncertainty, the present study adopted a qualitative research approach. The study's sample consisted of 28 full-time frontline employees from four public banks in India. Recruiting participants is often a key challenge in qualitative research. To address this, the authors employed the snowball sampling technique searching LinkedIn and Facebook for eligible frontline bank employees. Initially, 16 respondents were contacted and informed about the study's objectives; seven agreed to participate and subsequently assisted in recruiting an additional 17 participants, yielding a total of 33 respondents. The authors established three inclusion criteria for participant selection: respondents had to be full-time frontline employees at a public bank who regularly interact with clients, have at least five years of experience to ensure exposure to increasing economic uncertainty and be under 35 years old at the time of the interviews, representing mid-career professionals (refer table 1).

Table 1. Respondent Demographics

Experience (in years)	Gender	Education
5-6	Male	Masters
14-15	Male	Masters
6-7	Female	Masters
5-6	Male	Bachelors
9-10	Male	Masters
9-10	Female	Bachelors
12-13	Female	Masters
5-6	Male	Masters
8-9	Male	Bachelors
13-14	Male	Bachelors
10-11	Male	Masters
9-10	Male	Masters
7-8	Male	Masters
7-8	Male	Masters
5-6	Female	Bachelors
9-10	Male	Bachelors
7-8	Male	Bachelors
16-17	Male	Bachelors
13-14	Male	Masters
5-6	Male	Masters
11-12	Male	Masters
7-8	Female	Masters
5-6	Female	Masters
13-14	Male	Bachelors
7-8	Male	Bachelors
21-22	Male	Bachelors
10-11	Female	Masters
6-7	Male	Masters
6-7	Male	Bachelors
6-7	Male	Masters
9-10	Male	Masters
8-9	Female	Masters
8-9	Male	Masters

This bilingual approach reflected the respondents' professional environment, where their banking duties regularly require switching between languages (English, Hindi & natives) when interacting with clients and colleagues. Interviews were conducted online using Zoom & Google Meet, with each session lasting an average of 40 minutes. Prior to participation, respondents were briefed on the purpose of the study and assured of their anonymity throughout and after the research process. Consistent with general ethical research standards, participants were also informed of their right to skip any questions they found uncomfortable or overly sensitive. Research suggested that data saturation may be achieved after as few as 12 interviews in studies involving homogenous samples (Guest et al., 2006). In this study, saturation was reached by the 29th interview. Nonetheless, the researchers continued to probe for additional insights during the remaining interviews. Table 2 provides the set of interview questions.

Table 2. List of Interview Questions

Q. No.	Interview Questions
1	Can you describe the extent to which your bank supports you through continuous training, learning, coachingand motivational programs?
2	From your perspective, how are frontline employees like yourself usually managed within the bank?
3	From your experience, what HR-related strategies or practices has your bank put in place to support your performance during periods of economic uncertainty?
4	In what ways do you think your bank's management of frontline employees reflects (or fails to reflect) a strategic HR approach?
5	How do you think the way your bank manages employees through recruitment, placement, development and retention shapes overall performance on the frontline?
6	In what ways do you consider the learning, training and motivational initiatives offered by your bank to be beneficial (or not) for your work and performance?
7	How do the ongoing political and economic crises in India affect your performance and that of your colleagues?
8	How has your bank adapted its employee management strategies in response to economic uncertainty, compared with its practices beforehand?

DATA ANALYSIS

The data analysis process began with transcribing and coding the interviews, after which the coding was reviewed and feedback was provided. Emerging patterns were collaboratively identified and relationships within the data were explored. Following the analytical framework, the researchers concentrated on recognizing similarities across these patterns (Gioia et al., 2013), which were subsequently organized into first-order concepts. Once these initial concepts were established, the researchers engaged in a cyclical process, comparing their first-order concepts with insights drawn from the two guiding theories (street-level bureaucracy and social exchange) and the data collected from the interviews. This iterative process aimed to generate second-order themes (Gioia & Chittipeddi, 2017). Building on these themes, the authors ultimately derived aggregate dimensions that addressed the central research question (Hagen et al., 2018).

The analysis revealed three main categories of factors that contribute to the sustained performance of frontline employees during economic uncertainty: job-related (e.g., employees' discretionary authority, the nature of banking roles and recruitment of elite candidates), learning-related (e.g., continuous learning opportunities and resilience-building), and context-related (e.g., career support and enhanced financial rewards during periods of instability). The figure below (Fig. 1) depicts the first- and second-order conceptualizations along with their dimensional assemblage.

FINDINGS

This study builds on the calls for more empirical research on strategic human resource management (SHRM), with a particular emphasis on Indian contexts (Akwei & Nwachukwu, 2023; Mousa et al., 2023a; Mousa et al., 2023b). In light of the prevailing economic instability and the unpredictability of government policy decisions (Farooq et al., 2024), the research seeks to address the following question: How are frontline employees in Indian public banks strategically equipped to sustain their performance during periods of economic uncertainty? To explore this issue, the authors identify three central themes—job-related, learning-related and organization-related factors—which are viewed as the mechanisms enabling employees to adapt strategically to the challenges posed by the country's economic volatility.

All participants in this research were frontline employees in public banks, making them street-level bureaucrats with discretionary authority over whom to serve and in what manner (Brunetto et al., 2022). Despite the ongoing shortage of foreign currency in Indian banks (Devaux, 2023), these employees retain the power to determine the amount of foreign currency allocated to each client, provided it aligns with the bank's cash policy. This reflects the argument that the central challenge for street-level bureaucrats lies in addressing citizens' needs within the constraints of limited resources (Pedersen et al., 2020). Given that the core responsibilities of bank staff include managing client savings, loans and withdrawals, they have little opportunity to ease their workload.

Although frontline bank employees possess and exercise authority in their interactions with clients, they operate within a highly structured system. Their decisions must align with the broader policies established by senior personnel in areas such as credit, cash management, risk management, auditing, information technology and treasury. As a result, frontline staff base their judgments on knowledge and analyses generated by these specialized departments. This reflects the view that employees are better equipped to respond to challenges and even extreme circumstances when the organizational culture promotes risk-taking, adaptability and openness to change (Cooke et al., 2019).

Figure 1. Coding & Analysis Presentation

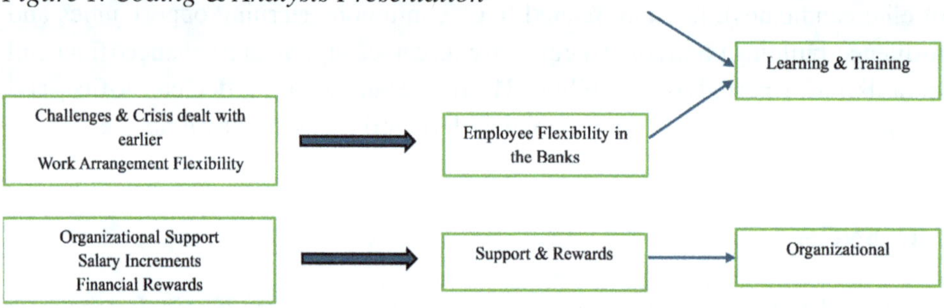

Source: Researchers' self-work

Research has argued that an organization's sustainability ultimately depends on its workforce (Kwong et al., 2021). In India, public banks restrict recruitment to top-ranking graduates from the faculties of commerce (business schools) or economics and political science. This selective approach demonstrates a strategic orientation toward identifying, developing, investing in and retaining talent capable of addressing both current and future challenges.

Ongoing learning plays a crucial role in strengthening the capabilities of bank employees. Katou (2013) noted that when organizations enhance employees' knowledge, skills and competencies through training, traditional HR functions can be transformed into more strategic practices. The Indian banks examined in this study recognize the motivational impact of learning, which fosters deeper employee engagement with their work environments (Cooke et al., 2021). Accordingly, these banks have established structured and sustained learning systems. In particular, their HR departments include specialized units dedicated to continuous staff training, enabling employees to perform effectively and remain prepared for unforeseen challenges.

Respondents emphasized that obtaining a Master of Business Administration (MBA) has become a priority for banking professionals. In India, both public and private universities provide MBA programs at relatively affordable costs, often delivered through weekend classes. Furthermore, banks across the public and private sectors increasingly view the MBA as a key requirement for employees aspiring to managerial roles. As a result, many bank employees gain exposure to the socio-cultural and economic challenges present in both global and local contexts through these programs. When questioned about whether pursuing an MBA was a personal decision or one influenced by the institution, respondents noted that banks actively encourage employees to enroll in such programs. They further explained that banks often support this process by subsidizing tuition costs or providing low-interest loans to cover the fees.

Employee resilience represents not only their capacity to cope with challenges but also the result of HR-related initiatives such as training, flexible work arrangements and transparent communication (Cooper et al., 2014; Frankl, 2017; Mousa & Samara, 2022). Respondents explained that although current economic instability poses a serious challenge for their banks, it feels less severe compared to earlier crises, including the 2011 revolution, the 2013 uprising, the violent demonstrations between 2013 and 2015 and the COVID-19 pandemic. Over time, employees have built significant resilience, shaped both by continuous learning and by navigating intense political and economic upheavals during the past decade. This accumulated experience enables them to view economic uncertainty as a manageable crisis that can be overcome with persistence and time.

Some respondents mentioned that their banks, in partnership with the government, initiated a media campaign to explain to both employees and clients that the current economic instability stems largely from the pandemic and the decline in tourism following several other issues. These campaigns have not only raised public awareness among Indian citizens but also strengthened their support for bank staff. As a result, conflicts between clients and employees are uncommon. Instead, clients often demonstrate solidarity in helping the country navigate its economic crisis. Bank employees, in turn, have translated this societal support into stronger commitment and higher levels of performance.

Amid economic uncertainty, India introduced a financial inclusion initiative for the period 2022–2025. To support this effort, banking staff were required to work extended hours, including weekends, to assist both individuals and businesses with opening accounts and accessing financial services. These measures resulted in additional monetary incentives for employees, alongside increased responsibilities and performance targets. Many employees viewed these financial benefits as a deliberate strategy for effective workforce management, which in turn motivated them to sustain high levels of performance during the challenging economic climate. The figure below (Fig. 2) depicts the findings of the study.

This study represents an early effort to explain how public institutions—specifically banks—adopt strategic approaches to manage their workforce and sustain performance during times of economic instability. It also adds to the broader international discourse on strategic human resource management (SHRM), which has gained prominence in recent years (Ghlichlee & Goodarzi, 2023). By concentrating on public banks, the paper highlights their capacity to grant frontline employees a level of discretionary authority, similar to other public sector organizations worldwide. This authority enables employees to determine how best to serve clients despite resource constraints, reinforcing the idea that the primary mission of public institutions is to uphold stable government–citizen relations (Farr-Wharton et al., 2021). Consequently, frontline staff who exercise this discretion are expected to prioritize citizen satisfaction (Mousa et al., 2023a; Mousa et al., 2023b). In contrast, private organizations focus predominantly on profit maximization rather than fostering such relationships.

The paper also focuses on India, a South-East Asian nation with one of the continent's largest populations. Asian countries vary significantly in terms of democratic governance, military influence, levels of corruption, public sector bureaucracy and the instability of their business environments (Gok & Gok, 2016; Pandit et al., 2018). In light of these differences, the study may inspire future research exploring how public sector employees in other Asian contexts are strategically managed, especially during periods of economic turmoil, military takeovers or civil unrest. The key theoretical contributions and practical implications are outlined below.

Figure 2. Stabilizing factors of public sector employees during economic variability

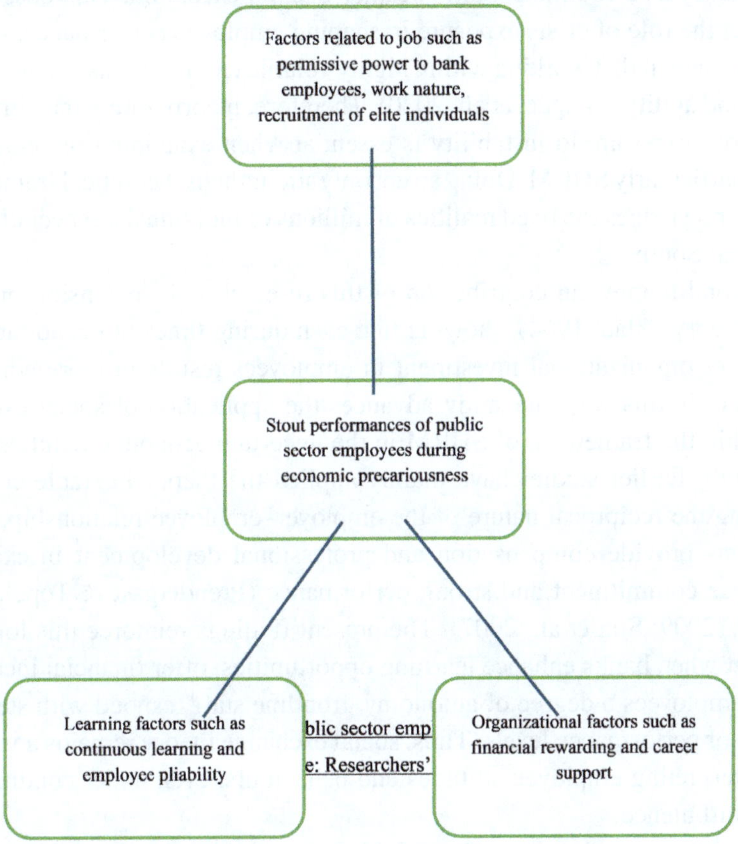

Source: Researchers' self-work

The primary theoretical contribution of this study is the identification of three groups of influencing factors: job-related (such as the discretionary authority of bank employees, the nature of banking work and the recruitment of highly skilled individuals), learning-related (including continuous professional development and employee resilience) and context-related (such as career support and enhanced financial incentives during economic instability). Together, these elements help explain why frontline banking employees maintain consistent performance even in times of uncertainty. Such strategic preparation can be understood as a response to numerous disruptive events over the past decade—ranging from socio-political upheavals, economic challenges to global health crises (Mousa & Abdelgaffar, 2023; Al Helou, 2024).

Repeated exposure to these crises has prompted banks to adopt strategic human resource management (SHRM) practices, ensuring that staff remain adaptable and well-prepared. Unsurprisingly, several interviewees described economic volatility in their country as a routine condition rather than an exception. This observation underscores the role of crisis exposure in shaping employee performance, as prior studies have shown that working within highly volatile environments enhances both resilience and agility (Gölgeci et al., 2020). Therefore, incorporating the dimension of continuous exposure to instability is essential when examining organizational practices, particularly SHRM. Doing so not only strengthens theoretical frameworks but also acknowledges the lived realities of millions of individuals, especially those in the Global South.

The second theoretical contribution of this research is its extension of social exchange theory (Blau, 1964), showing that even during times of economic instability, greater organizational investment in employees results in more consistent performance. In this way, the study advances the application of social exchange theory within the framework of SHRM in the uncertain economic realities of the Global South. Earlier studies have mainly applied the theory in stable contexts, emphasizing the reciprocal nature of the employer–employee relationship, where organizations provide compensation and professional development in exchange for employee commitment and strong performance (Prendergast & Topel, 1996; Shaw et al., 2009; Sun et al., 2007). The present findings reinforce this logic, revealing that when banks enhance learning opportunities, offer financial incentives and grant employees a degree of autonomy, frontline staff respond with steady or even superior performance levels. Thus, social exchange theory remains a valuable lens for interpreting employee attitudes and behaviours, even under conditions of economic turbulence.

The third theoretical contribution of this study emphasizes the role of public employees' discretionary power in enabling organizations to navigate turbulent and uncertain conditions. Although frontline staff possess the authority to shape aspects of their job and determine whom to serve and when (Brunetto et al., 2022), they also recognize the challenges faced by their clients—such as shortages of foreign currency—and therefore strive to deliver satisfaction despite constraints. This suggests that theorizing SHRM in the public sector of Global South economies should explicitly account for employees' discretionary authority. Furthermore, maintaining performance stability emerges as a vital consideration in such volatile contexts. In environments where growth is constrained or unattainable, sustaining a steady level of individual and organizational performance can itself be regarded as an achievement, serving as a foundation until conditions improve and opportunities for growth re-emerge.

Beyond theoretical contributions, this study also provides several practical implications. For organizations operating in developing economies and volatile environments, both in the public and private sectors, performance stability should be recognized as an important indicator of success, given the constraints imposed by high external uncertainty. In this regard, granting employees discretionary power, when accompanied by appropriate training, can serve as an effective mechanism for sustaining performance. Additionally, fostering continuous learning at both the individual and organizational levels become critical to achieving stability in such contexts. Drawing on best practices, such as those observed in the Indian public banking sector, may offer valuable guidance. Finally, enhancing awareness of SHRM and its benefits is essential for organizations in uncertain and highly volatile settings. Doing so can ease employee pressures, reduce turnover and foster greater motivation, even under challenging external conditions.

While this study opens multiple avenues for future inquiry, it is not without limitations. First, the analysis draws primarily on the perspectives of frontline employees, excluding insights from colleagues in other departments and senior management. As a result, some important dimensions of the relationship between SHRM and employee performance in public banks under economic uncertainty may have been overlooked. Second, since the data were collected during a period of severe economic instability in India, the socio-economic context may have shaped respondents' views, which in turn limits the broader generalizability of the findings.

Nonetheless, as an early attempt to examine the connection between SHRM and employee performance under uncertainty in India's banking sector, the study offers valuable directions for further research. Future studies could, for instance, investigate how SHRM practices evolve in response to employee performance, especially in countries frequently exposed to socio-political and economic disruptions. Comparative analyses between public and private organizations could also reveal key differences and commonalities in SHRM strategies across contexts. In addition, given the variation in the extent of discretionary power afforded to public employees across countries, further research is needed in diverse public service settings to assess both the benefits and drawbacks of such authority, particularly among staff with frequent citizen interaction. Finally, these questions could also be extended to private organizations in developing economies to explore whether unique patterns emerge in environments characterized by high volatility and uncertainty.

REFERENCES

Adeleye, I. (2011). Theorising human resource management in Africa: Beyond cultural relativism. *African Journal of Business Management, 5*(6), 2028–2029.

Akwei, C., & Nwachukwu, C. (2023). An exploration of contextual factors affecting the nexus of competitive strategy and human resource management practices in Nigeria's emerging economy context. *International Journal of Human Resource Management, 34*(16), 3079–3122. DOI: 10.1080/09585192.2022.2104128

Al Helou, E. (2024). Egypt's currency crisis threatens Red Sea projects. *Economy Middle East.* https://economymiddleeast.com/news/egypt-currency-red-sea/

Al Jazeera Staff. (2023). Mourning and worrying about the future in rural Egypt. *Al Jazeera.* https://www.aljazeera.com/features/2023/12/14/mourning-and-worrying-about-the-future-in-rural-egypt

. Anibaba, Y., & Adeleye, I. (2014). Strategic human resource management in Africa: Exploring institutional effects.

Arslan, A., Kamara, S., Golgeci, I., & Tarba, S. Y. (2022). Civil society organisations' management dynamics and social value creation in the post-conflict volatile contexts pre and during COVID-19. *The International Journal of Organizational Analysis, 30*(7), 20–33. DOI: 10.1108/IJOA-01-2021-2573

Baker, S., Bloom, N., & Davis, S. (2016). Measuring economic policy uncertainty. *The Quarterly Journal of Economics, 131*(4), 1593–1636. DOI: 10.1093/qje/qjw024

Bardoel, E. A., Pettit, T. M., De Cieri, H., & McMillan, L. (2014). Employee resilience: An emerging challenge for HRM. *Asia Pacific Journal of Human Resources, 52*(3), 279–297. DOI: 10.1111/1744-7941.12033

Blau, P. M. (1964). Exchange and power in social life. *Trans-Action.*

Bowen, D. E., & Ostroff, C. (2004). Understanding HRM–firm performance linkages: The role of the 'strength' of the HRM system. *Academy of Management Review, 29*(2), 203–221. DOI: 10.5465/amr.2004.12736076

Branicki, L., Steyer, V., & Sullivan-Taylor, B. (2019). Why resilience managers aren't resilient, and what human resource management can do about it. *International Journal of Human Resource Management, 30*(8), 1261–1286. DOI: 10.1080/09585192.2016.1244104

Britt, T. W., Shen, W., Sinclair, R. R., Grossman, M. R., & Klieger, D. M. (2016). How much do we really know about employee resilience? *Industrial and Organizational Psychology: Perspectives on Science and Practice*, *9*(2), 378–404. DOI: 10.1017/iop.2015.107

Brodkin, E. Z. (2011). Policy work: Street-level organizations under new managerialism. *Journal of Public Administration: Research and Theory*, *21*(2, Supplement 2), 253–277. DOI: 10.1093/jopart/muq093

Brogaard, J., & Detzel, A. (2015). The asset-pricing implications of government economic policy uncertainty. *Management Science*, *61*(1), 3–18. DOI: 10.1287/mnsc.2014.2044

Brunetto, Y., Xerri, M., & Farr-Wharton, B. (2022). Doing better with less: Do behavioural capabilities affect street-level bureaucrats' ability to deliver public value? *Public Management Review*, *26*(5), 1136–1155. DOI: 10.1080/14719037.2022.2133159

Chang, S., Gong, Y., Way, S. A., & Jia, L. (2013). Flexibility-oriented HRM systems, absorptive capacity, and market responsiveness and firm innovativeness. *Journal of Management*, *39*(7), 1924–1951. DOI: 10.1177/0149206312466145

Chartered Institute of Personnel and Development. (2017). *Strategic human resource management* (CIPD Factsheet). CIPD. https://www.cipd.co.uk/knowledge/strategy/hr/strategic-hrm-factsheet#6744

Chen, H., Chen, R., Bernard, S., & Rahman, I. (2019). US hotel industry revenue: An ARDL bounds testing approach. *International Journal of Contemporary Hospitality Management*, *31*(4), 1720–1743. DOI: 10.1108/IJCHM-01-2018-0031

Collins, C. J. (2021). Expanding the resource-based view model of strategic human resource management. *International Journal of Human Resource Management*, *32*(2), 331–358. DOI: 10.1080/09585192.2019.1711442

Cooke, F. L., Cooper, B., Bartram, T., Wang, J., & Mei, H. (2019). Mapping the relationships between high-performance work systems, employee resilience and engagement: A study of the banking industry in China. *International Journal of Human Resource Management*, *30*(8), 1239–1260. DOI: 10.1080/09585192.2015.1137618

Cooke, F. L., Xiao, Q., & Xiao, M. (2021). Extending the frontier of research on (strategic) human resource management in China: A review of David Lepak and colleagues' influence and future research direction. *International Journal of Human Resource Management*, *32*(1), 183–224. DOI: 10.1080/09585192.2020.1803949

Cooper, C. L., Liu, Y., & Tarba, S. Y. (2014). Resilience, HRM practices and impact on organizational performance and employee well-being. *International Journal of Human Resource Management*, *25*(17), 2466–2471. DOI: 10.1080/09585192.2014.926688

Coutu, D. L. (2002). How resilience works. *Harvard Business Review*, *80*(5), 46–56.

Delery, J., & Gupta, N. (2016). Human resource management practices and organizational effectiveness: Internal fit matters. *Journal of Organizational Effectiveness: People and Performance*, *3*(2), 139–163. DOI: 10.1108/JOEPP-03-2016-0028

Delery, J. E., & Doty, D. H. (1996). Modes of theorizing in strategic human resource management: Tests of universalistic, contingency, and configurational performance predictions. *Academy of Management Journal*, *39*(4), 802–835. DOI: 10.2307/256713

Delery, J. E., & Roumpi, D. (2017). Strategic human resource management, human capital and competitive advantage: Is the field going in circles? *Human Resource Management Journal*, *27*(1), 1–21. DOI: 10.1111/1748-8583.12137

Dello Russo, S., Mascia, D., & Morandi, F. (2018). Individual perceptions of HR practices, HRM strength and appropriateness of care: A meso, multilevel approach. *International Journal of Human Resource Management*, *29*(2), 286–310. DOI: 10.1080/09585192.2016.1165276

Devaux, P. (2023). *Egypt: Buying time*. BNP Paribas Economic Research. https://economic-research.bnpparibas.com/html/en-US/Egypt-Buyingtime-4/14/2023,48481

Dibben, P., Brewster, C., Brookes, M., Cunha, R., Webster, E., & Wood, G. (2017). Institutional legacies and HRM: Similarities and differences in HRM practices in Portugal and Mozambique. *International Journal of Human Resource Management*, *28*(18), 2519–2537. DOI: 10.1080/09585192.2016.1164225

DiMaggio, P. J., & Powell, W. W. (1991). The iron cage revisited: Institutional isomorphism and collective rationality in organizational fields. In Powell, W. W., & DiMaggio, P. J. (Eds.), *The new institutionalism in organizational analysis* (pp. 195–200). University of Chicago Press.

Ererdi, C., Nurgabdeshov, A., Kozhakhmet, S., Rofcanin, Y., & Demirbag, M. (2022). International HRM in the context of uncertainty and crisis: A systematic review of literature (2000–2018). *International Journal of Human Resource Management*, *33*(12), 2503–2540. DOI: 10.1080/09585192.2020.1863247

Español, M. (2023, June). Egypt remittances plunge amid economic uncertainty. *Al-Monitor*. https://www.al-monitor.com/originals/2023/06/egypt-remittances-plunge-amid-economic-uncertainty

Farooq, O., Jabbouri, I., & Naili, M. (2024). The nexus between economic policy uncertainty and access to finance: A study of developing countries. *International Journal of Managerial Finance*, *20*(1), 222–246. DOI: 10.1108/IJMF-11-2022-0507

Farr-Wharton, B., Brunetto, Y., Wankhade, P., Saccon, C., & Xerri, M. (2021). Comparing the impact of authentic leadership on Italian and UK police officers' discretionary power, well-being and commitment. *Policing*, *44*(5), 741–755. DOI: 10.1108/PIJPSM-09-2020-0156

Feng, X., Lo, Y. L., & Chan, K. C. (2019). Impact of economic policy uncertainty on cash holdings: Firm-level evidence from an emerging market. *Asia-Pacific Journal of Accounting & Economics*, *29*(2), 1–23. DOI: 10.1080/16081625.2019.1694954

Feng, Y. (2001). Political freedom, political instability, and policy uncertainty: A study of political institutions and private investment in developing countries. *International Studies Quarterly*, *45*(2), 271–294. DOI: 10.1111/0020-8833.00191

Flynn, A. (2022, November 14). Floating the pound: Currency devaluation in Egypt. *The American University in Cairo*. https://www.aucegypt.edu/news/floating-pound-currencydevaluation-egypt

Frankl, V. E. (2017). *Man's search for meaning*. Beacon Press.

Ghlichlee, B., & Goodarzi, A. (2023). Strategic human resource practices and new product development performance: The mediating role of intellectual capital. *Journal of Intellectual Capital*, *24*(3), 730–756. DOI: 10.1108/JIC-11-2020-0360

Ghoneim, E. (2023). [Article in Arabic]. *Veto Gate*. https://www.vetogate.com/4818653

Gioia, D. A., & Chittipeddi, K. (2017). Sensemaking and sensegiving in strategic change initiation. *Strategic Management Journal*, *12*(6), 433–448. DOI: 10.1002/smj.4250120604

Gioia, D. A., Corley, K. G., & Hamilton, A. L. (2013). Seeking qualitative rigor in inductive research: Notes on the Gioia methodology. *Organizational Research Methods*, *16*(1), 15–31. DOI: 10.1177/1094428112452151

Gittell, J. H., Cameron, K., Lim, S., & Rivas, V. (2006). Relationships, layoffs, and organizational resilience: Airline industry responses to September 11. *The Journal of Applied Behavioral Science*, *42*(3), 300–329. DOI: 10.1177/0021886306286466

Gok, G. O., & Gok, M. S. (2016). Emerging economies: Comparative analysis of MIST and IBSA. *Eurasian Journal of Soil Science*, *4*(2), 1–13. DOI: 10.15604/ejss.2016.04.02.001

Gölgeci, I., Arslan, A., Dikova, D., & Gligor, D. M. (2020). Resilient agility in volatile economies: Institutional and organizational antecedents. *Journal of Organizational Change Management, 33*(1), 100–113. DOI: 10.1108/JOCM-02-2019-0033

Gouldner, A. W. (1960). The norm of reciprocity: A preliminary statement. *American Sociological Review, 25*(2), 161–178. DOI: 10.2307/2092623

Guest, G., Bunce, A., & Johnson, L. (2006). How many interviews are enough? An experiment with data saturation and variability. *Field Methods, 18*(1), 59–82. DOI: 10.1177/1525822X05279903

Haddock-Millar, J., Sanyal, C., & Müller-Camen, M. (2016). Green human resource management: A comparative qualitative case study of a United States multinational corporation. *International Journal of Human Resource Management, 27*(2), 192–211. DOI: 10.1080/09585192.2015.1052087

Hagen, B., Zucchella, A., & Ghauri, P. N. (2018). From fragile to agile: Marketing as a key driver of entrepreneurial internationalization. *International Marketing Review, 36*(2), 260–288. DOI: 10.1108/IMR-01-2018-0023

Haque, A., & Khan, S. I. (2023). Promoting meaningfulness in work for higher job satisfaction: Will intent to quit make trouble for business managers? *Journal of Organizational Effectiveness: People and Performance, 10*(3), 455–476. DOI: 10.1108/JOEPP-02-2022-0020

Howie, L. (2007). The terrorism threat and managing workplaces. *Disaster Prevention and Management, 16*(1), 70–78. DOI: 10.1108/09653560710729820

Jackson, S. E., & Schuler, R. S. (1995). Understanding human resource management in the context of organizations and their environment. *Annual Review of Psychology, 46*(1), 237–264. DOI: 10.1146/annurev.ps.46.020195.001321

Jackson, S. E., Schuler, R. S., & Jiang, K. (2014). An aspirational framework for strategic human resource management. *The Academy of Management Annals, 8*(1), 1–56. DOI: 10.5465/19416520.2014.872335

Jiang, K., Lepak, D. P., Hu, J., & Baer, J. C. (2012). How does human resource management influence organizational outcomes? A meta-analytic investigation of mediating mechanisms. *Academy of Management Journal, 55*(6), 1264–1294. DOI: 10.5465/amj.2011.0088

Jiang, K., & Messersmith, J. (2018). On the shoulders of giants: A meta-review of strategic human resource management. *International Journal of Human Resource Management, 29*(1), 6–33. DOI: 10.1080/09585192.2017.1384930

Kabalina, V., Zelenova, O., & Reshetnikova, K. (2019). Contemporary human resource management practices in Russia: Flexibility under uncertainty. *International Studies of Management & Organization*, *49*(4), 422–440. DOI: 10.1080/00208825.2019.1646490

Katou, A. A. (2013). The link between HR practices, psychological contract fulfilment, and organisational performance in Greece: An economic crisis perspective. *Journal of Industrial Engineering and Management*, *6*(2), 568–594. DOI: 10.3926/jiem.501

Kim, S., & Wright, P. M. (2011). Putting strategic human resource management in context: A contextualized model of high commitment work systems and its implications in China. *Management and Organization Review*, *7*(1), 153–174. DOI: 10.1111/j.1740-8784.2010.00185.x

King, D. D., Newman, A., & Luthans, F. (2016). Not if, but when we need resilience in the workplace. *Journal of Organizational Behavior*, *37*(5), 782–786. DOI: 10.1002/job.2063

King, K. A. (2017). The talent climate: Creating an organisational context supportive of sustainable talent development through implementation of a strong talent system. *Journal of Organizational Effectiveness: People and Performance*, *4*(4), 298–314. DOI: 10.1108/JOEPP-03-2017-0023

Kuntz, J. R., Näswall, K., & Malinen, S. (2016). Resilient employees in resilient organizations: Flourishing beyond adversity. *Industrial and Organizational Psychology: Perspectives on Science and Practice*, *9*(2), 456–462. DOI: 10.1017/iop.2016.39

Kwong, C., Demirbag, M., Wood, G., & Cooke, F. L. (2021). Human resource management in the context of high uncertainties. *International Journal of Human Resource Management*, *32*(17), 3569–3599. DOI: 10.1080/09585192.2021.1966203

Lakshman, C., Wang, L., Adhikari, A., & Cheng, G. (2022). Flexibility-oriented HRM practices and innovation: Evidence from China and India. *International Journal of Human Resource Management*, *33*(12), 2473–2502. DOI: 10.1080/09585192.2020.1861057

Larsson, A. S., Martin, R., & Edwards, M. R. (2022). Insider econometrics meets people analytics and strategic human resource management. *International Journal of Human Resource Management*, *33*(12), 2373–2419. DOI: 10.1080/09585192.2020.1847166

Lee, J. H., Mustapha, A., & Hwang, J. (2019). Enhancing ethnic restaurant visits and reducing risk perception: The effect of information and protection motivation. *Journal of Hospitality and Tourism Insights*, *2*(4), 341–357. DOI: 10.1108/JHTI-10-2018-0068

Lepak, D. P., & Shaw, J. D. (2008). Strategic HRM in North America: Looking to the future. *International Journal of Human Resource Management*, *19*(8), 1486–1499. DOI: 10.1080/09585190802200272

Li, X., Qin, X., Jiang, K., Zhang, S., & Gao, F. Y. (2015). Human resource practices and firm performance in China: The moderating roles of regional human capital quality and firm innovation strategy. *Management and Organization Review*, *11*(2), 237–261. DOI: 10.1017/mor.2015.12

Lipsky, M. (1980). *Street-level bureaucracy: Dilemmas of the individual in public services*. Russell Sage Foundation.

Michaelson, R., & Farouk, M. (2023, May 8). Inflation, IMF austerity and grandiose military plans edge more Egyptians into poverty. *The Guardian*. https://www.theguardian.com/global-development/2023/may/08/inflation-imf-austerity-and-grandiose-military-plans-edge-more-egyptians-into-poverty

Miller, D. (1991). Stale in the saddle: CEO tenure and the match between organization and environment. *Management Science*, *37*(1), 34–52. DOI: 10.1287/mnsc.37.1.34

Mohnblatt, D. (2023, January 16). Egyptian economy continues to deteriorate with future uncertain. *The Media Line*. https://themedialine.org/by-region/egyptian-economy-continues-todeteriorate-with-future-uncertain/

Mousa, M. (2024a). From announcing their pregnancy to returning to work: The experience of pregnant street-level bureaucrats in non-Western public contexts. *Public Integrity*, •••, 1–17. DOI: 10.1080/10999922.2024.2304763

Mousa, M. (2024b). What determines the engagement of nurses in organizational learning post Covid-19? The role of street-level bureaucracy and Florence Nightingale theories. *Public Integrity*, •••, 1–16. DOI: 10.1080/10999922.2024.2348902

Mousa, M. (2025). Gig work, management education and changes in working conditions: A qualitative study. *Industrial and Commercial Training*, *57*(1), 82–98. DOI: 10.1108/ICT-07-2024-0066

Mousa, M., & Abdelgaffar, H. (2023). Career shock of hotel employees and their individual resilience: An exploratory study. *Consumer Behavior in Tourism and Hospitality*, *18*(2), 228–240. DOI: 10.1108/CBTH-06-2022-0134

Mousa, M., Avolio, B., & Pahlevan Sharif, S. (2023b). Emancipation and street-level bureaucracy in non-western contexts: The representation of neurodiverse individuals in public sector organizations. *Public Integrity*, *26*(4), 439–454. DOI: 10.1080/10999922.2023.2247867

Mousa, M., & Samara, G. (2022). Mental health of business academics within the COVID-19 era: Can meaningful work help? A qualitative study. *Employee Relations*, *44*(4), 764–784. DOI: 10.1108/ER-04-2021-0170

Mousa, M., Tarba, S., Arslan, A., & Cooper, C. (2023a). When extreme work becomes the norm: An exploration of coping strategies of public sector nurses. *Public Management Review*, *27*(1), 297–316. DOI: 10.1080/14719037.2023.2246493

Murphy, C., Klotz, A. C., & Kreiner, G. E. (2017). Blue skies and black boxes: The promise (and practice) of grounded theory in human resource management research. *Human Resource Management Review*, *27*(2), 291–305. DOI: 10.1016/j.hrmr.2016.08.006

Ogunyomi, P., & Bruning, N. S. (2016). Human resource management and organizational performance of small and medium sized enterprises (SMEs) in Nigeria. *International Journal of Human Resource Management*, *27*(6), 612–634. DOI: 10.1080/09585192.2015.1033640

Okpilike, M. E. (2012). The place of social interaction in the Nigerian school system: Implications for school life. *Developing Countries Journal*, *2*(10), 132–142.

Ozdemir, O., Han, W., & Dalbor, M. (2022). Economic policy uncertainty and hotel occupancy: The mediating effect of consumer sentiment. *Journal of Hospitality and Tourism Insights*, *5*(2), 253–273. DOI: 10.1108/JHTI-08-2020-0149

Paauwe, J. (2009). HRM and performance: Achievements, methodological issues and prospects. *Journal of Management Studies*, *46*(1), 129–142. DOI: 10.1111/j.1467-6486.2008.00809.x

Paauwe, J., Wright, P., & Guest, D. (2013). HRM and performance: What do we know and where should we go? In Paauwe, J., Wright, P., & Guest, D. (Eds.), *Human resource management and performance: Achievements and challenges* (pp. 1–15). Wiley.

Pandit, D., Joshi, M. P., Sahay, A., & Gupta, R. K. (2018). Disruptive innovation and dynamic capabilities in emerging economies: Evidence from the Indian automotive sector. *Technological Forecasting and Social Change*, *129*, 323–329. DOI: 10.1016/j.techfore.2017.09.035

Pedersen, L. H., Andersen, L. B., & Thomsen, N. (2020). Motivated to act and take responsibility: Integrating insights from community psychology in PSM research. *Public Management Review*, *22*(7), 999–1023. DOI: 10.1080/14719037.2020.1740307

Pollard, T. M. (2001). Changes in mental well-being, blood pressure and total cholesterol levels during workplace reorganization: The impact of uncertainty. *Work and Stress*, *15*(1), 14–28. DOI: 10.1080/02678370110064609

Prendergast, C., & Topel, R. H. (1996). Favouritism in organizations. *Journal of Political Economy*, *104*(5), 958–978. DOI: 10.1086/262048

Reade, C. (2009). Human resource management implications of terrorist threats to firms in the supply chain. *International Journal of Physical Distribution & Logistics Management*, *39*(6), 469–485. DOI: 10.1108/09600030910985820

Ren, Y., Guo, Q., Zhu, H., & Ying, W. (2019). The effects of economic policy uncertainty on China's economy: Evidence from time-varying parameter FAVAR. *Applied Economics*, *52*(29), 1–19. DOI: 10.1080/00036846.2019.1707475

Roumpi, D. (2023). Rethinking the strategic management of human resources: Lessons learned from Covid-19 and the way forward in building resilience. *The International Journal of Organizational Analysis*, *31*(1), 215–231. DOI: 10.1108/IJOA-09-2021-2974

Roumpi, D., & Delery, J. E. (2019). Strategic HRM: Where do we go from here? In Wilkinson, A., Bacon, N., Lepak, D., & Snell, S. (Eds.), *The Sage handbook of human resource management* (pp. 423–438). Sage. DOI: 10.4135/9781529714852.n25

Roumpi, D., Magrizos, S., & Nicolopoulou, K. (2020). Virtuous circle: Human capital and human resource management in social enterprises. *Human Resource Management*, *59*(5), 401–421. DOI: 10.1002/hrm.22002

Sahinoz, S., & Cosar, E. E. (2018). Economic policy uncertainty and economic activity in Turkey. *Applied Economics Letters*, *25*(21), 1517–1520. DOI: 10.1080/13504851.2018.1430321

Schalk, R. (2004). Changes in the employment relationship across time. In Coyle-Shapiro, J., Shore, L. M., Taylor, S., & Tetrick, L. E. (Eds.), *The employment relationship: Examining psychological and contextual perspectives* (pp. 284–311). Oxford University Press. DOI: 10.1093/oso/9780199269136.003.0013

Shaw, J. D., Dineen, B. R., Fang, R., & Vellella, R. F. (2009). Employee–organization exchange relationships, HRM practices, and quit rates of good and poor performers. *Academy of Management Journal*, *52*(5), 1016–1033. DOI: 10.5465/amj.2009.44635525

Sikora, D. M., Thompson, K. W., Russell, Z. A., & Ferris, G. R. (2016). Reimagining overqualified human resources to promote organizational effectiveness and competitive advantage. *Journal of Organizational Effectiveness: People and Performance*, *3*(1), 23–42. DOI: 10.1108/JOEPP-03-2015-0012

Storey, J., Ulrich, D., & Wright, P. M. (2019). *Strategic human resource management: A research overview*. Routledge. DOI: 10.4324/9780429490217

Sun, L. Y., Aryee, S., & Law, K. S. (2007). High-performance human resource practices, citizenship behavior, and organizational performance: A relational perspective. *Academy of Management Journal*, *50*(3), 558–577. DOI: 10.5465/amj.2007.25525821

The Statesman. (2023), available at: https://www.thestatesman.com/opinion/egypts-downturn-1503244320.html

Trading economics (2023), available at: https://tradingeconomics.com/egypt/unemployment-rate

Turhan, M. (2014). Organizational cronyism: A scale development and validation from the perspective of teachers. *Journal of Business Ethics*, *123*(2), 295–308. DOI: 10.1007/s10551-013-1839-3

Wallo, A., & Coetzer, A. (2023). Understanding and conceptualising the daily work of human resource practitioners. *Journal of Organizational Effectiveness: People and Performance*, *10*(2), 180–198. DOI: 10.1108/JOEPP-01-2022-0013

Wang, D., Tsui, A. S., Zhang, Y., & Ma, L. (2003). Employment relationships and firm performance: Evidence from an emerging economy. *Journal of Organizational Behavior*, *24*(5), 511–535. DOI: 10.1002/job.213

Williams, T. A., & Shepherd, D. A. (2016). Building resilience or providing sustenance: Different paths of emergent ventures in the aftermath of Haiti earthquake. *Academy of Management Journal*, *59*(6), 2069–2102. DOI: 10.5465/amj.2015.0682

World Bank. (2023). https://documents.worldbank.org/en/publication/documents-reports/documentdetail/099624304122329292/idu07c72dd550d99104e560a5fd0e79e14053665

Wright, P., & McMahan, G. (1992). Theoretical perspectives for strategic human resource management. *Journal of Management*, *18*(2), 295–322. DOI: 10.1177/014920639201800205

Wright, P. M., & Snell, S. A. (1998). Toward a unifying framework for exploring fit and flexibility in strategic human resource management. *Academy of Management Review*, *23*(4), 756–772. DOI: 10.2307/259061

Zahoor, N., Roumpi, D., Tarba, S., Arslan, A., & Golgeci, I. (2024). The role of digitalization and inclusive climate in building a resilient workforce: An ability–motivation–opportunity approach. *Journal of Organizational Behavior*, *45*(9), 1431–1459. DOI: 10.1002/job.2800

Zucker, L. G. (1991). The role of institutionalization in cultural persistence. In Powell, W. W., & DiMaggio, P. J. (Eds.), *The new institutionalism in organizational analysis* (pp. xx–xx). University of Chicago Press.

Chapter 3
Diversity, Equity, and Inclusion in the Service Economy

J. Shanthi Priya
http://orcid.org/0009-0000-1918-2260
VelTech Rangarajan Dr. Sagunthala R&D Institute of Science and Techology, India

K. R. Sowmya
Spectrum International University College, Malaysia

S. Raja
Veltech Rangarajan Dr. Sagunthala R&D Institute of Science and Technology, India

Abstract:

The study assesses the role of Service Economy in supporting diversity, inclusion, and equity in employee mental health in the Service Economy based on through an analysis of current literature it recreates the importance of well-being standards to effectively attract, support and upload a diverse workforce. Leadership is identified as a key driver in shaping organizational culture, with effective leaders serving as role models who promote values of respect, fairness, and inclusion. We have the opportunity human spirit, creativity, and a collective belief in a better future as powerful drivers of innovation. To create truly equitable Service Economy, it is critical to address the systems and processes that shape employee experiences. Trust in the process, transparency, and a commitment to the principles of equity are key to recovery and growth. Employers play a dual role they can either perpetuate or alleviate inequities, depending on how they respond to the unique experiences

DOI: 10.4018/979-8-3373-6395-0.ch003

of individuals based on intersecting social identities such as gender, age. Ensure clear standards for workplace counsellors, and a commitment to employee mental health these are essential in diverse work progress, diversity alone does not guarantee positive outcomes it must be ensure all employees feel valued and supported. Moreover, equity ensuring fair treatment, access, and opportunity is essential in addressing systemic and achieving meaningful representation across all levels of a Service Economy. Real transformation starts with understanding our own mental health tuning into self-awareness and aligning behaviour with intentional growth. When individuals show up with clarity, teams thrive through deeper connection, stronger collaboration, and shared purpose. This same mindset should drive how organisation craft their policies and shape decisions rooted in awareness, built on empathy, and designed for new impact. They contribute diverse, valuable and competitively relevant insights into how work truly gets done shaping how processes are designed, goals are achieved, tasks are framed, teams are built, ideas are communicated, and leadership is exercised.

1.INTRODUCTION:

This study aims to explore how setting standards for Service Economy well-being can improve the ability to attract and retain a diverse workforce. The Service Economy serves as a gateway to unlocking all opportunities by supporting a positive environment that drives employee engagement, inclusive and overall organizational success. It shows that developing and implementing effective Diversity, Equity, and Inclusion policies is Turning point. Every employee is entitled to a safe and healthy Service Economy, which enables them to perform efficiently. When mental health concerns go unacknowledged, individuals may experience a lack of support and a sense of disregard. In such environments, unfavourable leadership cultures can increase stress and negatively impact both employees and the overall Service Economy. To the individual's aspiration to be respected, recognized, and valued by others. Fulfilment in this area sense of accomplished.

Service Economy fairness includes justice in processes and procedures, which must be clearly defined in employer and employee agreements. Without such clarity, the work environment can become unstable. Differences in gender, age, status, disability, religion, and beyond. Differential treatment based on these differences can limit individuals' value-added input and devalue their unique skills and experiences. Leadership is central to moulding Service Economy culture effective leaders serve as a role models, and objectives aimed at driving motivation, strengthening employee connection and dedication. Granted that employees dedicate a significant part of their lives to work, it is crucial that the Service Economy upholds values of respect, fairness, and equal opportunity at both the individual and collective levels. Effective leadership cultivates a positive and supportive environment, while ineffective leadership can erode team unity and lower employees' sense of professional value.

These challenges underscore the importance of fostering a culture of respect, inclusive education, and equitable Service Economy practices. When effectively implemented, initiatives stimulate creatively and innovation by motivating individuals to acquire new skills and adopt to evolving situations. This, in turn, leads to higher employee satisfaction and personal growth.

In the context of Human Resources Management, organisations must prioritize foundational practices such as legal compliance, employee welfare, and development initiatives. This includes ensuring equal employment opportunities and maintaining occupational health and safety standards from the outset (Vasanthan et al 2025). When integrated effectively, diversity enhances organizational performance and support compliance with government regulations. By aligning with industry laws and standards, organization can drive development while addressing employee grievances and Service Economy disputes. Work-related stress is a significant factor in resignation intentions and poor mental health outcomes. Therefore, leadership must establish fair, supportive frameworks that promote mental well-being and provide equal opportunities for all employees. Establishing clear standards for the Service Economy and promoting supportive leadership are essential in diverse work environments. A diverse workforce alone does not guarantee positive outcomes; it must be accompanied by intentional inclusion practices that ensure all employees feel valved and supported.

Additionally, equity ensuring fair treatment, access, and opportunities is critical in addressing systemic barriers and achieving meaningful representation across all levels of the Service Economy. The success of any Service Economy is deeply rooted in the quality and commitment of its goals, Employees serve as the mainstay of the Service Economy achievement, and it is the management's responsibility to retain them by providing consistent motivation and support of recognition. Service Economy doctrines legal, ethical and justices fundamental to the success. It incorporates the acknowledge and support of individual difference, equitable access to opportunity, feel valued and included. In the contemporary era marked by globalization, technological advancement, the concepts of diversity, equity, and inclusion it ensures fair treatment, equal access to opportunity, and a sense of belonging for all employees' progress improve Service Economy effectiveness and reputation.

In recent decades, Service Economy have increasingly embraced approaches cantered on self-improvement, personal development, and personal leadership to enhance Service Economy performance .These methods emphasize for boosting overall effectiveness in the Service Economy and are applicable to both employees and Service Economy the growing popularity of personal development initiatives in mirrors a broader societal shift toward self-actualization and self-help movements, which aim to support individuals in achieving their fullest potential self-help and personal development was valued at with project, programs are delivered through various channels, workshops, books, digital tools making them widely accessible and adaptable across different professional settings. A culture of dedication and sustained effort across all levels is crucial for long-term success creates a positive environment.

Attracting top talent from around the employees reflects genuine changes within the Service Economy and highlights a commitment to practices. supporting in education fosters mutual respect and perspectives. During personnel leading to more effective and innovation outcomes. Meeting academic and professional standards also enhance an organisation's reputation and strengthens its brand image. Such environments encourage employees to contribute their best work. Establishing and supportive work settings ensures that employees feel valued and empowered. The positive Service Economy atmosphere requires more than recognizing individuals' achievements, systemic commitment to collaboration. The study dedicates to those working environments creates inspire positive way to admire the dedication of employees commit to achieves the goals. Empower employees to succeed and grow by providing guidance, continuous support, and opportunities for skill development. When employees' attitudes, capabilities, and available resources align with the demands of their roles, they are more likely to integrate smoothly into the work environment and perform with consistency and confidence. When there is a significant mismatch whether real or perceived between an individual and their work environment, stress inevitably rises. When there is a significant mismatch whether real between an individual and their work environment, stress inevitably rises.

Designation serves as a key structural element within an organisation, shaping how processes and roles are defined. However, relying solely on a controlling mindset to achieve alignment among employees is ineffective, especially if individuals do not perceive meaningfulness in their work. Control-based approaches may enforce compliance, but they rarely inspire genuine commitment or enthusiasm. True inspired action arises from intrinsic motivation, where employees feel personally connected to their tasks and Service Economy goals. This intrinsic drive fosters creativity, engagement, and higher performance, which cannot be achieved through control alone. Therefore, Service Economy seeking sustainable alignment and must focus on cultivating meaningful work experiences that motivate employees beyond mere compliance.

Relevance to current management practices: Often emphasizing similar dimensions such as inclusive leadership:

Multinational companies have taken the lead by establishing diversity committees and setting strategic benchmarks to promote diversity and inclusion within the Service Economy. This indicates a shift from merely meeting legal compliance in the short term to embracing a long-term commitment to valuing diversity.

The workforce of today still reflects the demographic growth brought about by the baby boomer period. An effective leader is someone who can inspire their team to reach peak productivity and efficiency. However, one can only motivate others with what they themselves understand and possess. To truly motivate employees, a leader must grasp the essence of motivation and how to apply it meaningfully.

Financial rewards such as salaries and benefits are often seen as standard and do not necessarily serve as primary motivators. In contrast, elements that uphold personal dignity though they may not carry monetary value can have a profound impact. Their presence can create a positive and motivating work environment, while their absence often leads to frustration and disengagement. To achieve this successful development, it needs to use the necessary leadership skills to build the knowledge base of the workforce, maintain their rights, and develop their motivation When there are leaders with knowledge, skills, experience, and perspective employees can be happy and motivated because such leaders are knowledge-based and positively respond well to the needs and interests of the employees population increase, because of the baby boomers era, is still present in today's workforce.

Objectives of the chapter: To prioritize the basic issues that add to employee motivation:

To prevent wrong decisions from being made.

- Planning to achieve the mission of the institution.
- To enable the institution to carry out its mission without interruption.
- To achieve the goals of the Service Economy on time.
- To determine which position to fill with employees.
- To assess whether the Service Economy plan can be completed on time.
- To determine the results of the work of the Service Economy and the scale of the resources used.
- To evaluate the performance of the employee and the success of the Service Economy.
- To identify the potential gap between employees and during the evaluation of the plan, if it is found that there is work that has not been done during the

implementation of the plan, it is necessary to include it in the plan or organize it to be done later.
- It believes that any employee can gain benefits as much as he/she does their work in a Service Economy.

Key insights statement of problem:

To gain clearer knowledge of Service Economy diversity, inclusion, and equity and how each is implemented within various Service Economy.

Given that research does not follow a one-size-fits-all model, this study specifically examines how perceive Service Economy diversity, equity, and inclusion.

I believe that an individual's educational background should not affect the assignment of duties and responsibilities within any Service Economy.

Not only does a diverse work environment matter, but an inclusive culture also plays a vital role in making employees feel respected and integrated into the Service Economy.

Queering Service Economy Design:

Employee level: outcomes such as commitment, unique identity, self-satisfied and achieve goals.

Work group level: outcomes are conflicts, creativity and common goals, Service Economy level: outcomes are brand visibility, competitiveness and success goals globally.

This suggests that creating a supportive atmosphere within a Service Economy involves acknowledging something beyond individual efforts. Service Economy reputation and brand image encourages them to contribute their best work settings to guarantee their employees. The measurement model of team spirit at work comprises three lower-order constructs engaging work, sense of community, and spiritual connection. The engaging work construct reflects team members' perceptions of meaningfulness in their work and their gratitude for opportunities to actively participate in tasks they find fulfilling.

Focusing on Individual Strength and Growth-Oriented Performance Systems:

Employee strength use, which refers to the actions employees take to utilize their original strength in the Service Economy, has secured growing interest among leadership and Service Economy dynamics. Growth-oriented performance system through one's attitude and actions than merely through words. Key qualities associated with mastery include a sense of freedom, fearlessness and boldness, ambition paired with diligent effort, a strong desire for success, and competence. Human resource management involves a combination of people-cantered practices that view employees as valuable resources and aim to foster sustain their motivation while toward workplace counsellors' objectives. To achieve successful development, it is essential to apply effective focusing on individual strength skills to build the Service Economy's knowledge, protect their rights, and enhance their motivation. When growth oriented possess the right knowledge, skills, experience and perspectives, employees tend to feel satisfied and motivated because these informed and responsive to their needs and interests. In this way, human resource management encompasses all aspects of how people are recruited, engaged, and supported within the workplace counsellors.

A lack of clarity or alignment regarding an employee's job responsibilities within the Service Economy can lead to conflict. Delivering excellence in satisfied so employees for success when it comes to workplace counsellor's frontline bound between employees and workplace counsellors' rules/regulations, such compliances with one would make more difficult with other. Support evidence based and with knowledge and skills relating to appeared favourable effect. The reward performance linkage suggest that individuals often develop a work for pay mindset tying their efforts directly to compensation. To ensure the team's sense of responsibility towards its work to accurately assess individual outcomes, it is important to avoid the role in an individual success or failure. Internal motivation is driven by elements as a sense of higher purpose, personal efficacy's, self-worth, self-interest a feeling of wholeness, and the self-actualization. The key advantage motivation is that it encourages individual to take full ownership of their performance and outcomes. In a three dimensions experienced meaningfulness, perceived responsibility for outcomes, awareness of results having clear feedback on performance systems.

The future of Fixing the System, Not the Person: Technology, Globalization, and the human experience:

For sustainable development, organisation must deploy transformational leadership practices that expand the intellectual capacity of employees, safeguard their Service Economy rights, and ignite intrinsic motivation. Leaders who exhibit a breadth of knowledge, experiential wisdom, and a holistic vision cultivate psychologically safe and supportive work environments.

Diversity, Equity, Inclusion principles must be introduced new term into foundational structures such as recruitment, training, leadership development, policy making and performance evaluation.

Effective leadership is essential for systematic change. Leaders are encouraged to model inclusive values, establish fair processes, and cultivate a in terms of mental health safe workplace counsellors. Helping employee branding, boosting employee engagement and team valued overall engagement. Employees and employee may not have sufficient understanding.

Supports dignity, fairness and employee voice, a positive, respectful environment fuels employee motivation, satisfaction and Service Economy success. Without role models and employee participations remains low. Do not be a mouthpiece less talk, more action in workplace counsellors. Diversity, Equity, Inclusion decades used as a lens to examine and challenges beliefs, practices, process, policies and values. To became impact of positive more creative, innovation they learn new skills and knowledge to current situations to increase the employee and self-satisfaction.to became impact of negative other hand high stress causes unpleasant situations that create of stress lack of motivation, lack of interest outcomes in workplace counsellors.

Work- based factors identified can be different make a leadership, and employees make a Service Economy should feel confident ensuring, fairly frameworks more mentally healthy. Everyone gets equal opportunities in the work and Service Economy insights retain talent by exploring can prioritize supportive workplace counsellors. Work related stress is strongly associated with resignation intentions, and a sign of mental health well-being reducing resignation rates. Today in the era of competitive environment, workforce becomes most difficult task, to be sustaining in this challenging motivated and skilful employee are essential is also explaining the relationship between leadership role motivates employee to work hard to achieve their stated goal's capable goal where one must learn to accept, respect processes unique qualities that when recognized and respected overall effectiveness to get positive results,

Therefore, this study will discuss the relationship Diversity, Equity, Inclusion and mental health in Service Economy towards achieving higher level of Service Economy and leadership direction of the employee.

2. CONCEPTUAL FRAMEWORK

The conceptual foundation of Diversity, Equity and Inclusion three core principles,

2.1 Diversity

Diversity refers to the wide range of unique qualities, characteristics, and dimensions that everyone possesses. This includes race, ethnicity, age, gender, religious beliefs, life experiences, and other personal attributes that contribute to the richness of any group or Service Economy includes both visible and invisible. Recognizes that everyone contributes a distinct perspective shaped by their identity and background (Jakhete et al 2025). Diversity is not just about representation it is environments with varied backgrounds and perspectives, varied identities and experiences, multifaceted nature of human.

2.2 Equity

Equity addresses systemic imbalances to provide fair access for all, fair treatment and opportunities, needs of individuals or groups, addressing structural and support so that everyone has a fair chance to succeed and fully participate, perform and thrive. acknowledge that historical and structural barriers exist for marginalized groups and seeks to remove them.

2.3 Inclusion

Inclusion ensures that every voice is acknowledged, valued, active engagement and empowerment of all individuals, regardless of their background or status fullest potential. While diversity represents the natural mix of people in a workplace counsellor, inclusion is the deliberate choice to make that mix work effectively. Encourages open communication, collaboration decision making and recognition of all voices. Inclusion transforms diverse groups into cohesive, high-performance teams by promoting mutual respect and shared purpose.

Figure 1.

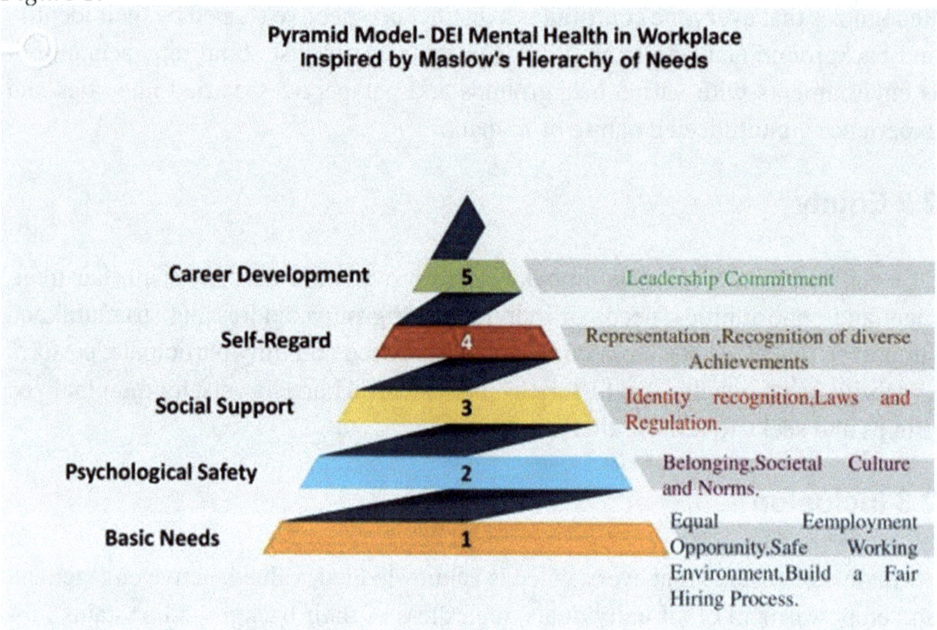

Source: Maslow (1943, 1954)

Employees who are their individual strength often experience heightened closely with the conceptualization of work engagement such as a dynamic, positive and dedication strength based contributes such Service Economy engagement by recognizing and valuing employee's unique strength aligning responsibilities facilitating. Discussions around strength development, an establishment of enhance through the identification, application and cultivation of employees encourage strength which is positively ensures that problem solving identities in the competitive environment.

Fair and respectful treatment highlights where you began; addressing safety and basic needs shows what has been effective; and providing opportunities for success reveals where the organization still needs to grow.

Figure 2.

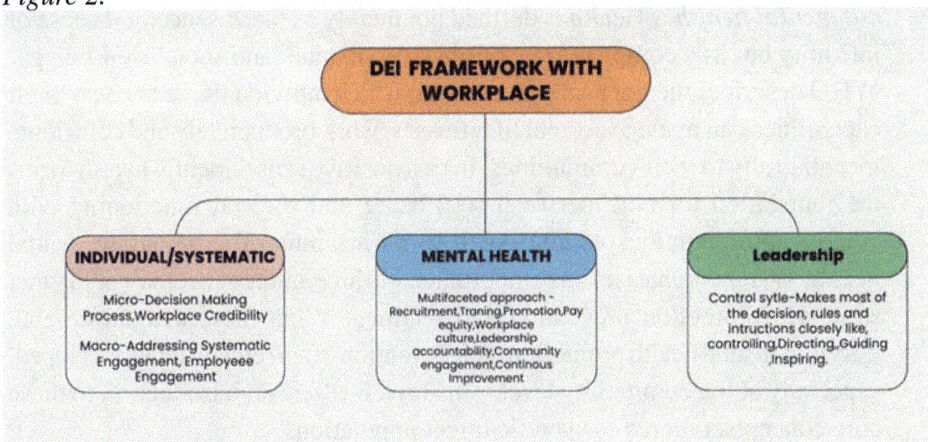

Source: created by author

2.4 Service Economy:

Service Economy are prepared to enhance their initiatives to meet commitments for boosting employee engagement. However, in some organizations, the quality of leadership fails to meet the standard expected, damaging their reputation.

The workplace promotes equal opportunity for all employees and upholds the principle of fairness in all aspects of employment. It strongly opposes favouritism or even the appearance of it.

These values are embedded in the organization's code of conduct and ethics. Personal backgrounds, social status, or cultural heritage do not influence workplace decisions, ensuring a respectful, unbiased, and peaceful working environment.

Engagement: A distinct powerful source of energy and motivation that stems from genuine passion and involvement in one's work.
Job satisfaction: A positive emotional response arising from favourable Service Economy conditions such as compensation, career opportunities and interpersonal relationship, often accompanied by a strong sense of belonging and attachment to the Service Economy

2.5 Mental health:

Establishing support networks for employees with shared traits or interests, offering a platform for representation and collective support.

The world health organisation (WHO) affirms that ***"there is no health without mental health".*** Health is defined not merely as the absence of disease or infirmity but as a complete state of physical, mental, and social well-being. **WHO** describes mental health as a state in which individuals are aware of their capabilities can manage normal life stresses, work productively and contribute meaningfully to their communities. In this positive sense, mental health forms the foundation for both personal well-being and societal functioning with cultural interpretations adding depth to its meaning. To strengthen mental health, WHO emphasizes the importance of three interconnected yet distinct strategies: promotion, prevention, and treatment. While these areas are crucial, efforts in mental health promotion and prevention often remain underdeveloped, especially at the community level. This review offers an introduction to these core concepts, tailored to specific target populations.

At any one time, a diverse set of individual, family, community and structural factors may combine to protect or undermine mental health. Although most people are resilient, people who are exposed to adverse circumstances including poverty, violence, disability and inequality are at higher risk of developing a mental health condition. Many mental health conditions can be effectively treated at relatively low cost, yet health systems remain significantly under resourced and treatment gaps are wide all over the world. Mental health care is often poor in quality when delivered.

2.6 Service Economy on their capacity to grasp the benefits of difference:

Employees do work in a Service Economy manner the responsible and are given opportunity to gain high learning knowledge in particular job role experts. Employees with different education levels can work together efficiency in the Service Economy. All the differences are not treated the same "the way of unique in working style "job role. Both the employers and all employees need to have an be willing to learn every day with each other to promote a positive, safe, and successful gathering. The upcoming generation lack to the old deal's individuals having different information to attain in the Service Economy goals. The literature reviews, clear policies deal employees focusing on individual strength and growth of success manner. Some of the costs or damages of what people do occur beyond their preview, and they either know or do not care about them in the Service Economy. Similar goals Service Economy values examine the confidence level observed analysis the activity and reflecting the employee's engagement. Equal opportunities for participation work together drive the reputation.

3.LITERATURE REVIEW

Equivalent entities are increasingly regarded as moral institutions advocating for the dignity, justice, and rightful place of the marginalized within the workforce. Their role extends to securing improved working and living conditions and ensuring fairness and equity in employment contexts. Moreover, efforts to self-confidence, encouraging sincerity and discipline and providing meaningful opportunities for career progression and growth.

Saxena (2014), in a study the literature emphasizes that workforce diversity comprising differences in age, gender, culture, religion and perception offers both opportunities and challenges. When managed effectively, diversity enhances innovation, creativity, problem solving and global competitiveness. However, poor diversity management can lead to communication barriers, interpersonal conflict, and reduced.

Chaudhry and Sharma (2017) states that in their study age diversity has a slight but significant influence on employee performance, with both young and experienced employees contributing uniquely to organisation success, Ethnic diversity shows a small yet definite positive correlation with performance, especially when organisations respect cultural identities and avoid discrimination. Educational diversity is stronger associated with better employee performance. Higher levels of education are associated with greater creativity, enhanced professionalism, and fewer counterproductive behaviors.

Inegbedion et al. (2020) in their study establishes that Service Economy diversity in the terms of race, gender, age, religion and cultural background has become a defining feature of modern organizations due to globalization. While diversity presents numerous challenges such as communication barriers discrimination and resistances to change, it also offers significant benefits like enhanced innovation, Broder perspectives, and improved Service Economy performance. Effective diversity management involves recognizing and valuing individual differences, promoting inclusion and addressing issues like marginalized cultural conflict.

Henry Inegbedion (2020) has further examined how diversity management affects organizational success, performance, and effectiveness. They emphasize that well-managed diversity improves innovation, teamwork, and competitiveness. Workforce diversity has become a defining feature of modern organizations, bringing both opportunities and challenges. It refers to the differences among employees stemming from various backgrounds, including gender, age, race, ethnicity, religion, physical ability, education, and culture. Such diversity enriches the Service Economy with multiple perspectives, skills, and problem-solving approaches, which can enhance creativity, innovation, and competitiveness. Highlighted both the benefits and challenges of diversity and stressed the need for proper management tools.

The International Labour Organization (ILO, 2021), reviewed Diversity and Inclusion through an online survey of 10,000 respondents across more than 40 countries and various sectors, encompassing small and medium-sized enterprises as well as large multinational corporations, with a focus on lower- to middle-income economies he study aims to generate fresh insights and understanding to better support enterprise in driving meaningful and lasting change in Diversity and Inclusion by examining.

Amirkhanyan, Krawczyk, and Wilamowski (2021) highlighted that men generally exhibit higher overconfidence than women across various contexts, including academics, finance and physical tasks. Culture factors, gender stereotypes, and task type influence these differences. Studies suggests that in more gender equal countries, both men and women tend to be less overconfident, reducing the gender gap. Overconfidence is linked to risky behavior and poor decision making, particularly among men. The authors use marathon pacing data as a novel and objective proxy to measure overconfidence across 70 countries, correlating it with national gender inequality indicators.

Rafaqat et al. (2022), reviewed studies that showed mixed but mostly positive effects of workforce diversity specifically age, gender, cultural, racial, and ethnic diversity on organizational performance. Many studies confirm that diversity can boost innovation, creativity, decision-making quality, and financial outcomes when well managed. However, some research finds negative or insignificant effects, especially when diversity leads to conflict, poor cohesion, or is not supported by inclusive practices. Overall, the balance and proper management of diversity are crucial for realizing its benefits for performance.

Solis-Grant et al. (2022) emphasized that inclusion education is a dynamic and evolving process rooted in equity, social justice, and human rights. Global declarations such as the universal declaration of human rights and UNESCO's initiatives have established inclusion as a core principle in education. While most inclusion research has focused on primary and secondary education, there is growing recognition of its importance in higher education, where diversity is increasing. Despite progress, inclusion in universities often lacks genuine institutional commitment, with policies sometimes serving more as symbolic gestures than transformative practices. Inclusion in higher education requires not just policy change but cultural transformation, involving all stakeholders' students, staff and administration.

Morris (2023), highlighted that cultural diversity in the Service Economy can enhance creativity, innovation, and overall business performance if properly managed. However, diversity also brings challenges such as communication barriers, misunderstandings, and potential conflicts. Research emphasizes that the key factor is not diversity alone but how managers implement strategies to promote inclusion, tolerance, and respect among employees. Effective management practices, clear policies, and cultural awareness training are crucial to harness the benefits of diversity and minimize drawbacks.

Leuhery (2024), this study reviews highlights that when leaders prioritize D&I, it creates a trickle-down effect, fostering inclusivity at all organizational levels (Guo et al. (2023)). For example, leadership buy-in is critical for the effective implementation of diversity training programs and inclusive policies. When employees observe that their leaders are genuinely committed to building an inclusive Service Economy, they more likely to engage with and support D&I initiatives (Atiku et al. (2024)). This alignment between leadership actions and organizational values reinforces the role of diversity and inclusion in driving business success.

Alshemmari and Al Monawer (2024), analyses the interplay between Service Economy diversity and innovation, and how they collectively impact organizational success with a specific focus on managers in the Kuwaiti banking sector. The research identifies various dimensions of diversity such as socio-economic status, religion, gender, ethnicity, and education and examines their role in fostering innovation and improving performance and leadership role in diversity-driven innovation requires further study.

Radhika and Mahalakshmi (2024), explored the role of Diversity, Equity, and Inclusion in shaping employee well-being. It examines how Diversity, Equity and Inclusion initiatives influence employee engagement, satisfaction, and productivity through both qualitative and quantitative methods, sense of belonging. Employees tend to feel more engaged when Diversity, Equity, and Inclusion (DEI) initiatives are implemented. Regarding equity perceptions, 83.3% of respondents believed their organization practiced fairness, mainly through performance-based promotions. Additionally, 40% of respondents emphasized the importance of inclusion in organizational decision-making processes.

Zhao et al. (2025), highlighted that while many D&I activities are widely used, the quality of evidence varies, and there remains a gap between academic knowledge and practical guidance for managers. Clearer, evidence-based frameworks are needed to help organizations choose interventions that genuinely improve inclusion and equity across diverse dimensions.

The reviewed studies collectively emphasize that workforce diversity, inclusion, and equity positively influence innovation, creativity, employee engagement, and organizational performance when managed effectively through inclusive leadership and fair policies. However, challenges such as communication barriers, discrimination, resistance to change, and lack of institutional commitment highlight the need for evidence-based diversity management practices and supportive organizational cultures.

4.DISCUSSION

The study aspires to provide new insights and understanding that will empower enterprise to drive meaningful and transformative advancements in Diversity, Equity and Inclusion by investigation.

This research will conduct a broad survey of Diversity and Inclusion literature alongside survey of 10,000 participants from more than 40 countries, covering various sectors that include small and medium-sized enterprises as well as large multinational corporations, with a particular focus on lower-to middle-income economies. The discussion draws on global perspectives, including WHO's Mental Health Action Plan (2013–2030) and the International Labour Organization's (ILO) efforts, emphasizing that mental health must be prioritized alongside Diversity, Equity, and Inclusion in all work environments. Addressing challenges such as resistance to change, resource constraints, and inconsistent leadership commitment is essential to ensure sustainable progress.

The International Labour Organization: This review publication trends sense of inspiration and possible overview promote well-being best practices. Additionally, changes for growth in professional, acknowledge, and work life balances improve employees 'engagement.

Challenges such as resistances to change, resources limitation process and through leadership commitment, employee engagement and emulation. Ensure that Diversity, Equity and Inclusion address multiple identity, principles reveals both challenges and opportunity. Integrating principles into essential intuitional activities such as recruitment, training, leadership growth, policy development, and evaluation is central to effective diversity management.

This study aims to provide deeper insights into how Diversity, Equity, and Inclusion can be leveraged to promote employee mental health and overall Service Economy well-being. It highlights the importance of embedding Diversity, Equity, and Inclusion principles into core organizational functions such as recruitment, leadership development, training, policymaking, and performance evaluation. Effective Diversity, Equity, and Inclusion strategies must address multiple intersecting identities and move beyond surface-level initiatives. The integration of Diversity, Equity, and Inclusion into institutional systems is essential for promoting equity, fair treatment, and a culture of inclusion.

The discussion stresses that inclusive, supportive, and mentally healthy Service Economys contribute significantly to employee engagement, innovation, and long-term organizational success. Real transformation requires leadership accountability, strategic alignment, and continuous evaluation of policies and practices. Overcoming these challenges requires persistent leadership accountability, strategic alignment, and a culture of continuous improvement. Furthermore, mental health support systems such as peer networks, psychological services, and wellness policies must be included in frameworks to ensure sustainability. Inclusive Service Economy foster a sense of belonging, boost employee engagement, and promote creativity and innovation.

5.CONCLUSION

As a result, organisations must embed fairness and respect into every aspect of their operations to foster environments that attract and retain diversity talent. The pursuit of truly inclusive Service Economy is an ongoing journey, despite this, the excepted outcomes rewards ranging from enhanced employee satisfaction and retention to improved organisational performance are undeniable. This study leaves readers with clear understanding of the critical need to integrate mental health considerations into leadership practices, positioning its findings within the border efforts to continuously improve Service Economy environments. In our review of the literature, we note several significant themes that should be reflected in the integrative model of diversity presented in, first it is the Service Economy context both internal and external plays a significant role in shaping the nature and impact of diversity.

A second theme, has been defined and measured in multiple ways, creating conceptual ambiguity and hindering the accumulation of knowledge the interactions within the levels of the realities of workplace counsellors. The third theme key, is the multifaceted effects of diversity, ranging from individual wellbeing and equal opportunity to performance and Service Economy success.

Recognizing and valuing diversity, advancing equity, and fostering are essential not only from an ethical standpoint but also as crucial elements for attracting and retaining talent in today's fast-changing landscape. As Service Economy evolve, sustained efforts are needed to tackle ongoing inequities and to build environments where individuals can engage fully and authentically, honouring their unique identities and personal goals. Diversity, Equity and Inclusion policies must extend beyond merely addressing inequalities, they should build systems that promote equal opportunity and transparent procedures, ensuring all employees are treated with dignity and respect. Disparities in treatment based on identity factors, such as gender, age, disability, or religion erode trust and can significantly contribute to mental health challenges. Sustainable progress requires ongoing learning, regular policy evaluation, collective commitment, leadership accountability, and a willingness to adapt. Inclusive Service Economy contribute to greater creativity, shaper problem solving, higher employee satisfaction, and stronger public trust, while reinforcing ethical standards and evidence-based practices.

Reward-performance and team's sense of responsibility towards its work he success or failure. Employees who possess creativity as a core strength excel in generating innovative solutions to complex Service Economy challenges. In contrast, those whose signature strength is perseverance demonstrate their best performance when pursuing long-term goals, especially in the face of obstacles and setbacks. Leadership is conveyed more through attitude and actions than through words Certain attributes connected with mastery include sense of freedom, fearlessness and hard work, thirst for success and competence human resource management is a mix of people management practices, and they recognize employees as resources and strive to achieve and maintain organizational goals that create and maintain their employees' motivation.

REFERENCES

Alshemmari, J. M. H. J., & Al Monawer, F. H. (2024). Analyzing the relationship between workplace diversity and innovation and its influence on organizational performance. *Journal of System and Management Sciences*, *14*(1), 471–489. https://doi.org/10.33168/JSMS.2024.0127

Amirkhanyan, H., Krawczyk, M. W., & Wilamowski, M. (2021). Gender inequality and national gender gaps in overconfidence. *PLoS One*, *16*(4), e0249459. https://doi.org/10.1371/journal.pone.0249459

Atiku, S. O., Omisore, B. O., & Akinyemi, A. I. (2024). Leadership commitment and employee engagement in diversity and inclusion initiatives. *International Journal of Organizational Leadership*, *13*(1), 45–60.

Chaudhry, S., & Sharma, D. (2017). Workforce diversity and employee performance: A study of organizational effectiveness. *International Journal of Human Resource Studies*, *7*(3), 45–58.

Guo, Y., Chen, X., & Zhang, L. (2023). Leadership commitment and inclusive workplace culture: Implications for diversity management. *Journal of Organizational Behavior*, *44*(2), 210–225.

Inegbedion, H., Sunday, E., Asaleye, A., Lawal, A., & Adebanji, A. (2020). Managing diversity for organizational efficiency. *SAGE Open*, *10*(1), 1–10. DOI: 10.1177/2158244019900173

International Labour Organization. (2021). *A literature review of diversity and inclusion in the workplace*. ILO.

Jakhete, M., Shende, P., Patil, P. A., Rana, V. S., & Raina, A. (2025). Synthesizing best practice frameworks for results measurement in multi-stakeholder social entrepreneurship initiatives. *Enterprise Development & Microfinance*, *35*(1), 140–158.

Leuhery, F. (2024). Leadership and diversity inclusion practices in modern organizations. *Journal of Human Resource and Sustainability Studies*, *12*(1), 55–70.

Maslow, A. H. (1943). A theory of human motivation. *Psychological Review*, *50*(4), 370–396. DOI: 10.1037/h0054346

Maslow, A. H. (1954). *Motivation and personality*. Harper & Row.

Morris, S. N. (2023). Cultural diversity in the workplace and the role of management. *American Journal of Industrial and Business Management*, *13*(5), 380–393. DOI: 10.4236/ajibm.2023.135024

Radhika, J., & Mahalakshmi, P. (2024). Diversity, equity, and inclusion practices and employee well-being. *International Journal of Management Research and Review*, *14*(2), 88–101.

Rafaqat, S., Rafaqat, S., Rafaqat, S., & Rafaqat, D. (2022). The impact of workforce diversity on organizational performance. *Journal of Economics and Behavioral Studies*, *14*(2), 39–50. DOI: 10.22610/jebs.v14i2(J).3301

Saxena, A. (2014). Workforce diversity: A key to improve productivity. *Procedia Economics and Finance*, *11*, 76–85.

Solis-Grant, M. J., Espinoza-Parcet, C., Sepulveda-Carrasco, C., Perez-Villalobos, C., Rodriguez-Nunez, I., Pincheira-Martinez, C., Gomez-Varela, J. P., & Aranguiz-Ibarra, D. (2022). Inclusion at universities: Psychometric properties of an inclusive management scale. *PLoS One*, *17*(1), e0262011. https://doi.org/10.1371/journal.pone.0262011

Vasanthan, R., Babu, M. N., Dzuvichu, K., Chong, T. S., Rana, V. S., & Singh, A. (2025). Bridging social norms theory and community mobilization: Pathways for overcoming gender stereotypes in women's economic empowerment programs. *Enterprise Development & Microfinance*, *35*(1), 159–176.

World Health Organization. (n.d.). Mental health: Strengthening our response. World Health Organization. https://www.who.int/news-room/fact-sheets/detail/mental-health-strengthening-our-response

Zhao, K., Hsieh, W., Faulkner, N., & Smith, L. (2025). Evidence-based diversity, equity, and inclusion frameworks in organizations. *Human Resource Development Review*, *24*(1), 15–31.

Chapter 4
Leadership Continuity and Capability:
Examining Succession Planning as a Strategic Imperative

Timcy Sachdeva
http://orcid.org/0000-0001-9978-9459
Vivekananda Institute of Professional Studies-TC, India

Ridhima Sharma
http://orcid.org/0000-0002-7851-0292
Vivekananda Institute of Professional Studies-TC, India

ABSTRACT

The research describes succession planning as a strategic imperative that is incorporated into governance, organizational culture, and long-term capability development, rather than a reactive human resources function. A comprehensive literature evaluation of fifty-two peer-reviewed publications published between 2010 and 2025 was conducted using the PRISMA approach in order to integrate current information on succession planning strategies, models, and outcomes. The review emphasizes the long-term significance of Rothwell's Succession Planning and Management (SPM) model and expands on it with a consolidated five-pillar framework that includes leadership. The findings indicate that firms with well-organized, inclusive, and strategically integrated succession plans had higher levels of leadership continuity, employee engagement, and organizational legitimacy.

DOI: 10.4018/979-8-3373-6395-0.ch004

INTRODUCTION

Maintaining performance and staying focused on goals despite leadership changes is more important in today's fast-paced corporate climate. Organizational resilience and competitiveness are now heavily influenced by leadership continuity, which was once seen as a minor administrative matter. As challenges arise from changing demographics, globalization, digitization, and the demands of many stakeholders, strategic succession planning is no longer only advised but is essential. The role of succession planning is shifting from that of a purely HR function to that of an essential part of corporate governance, talent management, and long-term strategy. There are major repercussions to unanticipated changes in leadership. When a senior leader leaves, whether willingly or not, it can lead to a loss of important institutional knowledge, harm to reputation, and major disruptions in operations (Payne et al., 2018). The lack of controlled succession procedures endangers not just continuity, but also adherence and economic responsibility, according to their study on public health organizations. These dangers aren't exclusive to any industry; they strike nonprofits, for-profits, and public institutions all the same, highlighting the necessity of institutional succession plans everywhere (Payne et al., 2018). Organizational performance and flexibility may both be enhanced through succession planning. Zafar and Akhtar (2020) state that good succession plans not only ensure a continuous flow of competent leaders but also boost morale, creativity, and advancement opportunities for current employees. According to Zafar and Akhtar (2020), these traits help create a pleasant workplace and lessen the impact of leadership changes. Organizational outcomes including operational stability, greater innovation potential, and cultural consistency are improved by succession planning, according to their study. Notwithstanding these benefits, many companies either don't plan for succession or utilize antiquated methods that depend only on replacement charts. Concerns about the erosion of meritocratic principles have kept many organizations, including public service organizations (Reid, 2005), from instituting systematic succession procedures. Public sector organizations are also seeing the need to adopt succession models that are influenced by the private sector. These models emphasize integrated human capital development and future readiness in response to rising leadership roles and retirement rates (Reid, 2005).

There has been a sea change in the current idea of succession with the reorientation of succession planning from an approach that is reactive and focused on positions to one that is proactive and centered around developing talent. Modern businesses see succession planning not as a means to prepare for the loss of key employees but as a chance to gradually enhance skills. This trend is corroborated by the results of a thematic research on succession planning procedures among CEOs in Ghana that was carried out by Coffie et al. (2022). While some companies acknowledge the strategic value of succession planning, their research shows that just a minority of those companies have comprehensive plans in place. Additionally, their research shows that boards of directors are crucial in implementing and promoting strategic succession plans (Coffie et al., 2022).

As part of a comprehensive succession plan, it is not enough to just fill open positions; leadership development must also be in line with the organization's purpose and objectives for the future. Groves (2007) and Ingale (2024) are among the scholars who contend that the process starts with a well-defined organizational goal and continues with the identification of the critical leadership skills needed to achieve that goal. In order to evaluate current talent pools and develop plans to help individuals with great potential improve, these abilities are employed as standards. The end game is to build a pipeline of future leaders that are committed to the same principles, culture, and goals as the company. Several elements are necessary for an all-encompassing succession planning approach. To identify future talent needs and possible succession planning failure areas, first-rate leadership forecasting is essential. As part of this process, it is necessary to think about different scenarios, demographics (such as recording when people are eligible to retire), and changes in the sector. Secondly, it needs to pay close attention to gap analysis and competency mapping. Find out if the individuals applying for critical jobs have the specific knowledge, abilities, and personality traits needed for the job with the help of these tools. Not only does this approach find possible heirs, but it also pinpoints places that need developmental funding to fill preparation shortages, as pointed out by Collings and Mellahi (2009). Thirdly, businesses should encourage learning and development methods include coaching, job rotation, mentorship, and action learning. Research shows that these strategies help students become better leaders. Research by Yadav et al. (2023) found that action learning programs can improve managerial abilities and cross-functional competence by putting high-potential employees in charge of solving strategic problems in real time. In addition to preparing people to take on leadership roles, these tactics boost loyalty among workers and help keep the company's culture alive. Fourth, programs for diversity, performance evaluation, and pay structure are all examples of strategic human resource systems that should be integrated with succession planning. By bringing HR and business goals into harmony, strategic alignment elevates succession planning to the level of an essential business function. The integration of management responsibilities, performance targets, and leadership pipeline goals may be enhanced by integrating succession planning into strategic planning frameworks, as stated by Meseguer-Sánchez et al. (2021) and Frasier (2019).

Strategic succession relies heavily on identifying high-potential individuals and developing individualized plans for their professional growth. Leadership evaluations, together with quantitative and behavioral performance metrics, enter the picture at this stage. Rosenzweig (2024) and Cadmus (2006) state that systematic assessments aid in career planning conversations by revealing underutilized ability. Aligning the company's objectives with the skills of its personnel is achieved through evaluations that are connected to the purpose and values of the organization. Having cultural alignment is also crucial. More and more, businesses are coming to the realization that technical expertise alone is not enough to make a good leader. In uncertain or ever-changing situations, it is helpful to have good interpersonal skills, the capacity to adapt, emotional intelligence, and a firm grasp of right and wrong. In succession planning, soft skills are equally significant as formal competence, according to Utaminingsih et al. (2024). Accordingly, all angles need to be considered and developed for succession management to be effective. It is important for succession plans to take external benchmarking and governance needs into account in addition to internal development. An even greater need for board monitoring arises in the event of a CEO or other C-suite executive's resignation. Insufficient board participation in succession planning puts long-term survival at risk for many firms in developing markets, according to Coffie et al. (2022). A key component of the duties of board members in organizations with developed governance frameworks is to assess, evaluate, and keep tabs on succession planning on a regular basis.

Strategic succession is enhanced by technology because it enables better decision-making. For future planning, readiness assessments, and leadership development investment decisions, digital dashboards, predictive analytics, and simulations driven by artificial intelligence (AI) could be useful tools. The usage of technology should not supplant human judgment, but rather augment it, as several authors have cautioned. Finding out if someone is motivated, culturally compatible, and a good fit still requires human judgment.

Last but not least, a viable succession plan may boost a company's credibility. It shows that the company is steady, future-oriented, and ready for anything to happen to its stakeholders including workers, investors, and regulators. Incorporating a plan for leadership transition into long-term messaging reinforces the company's reputation as a place where people can grow and adapt, especially in the face of uncertainty (Reid, 2005). When executed well, succession planning fosters not just a steady flow of leadership but also strategic flexibility, cultural authenticity, and the creation of value over the long run, according to the research. Organizations may strengthen their leadership pipelines and make them more resilient to change and more successful in the long run by integrating human capital systems, governance, strategic planning, and leadership development.

LITERATURE REVIEW

The academic discussion around succession planning has grown more intricate, painting a picture of it as an all-encompassing and strategic organizational strategy. The original intent of succession planning was to find people to take over senior positions. It has evolved into an all-encompassing approach that includes elements such as organizational resilience, strategy alignment, leadership development, and people recruiting. Many studies have utilized the resource-based view (RBV) of the company as their theoretical framework. It argues that human capital, and especially leadership potential, is a precious resource that, if properly identified, developed, and used, may lead to a competitive advantage in the long run (Siambi, 2022; Barney, 1991). Under these circumstances, succession planning is not only an administrative obligation, but rather a strategic capability that requires ongoing cultivation in order to facilitate future leadership transitions. Not only should the C-suite be included in succession planning, but other critical positions inside an organization should as well, according to a new research. According to Martin (2024), businesses that have clear succession plans tend to have more stable operations, less problems during transitions, and engaged employees. Based on their empirical study, clearly defined leadership routes boost motivation, retention, and the ability of internal candidates to take on more responsibility by intentionally developing their competencies. One of the most important parts of successful succession planning is integrating it with strategic talent management; say Schweitzer and Graebe (2024). According to them, organizations can keep their leadership in place and raise performance standards and professional rigor by implementing succession planning into accredited professional development programs like the ones provided by the American Nurses Credentialing Center (ANCC). Accreditation and long-term performance management are both enhanced by this strategic integration, which also involves succession.

Creating a framework for succession planning initiatives is another important point made in the research. This includes things like assignment rotation, mentorship programs, performance reviews, and leadership training. Technological integration, comprehensive performance rating systems, specialized training programs, staff retention strategies, and adaptive organizational structures are the five important enablers identified by Lakshmi (2024) as they pertain to business succession planning. This all-encompassing perspective mirrors the increasing agreement that succession planning ought to be perceived as an evolving framework that cultivates leadership preparedness on several fronts.

Additionally, frameworks for leadership development are crucial to good succession planning. Ananthi et al. (2023) found that leadership development and succession planning must happen simultaneously in Hindustan Unilever's succession plans. Incorporating these practices into company culture helps with generational shifts, encouraging creative problem-solving and reducing the impact of leadership changes that aren't anticipated. In order to foster leadership resilience across all levels of an organization, their research shows that structured growth procedures are crucial.

According to Siambi (2022), there are three primary models used in the field of succession planning: the organizational transition model, the human capital development model, and the resource-based alignment model. These views see succession planning as an evolving, policy-driven process with far-reaching consequences for holding on to people, maintaining performance, and preserving knowledge. According to Siambi (2022), a well-thought-out policy framework is required for smooth transitions, which go beyond simple identification and preparation. Such a framework should include succession into all aspects of strategic planning, governance, and change management. The execution of succession planning is still hindered by institutional and cultural hurdles. Even prosperous businesses expanding into new areas often lack clear strategies for future leadership, as pointed out by Coffie et al. (2022). Unfortunately, most of the time, their scope is either too limited or they just don't follow through. The importance of incorporating conversations about leadership succession into board agendas and strategic planning sessions is highlighted by this oversight. Furthermore, it necessitates a change in perspective on the part of businesses regarding leadership continuity, viewing it now not as a preventative measure but as an absolute need (Coffie et al., 2022).

In conclusion, the literature delves into the potential impact of technology on succession planning. Finding potential personnel, tracking their progress, and simulating leadership transition scenarios are all made easier with digital tools like talent analytics platforms, AI-driven evaluations, and predictive performance models. On the other hand, professionals say that AI shouldn't be used to supplant human judgment but to supplement it. Emotional intelligence, cultural fit, and adaptability are still hard to measure, yet they are crucial for a leader to succeed. The existing literature presents succession planning as an organized, systematic, and ever-changing process. No longer is it sufficient to choose prospective successors according on their length of service or how well they are thought to have performed. In its place, succession planning has to be closely tied to the organization's objectives, leadership style, governance structures, and ways of educating employees. According to the research, companies should build inclusive, future-oriented, and data-driven succession planning models that are built on competencies and can withstand both internal and external threats. The literature on succession planning also highlights the need of emotional intelligence (EI) and psychological readiness as key elements of a smooth leadership changeover. Newer studies reveal that relational traits, rather than technical competence or functional knowledge, are the most important for leadership success during and after changes. Especially in politically complicated and highly volatile organizational contexts, emotional intelligence—which encompasses self-awareness, empathy, and flexibility—has shown to be a robust predictor of success in the years following a succession. According to Siambi (2022), CEOs with high EI are better at handling interpersonal connections, overcoming opposition, and keeping morale high during times of transition. This, in turn, leads to easier organizational changes. These results are in line with the literature on organizational behavior, which establishes a connection between leaders' interpersonal skills and empathy and the growth of trust, which in turn leads to revolutionary transformation.

Succession planning is also heavily influenced by the organizational structure and the degree to which decision-making is decentralized. Flatter, team-based organizations are not well-suited to traditional succession models that rely on one-way pathways to leadership. Scholars like Kur and Bunning (2002) argue that instead of focusing on appointing a single successor, we should move toward establishing leadership roles that prioritize teams or cohorts. Modern theories of leadership, such dispersed and group leadership, are compatible with this paradigm. Leadership, according to these theories, is most effective when power is shared amongst people who have been well trained. In these types of systems, the goal of succession planning is not so much to identify a suitable replacement as it is to strengthen and institutionalize the leadership role throughout the whole business. Research on succession planning from an inclusive, equitable, and diverse perspective is also on the rise. Researchers found that without consideration of DEI, succession systems tend to reinforce structural injustices and make it harder to establish leadership that is representative of the population. Ananthi et al. (2023) states that leadership positions are underrepresented among women and people of color, especially in companies that uphold patriarchal values or have racial prejudices. In order to guarantee that underrepresented groups are recognized, mentored, and promoted through equitable access to leadership development opportunities, strategic succession planning should incorporate explicit DEI frameworks. This enhances creativity and decision-making while also satisfying ethical norms. In order to overcome difficult problems and align stakeholders, diverse leadership teams outperform homogenous ones.

In addition, studies conducted on nonprofits and public sector enterprises have shown unique challenges and shifts in succession planning approaches. Public businesses face obstacles such as bureaucratic red tape, limited funding, and hiring based on merit. In contrast, CEOs in private companies may be helped in their careers by financial incentives or shareholder mandates. In public organizations, succession planning is often underused due to people's fears of nepotism, a lack of long-term vision, and a reluctance to implement policies that identify leaders (Ramya et al., 2026). Other research, however, shows that these communities are becoming more strategic as a whole, especially as a large number of baby boomers enter retirement age. This has led innovative organizations to start building talent pools with tools like competence matrices, multi-tier mentoring, and scenario-based transition simulations. On occasion, laws passed by legislatures or certification bodies for professionals would back such endeavors. Mentoring and coaching are listed as important roles in the literature as well. It is most effective for succession planning to be implemented when high-potential individuals are given formal mentorship relationships and organized growth opportunities. Not only do mentors provide knowledge and advice on strategy, but they also impart the intangibles like the company's values, traditions, and informal power dynamics. To train future leaders in the intangible aspects of leadership, executive mentorship is essential, according to Fulmer and Conger (2004). Strategic thinking, stakeholder management, and dispute resolution are just a few examples of the kinds of competencies that may benefit greatly from coaching. Mentoring and coaching are cornerstones of many modern succession plans.

Recent studies have also highlighted the disparity between performance management and succession planning as a critical problem. Lakshmi (2024) argues that current methods of evaluating performance rely too much on past results, which can lead to the loss of future leaders with qualities like innovation, flexibility, and strategic vision. She suggests updating current assessment practices to incorporate more predictive indications of future performance in leadership roles, such as learning agility and potential. Behavioral assessments with numerous assessors and 360-degree feedback are becoming more popular, which supports this viewpoint. Managers' biases are lessened and a candidate's preparedness is more accurately shown in this way. A lot of companies' succession plans have changed because of the digital revolution. Predictive analytics and other cutting-edge tools have made it possible for businesses to simulate leadership scenarios, find high-potential employees, and forecast workforce changes. An example of a talent dashboard would be one that tracks employees' growth goals and notifies HR of any holes in the leadership pipeline. Even while these technologies make things more efficient and let people make decisions based on data, others worry that they may make people too reliant on statistics and dehumanize them. To avoid reducing leadership development to a series of algorithmic tests, Schweitzer and Graebe (2024) propose combining AI technologies with qualitative insights. Particularly when evaluating multi-faceted characteristics like cultural awareness, ethical compass, and interpersonal impact, they propose hybrid systems in which digital tools augment human judgment.

There is a growing body of research that calls for ERM and succession planning to work hand in hand. There is a serious threat to governance from sudden changes in leadership. Companies that fail to have a strategy in place for the future of leadership are more prone to break the rules, lose valuable institutional knowledge, and tarnish their reputation (Payne et al., 2018). By incorporating succession planning into risk management frameworks, organizations may better detect issues connected to succession, prepare for leadership departures, and put backup plans into action. A board of directors' succession planning should be a frequent topic of discussion and should be closely tied to the board's strategic supervision and fiduciary duties. Global and multiethnic contexts make succession planning more difficult. Global companies need to make sure their succession plans are localized to each region's own labor laws, cultural norms, and talent pool. Take leadership skills as an example. They might not be as important at Western headquarters as they are in emerging markets. In a world where academics advocate for "global-local alignment," different regions may adopt different approaches to implementing the same fundamental succession concepts. While making sure the strategy stays the same, this glocalized approach makes sure the culture and operations can change. In conclusion, academic studies have shown that succession planning is essential for developing corporate leaders and ensuring the smooth operation of any business. From DEI and digital transformation to organizational risk management and emotional intelligence, succession planning has grown into a complicated and dynamic system. To safeguard businesses against instability, revolution, and generational turnover, as well as to train individuals for leadership roles in the future, the current state of research necessitates models that are integrative, futuristic, and contextually aware.

CONCEPTUAL MODELS OF SUCCESSION PLANNING

Rothwell's Succession Planning and Management (SPM) Model

Rothwell's Succession Planning and Management (SPM) model is among the most widely utilized conceptual frameworks. This approach sees succession planning as a process that unfolds again and over, with five major steps: (1) determining which key positions are critical to the organization's success, (2) developing competency models for those positions, (3) examining internal talent pools to identify potential successors, (4) implementing targeted development programs such as coaching, mentoring, and job rotations, and (5) analyzing succession results to improve processes. The strength of Rothwell's approach is that it focuses on continuous growth and ensuring that the organization's plan and each individual's career path are in sync.

Integrated Strategic Succession Planning Framework (Synthesized)

Based on Rothwell's work, the literature review proposes a new conceptual model that incorporates contemporary strategic and contextual variables. This five-pillar integrated structure demonstrates how difficult succession planning is today:

1. Leadership Forecasting: using workforce analytics, demographic data, and scenario planning to predict what a firm will require in the future.
2. Identifying and nurturing talent through competency mapping, systematic examinations, mentoring, and rotating assignments to prepare future leaders.
3. Cultural Alignment: ensuring that diversity, equity, and inclusion are factored into succession planning so that leaders are representative and adaptive.
4. Governance and Accountability: appointing boards and executive committees to supervise operations and linking succession planning to enterprise risk management.
5. Strategic Integration: ensuring that succession planning aligns with other HR systems, performance management, and the organization's long-term objectives.

This integrated paradigm incorporates both classic succession management concepts and new difficulties that arise in today's society, such as globalization, digital transformation, and a diverse workforce. It also views succession planning as more than just recruiting fresh talent; it sees it as a means of remaining strong and adding value.

METHODOLOGY

This study used a systematic literature review (SLR) technique to investigate succession planning as a strategic imperative for leadership continuity and competency development. The SLR approach was chosen for its rigor, transparency, and replicability, which enable a full synthesis of current material and the identification of research requirements. To improve the reliability of the methodologies, the review process was built around the Preferred Reporting Items for Systematic Reviews and Meta-Analyses (PRISMA) framework.

RESEARCH DESIGN

The study methodology takes a qualitative interpretivist approach, recognizing that succession planning is a socially constructed process influenced by corporate culture, governance, and strategic objectives. Through a thorough examination of accessible materials, the study aims to capture a wide range of perspectives from various industries, geographical regions, and theoretical frameworks.

Strategy for Search

The literature search was conducted using major academic databases such as Scopus, Web of Science, ProQuest, and Google Scholar. The keywords included succession planning, leadership continuity, strategic human resource management, leadership development, and organisational resilience. To improve the findings, Boolean operators (AND, OR) were utilized. To ensure that the search remained current, it only looked at peer-reviewed journal articles and book chapters published between 2010 and 2025. The criteria for inclusion and exclusion

- Inclusion: Research on succession planning related to leadership continuity, organizational strategy, human capital development, governance, or performance outcomes.
- Exclusions include papers that merely discuss family-owned business succession without providing any strategic analysis, articles that are not written in English, and opinion pieces that lack empirical or theoretical support.

Screening and Selection Procedures

The PRISMA paradigm was used to document the research selection process. Initially, 1,248 records were discovered. After removing duplicates (n=312), the titles and abstracts were reviewed for relevance, and 456 articles were identified. We reviewed the whole content of these articles, and 78 of them met the conditions for inclusion. Following a thorough assessment of methodological quality and relevance, 52 publications were included in the final synthesis.

Data Extraction and Analysis

The study's aims, theoretical frameworks, methodology, setting, and outcomes were compiled into a matrix. Thematic synthesis was then used, following Braun and Clarke's (2006) six-phase approach of familiarization, coding, subject generation, theme review, theme definition, and report creation. We used NVivo software to sort and categorize qualitative data so that we could identify patterns and trends that occurred repeatedly.

Ethical issues

The study did not require formal ethical approval because it solely used secondary data that was already published. Accurate reference and honest portrayal of the writers' work ensured academic integrity.

Limitations

Relying on published literature may result in publication bias, as studies with positive outcomes are more likely to be published. Furthermore, eliminating research that is not in English makes it more difficult to adapt the findings to circumstances outside of the West. Nonetheless, the evaluation is more credible and repeatable since the technique is thorough and straightforward. In general, doing a PRISMA-guided systematic literature review provides a solid foundation for merging previous studies on succession planning. This enables the development of a theoretically solid and practically applicable framework for leadership continuity and organizational resilience.

FINDINGS

The results of the comprehensive literature review that was carried out using the PRISMA framework illuminate the theoretical and practical aspects of succession planning, which is a strategic necessity for maintaining leadership continuity. Succession planning is complex and ever-changing, according to an assessment of 52 scholarly articles. Incorporating it into broader strategy frameworks may boost organizational sustainability, employee engagement, and resilience right now. Complementing the results with the theoretical frameworks outlined in the literature helps to clarify them, especially Rothwell's SPM model and the integrated five-pillar framework. Leadership prediction, talent acquisition, cultural fit, accountability and leadership, and strategic integration were all covered by these models' analytic frameworks. Prerequisite for effective succession planning is leadership forecasting. Academics have repeatedly stressed the significance of preparing for leadership transitions well in advance of vacancies. Businesses that used workforce modeling, scenario-based forecasting, and demographic research were better prepared to deal with problems caused by staff retirements, sudden resignations, or hiring to fill additional positions due to growth. Studies have shown that predictive technology and workforce analytics are essential for spotting leadership gaps and making sure that succession plans are in accordance with the company's objectives for the future. This futuristic outlook is in line with Rothwell's idea, which states that succession is best seen as an ongoing cycle rather than a discrete occurrence. Recruitment and development of high-potential employees under regulated conditions is a second major issue. Using competency-based frameworks and rigorous evaluation procedures to identify individuals with leadership potential is the key to effective succession planning, according to the literature analysis. A number of strategies have been proposed to better prepare people for positions of increasing responsibility, including leadership academies, job rotation, executive coaching, and mentoring programs. Succession planning, when coupled with leadership development activities, boosts morale, retention, and the rate of internal promotions, according to many studies. To make sure that new leaders were ready to take over, and to help current leaders adapt and be ready for the future, succession planning and talent development worked hand in hand.

When asked about succession planning, many emphasized the importance of cultural congruence. In contrast to more hierarchical or closed cultures, organizations that are more open, developmental, and inclusive are better able to implement succession plans. Individuals react favorably and participate actively in leadership development activities when succession planning is portrayed as a chance for growth, rather than a politically charged process, as shown in the research. In addition, businesses were able to better reflect the variety of their stakeholders and achieve stronger inventive results after including diversity, equity, and inclusion (DEI) themes into succession planning. This boosted the representativeness of leadership pipelines. However, companies that fail to take DEI into account are more likely to uphold systemic inequality, which hinders leaders' ability to change, according to the research. Governance and accountability were found to be crucial for successful succession planning in the studies that were reviewed. Fewer interruptions and easier transitions were observed by organizations that incorporated board-level monitoring into their regular operations. This included creating succession guidelines, doing frequent progress assessments, and including succession planning into enterprise risk management. These actions reduce the reputational and operational risks of a leadership vacuum while simultaneously showing stakeholders that succession planning is an important strategic objective. In contrast, businesses that lacked formal structures for governance often used ad hoc or unstructured methods for succession planning, which left them vulnerable to leadership crises and produced results that were disjointed. Boards have a fiduciary duty to ensure a smooth transition of power in the event of an executive's departure, according to the literature on corporate governance.

One important takeaway is that HRM and larger organizational initiatives are the best places to implement succession planning. Studies show that companies do better in the long run when their succession plans, personnel strategies, and company strategies are all in sync with one another. In the healthcare industry, for instance, clinical competency frameworks and certification standards are interdependent on succession planning. In corporate contexts, it became a part of strategic goals and performance management systems. In addition to assisting CEOs in remaining in their roles, the incorporation of succession planning into strategic HR procedures enhanced the firm's credibility with regulators, investors, and workers. Strategic integration is essential to succession planning for the long run, according to the synthesised five-pillar framework, which is in line with this discovery.

There will always be problems with succession planning, no matter how good the processes get. Some of the main obstacles are anti-internal promotion attitudes in cultures that value external recruiting, a dearth of thorough data systems for evaluating leadership fitness, and inadequate funding for leadership development infrastructures. Some leadership pipelines do not have enough women or members of minority groups, which is a persistent problem with diversity. Additionally, succession is less helpful for planning when viewed as an event rather than an ongoing process. There are concerns raised in the literature regarding the use of technology. For example, while AI-based tools and predictive analytics do increase efficiency, there is a risk that leadership evaluations will become overly dependent on algorithmic results, which could lead to the omission of less quantifiable qualities like emotional intelligence, cultural fit, and ethical orientation.

RESULTS

The results show that strategic leadership management and organizational resilience rely heavily on succession planning. Proactivity, a focus on competencies, and harmony with corporate culture, governance, and strategy are the hallmarks of great succession systems, according to the report. Succession planning is a whole organizational competence, not just a way to replace leaders, as contrasted with models like the five-pillar integrated framework and Rothwell's cyclical SPM model. In addition to resolving existing problems, it anticipates and prepares for future ones, such as those caused by shifts in the workforce, technological advancements, and the elevated expectations of stakeholders for openness and participation.

Succession planning is now an integral part of organizational strategy, governance, and resilience, as shown in this comprehensive research review. Businesses may get a systematic knowledge of how to implement succession planning as a strategic necessity by analyzing these outcomes using Rothwell's Succession Planning and Management (SPM) model and the integrated five-pillar framework. Recognizing persistent problems and intricacies, this discourse offers a methodical evaluation of the results for theory, practice, and future studies.

Instead of seeing succession planning as an HR function in and of itself, the results demonstrate that it is best seen as an organizational capability. Succession planning may help organizations become more resilient and adaptable when they implement tactics like leadership forecasting, talent identification, and culture alignment. The resource-based view (RBV), which encourages this fresh perspective, sees human capital as an asset that may provide a company an edge in the market. Organizations may better respond to changes in the environment and in leadership when they incorporate succession planning into their long-term strategy and governance. The relevance of leadership prediction in succession planning has increased. By anticipating future leadership needs through scenario planning and workforce analytics, organizations may help avoid leadership shortages. Succession planning isn't only about finding new talent; it can also help lower organizational risk, as this study shows by tying forecasting to organizational resilience. Organizations may safeguard their leadership pipelines for the future by making forecasting an ongoing endeavor to guarantee that leadership development is in line with changing strategic goals.

Recognizing talent development as an investment in strategy is crucial due to the inseparable nature of succession planning and leadership development. According to the research, leadership pipelines cannot be established or maintained without structured development programs like as mentoring, coaching, and rotating assignments. Since this necessitates firms to allocate resources towards leadership development systems over the long term, it does have practical ramifications. The results also show that development can't be based on isolated events but must instead be ongoing and flexible, which is a key component of Rothwell's cycle model.

Succession planning relies heavily on cultural congruence, according to the results. Employee engagement and a more seamless transition are hallmarks of growth-oriented cultures that are open, welcoming, and inclusive of all. Succession is more difficult in societies that value hierarchy or politics. Maintaining strategic processes requires adherence to values, transparency, and inclusion, all of which are congruent with ideas of corporate culture. More and more people are getting the moral and performance demands of representative leadership when they include diversity, equality, and inclusion (DEI) into succession planning. In addition to advancing justice, diverse pipelines improve decision quality, provide fresh ideas, and build trust among stakeholders. The success or failure of a succession plan is heavily dependent on the board's responsibility and governance. Results showed less disruption and more continuity when boards were actively involved, when succession planning was integrated into risk management, and when monitoring systems were well-organized. This conclusion lends credence to the literature on corporate governance that characterizes board succession planning as a fiduciary duty. It also shows stakeholders how crucial succession planning is by highlighting its role in governance agendas. For boards, this means shifting their focus from monitoring leadership succession after the fact to proactively ensuring it.

According to the findings, succession planning is most effective when it is interconnected with other parts of the business. These parts include HR, SM, and TP. Because of this systemic coherence, succession planning is not seen as an independent activity but rather as an integral part of the whole company. The synthesised five-pillar structure, which encourages the merging of company strategy and succession planning, embodies this comprehensive perspective. Managers and lawmakers face this reality head-on and must monitor succession plans as part of their strategic performance evaluations to make sure they are in line with organizational objectives.

There are still problems that make succession less successful, according to study, even if there have been advancements. There are a number of issues, such as reliance on external recruitment, a lack of diversity in leadership pipelines, poor data systems, and inadequate financing for leadership development. More and more, AI and predictive analytics are being used, and this has both positive and negative consequences. While data-driven processes and analytics can increase productivity and accuracy, putting too much emphasis on quantitative metrics risks eroding important qualitative traits like emotional intelligence and cultural fit. The need of finding a middle ground between using technology and trusting human judgment is highlighted by this tension.

FUTURE IMPLICATIONS

There are a lot of potential areas for further research that the results point to. The first step is to conduct longitudinal studies to track the effects of succession planning on the resilience and performance of organizations across time. Additionally, research comparing different businesses and cultural regions might help illuminate the global adjustments needed for succession planning. Finally, research into the use of artificial intelligence (AI) for leadership assessment and prediction should focus on how this technology interacts with digital transformation and succession planning. Lastly, it would be beneficial for both firms to take a closer look at how diversity, equity, and inclusion (DEI) affect succession planning and how inclusive pipelines may improve performance and do the right thing.

This discussion places succession planning at the heart of strategic leadership management, based on theory and proved in reality. The combination of Rothwell's cycle model and the synthesized five-pillar framework demonstrates that succession planning is more than simply a means of replacing leaders; it is also a strategic and systemic competency. Effective succession systems improve organizational resilience, increase employee engagement, and strengthen governance integrity while addressing current issues like as diversity, digitization, and global uncertainty. The findings and interpretations provide both theoretical support and practical guidance for firms seeking to institutionalize succession planning as a strategic need.

CONCLUSION

This research proved that succession planning is an essential strategic competency that helps organizations remain resilient, maintain leadership, and prepare for the future, rather than just a minor HR function. The study positioned succession planning within both traditional and modern conceptual frameworks by utilizing data from more than fifty academic sources and conducting a thorough literature analysis informed by the PRISMA approach. A cycle framework for conceptualizing succession as a continuous process was offered by Rothwell's Succession Planning and Management (SPM) model. The five-pillar framework that was synthesized, on the other hand, provided support for this approach by incorporating modern necessities like as diversity, digital transformation, accountability in governance, and strategy alignment. If businesses want to be ready for demographic changes, industry evolutions, and changing skill demands, they need to start their succession planning with anticipatory leadership forecasting, according to the results. An important part of this process is still finding and developing talent. Systematic approaches like competence mapping, mentoring, coaching, and task rotation can help leaders get ready for the challenges they'll face in the future. To guarantee that leadership pipelines are diverse, flexible, and creative, cultural alignment is essential, especially through the use of DEI. The study also found that in order to prioritize succession planning, governance mechanisms are needed, especially active board monitoring. Last but not least, integrating succession planning into the larger organizational structures guarantees everything is consistent, legal, and valuable in the long run.

There are still very big problems that need fixing, notwithstanding these innovations. A lot of companies still consider succession planning as an afterthought, have weak data infrastructures, and underinvest in leadership development. To maintain the qualitative aspects of effective leadership—emotional intelligence, ethical orientation, and cultural compatibility—as digital technology continues to replace human judgment in forecasting and evaluation, a careful balance is required. To fix these problems, we have to change people's mindsets as well as the system itself. There are theoretical and practical aspects to this study. By fusing conventional wisdom with cutting-edge strategic frameworks, it theoretically adds to the body of work on succession planning. The organization considers succession planning to be an interdisciplinary skill that necessitates knowledge of culture, strategy, and leadership. In reality, it gives businesses a road map for creating succession plans that are proactive, inclusive, and intentional so they can weather the storms of changing demographics, new technology, and stakeholder expectations. Lastly, in order to create capacities for the future and guarantee leadership continuity, organizations should emphasize succession planning. Organizations may move succession planning from a reactive backup strategy to a proactive way of building resilience and producing value by using cyclical, integrated, and inclusive techniques. Research shows that companies with a well-thought-out succession plan are better able to weather leadership changes and thrive in more complicated and unpredictable business climates.

REFERENCES

Ananthi, P., Ramya, T. E., & Janani, R. (2023, June). Ensemble based intrusion detection system for IoT device. In *2023 International Conference on Sustainable Computing and Smart Systems (ICSCSS)* (pp. 1073-1078). IEEE. DOI: 10.1109/ICSCSS57650.2023.10169426

Barney, J. B. (1991). Firm resources and sustained competitive advantage. *Journal of Management*, *17*(1), 99–120. DOI: 10.1177/014920639101700108

Cadmus, E. (2006). Succession planning: Multilevel organizational strategies for the new workforce. *The Journal of Nursing Administration*, *36*(6), 298–303. DOI: 10.1097/00005110-200606000-00004 PMID: 16766908

Coffie, R. B., Odikro, D., & Turkson, J. K. (2022). A thematic approach to succession planning, leadership continuity, and organizational growth: Spotlight on chief executive officers in Ghanaian industry. *African Journal of Applied Research*, *8*(2), 83–100. DOI: 10.26437/ajar.31.10.2022.06

Collings, D., & Mellahi, K. (2009). Strategic talent management: A review and research agenda. *Human Resource Management Review*, *19*(4), 304–313. DOI: 10.1016/j.hrmr.2009.04.001

Frasier, N. (2019). Preparing nurse managers for authentic leadership: A pilot leadership development program. *The Journal of Nursing Administration*, *49*(2), 79–85. DOI: 10.1097/NNA.0000000000000714 PMID: 30664579

Fulmer, R. M., & Conger, J. A. (2004). Developing Leaders With 2020 Vision. *Financial Executive, 20*(5).

Groves, K. S. (2007). Integrating leadership development and succession planning best practices. *Journal of Management Development*, *26*(3), 239–260. DOI: 10.1108/02621710710732146

Ingale, A. (2024). Succession Planning And Leadership Development Are Important In Creating A Talent Pipeline Within Human Resource Management. Available at *SSRN* 5031223.

Kur, E., & Bunning, R. (2002). Assuring corporate leadership for the future. *Journal of Management Development*, *21*(10), 761–779. DOI: 10.1108/02621710210448039

Lakshmi, M. V. (2024). A study on strategic succession planning ensuring a pipeline of future leaders in workfreaks corporate services pvt ltd. *International Scientific Journal of Engineering and Management*, *03*(05), 1–9. DOI: 10.55041/ISJEM01790

Martin, D. C. (2024). Building Organizational Readiness through Effective Succession Planning.

Meseguer-Sánchez, V., Gálvez-Sánchez, F. J., López-Martínez, G., & Molina-Moreno, V. (2021). Corporate Social Responsibility and Sustainability: A Bibliometric Analysis of Their Interrelations. *Sustainability (Basel), 13*(4), 16–36. DOI: 10.3390/su13041636

Payne, R. A., Hovarter, R., Howell, M., Draws, C., & Gieryn, D. (2018). Succession planning in public health: Addressing continuity, costs, and compliance. *Nurse Leader, 16*(4), 253–256. DOI: 10.1016/j.mnl.2018.05.008

Ramya, M., Santhanakrishnan, C., Janani, M., & Poonkodi, S. (2026). A Comparative Analysis of Network Intrusion Detection Systems in Machine Learning and Deep Learning for Securing IoT devices. In *Improving Threat Detection, Network Security, and Incident Response With AI* (pp. 1-20). IGI Global Scientific Publishing.

Reid, M. (2005). Applying succession management benefits for leadership continuity. [JBER]. *Journal of Business & Economics Research, 3*(6). Advance online publication. DOI: 10.19030/jber.v3i6.2782

Rosenzweig, E. Q., Chen, X. Y., Song, Y., Baldwin, A., Barger, M. M., Cotterell, M. E., Dees, J., Injaian, A. S., Weliweriya, N., Walker, J. R., Wiegert, C. C., & Lemons, P. P. (2024). Beyond STEM attrition: Changing career plans within STEM fields in college is associated with lower motivation, certainty, and satisfaction about one's career. *International Journal of STEM Education, 11*(1), 15. DOI: 10.1186/s40594-024-00475-6

Schweitzer, K., & Graebe, J. (2024). Leadership Succession Planning for ANCC Accredited Providers in Nursing Continuing Professional Development. *Journal of Continuing Education in Nursing, 55*(7), 321–325. DOI: 10.3928/00220124-20240610-02 PMID: 38959097

Siambi, J. K. (2022). Leadership succession planning and organization transition: A review of literature. International Journal of Managerial Studies and Research, 10(3), pp. (16-30).

Utaminingsih, S., Hariyadi, A., & Sofiyati, D. (2024). Analysis of Learning Leadership Management Based on Soft Skill. *Uniglobal Journal of Social Sciences and Humanities, 3*(2), 18–25.

Yadav, P. V., Kollimath, U. S., Chavan, T. V., Pisal, D. T., Giramkar, S. A., & Swamy, S. M. (2023), Impact of Artificial Intelligence (AI) in Talent Acquisition Process: A study with reference to IT Industry, *International Conference on Intelligent and Innovative Technologies in Computing, Electrical and Electronics (IITCEE)*, Bengaluru, India, 2023, pp. 885-889, DOI: 10.1109/IITCEE57236.2023.10090973

Zafar, A., & Akhtar, G. K. H. (2020). Effect of succession planning on organizational growth. *Journal of Social Sciences and Humanities*, *59*(1), 21–33. DOI: 10.46568/jssh.v59i1.323

Chapter 5
The Ripple Effect of Employee Satisfaction on Hotel Performance:
A Focus on J&K's Hotel Industry

Sumaira Nissar
University of Kashmir, India

Qazi Ruban
http://orcid.org/0000-0001-9463-3594
Central University of Kashmir, India

Rameez Ahmad Mir
http://orcid.org/0009-0005-1442-4909
Central University of Kashmir, India

ABSTRACT

This study aims to identify various variables impacting employee's satisfaction levels and suggest training strategies for organizations to increase their employability, and to study the impact of employee satisfaction on the organizational performance. The research study tests the relationship between variables of employee satisfaction and performance in the hospitality sector. The premise of the relationship between levels of satisfaction and hospitality was also discussed. This research study was conducted to study the relationship between employee satisfaction and job performance in the hospitality sector. Employee satisfaction variables identified were subjected to exploratory factor analysis and tested after confirmatory factor analysis was done on variables. Performance variables about the hospitality sector were studied, and

DOI: 10.4018/979-8-3373-6395-0.ch005

items that impacted the hospitality sector were extracted. This research study conducted shows that there exists a positive relationship between variables of employee satisfaction and performance.

1. INTRODUCTION

The organizational culture, collective attitude, values, and satisfaction are an integral part of any organization. Employee satisfaction is an accumulation of positive and negative feelings that an employee gets towards her job; it is a kind of emotional response of an employee toward the job he/she is performing. A higher level of satisfaction is considered a pleasurable state of emotions resulting from the job. Employee satisfaction plays a critical role in maintaining the organizational success or performance of an organization. Employee satisfaction is also job satisfaction which states the extent of how happy an employee is with his/her job. It is critically important for an organization to know how to maintain the level of satisfaction among the employees to enhance organizational culture and increase the performance of the organization. The better culture and performance of an organization create a better reputation and pull out more profits. The hospitality industry is one of the growing industries across the globe and, along with tourism, is one of the largest employment-generating sectors in the world. Be it any sector one of the primary goals of any sector is to generate profits and the case is the same with the hospitality sector. Profitability is seen as organizational success or organizational performance. The organization's employees play a vital role in the performance and success of the organization; therefore, employee satisfaction influences the organization to a large extent. The hospitality industry is mainly a service industry which is dominated by the complexities of handling and managing guest experiences. Employees are the resource for an organization as they are the representatives of significant investments; they are the force for the execution and implementation of plans and policies. For the satisfaction of employees, often the top management organizes training and workshops and offers benefits and packages to keep the employees motivated and satisfied. The higher satisfaction level of employees often results in retaining the employees for a lengthy tenure.

The hotel industry is showing a rapid pace for development and is making a significant contribution to the upliftment of standards of food and accommodation, for maintaining the standards and to be in competition there are frequent pieces of training and short-term courses for the employees. In addition to this, there are food festivals and other events for recognizing the skills of employees of the hospitality industry; the recognition gives satisfaction to the employees.

2. REVIEW OF LITERATURE

In recent years, research on job satisfaction and organizational commitment has continued to evolve, incorporating new workplace dynamics such as remote work, employee empowerment, and technological change. A bibliometric review by Fitriani et al. (2024) examined 150 articles published between 2019 and 2024, highlighting the central role of job satisfaction and organizational commitment in shaping employee retention, leadership effectiveness, and workforce resilience. The study identified underexplored areas such as psychological empowerment, supervisor citizenship behavior, and the effects of inclusive leadership on satisfaction and commitment (Fitriani et al., 2024).

A comprehensive meta-analysis by Kosasih, Yohana, and Handaru (2024) further reinforced the positive correlation between job satisfaction and organizational commitment, reporting that satisfaction accounts for nearly half of the variance in commitment levels. The findings emphasized that while job satisfaction strongly influences commitment, external organizational and environmental factors also play a significant role in shaping employee attitudes (Kosasih et al., 2024).

Broadening this perspective, Reshma and Velmurugan (2024) conducted a systematic mapping of nearly 300 studies from 2014 to 2023, underscoring consistent associations between job satisfaction, turnover intention, performance, and workplace innovation. However, they cautioned that definitional inconsistencies and geographic clustering still limit the comparability of global findings. The study called for future research to examine how emerging organizational structures and digital work environments impact employee satisfaction and commitment (Reshma & Velmurugan, 2024).

At the organizational level, Verianto (2025) demonstrated that job satisfaction not only enhances employee performance directly but also strengthens organizational commitment, which in turn acts as a mediating factor improving overall productivity. This causal pathway suggests that commitment amplifies the effect of satisfaction on workplace outcomes, reinforcing the importance of integrated HR strategies (Verianto, 2025).

Finally, Cheng (2024) provided a conceptual synthesis of job satisfaction theories, outlining its key dimensions and emphasizing the need for future research to capture changing employee expectations in hybrid and flexible work arrangements (Cheng, 2024).

Mira Singh (1990) hypothesized that the satisfaction of a job is influenced by the involvement, participation, and occupational level in the job. According to the study of Balgir (1991), if the motivational factors suggested by Herzberg are achieved by the managers serving in the organizations in India, the satisfaction level of managers is higher. There are many studies conducted on employee satisfaction, job satisfaction, organizational culture and etc. In the year 1991, Mathew analyzed the link relating gratification and organizational commitment to a non-recursive model, which allowed parallel assessment of the effect of gratification on commitment and the effect of commitment on gratification. The study concluded that the two aforesaid variables were correlated but the effect of gratification on commitment was stronger. Mehra and Mishra 1991 conducted a study on 250 blue-collar industrial workers of UPTRON India Ltd to analyze the effect of mental health on the basic Job satisfaction-occupational stress relationship. Vasanthan et al 2025 recorded that mental health had a moderate effect on the basic Job Satisfaction-Occupational stress relationship. A study on academicians was carried out in 1992 by Dhar and Jain. The study examined the nature of the relationship between Job Satisfaction, Job Involvement, Age, and Length of service. It was concluded that involvement in jobs increases Job Satisfaction and vice-versa. Syeed 1992 tested the relationship between employee job satisfaction and organizational efficiency. 44 supervisors of the public sector from a single unit of the company were randomly selected for the study. The main purpose of the study was to link satisfaction with organizational efficiency along with personal characteristics like age, education, pay, and length of service. The study revealed that Job satisfaction facets had more explanatory power than the personal attributes of respondents. It was concluded from the study that human resource development policies and practices created a better environment for employees, resulting in greater satisfaction which in turn enhanced Organizational efficiency. According to Heskett et al. 1994 the service profit chain that explains the rate of growth and profits depends on customer loyalty which comes from satisfaction. According to the study by Khan and Ahmed, 2013, the level of job satisfaction of library professionals serving in Public Sector Universities of Pakistan was measured. It was found that although the employees were quite satisfied with the job description, they were disappointed with supervision policies, benefits, perks, promotions, etc. In 1997, Rama Devi conducted a study on the faculties of two universities in Andhra Pradesh on Job satisfaction and their stance on the management of the universities. 200 members of the teaching faculty, 100 from each university were randomly chosen for the study. The study revealed that the factors such as freedom in the job, the scope for self-improvement, income, and job security were causing satisfaction, while bureaucratic rules, no recognition for work, and routine work were causing dissatisfaction to them. In 2008, Liu explored the generality of Public Service Motivation and also investigated the association between each dimension of public servant's job satisfaction and public service motivation. Various techniques like confirmatory and exploratory factors were applied to survey data of 191 public servants in China. It was found that public service motivation existed in China, but the generalizability of the construct was limited. Out of four dimensions, three dimensions (attraction to public policy making, commitment to the public interest, and self-sacrifice) existed in China, but the fourth dimension was not confirmed. The study of Ram and Choudhury 2010, investigated the association between organizational climate and job satisfaction in various libraries in New Delhi. A total number of 228 questionnaires were distributed and collected from the staff of different libraries. The study, at last, revealed that job satisfaction is positively correlated with organizational climate. In 2011, Rane researched the significance of employee job satisfaction. According to his study, it is very important for an organization to satisfy its employees in order to increase productivity and survive in intense competition. He emphasizes the fact that high levels of job satisfaction are achieved only when employees feel free at work. His work concluded with the findings that an organization can improve its performance by focusing on employees' needs like providing a positive work environment, the appreciation of the performance, personal recognition of employees by the management, employee participation in decision making, providing training facilities to improve worker's skills and potentials. Spector 1997 says satisfaction among employees is how people look at their job and how they feel about it; Ellickson and Logsdon 2002 shared a similar view about employee satisfaction. Various studies and researches about employee satisfaction in hospitality suggest that satisfaction among the employees leads to guest satisfaction, and it results in more profitability; Bach & Milman 1996.As per the research carried out by Bellou in 2009 in Greece. The aim of the study was to examine the impact of age and gender on the relationship between job satisfaction and organizational culture. He collected data by distributing 125 questionnaires from three Public Hospitals. He analyzed the data using certain statistical techniques like regression analysis, tests, descriptive statistics, etc. Later on it was found that gender and age of employees actually do affect job satisfaction.

A research article based on understanding employees' attitudes and job satisfaction was provided by Sarri and Judges in 2004. As Per the survey performed by Castro and Martin (2004), 696 questionnaires were analyzed to find out the relationship between organizational climate and job satisfaction. It further concluded that the employee's perceptions of the work environment influenced their level of job satisfaction. The article highlighted three gaps that existed between human resource practice and scientific research in the area of employee attitudes in general and most focal employee attitude in particular – Job satisfaction: the reason for employee behavior, the result of positive or negative job satisfaction, and also how to study and persuade employee attitudes. As per Lu, While, & Barriball, 2005 traditionally employee satisfaction was confined to feelings that the employee had for his/her job and but Spector, 1997 suggests it's the nature of the job along with the expectations of employees that lead to satisfaction. According to the review of Hertzberg, 2008 the employees of hotels need a sound amount of social interaction and a monetary reward to remain motivated. Kumar et al. 2013 examine various parameters that influence employees' satisfaction in jobs like the operational jobs in back houses of hotels. Job satisfaction has been an essential issue for the hospitality industry as its employee satisfaction that gives the right idea of customer satisfaction; therefore, the hoteliers try their best to create a system that gives the employees satisfaction Gallardo et al., 2010.

3. OBJECTIVES

1. To identify the key variables influencing the satisfaction levels of employees in the hospitality sector.
2. To propose effective training and development strategies aimed at enhancing employee skills and employability.
3. To study the impact of employee satisfaction on overall organizational performance.

4. METHODOLOGY

The present study adopted a quantitative research design to investigate the relationship between employee satisfaction and performance in the hospitality sector of Jammu & Kashmir. A structured questionnaire was employed as the primary data collection instrument. The survey was administered across four districts of the state, targeting staff members employed in major hotels. A total of 300 questionnaires were distributed, out of which 256 were successfully returned, yielding a response rate of 85.3%. The final sample comprised 189 male and 67 female employees, ensuring adequate representation of both genders.

The questionnaire was systematically designed and divided into three sections. The first section captured demographic information of the respondents, including age, gender, education, job position, and years of service. The second and third sections comprised items measuring the core variables of the study: employee satisfaction and employee performance. All responses were recorded using a six-point Likert scale ranging from *Strongly Agree* (1) to *Strongly Disagree* (6), thereby eliminating the possibility of a neutral midpoint and encouraging respondents to express a definitive opinion.

Employee satisfaction was measured using the standardized instrument developed by Paul E. Spector (1997). The scale consisted of 36 items encompassing multiple dimensions of job satisfaction, such as pay, promotion, supervision, benefits, contingent rewards, operating procedures, coworkers, nature of work, and communication. Each construct was assessed through four items, with a mix of positively and negatively worded statements to reduce response bias. Reverse scoring was applied where appropriate.

Employee performance was measured through scale items designed to assess individual perceptions of task accomplishment, efficiency, and contribution to organizational goals. The scale was adapted to align with the hospitality industry context, ensuring relevance and validity. Prior to the main survey, the questionnaire was pre-tested with a small subset of respondents to verify clarity, comprehensibility, and reliability of the items. Data obtained were coded and analysed using statistical tools to explore the relationships among the variables under study.

5. ANALYSIS AND PROCESSING OF DATA:

Data gathered from the questionnaires were processed and analyzed with the help of a statistical software package SPSS 21.0 using various descriptive and analytical tools e.g.; Chronbach's Alpha, Exploratory Factor Analysis, Correlation, and Regression analysis to achieve the objectives of the research study.

Nine constructs each containing four items of the scale are given below in a table. Chronbach Alpha coefficients of the constructs were extracted.

5.1 Reliability

Chronbach Alpha was used to determine the reliability coefficient of the variables. It was observed that the Alpha coefficient of groups was >0.6 and the total item correlation of variables was >0.3, which is a prerequisite for subjecting the data for further analysis. The data can be subjected to exploratory factor analysis since the job satisfaction scale has Chronbcah's Alpha coefficient of 0.81.

5.2 Descriptive Statistics

Table 1. Mean Scores

Variable	Mean Score
Pay	4.01
Promotion	4.50
Supervision	3.65
Fringe Benefits	4.01
Contingent Rewards	3.95

continued on following page

Table 1. Continued

Variable	Mean Score
Operating Procedures	3.96
Coworkers	4.67
Nature of Work	3.99
Communication	2.69

Table 2.

Variables	Mean	Std. Deviation	Minimum	Maximum
Employee satisfaction	3.73	0.610	1.33	3.90
Performance	3.57	0.573	1.51	3.92

5.3 Exploratory Factor Analysis

KMO measure of sampling adequacy was 0.853 and observed variables have no inter-item correlation at sig= 0.005, this indicates that exploratory factor analysis is appropriate. With principal component extraction method and varimax rotation Eigen value of 2.432 was extracted. Furthermore, factor loadings of items were high. Thus the scale was further subjected to the consequent analysis.

5.4 Correlation Analysis

Analysis of the correlation between market orientation and organizational performance shows a positive and significant relationship between market orientation and performance.

Correlation analysis of the data reveals that the hypotheses stand accepted infer that a positive and significant relationship exists between employee satisfaction and performance. Correlation quotient $r = 0.357$ and p- value $= 0.041$ establishes the two variables' existing significant and positive relationship.

Table 3.

variables	Performance	
	Correlation Quotient	P-Value
Employee satisfaction	0.357	0.041

Source: Paul E. Spector (1997) scale of Employee Satisfaction.

5.5 Multiple Regression Model

After exploratory factor analysis, correlation analysis assessed the fitness to include the components in the regression model.

Dependent variables: Performance.
Independent variables: Pay, Promotion, Supervision, Fringe Benefits, Contingent Rewards, Operating Procedures, Coworkers, Nature of Work, and Communication.

Correlation matrix results show that the items about Pay, Promotion, Supervision, Fringe Benefits, Contingent Rewards, Operating Procedures, Coworkers, Nature of Work, and Communication are closely correlated with the employee satisfaction variable with a significance level of 5%.

5.5 Regression Analysis

For carrying out regression analysis, enter method was selected. Regression analysis results are shown in the table below.

Table 4.

R	R^2	Adjusted R Square	Durbin-Watson
0.49	0.2401	0.240	1.291

Based on the data obtained from the regression analysis there exists a positive correlation between employee satisfaction and performance of an organization.

6. STRATEGIES FOR IMPROVING EMPLOYABILITY

The human resource management of all organizations prioritizes ways to ensure more employee satisfaction so that the human resource is used to its best. Every organization tries to find the best ways to get higher production, to create a healthy work culture, policymakers need to draft and adopt strategies for training to increase employability. The various strategies that can adopt to increase employability are as follows:

1. Regular training and skill orientation programs.

2. Giving employees genuine care regarding their level of engagement at the workplace.
3. More empowerment of employees.
4. Personal growth and opportunities for continued learning.
5. Positive and genuine feedback will make employees more comfortable.
6. Clear communication and discussions with the employees.
7. Sophisticated workplace conditions.
8. More focus on employees' expectations and keeping a belief in employees.
9. Equality in treating the employees.
10. Job security is the key factor in increasing employability.
11. Installation of sound and latest information technology system.
12. Perks, bonuses, and incentives.

Every organization aims for sustainable employability and try best to adopt the strategies that help in achieving and improving the employability.

7. CONCLUSION

Employee satisfaction is usually attributed to various internal and external factors which influence the behavior of employees. It is the way employees of a hotel feel and perceives various dimensions and how these dimensions impact their job. All organizations, mainly the service sector, must be proactive in developing strategies to strengthen the work culture and enhance employee morale to keep the satisfaction level high. On the other hand, give positive results in productivity and help in customer retention. Employee satisfaction in hotels represents the most complex area faced by the manager at present in managing the hotel's employees. A good work atmosphere and healthy work culture give an increase in satisfaction of employees and also improve job performance. Arnett (2002) states that employees who give positive feedback to their seniors are likely to be more satisfied with their jobs. Chi & Gursoy argue the more satisfied employees are always in love with providing better services to guests. Yang (2010) discussed employee satisfaction as a vital contributor to positive results for hotels.

Management of hotels needs to realize and understand the factors and dimensions that play a critical role in maintaining employee satisfaction. Further, the hotels need to provide healthy and safe work culture and also must give proper recognition to employees by involving them in decision-making and other things like capacity building training programs and providing regular incentives to get better results.

REFERENCES

Arnett, J. J. (2002). The psychology of globalization. American psychologist, 57(10). *The American Psychologist, 57*(10), 774–783. DOI: 10.1037/0003-066X.57.10.774 PMID: 12369500

Bach, S. A., & Milman, A. (1996). A novel technique for reviewing a hospitality management curriculum. *Hospitality & Tourism Educator, 8*(1), 37–40. DOI: 10.1080/23298758.1996.10685709

Barroso Castro, C. M., Martín Armario, E., & Martín Ruiz, D. (2004). The influence of employee organizational citizenship behavior on customer loyalty. *International Journal of Service Industry Management, 15*(1), 27–53. DOI: 10.1108/09564230410523321

Bellou, V. (2009). Profiling the desirable psychological contract for different groups of employees: Evidence from Greece. *International Journal of Human Resource Management, 20*(4), 810–830. DOI: 10.1080/09585190902770711

Ellickson, M., & Logsdon, K. (2002). Determinants of job satisfaction of municipal government employees. *Public Personnel Management, 31*(3), 343–358. DOI: 10.1177/009102600203100307

Fitriani, N., & Sudiarditha, I. K. R. (2024). Uncovering Research Clusters in Job Satisfaction and Organizational Commitment: A VOSviewer Approach. *International Journal of Research and Review, 11*(6), 536–545. DOI: 10.52403/ijrr.20240659

Gallardo, E. S.-C.-G., Sánchez-Cañizares, S.-M., López-Guzmán, T., & Margarida Nascimento Jesus, M. (2010). Employee satisfaction in the Iberian hotel industry: The case of Andalusia (Spain) and the Algarve (Portugal). *International Journal of Contemporary Hospitality Management, 22*(3), 321–334. DOI: 10.1108/09596111011035936

Kosasih, F. G., Yohana, C., & Handaru, A. W. (2024). Job Satisfaction and Organizational Commitments: A Meta-Analysis. *EARTH SCIENCES AND HUMAN CONSTRUCTIONS, 4*, 43–50. DOI: 10.37394/232024.2024.4.5

Liu, B. T. (2008). Public service motivation and job satisfaction in chaina: An investigation of generalisability and instrumentality. *International Journal of Manpower, 29*(8). Advance online publication. DOI: 10.1108/01437720810919297

Lu, H. W., While, A. E., & Louise Barriball, K. (2005). Job satisfaction among nurses: A literature review. *International Journal of Nursing Studies, 42*(2), 211–227. DOI: 10.1016/j.ijnurstu.2004.09.003 PMID: 15680619

Mehra, G. (1991). Mental Health as a moderator variable of intrinsic job satisfaction and occupational stress. *Psychological Studies*.

Rane, D. (2011). Employee Job Satisfaction: An essence of organization. *HRM Review*, *11*(27), 10–16.

Reshma, J., & Velmurugan, G. (2024). Organisational and Job Satisfaction: A Decade of Research Trends, Systematic Mapping, and Bibliometric Analysis. *International Journal of Computational and Experimental Science and Engineering*, *11*(1). Advance online publication. DOI: 10.22399/ijcesen.741

Singh, M. (1990). Job satisfication, Job involvement and Participation amongest different categories of bank employees. *Journal of the Indian Acedamy of applied. Psychology (Savannah, Ga.)*.

Spector, P. E. (1997). *Job satisfaction: Application, assessment, causes, and consequences* (Vol. 3). Sage. DOI: 10.4135/9781452231549

Spector, P. E. (1997). Job satisfaction: Application, assessment, causes, and consequences. *Sage (Atlanta, Ga.)*, *3*, •••. DOI: 10.4135/9781452231549

Vasanthan, R., Nath Babu, M., Dzuvichu, K., & Chong, T. S., Singh Rana, V., & Singh, A. (2025). Bridging Social Norms Theory and Community Mobilization: Pathways for Overcoming Gender Stereotypes in Women's Economic Empowerment Programs. *Enterprise Development & Microfinance*, *35*(1), 159–176. Retrieved from https://papjournals.com/index.php/edm/article/view/13

Yang, K., & Kassekert, A. (2010). Linking management reform with employee job satisfaction: Evidence from federal agencies. *Journal of Public Administration: Research and Theory*, *20*(2), 413–436. DOI: 10.1093/jopart/mup010

Chapter 6
Positioning Education in the Service Economy: A Cross-Disciplinary Framework for Self-Regulation, Emotional Labour, and Resilient Engagement

Giselle Phillips
http://orcid.org/0009-0002-2145-0070
University of the West Indies, Trinidad and Tobago

ABSTRACT

This chapter explores the positioning of education within the contemporary service economy, proposing a cross-disciplinary framework that integrates self-regulation, emotional labour and resilient engagement. Education increasingly conceptualised as a service, demands that educators navigate complex interpersonal and emotional dynamics while fostering meaningly learner outcomes. The chapter examines how adherence to display rules and the strategic management of emotions through surface and deep acting shape professional experiences, engagement and well-being. Self-regulation emerges as a central mechanism enabling educators to manage emotional dissonance, and sustain resilient engagement. Drawing on a combination of theoretical perspectives, empirical evidence, and illustrative case studies, the chapter highlights the interconnections between emotional labour, and educator resilience. The chapter provides a nuanced framework for enhancing educational service quality, teacher well-being and sustainable professional engagement in complex learning environments.

DOI: 10.4018/979-8-3373-6395-0.ch006

INTRODUCTION

The twenty first century has witnessed an unmistakable economic shift in which services have eclipsed manufacturing as the primary driver of global growth. Education, long regarded as a public good and an engine for social mobility, now occupies position within this service economy. No longer confined to the realm of civic responsibility or state provision, education increasingly operates as a competitive marker in which institutions, teacher and students engage in transactions that resemble those of hospitality, healthcare and retail industries. Universities recruit international students, schools advertise distinctive, 'customer experiences', and learners evaluate programs as consumers who weigh cost, flexibility and perceived return on investment. This economic reframing is not merely semantic, it fundamentally reshapes the expectations placed on educators and students alike, demanding a new understanding of emotional and psychological dynamics of teaching and learning.

With this evolving landscape, three interrelated constructs, self-regulation, emotional labour and resilient engagement emerge as critical for sustaining high quality educational experiences. Service work in any sector requires workers to manage their emotions in ways that align with organisational display rules a process Hochschild (1983) famously described as emotional labour. Teachers, administrators and even students perform similar work when they suppress frustration, display enthusiasm or maintain composure in the face of diverse classroom demands. Yet, emotional labour in education remains underexamined relative to hospitality or healthcare, despite growing evidence that is contributes to burnout, turnover intentions and diminished well-being (Brotheridge & Grandey, 2002; Yin et al., 2019). Understanding how emotional labour operates in educational settings is therefore essential for developing strategies that protect the psychological health of both staff and learners. Closely linked to emotional labour is the capacity of self-regulation, defined as the ability to monitor and adjust one's thoughts, emotions and behaviours to achieve the desired goals (Zimmerman, 2002). Teachers must regulate their responses to challenging classroom interactions whilst students must manage motivation, attention and affect to persist in complete learning tasks. Self- regulation serves as both a protective factor and a performance enhancer, it buffers individuals against the stress of constant emotional display and supports sustained engagement with challenging content. Recent advances in educational psychology highlight the importance of self-regulated learning strategies, such as goal setting, self-monitoring and reflection, in promoting academic achievement and lifelong adaptability (Panadero, 2017). These findings position self-regulation as a core competence for thriving in a service oriented educational economy.

However, neither emotional labour nor self-regulation alone guarantees long term success or wellbeing. The increasing volatility of the service economy demands resilient engagement, a construct that captures to ability to remain committed, energised and adaptive despite setbacks. Resilience extends beyond mere coping, it involves proactive resource building, flexible thinking and the cultivation of positive affect even in the presence of chronic stressors (Masten, 2014). In educational settings, resilient engagement allows teachers to sustain passion for their work despite systematic pressures such as standardised testing, budget constraints and shifting policy mandates. For students, resilience supports persistence through academic failure, social challenges and rapidly changing labour market expectations. Developing resilience thus represents both a psychological necessity and a strategic advantage in a knowledge economy where continuous learning is paramount.

Taken together, these constructs illuminate a central paradox of contemporary education, while the service economy celebrates personalisation, flexibility and human connection, it simultaneously intensifies the emotional and cognitive demands placed on those who deliver and consume educational services. Teachers are expected to perform with unwavering positivity, students to self-manage their learning journeys, and institutions to provide ever-increasing value with limited resources. Without intentional frameworks for understanding and supporting these demands, the service orientation of education risks eroding the very human capacities it relies upon. This chapter responds to that challenge by proposing a cross-disciplinary framework that integrates insights from human resource management (HRM), organizational behaviour, educational psychology, and sociology. By examining education through the lens of the service economy we can identify structural parallels with other service industries and adapt proven strategies for emotional regulation, employee well-being and resilience training. At the same time, education offers unique opportunities to extend these theories particularly in its dual role as both a workplace and a developmental context for learners.

CHAPTER ROADMAP

The chapter unfolds in six sections. The first situates education within the broader trajectory of the global service economy, highlighting market dynamics that have transformed educational institutions into service providers. The second examines emotional labour in teaching and learning, drawing on seminal and contemporary research to reveal its hidden costs and potential benefits. The third explores self-regulation as a critical competence for both educators and students, while the fourth introduces the concept of resilient engagement as a key outcome of effective self-regulation and emotional management. The fifth section presents a cross disciplinary framework that syntheses three constructs into a coherent model offering visual representations and actionable principles. The final section discusses the implications for policy, institutional practice and future research, emphasising the need for systemic interventions that foster emotional intelligence and sustainable engagement across all levels of education.

By positioning education as a pivotal actor in the service economy and highlighting the intertwined roles of self-regulation, emotional labour and resilient engagement, this chapter aims to bridge disciplinary silos and provide a foundation for evidence-based strategies that promote both human flourishing and organisational effectiveness. In doing so, it invites educators, policy makers and researchers to rethink education not only as a site of knowledge transmission but also a dynamic service arena in which emotional and psychological capacities are as vital as cognitive skills.

THE SERVICE ECONOMY AND EDUCATION

The Global Shift to a Service Economy

From Industrial Production to a Service World

Over the last half-century, the global economy has experienced profound reordering of productive activity, commonly referred to as the shift from an industrial to a service economy. In the immediate post World War II period, most advanced economies were dominated by manufacturing, heavy industry and agriculture. Today, services such as finance, healthcare, tourism, digital platforms and importantly education account for more than 70 percent of GDP in most OECD member states and over 65 percent of global employment (OECD, 2022). Similar patterns are emerging in middle-income economies where manufacturing is no longer the singular route to prosperity (UNCTAD, 2021). This transformation is not simply a change in industrial composition; it represents a fundamental redefinition of how societies create wealth and how people experience work.

Multiple forces underpin this global reorientation.

- **Technological automation** has reduced the labour intensity of manufacturing, displacing routine tasks.
- **Global supply chains** allow goods to be produced in lower-cost regions, further shrinking domestic manufacturing employment in high income countries.
- **Rising household incomes** generate consumer demand for knowledge, health. Leisure and personal services.
- **Digitization and the knowledge economy** privilege information processing, creativity and human interaction over physical production (Powell & Snellman, 2004).

The cumulative effect is a world where intangible value creation from streaming entertainment to advanced education outpaces the production of tangible goods.

Distinctive Characteristics of Service Work

Services differ from goods in ways that profoundly shape the nature of labour and organisational practices (Zeithaml et al., 2020). First, services are intangible: their value resides in experiences, relationships and knowledge rather than physical artefacts. Second, production and consumption are typically simultaneous. A lecture, counselling session or hotel stay is created and consumed in real time, leaving little opportunity for quality inspection before delivery. Third, services are heterogeneous and co-produced. Outcomes depend on the active participation of both provider and recipient; the quality of a tutoring session, for instance reflects not only the instructor's skill but also the student's engagement.

These features create distinctive labour demands. Service workers must be skilled in interactional competence, emotional display and adaptive problem solving. They are often expected to project warmth, enthusiasm and reliability regardless of internal feelings, a phenomenon a sociologist Arlie Hochschild (1983) famously termed emotional labour. Unlike a factory worker whose output can be measured in units, a teacher or healthcare provider is judged through subjective indicators such as client satisfaction, trust or engagement. Because each encounter is unique, workers require high levels of self-regulation (Bandura, 1991) to monitor their emotion, maintain composure and adjust in real time.

Global Illustrations of the Service Shift

The global scale of this transformation is evident across diverse contexts. In Singapore, government policy deliberately repositioned the economy away from manufacturing toward finance, education and high value business services. By 2023, services represented nearly 75 percent of Singapore's GDP with education promoted as a strategic export through international branch campuses and student recruitment. In India, the rise of information technology and business process outsourcing created millions of service jobs in call centres, software development and online education platforms such as BYJU's and Vedantu, illustrating how digitisation enables service exports without physical relocation. In Nordic countries, public services such as education and healthcare have become major employment engines demonstrating that service expansion is not solely market-driven but also propelled by welfare-state commitments. The COVID-19 pandemic further underscored the resilience and adaptability of the service economy. While tourism and hospitality initially contracted, digital services including online education expanded rapidly accelerating pre-existing trends towards remove delivery and hybrid work.

Education as a Service Industry

Among all service domains, education occupies a particularly revealing position. Traditionally framed as a public good and a vehicle for nation building, education increasingly functions as a competitive, globally traded service. Universities recruit fee paying international students, compete for world rankings and diversify revenue streams through executive education and online programs (Marginson, 2016). For example, the United Kingdom's higher education sector generated £25.6 billion in export earning in 2022, largely from international tuition fees and transnational programs (UK Department of Education, 2023). Australia similarly brands education as its fourth largest explore industry with international students contributing billions to the national economy.

At the primary and secondary levels, service logics are equally evident. Public school systems adopt customer-satisfaction metrics such as parent surveys and student engagement scores. Charter schools in the United States market themselves on differentiated, 'service packages', promising personalised learning experiences. The global tutoring industry estimated at US $200 billion annually illustrates the commercialisation of supplemental education where families purchase bespoke learning services to gain competitive advantage. The intangibility and co-production of educational outcomes align perfectly with service characteristics. Knowledge cannot be stockpiled like manufactured goods. Learning emerges through the dynamic interaction of teacher and student. A university lecture is valuable not merely for the transfer of information but for the experience of critical discourse, mentorship and community. As a result, the 'product' of education is inseparable from the relational processes through which it is delivered.

Digital Service Turn in Education

The service framing of education is intensified by the rapid expansion of digital learning platforms. Massive online courses (MOOCs), virtual tutoring apps and AI driven adaptive learning systems allow education to scale globally. For example, China's TAL Education and India's BYJU'S each serve tens of millions of users across multiple countries. While digital platforms automate certain tasks, grading quizzes, scheduling reminders, they heighten the need for human educators to provide emotional presence and personalised feedback that technology cannot replicate. The hybrid future of education therefore magnifies the importance of self-regulation and emotional labour rather than diminishing it.

Conceptual Bridge to the Cross-Disciplinary Framework

Recognizing education as part of the service economy is more than a descriptive exercise. It is the conceptual foundation for the cross disciplinary framework proposed in this chapter. The global shift explains why skills such as emotional intelligence, self-regulation and resilient engagement are no longer, 'soft' but strategically essential. Whether in a Singaporean polytechnic adapting to internation student markets, a US public school integrating customer service surveys or an African university leveraging online platforms, educators must navigate the same service-driven imperative which are to maintain high quality interactions, manage emotions and foster sustainable engagement under conditions of uncertainty.

These realities call for theoretical tools that cross traditional disciplinary boundaries, drawing from psychology to understand self-regulation, from sociology to analyse emotional labour and from management studies to design organisational support. The following subsections build on this service economy context to examine self-regulation as a core competence, emotional labour as structural expectation and the mechanisms through which educators can cultivate resilient engagement in an era where education is both a public mission and a competitive service industry.

EMOTIONAL LABOUR IN EDUCATION

Conceptual Foundations

The concept of emotional labour was first articulated by Arlie Hochschild (1983) to capture how workers manage their feelings and emotional expressions to meet the 'display rules' of their occupation. Unlike physical or cognitive labour, emotional labour requires employees to evoke or suppress emotions so that customers, clients or students experience a desired emotional climate.

Hochschild distinguished two primary strategies of emotional regulation:

- **Surface acting**, in which individuals alter outward expressions (e.g., smiles, tone of voice) while inner feelings remain unchanged
- **Deep acting**, in which individuals attempt to align internal emotions with required displays, genuinely feeling the required affect.

Both strategies can achieve compliance with institutional expectations but differ in psychological cost. Surface acting often leads to emotional dissonance, a mismatch between felt and expressed emotions associated with burnout and diminished well-being (Brotheridge & Grandey, 2002). Deep acting, though more authentic, requires sustained cognitive effort and can also be exhausting. Education is a prototypical high contact service where emotional labour is inevitable. Teachers, administrators and students must continually manage relationships and emotions to sustain engagement and learning. Societal expectations of care, fairness and professionalism amplify the need for emotional regulation and make it central educational practice.

TEACHERS, ADMINISTRATORS AND STUDENTS AS EMOTIONAL LABOURERS

Teachers

Teaching involves intensive, daily interpersonal contact in classrooms, laboratories and online environments. Educators must maintain engagement, respond to students' emotional cues, and project patience and enthusiasm even when facing disruptive behaviours, administrative pressure or personal fatigue. Research shows that positive teacher emotions enhance student motivation and academic achievement (Frenzel, 2014). Yet sustaining this positivity requires constant regulation. Teachers often engage in surface acting when masking frustration or disappointment and in deep acting when attempting to cultivate genuine empathy for struggling students.

Examples abound globally:

- **South Korea's hagwon system** demands charismatic, high- energy performances late into the night, forcing teachers to mask fatigue to retain enrolments (Kim, 2016).
- In **UK and Australian universities,** student satisfaction surveys and market pressures compel lecturers to remain upbeat and approachable, linking emotional displays to career advancement (Kinman & Wray, 2018).
- In **resource- constrained Sub-Saharan schools,** teachers often provide emotional support for students affected by poverty or conflict, sustaining hope under challenging conditions (Bennell & Akyeampong, 2007).

While emotional labour can strengthen professional identity when aligned with personal values, chronic surface acting predicts burnout, depersonalization and turnover (Taxer & Frenzel, 2015).

Administrators and Support Staff

Administrators, principals, deans, student-affairs officers, academic advisors, also engage in high levels of emotional labour. They mediate conflicts among faculty, negotiate with parents or governing boards, and reassure anxious students. Academic advisors in U.S. community colleges, for example, routinely counsel first-generation students dealing with housing insecurity or mental health crises, balancing empathy with institutional policy (Rodriguez-Keyes et al., 2021). Leader must project optimism and stability even during crises such as funding cuts or campus emergencies.

Supportive leadership, clear display rules and recognition of emotional contributions can mitigate negative outcomes (Leithwood et al., 2020). Without such supports, administrators face heightened risk of stress and presenteeism.

Students

Students themselves are not exempt. Particularly in service oriented, marketized education systems, students often management emotions to meet peer and faculty expectations. International students may ask loneliness to fit in, while gradate students may suppress anxiety to appear competent. In competitive programs, students may engage in surface acting to maintain group harmony or secure recommendations. This 'hidden curriculum' of emotional labour influences persistence and academic success.

Cross- Sector Comparisons

Placing educational emotional labour alongside other service occupations clarifies both commonalities and distinctive features.

- **Healthcare**- Nurses and physicians manage fear and suffering while projecting calm reassurance. Like teachers, they must balance empathy with professional boundaries. However, healthcare emotional labour often deals with acute life and death stakes, whereas education focuses on long-term development relationships (Grandey et al., 2013).
- **Hospitality and Retail**- Service workers are expected to create pleasant customer experiences, similar to teachers' need to maintain positive classroom climates. Yet teachers' emotional displays are tied not only to satisfaction but also to learning outcomes and moral development (Noddings, 2013).
- **Social Work**- Social workers, like teachers, provide care and guidance but often in crisis situations. Education differs in its dual role as both a public good and a commodified service, blending moral mission with marker pressures (Marginson, 2016).

These comparisons underscore that emotional labour is a structural requirement across service industries but in education it intersects uniquely with identity formation, moral expectations and evaluative authority. Teachers' emotional work directly shapes cognitive outcomes, making it central to institutional success and societal development.

Coping Self- Regulation and Organisational Support

Because motional labour is inescapable, educators and students require strategies to manage it effectively.

- Individual strategies include mindfulness, cognitive reappraisal, job crafting and boundary management all of which help algin internal states with external demands (Roeser et al., 2013; Bakker et al., 2012).
- Organisational interventions such as mentoring, recognition of emotional contributions in performance evaluations and reasonable workloads reduce emotional dissonance and foster resilience (Leithwood et al., 2020).
- Digital contexts present new challenges. Online teaching compresses emotional cues and extends work hours, producing 'Zoom fatigue' (Bailenson, 2021). At the same time, analytics and multimedia tools can support innovative emotional engagement.

Summary

Emotional labour is a defining feature of education in the service economy. Teachers, administrators and students all regulate emotions to create positive learning environments, satisfy institutional expectations and navigate market pressures. While such labour can enrich professional identity and student engagement, it also carries risks of burnout and turnover when unsupported. Comparing education with other service sectors highlights its unique moral and development stakes, reinforcing the need for cross disciplinary strategies that integrate sociology, psychology and organisational studies.

The next section explores self-regulation as a core competence, detailing mechanisms that enable educators t convert emotional labour from a source of strain into a driver of resilient management.

SELF- REGULATION AS A CORE COMPETENCE

As education becomes increasingly service-oriented, the ability of teachers, administrators and students to self-regulate emotions, cognitions and behaviors emerges as a defining professional and personal competence. Self-regulation enables individuals to maintain well-being, deliver high-quality service and sustain performance in the face of the emotional demands characteristic of service economies. This section examines the theories of self-regulation explores their applications in education and reviews measurements and interventions that can strengthen this critical capacity.

Theories of Self-Regulation

Self-regulation refers to the processes by which individuals plan, monitor, and adjust their thoughts, emotions, and actions to achieve goals (Carver & Scheier, 2016; Zimmerman, 2000). Across psychology and management, several influential theoretical models provide a conceptual foundation.

Social- Cognitive Theory and Cyclical Models

Zimmerman (2000) describes self-regulation as a cyclical process comprising three interrelated phases: forethought, performance control and self-reflection. In the forethought phase, individuals set goals and plan strategies. During performance control, they monitor progress, employ cognitive or behavioural tactics, and adjust efforts as needed. The self-reflection phase involves evaluation outcomes, attribution success or failure and feeding insights back into future forethought. This cyclical model underscores the dynamic nature of self-regulation and its responsiveness to feedback.

Control Theory

Carver and Scheier (2016) conceptualise self-regulation as a feedback loop. Individuals compare current states to desired standards and discrepancies trigger behavior to reduce the gap. The model highlights the motivational force of perceived discrepancies, explaining why clear performance standards (e.g., academic rubrics or teaching benchmarks) can drive adaptive self-regulatory responses.

Emotion Regulation Models

Given education's service orientation, emotional processes are central. Gross's (2015) process model identifies strategies such as cognitive reappraisal (changing one's interpretation of a situation) and expressive suppression (inhibiting outward emotional displays). Research shows the reappraisal tends to product positive outcomes, reduced stress and burnout, improve relationships while chronic suppression predicts emotional exhaustion (Grandey & Gabriel, 2015).

Self- Determination Theory (SDT)

Deci and Ryan's SDT adds a motivational dimension, emphasising that self-regulation flourishes when individuals experience, autonomy, competence and relatedness (Ryan & Deci, 2000). Educational environments that satisfy these psychological needs enable deeper internationalisation of goals and more sustainable regulation of learning and professional performance.

Applications in Education

The service economy demands that educators and learner manage complex interactions, sustain engagement and adapt to rapidly changing conditions. Within this context, self-regulation operates at multiple levels, teachers, administrators and students, each requiring tailored applications.

Teachers

Teachers are frontline service providers who must balance instructional quality, student relationships and institutional expectations. Self-regulation allows them to project enthusiasm and patience even when personally fatigued. Studies show that teachers who employ cognitive reappraisal report higher job satisfaction and lower burnout compared to those who rely on suppression (Taxer & Frenzel, 2015).

Example: A high school English teacher facing a disruptive class might reframe student restlessness as a signal to adjust lesson pacing rather than as disrespect, thereby reducing frustration and maintaining instructional focus.

Practical strategies include pre-lesson goal setting, mindfulness-based stress reduction and peer reflection groups. School policies that allow for planning time and encourage collegial support create the environmental scaffolding for such self-regulation (Brotheridge & Grandey, 2002).

Administrators

Administrators navigate conflict amongst staff, mediate parental concerns and respond to shifting policy directives. Self-regulation enables them to remain impartial and maintain trust. Leadership research demonstrates that principals who engage in deliberate emotional regulation, particularly cognitive reappraisal and problem focus coping which foster more positive organisational climates (Boyatzis et al., 2013).

Example: A principal dealing with a sudden budget cut might slow decision-making, consult stakeholders and employ mindfulness techniques to prevent reactive responses.

Leadership development programs increasingly incorporate emotional intelligence training, reflective coaching and scenario-based simulations to enhance self-regulatory skills.

Students

For students, self-regulation underpins academic achievement and socioemotional growth. Zimmerman's (2000) model identifies goal setting, strategic action and self-monitoring as key. Students who can plan, persist and adapt are better equipped to meet the demands of project-based-learning and continuous assessment typical of service-oriented economies.

Digital learning intensifies these needs. Online courses require sustained attention and emotion regulation in the absence of face-to-face instructor cues (Winne & Hadwin, 2013). Program that teach metacognitive strategies, provide immediate feedback and foster growth mindsets significantly enhance student self-regulatory skills (Panadero, 2017).

Example: Learning management systems that prompt students to track progress and reflect on learning outcomes can strengthen their capacity for self-regulation in real time.

Organisational Environment

Although self-regulation is an individual competence it is strongly shaped by organisational culture. Supportive leadership, manageable workloads and professional learning communities (PLCs) create conditions where self-regulation can thrive (Vescio et al., 2008). Conversely, punitive accountability regimes or chronic resources scarcity undermine regulation and increase burnout.

Measurements and Interventions

Assessing and cultivating self-regulation is essential for evidence-based practice. Researchers and partitioners use a combination of self-report instruments, behavioural indicators and technology-enhanced analytics.

Measurements

1. Self-Report Scales
    - *Self- regulation Questionnaire (SRQ)* measures goal setting, monitoring and self-evaluation (Brown et al., 1999).

- *Emotional Regulation Questionnnaire (ERQ)* assesses reappraisal and suppression strategies (Gross & John, 2003).
- *Motivated Strategies for Learning Questionnnaire (MSLQ)* evaluates students' metacognitive regulation and motivational beliefs (Pintrich, 2000).

2. Behavioral and Performance Indicators
   Observing persistence on tasks, accuracy of self-predicted grades, or time on task in digital platforms provides objective measures of self-regulation.
   Example: Learning analytics in online courses can track log-ins, pacing and self- initiated revisions as proxies for regulatory behavior.
3. Physiological Measures
   Heart rate variability and cortisol levels are emerging biomarkers for stress regulation, particularly in teacher burnout studies (Roeser et al., 2013).

Interventions

Effective interventions target both individual skills and systemic supports.

Individual- Level Interventions

- **Mindfulness- Based Programs:** Reduce stress and enhance emotion regulation for teachers and students (Jennings et al., 2017).
- **Cognitive-Behavioral Training:** Teaches reappraisal strategies and coping skills to prevent emotional exhaustion.
- **Metacognitive strategy instruction:** Guides students to set goals, monitor comprehension and adjust strategies during learning.

Organisational Interventions

- **Professional Learning Communities (PLCs):** Facilitate collaborative goal setting and shared accountability, enhancing collective regulation (Vescio et al., 2008).
- **Leadership Coaching:** Builds principals' capacity for reflective decision making and emotional intelligence (Boyatzis et al., 2013).
- **Technology- Enabled Supports**: AI- driven dashboards provide real time feedback to students and teachers, prompting self-monitoring and timely adjustments.

Cross- sector lessons reinforce these approaches. Healthcare uses structured debriefing sessions to help staff process high stress events (Mealer et al., 2012). Hospitality industries integrate emotional intelligence training to improve service quality (Kim et al., 2012). Education can adapt these models to strengthen self-regulation while respecting its dual mission of cognitive development and emotional growth.

Key Takeaways

- Self-regulation is a dynamic system of cognitive, emotional and motivational mechanisms that sustain performance in the service economy.
- Teachers, administrators and students each require context specific self-regulation strategies to manage emotional labour and maintain engagement
- Reliable measurement tools and multi-level interventions enable educators and policy makers to assess, cultivate and sustain self-regulatory competence.

Summary

The cultivation of self-regulation establishes a psychological foundation on which sustainable engagement can flourish. Yet, as service-oriented education systems continue to face rapid technological change, resource constraints and shifting emotional demands the ability to regulate one's own thoughts and feelings while essential may not be sufficient to ensure long term professional vitality. What educators, administrators send students increasingly require is the capacity to remain resiliently engaged, to recover from setbacks, sustain motivation during uncertainty and channel regulated emotions into constructive action. The following section therefore examines *Resilient Engagement in Education*, exploring how self-regulation interacts with resilience processes to protect well-being and enhance performance in an era of contact disruption.

BUILDING RESILIENT ENGAGEMENT

Defining Resilient Engagement

Resilient engagement describes the ability of educators, administrators and students to sustain high-quality participation in teaching and learning despite chronic stressors and unexpected disruptions. Unlike simple persistence which implies merely staying in the job or remaining enrolled resilient engagement combines vigor, dedication and adaptive recovery. If reflects a state in which individuals maintain enthusiasm, professional commitment and constructive relationships even when facing structural challenges such as policy volatility, digital overload or public health crises.

Three conceptual streams converge in this construct:

1. **Psychological resilience:** the capacity to bounce back from adversity and to learn from setbacks (Masten, 2014).
2. **Work engagement**: a positive, fulfilling state of vigor, dedication and absorption that predicts performance and well- being (Schaufeli & Bakker, 2004).
3. **Self-regulation:** the ongoing monitoring and adjustment of thoughts, emotions and behaviors to achieve personal and professional goals (Zimmerman & Schunk, 2011).

In education, a sector that increasingly resembles a high contact service industry, these elements are interdependent. Teachers who regulate their emotions and reflect on practice are better able to maintain enthusiasm when confronted with large classes or demanding parents. Students who cultivate metacognitive awareness can recover quickly after disappointing grades. Administrators who manage their own stress communicate stability to staff, reinforcing collective morale. Resilient engagement therefore represents more than an individual trait, it is adynamic process shaped by internal resources and external conditions. It enables educators and learners not only to withstands challenges but to convert them into opportunities for growth, creativity and institutional learning.

Drivers of Resilience

Resilient engagement does not emerge in a vacuum. It is activated by interacting individual, interpersonal and institutional drivers that together create a climate where energy and commitment can be sustained.

Individual Drivers

- **Meaning-Making and Cognitive Appraisal**

  Teachers who interpret stressors as opportunities to refine their pedagogy exhibit lower burnout and stronger job satisfaction (Folkman & Moskowitz, 2000).

  For example, a mathematics instructor who views curriculum reforms as a chance to introduce real-world problem solving is more likely to remain engaged than one who interprets reforms as mere bureaucratic interference.
- **Emotion Regulation**

  Effective strategies such as cognitive reappraisal or mindfulness allow educators to manage frustration during classroom disruptions and maintain instructional quality.
- **Growth Mindset and Grit**

Belief that abilities can be developed (Dweck, 2006) supports perseverance through failed lesson plans or grant rejections.

Interpersonal Drivers

- **Peer Support Networks**
  Collegial relationships buffer stress by normalizing difficulties and offering practical help. Regular "lesson study" meetings, for example, create safe spaces for collective problem solving.
- **Leader-Member Exchange**
  Supportive leadership that models emotional balance increases staff engagement even in high pressure reforms (Leithwood et al., 2020).

Institutional Drivers

- **Flexible Policies and Workload Design**
  Rotational timetable, hybrid teaching options and recovery breaks enable staff to manage peak periods.
- **Recognition of Emotional Labour**
  Evaluation system that acknowledge relational work such as mentoring and parent engagement validate that invisible care work that sustains education quality.

These drivers are mutually reinforcing. A teachers personal mindfulness practice (individual) gains traction when leaders schedule reflection periods (institutional) and colleagues share coping strategies (interpersonal).

Case studies

Cross sector comparisons reveal that education can borrow proven resilience strategies from other service domains. The following detailed case studies illustrate how resilient engagement can be cultivated through intentional design.

Healthcare: 'Schwartz Rounds' for Emotional Processing

Context.

Hospitals worldwide have implementation Schwartz Rounds structured group discussions that allow healthcare workers to share the emotional impact of patient care.

Educational Adaptation.

Following a devasting earthquake in Nepal (2015), several Kathmandu secondary schools piloted weekly *Teacher Reflection Circles* inspired by hospital rounds. Facilitated by trained counsellors, teachers met for 45-minute sessions to discuss fears, grief and classroom challenges. Survey data collected by a local NGO showed a 35% reduction in self-reported secondary trauma and faster classroom stabilization compared with schools without the program. Teachers credited the circles with restoring a sense of professional purpose, enabling them to focus on rebuilding curriculum and student morale.

Aviation: Crew Resource Management (CRM) for Crisis Readiness

Context.

Airlines use CRM training to cultivate shared situational awareness and rapid decision-making under stress.

Educational Adaptation.

A Canadian school district incorporated CRM principles into 'Classroom Response Team' to management violent incidents and sudden lockdowns. Teachers and support staff rehearse clear communication protocols and role flexibility mirroring cockpit procedures. During a real lockdown in 2022, response teams successfully evacuated students with minimal panic and staff reported lower post incident anxiety. The structured drills reinforced collective confidence, demonstrating that resilience is not only psychological but procedural.

Technology Sector: Agile Sprints During the COVID- 19 Pivot

Context.

Technology companies rely on agile sprints, short, iterative work cycles to remain productive amid constant change.

Educational Adaptation.

During the pandemic, a large U.S. urban district created multi-disciplinary 'scrum teams' of teachers, IT staff and counsellors. Teams met virtually each week to identify obstacles in remove learning such as digital equity gaps or inconsistent student engagement. Through rapid prototyping they introduced real-time solutions: distributing WI-FI hotspots, redesigning asynchronous lesson templates and creating a peer tutoring application. Internal evaluations showed a 20% increase in student login rates and 1 significant drop in teacher burnout compared with neighbouring districts that used top-down mandates.

Hospitality Industry: Emotional Recovery Rooms

Context.

High-end hotels provide staff with 'recovery room', quiet spaces for decompression after difficult guess interactions.

Educational Adaptation.

A New Zealand primary school established a *Resilience Room* stocked with sensory aids, soft lighting and brief mindfulness recordings. Teachers could sign up for 10-minute sessions between classes without stigma. Usage logs indicated high uptake during parent-teacher conference weeks and follow up surveys revealed decreased afternoon stress and improved instructional presence. Administrators noted a drop in unplanned sick leave during high pressure periods.

Higher education: Student Peer Support Pods

While many interventions focus on teachers, students also require resilient engagement. At a mid-sized UK university, first-year engineering students were organisation into 'Peer Pods' of six members who met weekly to share academic and emotional challenges. Facilitators trained in motivational interviewing guided sessions. By semester's end, participating students displayed a 15% higher retention rate and reported stronger belonging compared to non-participants, underscoring the role of social connection in resilience.

These cases reveal a pattern, resilient engagement is not merely an individual attribute but a designed capacity supported by protocols, spaces and cultures that legitimize recovery and continuous improvement.

Implications for Educational Policy and Practice

The case studies highlight several policy levers:

- **Institutionalize Recovery Spaces and Reflection Periods**
  Schools can dedicate physical or temporal space for emotional decompression, modelled after healthcare and hospitality sectors.
- **Integrate Crisis-Preparedness Training**
  Borrowing CRM practices prepares educators to remain composed and effective during emergencies.
- **Adopt Agile Improvement Cycles**
  Agile methods allow rapid, collaborative responses to curriculum changes or technological disruptions.
- **Support Peer Networks**
  Student and teacher peer-support pods reinforce belonging, which is strongly linked to resilience.

Implementing these strategies required leadership commitment and resource allocation. Programs such as mindfulness workshops or resilience rooms will falter if workloads remain excessive or if emotional labour continues to be undervalued in promotion criteria.

Challenges and Future Directions

Despite promising innovations, several obstacles persist:

Measurement Limitations- Resilience and engagement are often assessed via self-report, raising concerns about social desirability bias.
Cultural Variability- Strategies effective in Western contexts may not directly translate to collectivist societies with different norms of emotional expression.
Policy Pressures- High-stakes testing can undermine recovery periods and collaborative practices.

Future research should employ longitudinal, multi-level designs to understand how individual, team and system interventions interact over time. Emerging tools such as wearable stress sensors and AI-assisted workload analytics may allow real-time monitoring and personalised support but ethical safeguards with critical.

Summary

Resilient engagement is not an innate personality trait but a multifaceted, designable process rooted in self-regulation, supportive relationships and enabling institutions. Lessons from healthcare, aviation, technology, hospitality and higher education show that resilience can be engineered through deliberate structures reflection circles, agile teams, decompression spaces and peer pods. By embedding these mechanisms into the daily life of schools and universities, educational leaders can cultivate environments where teachers and students not only withstand the pressures of the service economy but thrive within it.

A CROSS- DISCIPLINARY FRAMEWORK

Positioning education within the service economy requires an approach that moves beyond the single-discipline explanations of teacher and student experience. The intertwined demands of self-regulation, emotional labour and resilient engagement are not merely psychological phenomenon, they are shaped by organisational policies, labour marker dynamics and sociocultural expectations. A cross-disciplinary framework provides the conceptual breadth needed to capture these interactions and to guide actionable interventions. The framework proposed here draws on human resource management, organisational behaviour, educational psychology and sociology to illuminate how individual capacities and structural conditions jointly sustain or undermine well being and performance in education.

Conceptual Foundations

The service economy lens frames education as a context in which the 'product' is co- created by providers and recipients. Teachers deliver instruction, but the quality of the 'service encounter' depends on student participation and emotional engagement, paralleling customer experiences in hospitality or healthcare. From HRM, concepts such as emotional intelligence, employee engagement and job crafting highlight how workers manage affective interactions to create value (Grandey & Melloy, 2017). Organisational behaviour research contributes theories of job demands- resources (JD-R), which explain how work environments create strain and foster motivation depending on the balance between demands (e.g., emotional display rules) and resources (e.g., autonomy, social support) (Bakker & Demerouti, 2017). Educational psychology adds models of self-regulated learning, emphasising goal setting, self-monitoring and adaptive strategies (Zimmerman, 2002). Finally, sociology underscores the macro forces, neoliberal governance, marketization and cultural norms, that define what emotions are valued and which regulatory strategies are rewarded in educational settings.

Integrating these strands reveals three central propositions. First, self-regulation functions as both a personal resources and a mediator of organizational demands. Second, emotional labour represents a key job demand that can either deplete or enrich depending on the availability of resources and the authenticity of emotional expression. Third, resilient engagement emerges as the adaptive outcome when self-regulation effectively manages emotional labour in supportive contexts.

Integrative Model

The education service economy demands a nuanced understanding of how self-regulation, emotional labour, and resilient engagement interact. Self-regulation provides the cognitive scaffolding for managing effort and persistence, while emotional labour ensures the appropriate expression of feeling rules within student and stakeholder interactions. Resilient engagement emerges as the sustaining force that protects professionals from burnout and supports long-term service quality. The interconnections among these three core constructs are summarized in Figure 1, which presents a triadic framework linking self-regulation, emotional labour, and resilient engagement.

Figure 1. Cross-Disciplinary Triadic Framework of Self-Regulation, Emotional Labour, and Resilient Engagement.

Core components of the Framework

Self- Regulation as a Foundational Resource

Self-regulation is conceptualised here as a multidimensional capacity encompassing emotional control cognitive monitoring and behavioural adjustment. Drawing on Bandura's (1991) social cognitive theory, self- regulation involves forethought (planning and goal setting), performance control (self-monitoring and strategy use), and self-reflection (evaluation and adaptation). In the educational service economy, these skills allow teachers to management classroom disruptions, maintain instructional quality under policy pressure and recover from emotionally charged encounters. For students, self-regulation supports sustained motivation in self-paced or hybrid learning environments where external monitoring is limited. HRM research parallels these insights by demonstrating that self-regulatory capacities predict employee adaptability and service quality across sectors (Pulakos et al., 2000). Tus, self-regulation functions as the primary psychological resource that enables individuals to cope with emotional labour demands and to persist in the face of instructional expectations.

Emotional Labour as a Central Job Demand

Emotional labour refers to the process of managing emotions to meet organisation a display rules (Hochschild, 1983). In education, these rules often require teachers to exhibit enthusiasm, warmth and patience regardless of personal feelings or situation stressors. Students, particularly those in service- oriented disciplines such as nursing or hospitality, may also ne required to project professionalism and empathy during practicum placements. Organisational behaviour literature distinguishes between surface acting, faking or suppressing emotions and deep acting aligning internal feelings with required displays (Grandey, 2000). Surface acting tends to deplete psychological resources, leadings burnout and depersonalisation, whereas deep acting can foster authentic connections and job satisfaction (Brotheridge & Grandey, 2002). Applying the JD-R model, emotional labour represents a high-demand condition that necessitates robust self-regulatory resources and institutional supports to avoid strain.

Resilient Engagement as the Desired Outcome

Resilient engagement is defined as a sustained state of energy, dedication and absorption in one's works or studies, accompanied by the capacity to adapt and recover from setbacks (Masten, 2014). It extends beyond traditional notions of engagement by incorporating the ability to thrive under pressure. Within the JD-R framework, resilient engagement emerges when job resources such as supportive leadership, professional development opportunities and collegial networks, offset the demands of emotional labour. Educational psychology provides complementary evidence that self- regulation strategies (e.g., cognitive reappraisal, adaptive goal revision) promote resilience by facilitating positive emotion and flexible problem solving (Panadero, 2017). In this framework, resilient engagement represents the outcome of successful alignment between personal resources and structural conditions.

Interactions and Feedback Loops

The proposed model emphasises that these three components are mutually reinforcing rather than linear. Self- regulation enables effective emotional labour by allowing individuals to choose deep acting over surface acting, which in turn preserves energy for continued engagement. Resilient engagement feeds back into self-regulation by building confidence and expanding coping repertoires. Conversely, chronic emotional labour without adequate resources can erode self-regulation, leading to disengagement or burnout. These feedback loops underscore the importance of ongoing monitoring and dynamic interventions rather than one-time training. This conceptual model illustrates the reciprocal relationships among self-regulation, emotional labour, and resilient engagement within the education service economy. The triangular structure highlights the mutually reinforcing dynamics that sustain professional well-being and service quality.

Organisational and Policy Levers

A cross disciplinary perspective highlights several leverage points for practice and policy:

1. Job Design and Resource Allocation
   HRM research demonstrates that autonomy, clear role expectations and access to supportive supervision buffer the effects of emotional labour. Educational leaders can apply these principles by granting teachers greater decision-making authority, ensuring manageable class sizes and providing mentoring systems for both faculty and students.
2. Training for Emotional Intelligence and Self-Regulation
   Evidence for service industries shows that targeted training in emotional intelligence improves customer satisfaction and employee well-being (Kernbach &Schutte, 2005). Teacher education and professional development programs can integrate modules on mindfulness, cognitive reappraisal and stress management to strengthen self-regulatory capacity.
3. Culture and Display Rule Negotiation
   Sociological analyses reveal that organisational cultures shape which emotions are valued and how they are expressed. Institutions can create more humane display rules by encouraging authentic emotional expression and recognising the emotional complexity of teaching and learning.
4. Data- Informed Monitoring

Borrowing from HR analytics, educational institutions can implement regular climate surveys or well being assessments to detect early signs of burnout or disengagement, enabling timely interventions.

Multi-Disciplinary Insights- Implications for Cross-Sector Learning

The service economy perspective encourages education to learn from and contribute to other sectors. For example, healthcare's emphasis on compassion fatigue and hospitality's focus on customer experience offer transferable insights for managing emotional labour. Conversely, education's developmental mission provides a unique context for cultivating self-regulation and resilience not only in employees but also in further service workers across industries. This bidirectional exchange reinforces the value of cross-disciplinary thinking in designing sustainable educational systems.

Figure 2. Process Flow of Self-Regulation, Emotional Labour, and Resilient Engagement in the Education Service Economy.

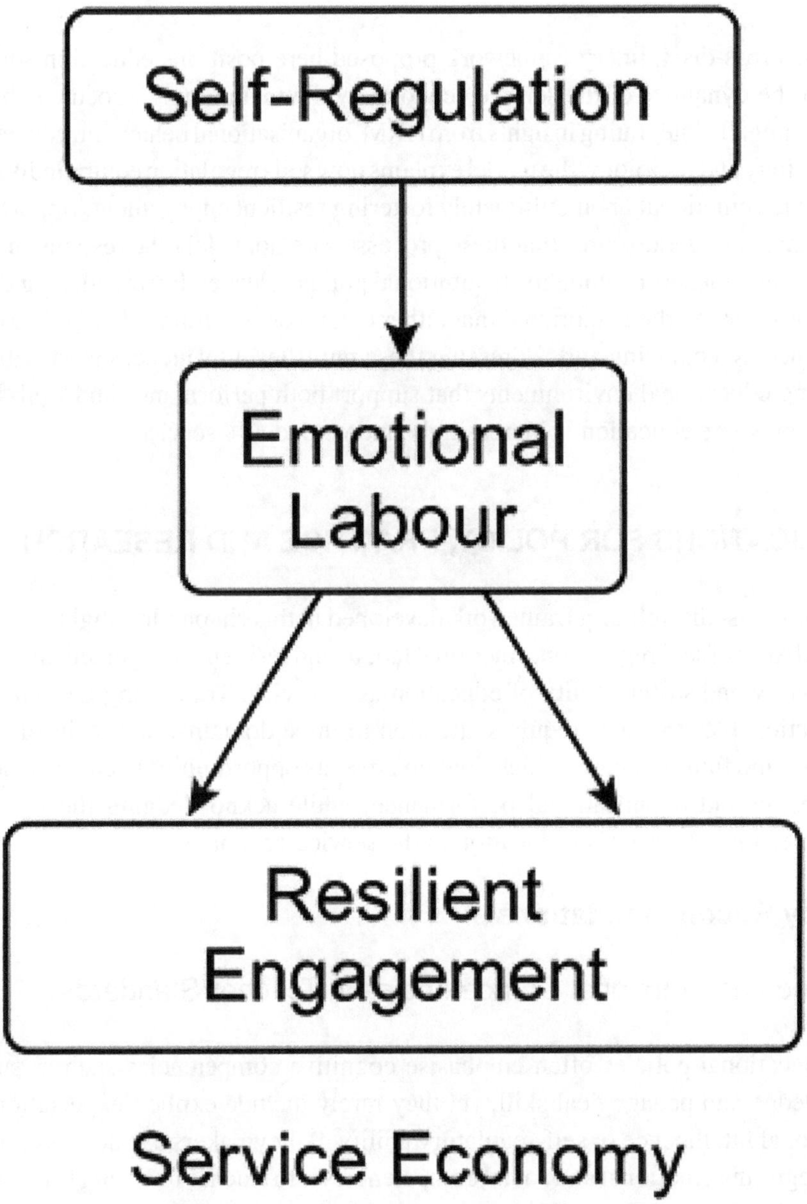

The flowchart depicts the directional mechanisms through which self-regulation informs emotional labour strategies, which in turn foster resilient engagement and adaptive outcomes in service-oriented educational contexts.

Summary

The cross-disciplinary framework proposed here positions education squarely within the dynamics of the service economy while maintaining a focus on human flourishing. By integrating insights from HRM, organisational behaviour, educational psychology and sociology, the model explains how self- regulation equips individuals to manage emotional about, ultimately fostering resilient engagement. Importantly, the framework underscores that these processes are not solely the responsibility of individuals teachers or students. Institutional policies, leadership practices and societal norms create the conditional that either enable or constrain self-regulation and resilience. Recognising and addressing these multi-level influences is essential for building educational environments that support both performance and well- being in an era where education is increasingly understood as a service.

IMPLICATIONS FOR POLICY, PRACTICE AND RESEARCH

The cross- disciplinary framework developed in this chapter highlights the intertwined roles of self-regulation, emotional labour and resilient engagement in shaping the quality and sustainability of education as a service. Translating these insights into actionable strategies requires attention to three domains: policy, institutional practice and future research. Each domain presents opportunities to enhance human well-being and organisational performance, while acknowledging the structural pressures that characterise education in the service economy.

Policy Recommendations

Embedding Emotional Competencies in Teacher Standards

Educational policies often emphasise cognitive competencies such as subject knowledge and pedagogical skill, yet they rarely include explicit expectations for emotional intelligence or self-regulatory ability. Policymakers can address this gap by integrating emotional and social competencies into teacher licensing frameworks and professional standards. For example, standards might require demonstrated proficiency in emotion regulation strategies, conflict management and empathy skills that research consistently links to classroom effectiveness and student outcomes (Jennings & Greenberg, 2009).

Funding for Well-Being and Resilience Programs

The shift toward market-based funding models has placed increasing financial strain on schools and universities, often limiting investment in staff and student well-being. National and regional education authorities can counteract these pressures by allocating dedicated funds for programs that build self-regulation and resilience. Evidence based interventions such as mindfulness training and peer support networks have shown positive effects on both teacher retention and student engagement (Klusmann et al., 2016). Policy mandates that secure consistent funding for such programs can help institutionalised these benefits.

Regulation of Emotional Labour Expectations

In many service industries, labour regulations limit excessive emotional demands by defining safe workloads and providing rights to psychological rest. Similar protections could be extended to education through guidelines that limit mandatory after-hours communication, require regular mental-health assessments and enforce reasonable class sizes. Such measures recognize emotional labour as a legitimate occupational demand rather than an invisible personal responsibility.

Practice Recommendations

Leadership for Emotional Climate

Institutional leaders play a pivotal role in shaping the emotional climate of schools and universities. Research from organisational behavior underscores that transformational leadership characterised empathy, vision and individualised support, buffers the negative effects of emotional labour (Breevaart et al., 2014). Leaders can model authentic emotional expression, encourage open dialogue about stress and prioritize well bring in performance evaluations. Simple practices such as regular check ins and transparent communication can signal that emotional health is valued alongside academic outcomes.

Professional Development for Self-Regulation

Professional development program can incorporate training modules on self-regulation strategies such as cognitive reappraisal, goal setting and adaptive problem solving. Workshops might combine theoretical instruction with experiential exercises including role play scenarios that mimic emotionally charged classroom interactions. By practicing these techniques in low stakes settings, teachers and administrators can strengthen their capacity to respond effectively when real challenges arise.

Student Centered-Interventions

Students, like educators, face growing demands for emotional labour, whether in group projects, service-learning experiences or customer facing practicum placements. Universities can support students by embedding self-regulation training into the curricula, offering resilience workshops and creating peer mentoring systems. Programs such as structured reflection journals, learning analytics dashboards and guided mindfulness sessions have demonstrated efficacy in enhancing students' self-awareness and emotional control (Panadero, 2017).

Data- Driven Monitoring and Early Intervention

Adapting methods from HR analytics, educational institutions can employ regular climate surveys, well-being assessments and engagement metrics to detect early signs of burnout or disengagement. These data can guide targeted interventions such as workload adjustments, counselling referrals or team-based problem solving. Importantly, data collection should be transparent and voluntary with clear protocols for privacy protection.

Research Agenda

Despite growing recognition of the emotional dimensions of education, significant gaps remain in the empirical literature. A robust research agenda should address the following priorities:

1. Longitudinal Pathways of Emotional Labour

   Most studies of teacher or student emotion rely on cross-sectional designs, limiting causal inference. Longitudinal research is needed to examine how emotional labour demands accumulate over time, how self-regulation mediates these effects and how resilience develops as a dynamic process.
2. Cross- Cultural Comparisons

   Emotional display rules and regulatory strategies are deeply shaped by cultural norms. Comparative studies across national contexts can reveal how service economy pressures interact with local traditions of teacher-student relationships and emotional expression.

3. Intervention Efficacy and Mechanisms

   While interventions such as mindfulness training show promise, more rigorous experimental studies are required to identify which components drive change. Mixed methods design combining quantitative outcome and qualitative narrative scan capture both the measurable effects and the lived experiences of participants.

4. Technology- mediated Emotional Labour

   The rise of online and hybrid education introduces new emotional challenges including the need to convey warmth through digital platforms and to self-regulate in the absences of immediate social feedback. Future research should investigate how virtual environments reshape the dynamics of emotional labour and engagement.

5. Organizational- Level Models

   Most research focuses on individuals, yet the service economy operates through institutions and policy systems. Multi- level modelling can examine how organisational culture, leadership practices and funding structures influence the interplay of self-regulation, emotional labour and resilience.

Integrating Policy, Practice and Research

A key insight of this chapter is that policy, practice and research are not isolated silos but mutually reinforcing components of a service-oriented education system. Policy mandates create the conditions for institutional investment in well-being, practice innovations provide the contexts for testing and refining interventions, and research generates the evidence base that informs policy revisions. For example, a national policy requiring teacher well being assessments might prompt universities to implement new data collection systems which in turn supply researchers with longitudinal datasets for evaluation effectiveness of resilience programs.

Summary

The service economy's influence on education is not a passing trend but a structural transformation that demands new approaches to human development and organisational management. By applying the cross disciplinary framework introduced in this chapter, policy makers can craft regulations that recognise emotional labour as legitimate work, institutions can design professional develop programs that strengthen self-regulation, and researchers can build evidence for interventions that promote resilient engagement. Together these efforts can create an educational ecosystem that not only meets the economic imperatives of a service driven world but also safeguards the psychological health and professional sustainability of the people who make education possible.

CONCLUSION

This chapter argued that education, increasingly embedded within the logic of the service economy, demands a new framework for understanding and supporting the people who teach, learn and lead within it. Across the sections, three interwoven concepts, self-regulation, emotional labour and resilient engagement emerged as the critical capacities that enable educators and students to thrive describe the volatility, uncertainty and relational intensity of contemporary schooling. The discussion of self-regulation demonstrated that effective educational actors are not merely transmitters or recipients of knowledge; they are active managers of their own cognition, motivation, and emotions. Theories such as Zimmerman's cyclical model and Bandura's social cognitive perspective illustrate how goal setting, monitoring, and reflective adaptation allow both teachers and students to sustain learning and performance. Applications in classrooms from structured metacognitive prompts to mindfulness-based interventions show that self-regulation can be cultivated rather than assumed. The examination of emotional labour highlighted the invisible work of managing feelings to meet institutional and stakeholder expectations. Whether in the warmth required of a primary school teacher or the calm neutrality demanded of a university administrator, emotional labour sustains relationships but also creates risks of burnout when left unacknowledged. Recognizing this labour through policy, professional development, and collegial support is therefore not a peripheral concern but a central condition for educational quality.

Finally, the exploration of resilient engagement demonstrated how self-regulation and emotional labour coalesce into sustained, adaptive participation. Resilience was shown to be neither an innate trait nor a simple act of perseverance, but a designable process supported by individual skills, interpersonal networks, and institutional structures. Detailed case studies, from teacher reflection circles inspired by healthcare's Schwartz Rounds, to agile response teams borrowed from the technology sector, illustrated how deliberate practices can transform stress into learning and disruption into innovation. Taken together, these strands reveal a powerful insight: the service economy does not merely impose new demands on education; it also offers transferable strategies for meeting them. Hospitals, airlines, technology firms, and hospitality enterprises have all developed mechanisms to support emotional balance, collaborative problem-solving, and continuous improvement. When adapted thoughtfully, these approaches can help schools and universities create cultures where teachers and students are not only protected from burnout but positioned for growth. For policy makers, the implications are clear. Resilient engagement will not flourish in environments of excessive workload, rigid accountability or neglected well-being. Investment in professional learning communities, flexible scheduling, recovery spaces, and recognition of emotional labour is essential. For practitioners, the chapter underscores the value of self-awareness, peer connection, and proactive coping strategies as everyday disciplines rather than emergency measures.

In sum positioning education within the service economy is not merely a descriptive exercise, it is a call to action. By embedding self-regulation, acknowledging emotional labour and engineering resilient engagement into the core of educational practice and policy, leaders can transform schools and universities into adaptive, humane, and high-performing institutions. Such transformation ensures that education remains not only a driver of economic vitality but also a source of personal growth, collective resilience, and societal well-being.

REFERENCES

Bailenson, J. N. (2021). Nonverbal overload: A theoretical argument for the causes of Zoom fatigue. *Technology, Mind, and Behavior*, *2*(1), 1–6. DOI: 10.1037/tmb0000030

Bakker, A. B., & Demerouti, E. (2017). Job demands–resources theory: Taking stock and looking forward. *Journal of Occupational Health Psychology*, *22*(3), 273–285. DOI: 10.1037/ocp0000056 PMID: 27732008

Bakker, A. B., Tims, M., & Derks, D. (2012). Proactive personality and job performance: The role of job crafting and work engagement. *Human Relations*, *65*(10), 1359–1378. DOI: 10.1177/0018726712453471

Bandura, A. (1991). Social cognitive theory of self-regulation. *Organizational Behavior and Human Decision Processes*, *50*(2), 248–287. DOI: 10.1016/0749-5978(91)90022-L

Bennell, P., & Akyeampong, K. (2007). *Teacher motivation in Sub-Saharan Africa and South Asia. Educational Papers, 71*. Department for International Development.

Breevaart, K., Bakker, A. B., Hetland, J., Demerouti, E., Olsen, O. K., & Espevik, R. (2014). Daily transactional and transformational leadership and daily employee engagement. *Journal of Occupational and Organizational Psychology*, *87*(1), 138–157. DOI: 10.1111/joop.12041

Brotheridge, C. M., & Grandey, A. A. (2002). Emotional labor and burnout: Comparing two perspectives of "people work.". *Journal of Vocational Behavior*, *60*(1), 17–39. DOI: 10.1006/jvbe.2001.1815

Carver, C. S., & Scheier, M. F. (2016). *Perspectives on personality* (8th ed.). Pearson.

Deci, E. L., & Ryan, R. M. (2000). The "what" and "why" of goal pursuits: Human needs and the self-determination of behavior. *Psychological Inquiry*, *11*(4), 227–268. DOI: 10.1207/S15327965PLI1104_01

Dweck, C. S. (2006). *Mindset: The new psychology of success*. Random House.

Folkman, S., & Moskowitz, J. T. (2000). Positive affect and the other side of coping. *The American Psychologist*, *55*(6), 647–654. DOI: 10.1037/0003-066X.55.6.647 PMID: 10892207

Frenzel, A. C. (2014). Teacher emotions. In Linnenbrink-Garcia, E. A., & Pekrun, R. (Eds.), *International handbook of emotions in education* (pp. 494–519). Routledge.

Grandey, A. A. (2000). Emotion regulation in the workplace: A new way to conceptualize emotional labor. *Journal of Occupational Health Psychology*, *5*(1), 95–110. DOI: 10.1037/1076-8998.5.1.95 PMID: 10658889

Grandey, A. A., Diefendorff, J. M., & Rupp, D. E. (2013). *Emotional labor in the 21st century*. Routledge. DOI: 10.4324/9780203100851

Grandey, A. A., & Melloy, R. C. (2017). The state of the heart: Emotional labor as emotion regulation reviewed and revised. *Journal of Occupational Health Psychology*, *22*(3), 407–422. DOI: 10.1037/ocp0000067 PMID: 28150996

Gross, J. J. (2015). Emotion regulation: Current status and future prospects. *Psychological Inquiry*, *26*(1), 1–26. DOI: 10.1080/1047840X.2014.940781

Hochschild, A. R. (1983). *The managed heart: Commercialization of human feeling*. University of California Press.

Jennings, P. A., & Greenberg, M. T. (2009). The prosocial classroom: Teacher social and emotional competence in relation to student and classroom outcomes. *Review of Educational Research*, *79*(1), 491–525. DOI: 10.3102/0034654308325693

Kernbach, S., & Schutte, N. S. (2005). The impact of service provider emotional intelligence on customer satisfaction. *Journal of Services Marketing*, *19*(7), 438–444. DOI: 10.1108/08876040510625945

Kim, J. (2016). Private tutoring and emotional labor in South Korea. *Asia Pacific Journal of Education*, *36*(4), 552–568.

Kim, T., Yoo, J. J. E., & Lee, G. (2012). Emotional intelligence and emotional labor acting strategies among frontline hotel employees. *International Journal of Contemporary Hospitality Management*, *24*(7), 1029–1046. DOI: 10.1108/09596111211258900

Kinman, G., & Wray, S. (2018). Presenteeism in academic employees: Examining the role of work-related stressors. *Higher Education Research & Development*, *37*(3), 518–531.

Klusmann, U., Richter, D., & Lüdtke, O. (2016). Teachers' emotional exhaustion is negatively related to students' achievement: Evidence from a large-scale assessment study. *Journal of Educational Psychology*, *108*(8), 1193–1203. DOI: 10.1037/edu0000125

Leithwood, K., Sun, J., & Pollock, K. (2020). *How school leaders contribute to student success: The four paths framework*. Springer.

Marginson, S. (2016). High participation systems of higher education. *The Journal of Higher Education*, *87*(2), 243–271. DOI: 10.1080/00221546.2016.11777401

Masten, A. S. (2014). *Ordinary magic: Resilience in development.* Guilford Press.

Noddings, N. (2013). *Caring: A relational approach to ethics and moral education* (2nd ed.). University of California Press.

Organisation for Economic Co-operation and Development. (2022). *OECD services trade restrictiveness index.* OECD Publishing.

Panadero, E. (2017). A review of self-regulated learning: Six models and four directions for research. *Frontiers in Psychology, 8*, 422. Advance online publication. DOI: 10.3389/fpsyg.2017.00422 PMID: 28503157

Pintrich, P. R. (2000). The role of goal orientation in self-regulated learning. In Boekaerts, M., Pintrich, P. R., & Zeidner, M. (Eds.), *Handbook of self-regulation* (pp. 451–502). Academic Pres. DOI: 10.1016/B978-012109890-2/50043-3

Powell, W. W., & Snellman, K. (2004). The knowledge economy. *Annual Review of Sociology, 30*(1), 199–220. DOI: 10.1146/annurev.soc.29.010202.100037

Pulakos, E. D., Arad, S., Donovan, M. A., & Plamondon, K. E. (2000). Adaptability in the workplace: Development of a taxonomy of adaptive performance. *The Journal of Applied Psychology, 85*(4), 612–624. DOI: 10.1037/0021-9010.85.4.612 PMID: 10948805

Rodriguez-Keyes, E., Schneider, D., & Keenan, E. K. (2021). Emotional labor in online teaching: Faculty experiences during COVID-19. *Journal of Social Work Education, 57*(Suppl. 1), 123–136.

Roeser, R. W., Skinner, E., Beers, J., & Jennings, P. A. (2013). Mindfulness training and teachers' professional development: An emerging area of research and practice. *Child Development Perspectives, 6*(2), 167–173. DOI: 10.1111/j.1750-8606.2012.00238.x

Schaufeli, W. B., & Bakker, A. B. (2004). Job demands, job resources, and their relationship with burnout and engagement: A multi-sample study. *Journal of Organizational Behavior, 25*(3), 293–315. DOI: 10.1002/job.248

Taxer, J. L., & Frenzel, A. C. (2015). Facets of teachers' emotional lives: A quantitative investigation of teachers' genuine, faked, and hidden emotions. *Teaching and Teacher Education, 49*, 78–88. DOI: 10.1016/j.tate.2015.03.003

UNCTAD. (2021). *World investment report 2021: Investing in sustainable recovery.* United Nations.

Yin, H., Huang, S., & Wang, W. (2019). Work environment characteristics and teacher well-being: The mediation of emotion regulation strategies. *International Journal of Environmental Research and Public Health, 16*(23), 4717. DOI: 10.3390/ijerph16234717 PMID: 31779268

Zeithaml, V. A., Bitner, M. J., & Gremler, D. D. (2020). *Services marketing: Integrating customer focus across the firm* (8th ed.). McGraw-Hill.

Zimmerman, B. J. (2002). Becoming a self-regulated learner: An overview. *Theory into Practice, 41*(2), 64–70. DOI: 10.1207/s15430421tip4102_2

Zimmerman, B. J., & Moylan, A. R. (2009). Self-regulation: Where metacognition and motivation intersect. In Hacker, D. J., Dunlosky, J., & Graesser, A. C. (Eds.), *Handbook of metacognition in education* (pp. 299–315). Routledge.

Zimmerman, B. J., & Schunk, D. H. (2011). *Handbook of self-regulation of learning and performance.* Routledge.

KEY TERMS AND DEFINITIONS

Burnout: A state of chronic physical, emotional and mental exhaustion resulting from prolonged stress and emotional labour.

Cognitive Reappraisal: A self-regulation strategy involving reframing a situation to alter its emotional impact.

Deep Acting: Attempting to align internal emotions with required emotional expressions, reducing dissonance and fostering authentic interactions.

Display Rules: Organisationally or culturally prescribed norms dictating hoW individuals should express emotions in professional or social settings.

Education as a Service: The conceptualisation of education not merely s content delivery but as an interactive service involving engagement, responsiveness and relational labour between educators and learners.

Emotional Dissonance: The psychological tension that occurs when there is a mismatch between felt emotions and required emotional expressions.

Emotional Labour (EL): The process by which individuals manage and sometimes suppress or amplify emotions to meet organisational or professional expectations particularly in service roles.

Resilient Engagement: The sustained ability to invest effort, maintain motivation and recover from challenges while actively participating in professional or learning activities.

Self: Regulation: The capacity to monitor, control and adjust one's thoughts, emotions and behaviours to achieve personal and professional goals.

Service Economy: An economy system where the primary value is generated through services rather than goods, emphasising human interaction, client satisfaction and relational competencies.

Service Orientation: A professional mindset emphasizing responsiveness, empathy and quality interactions with clients or stakeholders.

Surface Acting: Modifying outward emotional expressions without changing internal feelings often leading to emotional dissonance.

Chapter 7
Emotional Intelligence and Soft Skills Development:
Strategic Assets in the Modern Service Economy

Saima Khan
http://orcid.org/0009-0008-6402-3734
Zayed University, UAE

Elsayed Mahmoud
http://orcid.org/0009-0007-4848-6643
City University, Ajman, UAE

ABSTRACT.

In today's fast-paced service-driven economy, technical expertise alone no longer guarantees success. Increasingly, it is the human side of work—our ability to understand emotions, communicate effectively, adapt, and build meaningful relationships—that drives real value within organizations. This chapter explores how emotional intelligence, and soft skills have become essential elements of strategic human resource development, especially in industries where service quality and customer experience are paramount. Rather than viewing soft skills as secondary or innate traits, the chapter highlights their growing significance as learnable, measurable competencies that contribute directly to employee performance, leadership effectiveness, and organizational resilience. Drawing from psychological theories and contemporary HR frameworks, the discussion examines how these capabilities can be purposefully cultivated through recruitment strategies, staff training, coaching programs, and performance evaluations.

DOI: 10.4018/979-8-3373-6395-0.ch007

1. INTRODUCTION

The modern service-oriented economy has shifted organizational priorities, placing greater emphasis on human-centric skills alongside technical expertise. While traditional models focused on efficiency and specialized knowledge, today's interconnected environment highlights the importance of interpersonal skills, adaptability, and emotional intelligence. Service sectors such as healthcare, education, hospitality, and customer relations depend on the quality of human engagement. Within these domains, employees are expected to not only fulfill their operational obligations but also to establish enduring professional relationships, navigate interpersonal conflicts, exhibit empathetic sensitivity to diverse needs, and engage in meaningful client interactions.

This chapter contends that Emotional Intelligence (EI) and soft skills have moved beyond their traditional role as supplementary competencies, becoming essential strategic imperatives for maintaining organizational performance and achieving competitive advantage. Emotional intelligence, initially defined by Salovey and Mayer (1990) and further developed by Goleman (1995), refers to the ability to accurately perceive, interpret, regulate, and utilize emotions effectively. Soft skills, including effective communication, teamwork, adaptability, and critical problem-solving, significantly influence the quality of interpersonal collaboration and service delivery. Integrating these competencies into human resource frameworks enables organizations to more effectively address volatility, technological change, and the challenges of global competition.

Informed by organizational behavior research, psychological theory, and illustrative case studies, the main objective of this chapter is to conduct a thorough analysis of the role that soft skills and emotional intelligence (EI) play in the modern service economy. This discussion highlights the systematic cultivation, rigorous assessment, and strategic integration of these competencies into human resource policies, thereby reinforcing their role as essential pillars of organizational adaptability and long-term resilience.

1.1. Importance of Human-Centered Skills in Service Economies

The rise of the service sector in the twenty-first-century global economy has redefined value creation, shifting focus from material production to the quality of human interactions. Recent World Bank statistics (2023) show that services now employ most of the world's workforce and account for over 65% of global GDP, underscoring their critical role in social and economic development. In this context, the success of service delivery goes beyond technical proficiency; it depends on employees' ability to communicate, manage emotions, and navigate complex interpersonal interactions. Human-centered capabilities—most prominently emotional intelligence (EI) and a wide spectrum of soft skills—therefore constitute not peripheral attributes but critical determinants of organizational competitiveness, resilience, and long-term sustainability.

Contrary to technical knowledge, which can be codified and standardized, human-centered skills are intrinsically relational and context-dependent. They modify the way employees interact with customers, colleagues, and stakeholders. Scholars have consistently argued that while "hard" skills might secure initial employment, "soft" skills determine long-term success in both individual careers and organizational performance (Andrews & Higson, 2008). In the service economy, where customer satisfaction, trust, and loyalty are central, the human dimension of work becomes not a peripheral add-on but a strategic necessity.

1.2. Shifting HR Priorities Beyond Technical Competence

Human resource management (HRM) has experienced a significant transformation in recent decades. Human resource policies and procedures have long placed an emphasis on technical proficiency, job-specific training, and measurable outcomes. Globalization, technological disruption, and demographic changes have fundamentally transformed the nature of work. According to the World Economic Forum's 2020 Future of Jobs Report, over 40% of fundamental work skills will shift by 2030, with creativity, flexibility, emotional intelligence, and critical thinking ranking among the most in-demand competencies.

There is a growing recognition among current enterprises that employees endowed with emotional and interpersonal competencies are more adept at navigating ambiguity, mediating conflicts, and fostering collaborative organizational cultures. Human resource strategies are progressively oriented toward cultivating these "human" skills to complement technical expertise. Exemplars such as Google and Deloitte emphasize "learning agility" and collaborative leadership in recruitment and promotion, reflecting a strategic shift toward capabilities that remain resilient to automation, outsourcing, and rapid technological change (Chamorro-Premuzic, 2019).

This change is additionally supported by empirical data. According to a meta-analysis conducted by Joseph and Newman (2010), emotional intelligence significantly contributes to the variance in job performance across various industries, especially in roles related to service. Additionally, the OECD (2019) has conducted research that indicates that soft skills, including communication, collaboration, and problem-solving, have a stronger correlation with employability and career advancement than numerous technical skills.

1.3. Theoretical Foundations of Emotional Intelligence

The increasing focus on emotional intelligence is backed by various theoretical frameworks. Salovey and Mayer (1990) initially defined emotional intelligence as the capacity to recognize, comprehend, and manage emotions in both oneself and others. Their ability model conceptualizes EI as a type of intelligence that can be evaluated and cultivated in a systematic manner.

Building upon this foundational work, Daniel Goleman (1995) highlighted the mixed model, which incorporates both emotional competencies (such as self-awareness and empathy) and associated soft skills (such as leadership and conflict management). Goleman's research underscored the critical role of EI in workplace success, particularly in relation to effective leadership and team performance.

Bar-On (1997) proposed the trait model, highlighting a broader range of emotional and social competencies, including adaptability, stress management, and interpersonal skills. His Emotional Quotient Inventory (EQ-i) emerged as one of the initial standardized assessments of EI carried out within organizational contexts.

Collectively, these frameworks highlight the complex characteristics of EI and its relevance to HRM. Through the combination of skills, personality characteristics, and behavioral competencies, HR professionals acquire resources for evaluating and developing emotional intelligence within talent management approaches.

1.4. Soft Skills Frameworks in the Global Context

Soft skills encompass more than emotional intelligence; they also involve abilities like adaptability, critical thinking, collaboration, and ethical decision-making. UNESCO (2017) identifies these as "21st-century skills," which are crucial for successfully operating within a knowledge-driven, global economy. Comparably, the OECD Learning Compass (2019) highlights how cognitive, social, and emotional skills interact to support employment and lifelong learning.

The 2020 categorization by the World Economic Forum notably emphasizes the need of soft skills like creativity, emotional intelligence, and interactive learning for the workforce of the future. These frameworks offer HR professionals standards for creating recruitment, training, and performance management systems that foster comprehensive employee development.

Crucially, soft talents are more than just attractive "extras." They are progressively acknowledged as a form of strategic capital, serving as a source of competitive advantage within service-oriented economies. Unlike technical abilities, which may become obsolete as technology advances, soft skills are long-lasting and adaptable across positions and sectors, making them an important investment for businesses.

1.5. Cross-Cultural Perspectives

A significant aspect of EI and soft skills is their variation across cultures. The GLOBE research (House, 2004) and Hofstede's (1980) framework of cultural dimensions show that regional differences in emotional competence manifestations are substantial. For instance, in collectivist societies like Japan or China, the emphasis is on group cohesion and harmony, which influences the manner in which empathy and collaboration are exhibited. Conversely, individualistic cultures such as the United States tend to prioritize assertiveness and direct communication as signs of effective interpersonal abilities.

HR managers in multinational organizations must adapt EI and soft skills frameworks to accommodate cultural differences while upholding global service standards. For example, feedback methods effective in North America, such as direct criticism, may be viewed as disrespectful in certain regions of Asia. This underscores the necessity for culturally aware HR strategies that integrate emotional intelligence development into wider diversity and inclusion frameworks.

1.6. Empirical Evidence Linking EI, Soft Skills, and HR Outcomes

Empirical research increasingly supports the strategic significance of emotional intelligence and soft skills. Lopes et al. (2006) demonstrated that employees exhibiting elevated emotional intelligence experienced enhanced social interactions in the workplace, which contributed to improved team performance. Research in the hospitality sector shows that employees with high emotional intelligence enhance customer satisfaction and encourage repeat business (Kim, Oh, & Lee, 2019).

Quantitative data reinforces these findings. A global survey conducted by LinkedIn (2019) found that 92% of talent professionals and hiring managers consider soft skills to be as important or more important than hard skills. Furthermore, according to the Hay Group (2018), leaders with high EI outperformed those with lower EI by 20%.

These data points demonstrate that EI and soft skills are not abstract constructs but measurable competencies with tangible impacts on organizational outcomes such as employee engagement, retention, customer loyalty, and profitability.

1.7. Toward a Human-Centered HR Paradigm

The increasing acknowledgment of human-centered skills indicates a significant change in human resource management. Organizations now recognize employees not merely as resources to manage, but as comprehensive contributors whose emotional and interpersonal skills are essential for effective service delivery. This corresponds with innovative HR frameworks like "human-centric leadership" and "employee experience design," which prioritize well-being, engagement, and emotional health in organizational strategy (Meijerink & Keegan, 2019).

With the ongoing growth of the service economy, HR professionals face the challenge of creating systems that incorporate emotional intelligence and soft skills development throughout the entire employee lifecycle, including recruitment, onboarding, training, performance management, and leadership development. This manuscript's subsequent chapters will analyze the theoretical foundations, strategic significance, and practical uses of emotional intelligence and soft skills, emphasizing their importance in developing resilient, adaptable, and high-performing service organizations.

2. UNDERSTANDING EMOTIONAL INTELLIGENCE AND SOFT SKILLS

Emotional Intelligence (EI) and soft skills are becoming increasingly recognized as essential competencies for achieving success in service-oriented organizations. In order to situate these ideas in the context of the strategic human resources (HR) framework, it is essential to define them, investigate their theoretical foundations, and comprehend their real-world applications. Although technical skills are essential, the relational and emotional aspects of human interaction play a crucial role in the effectiveness of service delivery and the maintenance of competitive advantage within organizations.

2.1. Defining Emotional Intelligence

Salovey and Mayer (1990) first introduced the concept of Emotional Intelligence, defining it as "the ability to monitor one's own and others' feelings and emotions, to discriminate among them, and to use this information to guide one's thinking and actions" (p. 189). Their framework defined emotional intelligence as a collection of cognitive skills associated with emotional processing, aligning it with conventional perspectives on intelligence.

Since then, several models of EI have been developed, reflecting different emphases on ability, traits, and competencies:

- The Ability Model (Salovey & Mayer, 1997): This model conceptualizes EI as a mental ability equivalent to IQ. The framework comprises four components: recognizing emotions, utilizing emotions to enhance cognitive processes, comprehending emotions, and regulating emotions. The Mayer-

Salovey-Caruso Emotional Intelligence Test (MSCEIT) is commonly used to assess Ability EI.

- The Mixed Model (Goleman, 1995, 1998): Daniel Goleman brought global attention to emotional intelligence by associating it with workplace performance. The model highlights emotional competencies, including self-awareness, self-regulation, motivation, empathy, and social skills. Goleman posited that EI constitutes approximately 90% of the variance between exceptional and average leaders.
- The Trait Model (Bar-On, 1997): Reuven Bar-On identified emotional intelligence as a collection of emotional and social skills that enhance overall psychological health. The Emotional Quotient Inventory (EQ-i) assesses characteristics including adaptability, stress management, and interpersonal relationships.
- Integrative Approaches: More recently, scholars like Mayer, Roberts, and Barsade (2008) have emphasized the need to bridge these models by recognizing EI as a combination of measurable cognitive abilities, personality dispositions, and observable behaviors.

These theoretical frameworks highlight that EI is not a single, fixed construct but a multidimensional capacity that influences how individuals perceive themselves, interact with others, and navigate complex workplace dynamics. In HR contexts, EI has been linked to job performance, leadership effectiveness, teamwork, and employee well-being (Joseph & Newman, 2010).

2.2. Defining Soft Skills

A collection of behavioral, interpersonal, and non-technical capabilities known as "soft skills" help people communicate, work together, be flexible, and solve problems (Robles, 2012). Contrarily, hard skills, which are generally specific to particular tasks, quantifiable, and associated with technical expertise, soft skills are transferable across industries and situations.

Examples of soft skills include:

- Interpersonal skills: communication, active listening, and cultural competence.
- Cognitive skills: critical thinking, problem-solving, and creativity.
- Self-management skills: adaptability, resilience, and time management.
- Leadership-related skills: team building, conflict resolution, and influence.

Global frameworks highlight the strategic importance of these competencies. For instance:

- The World Economic Forum (2020) identifies complex problem-solving, critical thinking, and emotional intelligence among the top skills for the future workforce.
- The OECD's Learning Compass 2030 emphasizes "transformative competencies" such as responsibility, collaboration, and reflective thinking as essential for navigating uncertain global contexts (OECD, 2019).
- UNESCO (2017) underscores the role of soft skills in promoting lifelong learning and sustainable development, particularly in knowledge economies.

Soft skills have been demonstrated to affect employability. A 2019 LinkedIn survey revealed that 92% of talent professionals regard soft skills as equally or more significant than hard skills in the hiring process. Additionally, a report by McKinsey (2021) indicated that the demand for social and emotional skills is expected to increase by 24% by 2030, significantly exceeding the demand for various routine technical skills.

These findings indicate that organizations must prioritize soft skills development as a long-term strategic investment.

2.3. The Interconnection of EI and Soft Skills

Although EI and soft skills are frequently regarded as separate entities, they are fundamentally linked. Emotional intelligence serves as the psychological basis for various soft skills. For instance:

- Conflict management (soft skill) requires emotional regulation and empathy (EI dimensions).
- Effective communication (soft skill) depends on emotional awareness, active listening, and perspective-taking (EI capacities).
- Leadership (soft skill) is strengthened by EI competencies such as motivation, influence, and relationship management.

Empirical research strongly supports this interdependence. Lopes et al. (2006) demonstrated that individuals with high emotional intelligence engage in more prosocial behaviors, enhancing teamwork and collaboration, which are critical soft skills. Additionally, Côté and Miners (2006) found that emotional intelligence (EI) compensates for lower cognitive intelligence in predicting work success, especially in roles requiring significant interpersonal interaction.

This implies that HR practitioners should consider soft skills and emotional intelligence (EI) as complementary training areas rather than as distinct training areas. Initiatives aimed at enhancing emotional awareness also bolster communication, collaboration, and adaptability. In contrast, leadership training focused on soft skills tends to improve emotional intelligence abilities indirectly.

2.4. Cross-Cultural Perspectives

The interpretation and application of EI and soft skills vary across cultural contexts. Hofstede's cultural dimensions theory (Hofstede, Hofstede, & Minkov, 2010) and the GLOBE study (House, 2004) highlight significant cultural differences in how emotional and interpersonal competencies are valued.

- Collectivist cultures (e.g., China, Japan, Middle East): Emphasize empathy, harmony, and group cohesion. Employees are expected to regulate emotions to maintain relational harmony.
- Individualist cultures (e.g., United States, Western Europe): Value assertiveness, independence, and critical thinking. Direct communication and self-expression are viewed as signs of competence.
- High-context cultures (e.g., Arab Gulf, East Asia): Depend heavily on non-verbal cues, requiring employees to be adept at reading subtle emotional signals.
- Low-context cultures (e.g., Germany, North America): Prioritize explicit communication, requiring clarity and assertiveness in interpersonal exchanges.

Cultural nuances in multinational organizations create both opportunities and challenges for HR professionals. Culturally diverse teams can utilize a variety of emotional intelligence and soft skills, which can improve creativity and problem-solving capabilities. Conversely, discrepancies in expectations regarding emotional expression or communication styles can result in misunderstandings and conflict.

Evidence substantiates this complexity. Research conducted by Shaffer et al. (2012) indicated that expatriates possessing greater cultural intelligence and emotional intelligence adapted more successfully during international assignments. Gunkel (2016) similarly discovered that emotional intelligence influenced leadership effectiveness variably across cultures, exhibiting more pronounced effects in collectivist societies.

These results highlight the significance of culturally aware HR practices that uphold international service standards while customizing performance management, training, and evaluation to local standards.

3. THE STRATEGIC VALUE OF EMOTIONAL INTELLIGENCE

Emotional Intelligence (EI) holds significant strategic value for organizations, particularly within the modern service economy where interpersonal interactions define service delivery and customer satisfaction. EI functions as both a personal characteristic and a shared organizational resource that influences leadership, employee involvement, and the overall quality of service delivery. The significance of EI goes beyond frontline service contacts to the whole corporate atmosphere, making it a cornerstone of long-term human resource management.

3.1. Emotional Labor and Service Performance

In service-oriented positions, workers often participate in what Hochschild (1983) referred to as emotional labor, which involves managing emotions to align with organizational standards. Employees frequently need to exhibit particular emotions, including cheerfulness in customer service, compassion in healthcare, or neutrality in conflict resolution. Emotional labor encompasses both surface acting (faking or suppressing emotions) and deep acting (authentically aligning their internal emotions with the expected expressions).

Research has demonstrated that surface acting, while common, is associated with emotional exhaustion and burnout (Grandey, 2000; Hülsheger & Schewe, 2011). In contrast, deep acting tends to produce more authentic service interactions and is linked to higher customer satisfaction. EI plays a critical role in determining how effectively employees manage emotional labor. Employees with high EI are better able to recognize emotional cues, regulate their own responses, and engage in deep acting rather than relying on surface-level performance.

Research in the hospitality industry indicates that frontline employees possessing elevated emotional intelligence provide service experiences that result in increased customer return rates and enhanced brand loyalty (Kim, Oh, & Lee, 2019). Emotionally intelligent nurses in healthcare experience reduced stress and increased job satisfaction, leading to enhanced patient care outcomes (Codier et al., 2019). In call centers, where employees frequently encounter difficult customers, emotional intelligence mitigates turnover caused by stress by allowing staff to sustain composure and empathy (Zapf, 2002).

Thus, emotional labor is not just a personal challenge; it is a crucial strategic concern for human resources. Organizations that recognize and tackle the emotional difficulties linked to service roles—through stress management programs, resilience training, and promoting emotionally intelligent leadership—build more sustainable and resilient workforces.

3.2. EI and Effective Leadership

Leadership in the service economy requires more than technical expertise; it demands emotional acumen. Goleman, Boyatzis, and McKee (2013) argue that emotionally intelligent leaders can inspire trust, articulate compelling visions, and cultivate positive work environments. Such leaders demonstrate four core competencies:

1. Self-awareness – understanding one's emotions and their impact.
2. Self-management – controlling impulses and adapting to change.
3. Social awareness – empathizing with others and recognizing social cues.
4. Relationship management – inspiring, influencing, and resolving conflict constructively.

These competencies align closely with transformational leadership, which emphasizes vision, inspiration, and individualized consideration of employees. Barling, Slater, and Kelloway (2000) found that EI is strongly associated with transformational leadership behaviors, which are in turn linked to innovation, employee commitment, and adaptability.

This dynamic is underscored by industry examples. In hospitality, managers with emotional intelligence cultivate warm and attentive cultures, leading to customer experiences that surpass expectations. School leaders with strong EI foster trust with staff and students, enhancing academic success and well-being (Brackett & Rivers, 2014). In corporate service sectors, leaders with strong emotional intelligence excel at managing diverse teams, a vital skill in global markets.

Emotional intelligence in leadership is not a natural trait; it can be cultivated through coaching, mentoring, and organized training. HR departments that focus on EI-driven leadership development prepare future leaders with both strategic insight and the emotional skills necessary to lead teams through unpredictable situations.

3.3. EI as a Predictor of Employee Performance

Beyond leadership, EI has been extensively researched as a predictor of professional achievement. With almost 15,000 participants, O'Boyle, Humphrey, Pollack, Hawver, and Story (2011) conducted a meta-analysis and found that emotional intelligence (EI) is positively correlated with performance in all job categories, with especially substantial benefits in occupations involving interpersonal contact that are connected to services.

EI influences performance in several ways:

- Stress management: Employees with high EI are more resilient to workplace pressures, reducing absenteeism and turnover (Slaski & Cartwright, 2002).
- Conflict resolution: EI enhances negotiation and problem-solving, allowing employees to address conflicts constructively.
- Customer interaction: EI enables employees to perceive customer emotions accurately, tailor responses, and build trust, leading to higher satisfaction and loyalty.
- Teamwork: EI fosters empathy and cooperation, which improves collaboration and innovation within teams.

For example, Research in the financial services sector revealed that advisors with elevated emotional intelligence had better client retention and sales outcomes due to their ability to foster stronger relationships (Rozell, Pettijohn, & Parker, 2006). In education, instructors who possess a higher level of EI establish classroom environments that are conducive to student engagement and academic success.

3.4. EI and Organizational Climate

At the organizational level, EI influences the overall climate and culture, extending beyond individual contributions. An emotionally intelligent environment incorporates trust, empathy, and open communication into everyday behaviors. Carmeli (2003) discovered that organizations exhibiting high collective emotional intelligence promote greater employee commitment, job satisfaction, and organizational citizenship behaviors.

Such environments promote psychological safety, enabling employees to express ideas, take risks, and admit mistakes without fearing negative consequences (Edmondson, 1999). Psychological safety is crucial in service industries because negligence can greatly affect service quality, and employees must swiftly adapt to customer needs.

Organizations with emotionally aware cultures are also more resilient in times of crisis. For instance, during the COVID-19 epidemic, businesses that prioritized flexible work schedules, employee well-being initiatives, and compassionate communication were better equipped to maintain service quality and staff morale.

HR practices are crucial for integrating EI into the organizational culture. Recruitment methods that evaluate empathy and teamwork, training initiatives that enhance communication skills, and evaluation systems that recognize collaboration foster an environment conducive to emotional intelligence. When EI is integrated into HR systems, it transforms into a shared organizational resource instead of being just an individual characteristic.

4: SOFT SKILLS AS STRATEGIC CAPITAL

In the knowledge- and service-based economy, soft skills represent a form of strategic capital that is just as vital as technical expertise. While hard skills enable employees to perform specific tasks, soft skills determine how effectively they collaborate, adapt, and contribute to organizational goals. In this sense, soft skills can be conceptualized as human capital that generates value through relational and adaptive capabilities.

The World Economic Forum (2020) highlights that competencies such as problem-solving, creativity, and communication will be highly sought after by 2030. The OECD (2019) similarly identifies "transformative competencies," including collaboration, adaptability, and reflective thinking, as crucial for sustainable growth. According to UNESCO (2017), interpersonal and emotional skills are essential for lifelong learning and employability, especially within globalized service economies. These frameworks emphasize that soft skills are essential; they are key factors in organizational resilience and competitive advantage.

4.1. Communication as a Core Asset

Effective communication is consistently ranked among the most critical soft skills in the workplace (Robles, 2012). In service industries, communication extends beyond information transfer; it involves active listening, empathy, clarity, and responsiveness.

- Healthcare: The capacity of a doctor to empathetically communicate diagnosis and treatment choices may help patients follow medical recommendations. Research shows that good communication between patients and healthcare professionals greatly lowers malpractice claims and improves patient satisfaction (Levinson, Roter, Mullooly, Dull, & Frankel, 1997).
- Hospitality: Frontline staff often manage tense situations, such as customer complaints. Employees who combine empathy with clear communication can turn dissatisfied customers into loyal ones. Marriott International, for example, invests heavily in communication training to ensure service consistency across its global hotels.
- Education: Teachers' communication skills influence not only knowledge transfer but also student engagement, motivation, and classroom climate. Brackett and Rivers (2014) found that emotionally intelligent teachers who communicate effectively foster higher academic performance and social well-being among students.

Communication encompasses digital platforms as well. The increase in hybrid work has made effective communication via emails, video calls, and collaborative tools crucial. Miscommunication in online settings can result in disengagement and conflict, highlighting the importance of communication training in HR strategies.

4.2. Adaptability and Resilience

The swift advancement of technology, globalization, and crises such as the COVID-19 pandemic necessitate adaptability as an essential skill for the workforce. Adaptability denotes the capacity to modify oneself in response to new roles, expectations, and environments, whereas resilience signifies the ability to swiftly rebound from stress or setbacks.

- Pulakos et al. (2000) define adaptability as involving problem-solving in unfamiliar contexts, acquiring new technologies, and managing uncertainty.
- According to a McKinsey (2021) analysis, companies employing flexible workers had a 1.5-fold higher chance of outperforming their rivals during the pandemic.

Industry examples:

- IT services: With constant technological upgrades, IT professionals must continuously learn and adapt. Firms like IBM and Microsoft prioritize adaptability in their competency models.
- Healthcare: The pandemic required healthcare workers to rapidly adjust to new protocols, telemedicine platforms, and crisis conditions. Resilience training programs helped prevent burnout and sustain performance (Shanafelt et al., 2020).
- Customer service: Employees in call centers frequently face unpredictable client demands. Adaptability enables them to adjust tone, language, and solutions in real time.

HR plays an important role in building adaptation by offering continuous learning opportunities, encouraging job rotation, and implementing resilience training programs. Integrating adaptability in performance and appraisals promotion criteria enhances its recognition as a valuable organizational asset.

4.3. Problem-Solving and Critical Thinking

Service roles frequently offer employees unique challenges that demand innovative solutions. Critical thinking, which involves objectively analyzing information and making informed decisions, is becoming more important in service industries due to evolving customer expectations and complex issues.

- Ennis (2011) describes critical thinking as an evaluative process involving analysis, inference, and logical reasoning.
- A World Economic Forum (2020) survey placed problem-solving and critical thinking as the top two skills for the future of work.

Industry applications:

- Customer service: Representatives frequently encounter unexpected complaints that cannot be resolved through standard procedures. Problem-solving skills enable them to devise customer-focused solutions, enhancing loyalty.
- Education: Teachers use critical thinking to tailor strategies for diverse learners, ensuring inclusive classrooms.
- Aviation: Pilots and crew members engage in critical decision-making under pressure, where problem-solving skills can prevent accidents.

Organizations that promote problem-solving foster cultures of innovation and ongoing enhancement. HR can facilitate this by developing training that prioritizes scenario-based learning, cross-functional collaboration exercises, and case study analysis. Additionally, businesses that incentivize creative ideas cultivate a workforce that perceives challenges as opportunities instead of barriers.

4.4. Collaboration and Teamwork

Service delivery is typically a team effort, necessitating collaboration among various teams and departments. Teamwork requires trust, respect, and a unified effort towards common objectives.

- Salas, Sims, and Burke (2005) argue that effective teamwork depends on shared mental models, communication, and adaptability.
- The Gallup Organization (2019) found that organizations with highly engaged teams report 21% higher profitability and 17% higher productivity compared to disengaged teams.

Examples:

- Healthcare: Interdisciplinary teamwork between doctors, nurses, and technicians reduces medical errors and improves patient outcomes.
- Aviation: Crew resource management (CRM) programs emphasize communication and collaboration to prevent accidents.
- Hospitality: Coordinated teamwork between housekeeping, front-desk, and food services ensures seamless customer experiences.

HR may foster teamwork by insisting on team-based performance indicators, providing cross-training, and encouraging diversity and inclusion efforts. Collaborative organizations are better able to handle complexity and adapt to changing customer demands.

4.5. Soft Skills in Job Design and Team Building

Soft skills function as strategic assets when incorporated into team frameworks and employment models, alongside individual abilities. Current job roles require not only task completion but also the management of interpersonal relationships. For example, customer-facing roles in finance or hospitality prioritize empathy and communication as job requirements.

Team building activities and HR procedures that incorporate EI and the development of soft skills improve group cohesion and profitability. Instruments like 360-degree feedback, competency-based interviews, and psychometric assessments enable HR professionals to assess soft skills in the context of recruitment and performance evaluations.

Furthermore, organizations that incentivize collaborative behaviors—via recognition programs or promotion opportunities—indicate that soft skills are essential rather than peripheral to career progression. This promotes a workforce in which employees actively develop and utilize these skills for their professional advancement.

4.6. Global and Regional Perspectives

Soft skills, like EI, manifest differently across cultural and regional contexts.

- North America & Western Europe: Emphasize assertiveness, critical thinking, and innovation.
- Asia-Pacific: Value harmony, respect, and collective decision-making, with soft skills aligned to teamwork and group cohesion.

- Middle East: Hospitality and service sectors prioritize empathy and relationship-building, rooted in cultural traditions of generosity.
- Africa: Adaptability and resilience are emphasized in economies marked by volatility, while communal values shape collaboration.

These regional nuances require HR strategies to be context sensitive. Multinational corporations must adapt their competency frameworks while maintaining consistency in global service standards.

5: HR STRATEGIES FOR CULTIVATING EI AND SOFT SKILLS

Recognizing the strategic relevance of EI and soft skills, HR professionals must develop purposeful methods to foster such abilities across the workforce. The incorporation of EI and soft skills into HR practices necessitates a structured method that encompasses recruitment, training, performance management, and organizational culture. When strategically integrated, these competencies improve employee performance and bolster organizational resilience, adaptability, and service excellence.

5.1. Recruitment and Onboarding

The recruitment process serves as a key entry point to organizational culture, providing an essential opportunity to identify candidates possessing strong emotional intelligence and soft skills. Historically, recruitment emphasized technical qualifications; however, progressive organizations are increasingly adopting competency-based hiring to assess interpersonal and emotional skills.

Assessment tools and practices include:

- Behavioral interviews: Asking candidates to provide examples of past experiences dealing with conflict, teamwork, or adaptability.
- Situational judgment tests (SJTs): Presenting candidates with hypothetical workplace scenarios to evaluate empathy, decision-making, and communication skills (Lievens & Sackett, 2012).
- Psychometric assessments: Instruments such as the EQ-i 2.0 (Bar-On, 1997) or MSCEIT (Mayer et al., 2008) assess emotional intelligence dimensions directly.
- Gamified recruitment tools: Emerging technologies allow organizations to evaluate EI through simulations, role-play, and AI-driven behavioral analysis.

Global examples:

- Google uses behavioral interviewing to assess problem-solving and collaboration, ensuring cultural fit and teamwork skills.
- Emirates Airlines evaluates adaptability, empathy, and communication in its rigorous cabin crew selection process, recognizing that EI is central to passenger experience.

Onboarding:

Once recruited, onboarding must emphasize the significance of EI and soft skills. Organizations can enhance orientation by including sessions on values like empathy, collaboration, and appreciation for diversity, rather than just focusing on compliance and technical information. Onboarding programs consisting of team activities, role-play, and emotional awareness workshops demonstrate to new employees that emotional intelligence is integral to the company culture.

5.2. Training and Development

Unlike IQ, EI and soft skills are learnable and developable (Cherniss & Goleman, 2001). Training interventions are critical for equipping employees with competencies that enhance interpersonal effectiveness and adaptability.

Methods of training include:

- Workshops and seminars: Focused on communication, emotional regulation, and conflict resolution.
- Role-playing scenarios: Allow employees to practice empathy and negotiation in realistic contexts.
- Simulations and case studies: For example, hospitality workers can simulate challenging customer interactions.
- Digital learning platforms: Scalable, interactive modules accessible across global workforces.
- Experiential learning: Outdoor team building and service-learning projects that develop collaboration and adaptability.

Evidence:

A meta-analysis by Kotsou et al. (2019) found that EI training interventions significantly improve self-awareness, emotional regulation, and social functioning across organizational contexts.

Examples:

- Mayo Clinic (USA): Introduced empathy and communication training for physicians, improving patient satisfaction scores.
- Accenture: Provides blended learning programs combining online modules and coaching to build critical thinking and interpersonal skills for consultants.

HR leaders must also design tailored interventions for different employee levels—frontline staff, middle managers, and executives—since EI and soft skills manifest differently depending on role requirements.

5.3. Coaching and Mentoring

Coaching and mentoring programs provide individualized, relationship-based support for EI and soft skills development.

- Coaching: Focuses on structured, short-term, goal-oriented development. Coaches help employees identify blind spots, enhance self-regulation, and refine communication styles (Boyatzis, Smith, & Blaize, 2006). For example, managers may undergo executive coaching to improve empathy in leadership.
- Mentoring: Long-term relationships between experienced professionals and junior employees foster role modeling of emotionally intelligent behaviors. Mentors transmit both tacit knowledge and interpersonal norms that shape organizational culture.

Benefits:

- Improves leadership development by integrating EI into succession planning.
- Provides personalized development beyond one-size-fits-all training.
- Encourages reflective learning and emotional self-awareness.

Examples:

- Deloitte's "Women in Leadership" program pairs emerging leaders with senior mentors to cultivate resilience, confidence, and influence.
- Starbucks incorporates coaching into its leadership model, emphasizing empathy, servant leadership, and customer connection.

When coaching and mentoring are supported by HR policies and recognized in performance appraisals, they contribute to a strong developmental culture that sustains EI and soft skills across generations of employees.

5.4. Performance Management and Feedback Culture

Performance management systems must expand beyond technical outputs to assess and reward EI and soft skills.

Incorporation into appraisals:

- Competency frameworks can include empathy, adaptability, collaboration, and communication.
- 360-degree feedback systems allow employees to receive input from peers, subordinates, and supervisors, providing holistic insights into soft skill performance.

Feedback culture:

Regular, constructive feedback fosters growth in emotional awareness and interpersonal skills. London and Smither (2002) argue that emotionally intelligent feedback—delivered empathetically and with relational sensitivity—improves receptivity and accelerates learning.

Organizational examples:

- Adobe replaced annual performance reviews with a "Check-In" system, emphasizing continuous feedback and coaching.
- Microsoft transformed its appraisal system to prioritize collaboration and growth mindset, rewarding teamwork alongside technical results.

Feedback cultures also promote psychological safety, enabling employees to engage in honest conversations, admit mistakes, and experiment without fear—key drivers of innovation and adaptability.

5.5. Embedding EI and Soft Skills into Organizational Culture

For sustainable impact, EI and soft skills must be integrated into the very fabric of organizational culture. HR plays a central role by aligning values, leadership behaviors, and reward systems with emotional and interpersonal competencies.

Strategies include:

- Values alignment: Articulating empathy, respect, and collaboration in mission statements and HR policies.
- Recognition programs: Rewarding employees who exemplify emotionally intelligent behaviors, such as resolving conflicts constructively or supporting colleagues.
- Leadership modeling: Senior leaders must "walk the talk" by demonstrating EI in decision-making and communication.
- HR policies: Flexible work arrangements, wellness programs, and diversity initiatives reinforce the importance of human-centered practices.

Case Example Zappos:

A cultural cornerstone of Zappos is the institutionalization of customer service excellence and empathy. Employees are encouraged to exceed expectations in customer service, showcasing a culture that values emotional intelligence and soft skills alongside efficiency and sales.

Case Example – Emirates Airlines:

Cultural embedding of EI is evident in the airline's service philosophy, where empathy, adaptability, and communication form the foundation of the global customer experience.

By embedding EI and soft skills into cultural DNA, organizations create human-centered workplaces that sustain both performance and employee well-being.

5.6 ROI of EI and Soft Skills Development

One of the barriers HR leaders' faces is skepticism regarding the tangible return on investment (ROI) of EI and soft skills initiatives. However, research consistently shows positive outcomes:

- Hay Group (2018): Leaders with high EI outperform peers by 20%.
- Talent Smart (2019): EI accounts for 58% of performance in all job types.
- Gallup (2019): Teams with strong collaboration and engagement (linked to EI and soft skills) report 21% higher profitability.

Organizations that invest in EI and soft skills see measurable improvements in employee retention, customer loyalty, and productivity, making such programs both strategic and financially viable.

6: CASE STUDIES AND INDUSTRY EXAMPLES

The importance of Emotional Intelligence (EI) and soft skills is particularly clear when examined in certain service sectors. Every sector showcases unique methods by which emotional and interpersonal skills lead to quantifiable results for employees, customers, and organizations. Upon analyzing both successful and problematic cases across industries, it is evident that emotional intelligence (EI) and soft skills are not ancillary qualities, but strategic determinants of long-term profitability, employee retention, and service delivery.

6.1 Healthcare

Healthcare professionals constantly navigate emotionally charged interactions with patients and families. Empathy, active listening, and emotional regulation are vital for building trust and improving patient satisfaction. Codier, Freel, Kamikawa, and Morrison (2019) found that higher EI among nurses correlated with reduced burnout, greater resilience, and better patient-centered care outcomes.

> Case Example – Mayo Clinic (USA): Mayo Clinic has long invested in communication and empathy training for physicians. By embedding EI into its professional development, it reduced malpractice claims and improved patient satisfaction scores. For example, physicians who received EI training reported significantly higher patient adherence to treatment plans.

Case Example – UK NHS (National Health Service): Within the NHS, programs focused on "compassion in practice" emphasize empathy and communication as central competencies. Hospitals adopting EI-based training reported improved staff morale, lower turnover, and higher patient satisfaction ratings (Health Education England, 2017).

By contrast, hospitals with limited investment in EI often experience higher staff burnout and strained patient-provider relationships. The COVID-19 pandemic underscored the need for resilience and empathy, as emotionally intelligent healthcare teams adapted more effectively to crisis conditions than those without such training.

6.2 Education

Teachers serve not only as knowledge transmitters but also as emotional role models. EI enhances classroom management, student engagement, and conflict resolution. Brackett and Rivers (2014) found that programs training educators in self-awareness and relationship management significantly improved student academic outcomes and emotional well-being.

Case Example – Finland's Education System: Finland integrates soft skills development into its curriculum, emphasizing empathy, collaboration, and resilience alongside academic knowledge. Teachers are trained not just in pedagogy but also in emotional competence, which helps sustain Finland's reputation for high-quality, inclusive education (Sahlberg, 2011).

Case Example – U.S. "RULER Program": Developed by Yale's Center for Emotional Intelligence, the RULER program trains educators and students in Recognizing, Understanding, Labeling, Expressing, and Regulating emotions. Schools implementing RULER show reduced bullying, improved classroom climate, and stronger academic outcomes.

In contrast, educational institutions that fail to prioritize EI often struggle with high teacher burnout, poor classroom climate, and disengaged students. This underscores the need to view EI not as an add-on but as a core teaching competency.

6.3 Hospitality

In hospitality, customer satisfaction hinges on frontline workers' ability to manage emotional labor. Employees are frequently required to "act happy" or "stay calm" in stressful situations. Kim, Oh, and Lee (2019) found that hotel employees with higher EI create more authentic service experiences, resulting in stronger customer loyalty and repeat business.

> Case Example – Marriott International: Marriott invests in EI-based training to equip staff with communication and problem-solving skills. By empowering employees to make emotionally intelligent decisions—such as resolving complaints without rigid protocols—the company has built strong global brand loyalty.
> Case Example – Ritz-Carlton: Ritz-Carlton empowers staff to spend up to $2,000 per guest to resolve service failures, emphasizing empathy and initiative. This policy reflects the organization's belief that emotionally intelligent employees who act with empathy and autonomy enhance customer experiences.

On the other hand, hospitality providers that fail to cultivate EI face service breakdowns. For example, poor conflict management by frontline staff can escalate customer complaints, leading to negative online reviews and reputational damage.

6.4 Customer Service and Retail

Customer service representatives are often the face of organizations, tasked with diffusing conflict and addressing complaints. EI and problem-solving skills enable employees to handle high-stress interactions constructively.

> Case Example – Zappos: Zappos has become a global benchmark for customer service excellence by embedding empathy and adaptability into employee training. Staff are encouraged to spend as much time as necessary on calls to build genuine connections, rather than following rigid scripts. This emotionally intelligent approach has created a loyal customer base and differentiated the brand.
> Case Example – Starbucks: Starbucks emphasizes "customer connection" as a core value. Employees are trained to engage authentically with customers, which has built a sense of community around the brand. During the 2008 financial crisis, Starbucks reinforced its EI culture by retraining staff in customer service empathy, which helped it recover customer trust.

Conversely, retail companies that neglect EI often experience employee disengagement, high turnover, and poor customer satisfaction. For instance, high-pressure sales environments that prioritize technical performance over interpersonal skills may achieve short-term gains but suffer long-term reputational decline.

6.5 Aviation

Aviation is a sector where EI and teamwork are literally matters of life and death. Pilots, cabin crew, and ground staff must collaborate under high pressure, often in unpredictable circumstances.

Case Example – Crew Resource Management (CRM): Developed after aviation accidents in the 1970s, CRM emphasizes communication, collaboration, and emotional regulation in cockpit crews. Studies show CRM significantly reduces human error by improving EI-related competencies such as conflict management and situational awareness (Salas et al., 2006).
Case Example – Emirates Airlines: Emirates integrates EI and soft skills training into cabin crew recruitment and development. Emphasis is placed on cultural sensitivity, empathy, and adaptability, as crews serve highly diverse international passengers. This investment has contributed to Emirates' global reputation for service excellence.

6.6 IT and Technology Services

Although often associated with technical expertise, IT and tech services increasingly rely on soft skills. IT consultants, project managers, and support staff must translate complex technical information into solutions that clients can understand and trust.

Case Example – IBM: IBM integrates EI into its leadership development programs, emphasizing empathy, collaboration, and adaptability in managing global client relationships. This shift recognizes that technology solutions succeed only when supported by trust-based human interactions.
Case Example – Infosys (India): Infosys provides training in communication and cultural competence for its engineers working on global projects. This ensures smoother collaboration with international clients and reduces cross-cultural misunderstandings.

6.7 Cross-Industry Patterns

Across industries, three key patterns emerge:

1. EI reduces burnout and improves well-being. Healthcare and education show that emotionally intelligent employees experience lower stress and create healthier environments.

2. EI enhances customer satisfaction and loyalty. Hospitality, retail, and aviation demonstrate that empathy and communication directly impact brand reputation and repeat business.
3. EI fosters innovation and adaptability. In IT and professional services, soft skills complement technical expertise, enabling organizations to thrive in globalized markets.

6.8 Success vs. Failure: Lessons Learned

- Success: Starbucks, Zappos, and Mayo Clinic demonstrate how embedding EI into training and culture strengthens long-term performance.
- Failure: Organizations that treat employees as replaceable "service machines" often face disengagement, high turnover, and reputational decline. For example, several fast-food chains with rigid scripts and minimal EI training have faced negative publicity over poor customer interactions.

7: CHALLENGES AND CONSIDERATIONS

Although emotional intelligence and soft skills are increasingly acknowledged as vital assets in today's service economy, incorporating them into human resource management poses significant challenges. In contrast to technical skills that are clear, quantifiable, and typically uniform across sectors, soft skills and emotional intelligence are complex, reliant on context, and influenced by personal traits, cultural standards, and specific situations. As organizations work to integrate these competencies into hiring, development, and performance systems, HR managers and leaders must address several key factors.

7.1 Measuring Soft Skills and Emotional Competencies

Evaluating emotional intelligence and soft skills presents a major challenge. Conventional performance evaluation techniques, like numerical metrics, task completion rates, or technical certifications, do not adequately reflect the depth of interpersonal skills or emotional intelligence. Psychometric tools such as the Emotional Quotient Inventory (EQ-i) and the Mayer-Salovey-Caruso Emotional Intelligence Test (MSCEIT) provide frameworks for assessing emotional intelligence, but their relevance in various workplace settings is complex. Joseph and Newman (2010) indicate that while these tools can serve as useful benchmarks, they fall short in addressing situational nuances, individual differences, and cultural factors affecting emotional expression and interpersonal behavior.

Additionally, turning assessment results into effective HR strategies continues to be a significant challenge. HR managers might find it challenging to create focused interventions without reducing complex human behaviors to oversimplified terms. Scoring low on self-awareness doesn't necessarily mean there's a problem; it could simply be influenced by the context of emotional expression or workplace stressors. Organizations ought to combine standardized assessments with observational methods, 360-degree feedback, coaching, and reflective practices to obtain a complete understanding of employees' emotional and interpersonal abilities. At that stage, development programs can be tailored to address specific needs and organizational objectives effectively.

7.2 Cultural Variability

The implementation of EI and soft skills frameworks is further complicated by cultural diversity. Emotional expression, communication methods, and social norms vary greatly between cultures, and what is seen as a strength in one context may be viewed differently in another. Assertiveness is typically regarded in Western service economies as a sign of confidence and active participation. East Asian cultures often emphasize harmony, indirect communication, and group cohesion rather than direct assertiveness (Matsumoto & Hwang, 2019).

This cultural diversity requires a flexible and context-aware method for developing soft skills programs. Multinational organizations cannot enforce a uniform set of interpersonal skills worldwide without the risk of misunderstandings, reduced employee engagement, or potential conflict. Soft skills frameworks should be tailored to fit local cultural norms while still aligning with core service standards and organizational values. Training programs, assessment tools, and performance metrics must embody this balance by including culturally relevant scenarios, case studies, and role-playing exercises that enable employees to apply emotional intelligence in authentic and effective ways.

7.3 Organizational Resistance

Even when measurement tools and culturally adapted frameworks are in place, organizational resistance can impede the integration of EI and soft skills. Resistance can arise at various levels. Leadership might consider the development of soft skills as less important than operational efficiency, technical skills, or financial results. Employees used to transactional HR practices that prioritize task completion might view training programs centered on self-reflection, emotional awareness, or interpersonal growth as unnecessary or intrusive.

Addressing this resistance necessitates strategic alignment with the organization and effective communication of advantages. Organizations need to show that investing in emotional intelligence and soft skills directly influences employee engagement, customer satisfaction, innovation, and financial performance. Case studies demonstrating enhanced team collaboration, decreased conflict, and increased client retention after EI-based interventions can aid in gaining leadership support. Involving employees in the design and implementation of development programs creates ownership and reduces skepticism, transforming potential resistance into active engagement.

7.4 Strategies for Addressing Challenges

Addressing these challenges effectively requires a multifaceted approach:

1. Holistic Assessment: Combine psychometric tools with behavioral observations, 360-degree feedback, mentoring, and reflective exercises to capture a comprehensive picture of emotional and interpersonal competencies.
2. Cultural Adaptation: Develop culturally sensitive training modules, scenario-based exercises, and evaluation methods that respect local norms while maintaining organizational standards.
3. Evidence-Based Advocacy: Use data, case studies, and measurable outcomes to demonstrate the tangible benefits of soft skills and EI, securing executive support and resource allocation.
4. Integration with Organizational Strategy: Align soft skills initiatives with broader HRM strategies, performance metrics, and leadership development programs to ensure they are perceived as essential rather than optional.
5. Change Management: Engage employees in co-creating programs, communicate the purpose clearly, and provide ongoing support to foster acceptance and sustained behavioral change.

By addressing these challenges with thoughtful design, cultural sensitivity, and strategic alignment, organizations can move beyond viewing EI and soft skills as abstract concepts and fully integrate them as critical components of human capital development. Doing so not only enhances individual performance but also strengthens organizational resilience, adaptability, and long-term competitiveness in the service economy.

8: STRATEGIC RECOMMENDATIONS

To fully realize the benefits of emotional intelligence (EI) and soft skills, organizations must embed them at both cultural and structural levels. While technical skills remain essential, it is the human-centered competencies of empathy, adaptability, and collaboration that distinguish high-performing service organizations from average ones. Strategic recommendations for HR practitioners and organizational leaders focus on four interconnected areas: integrating soft skills into culture, embedding EI in HR policies, developing leadership pipelines, and leveraging technology to scale human-centered learning.

8.1 Integrating Soft Skills into Organizational Culture

Organizational culture shapes how employees behave, interact, and perceive their roles. For EI and soft skills to have sustainable impact, they must be institutionalized in cultural values and everyday practices.

Practical approaches include:

- Aligning mission statements and values: Organizations should explicitly articulate empathy, collaboration, and respect as part of their corporate identity. For instance, Southwest Airlines emphasizes a "people-first" culture that prioritizes employee happiness, which translates into exceptional customer service.
- Recognition and storytelling: Recognition programs can spotlight employees who demonstrate EI—such as resolving conflicts, going beyond to help customers, or supporting colleagues during stress. Storytelling reinforces these values across the organization.
- Cultural rituals: Regular team check-ins, well-being initiatives, and employee resource groups can embed EI into the day-to-day work environment.

Emotionally intelligent cultures have been shown to have more potential for creativity, fewer turnover, and increased work satisfaction (Carmeli, 2003). Global organizations must adapt locally to embed culture effectively. Empathy can be expressed differently in Japan than in the United States, necessitating leaders to adapt emotional intelligence to cultural norms.

8.2 Embedding EI in HR Policies

For EI and soft skills to be treated as strategic capital, they must be integrated into HR systems that govern recruitment, performance management, and promotions.

Recruitment:

- Use behavioral interviews that probe candidates' interpersonal competencies ("Tell me about a time you resolved a workplace conflict").
- Deploy situational judgment tests (SJTs) to evaluate how applicants respond to emotionally complex scenarios (Lievens & Sackett, 2012).
- Leverage psychometric tools such as the EQ-i 2.0 or MSCEIT to provide objective assessments.

Performance appraisals:

Traditional appraisal systems focused almost exclusively on technical performance. To embed EI, organizations should evaluate employees on criteria such as:

- Collaboration and teamwork
- Empathy in customer interactions
- Conflict resolution skills
- Adaptability under pressure

Examples:

- Microsoft redesigned its appraisal system to prioritize collaboration and "growth mindset" over individual technical output.
- Adobe replaced annual reviews with continuous "check-ins," encouraging managers to provide empathetic, developmental feedback.

Embedding EI in HR policies ensures that employees view these competencies not as optional "extras" but as core criteria for career advancement.

8.3 Building Emotionally Intelligent Leadership Pipelines

Leadership pipelines must be reimagined to prioritize relational and emotional competencies alongside technical expertise. Research demonstrates that emotionally intelligent leaders are better at motivating employees, managing change, and fostering resilience (Goleman, Boyatzis, & McKee, 2013).

Key strategies:

- Succession planning models that identify and promote leaders with demonstrated EI. This can include 360-degree feedback and peer evaluations that highlight relational strengths.
- Leadership development programs emphasizing self-awareness, emotional regulation, empathy, and inclusive leadership. For example, Deloitte's "Leadership Academy" integrates EI into all executive training modules.
- Mentoring and coaching: Senior leaders should model emotionally intelligent behaviors and mentor emerging leaders. This accelerates cultural transfer and builds continuity.

  Case Example – Google: Google's leadership framework "Project Oxygen" identified that the most effective managers were not those with superior technical knowledge but those who excelled in coaching, communication, and empathy. As a result, Google restructured its leadership development to emphasize EI and soft skills.

  Case Example – Emirates Airlines: Emirates incorporates cultural intelligence and EI in developing global leaders who manage highly diverse international crews, recognizing that leadership in service industries is rooted in empathy and cross-cultural sensitivity.

By institutionalizing EI within leadership pipelines, organizations build resilient leaders who can guide teams through uncertainty and change.

8.4 Leveraging Technology and Digital Tools

Technology offers innovative ways to train, measure, and scale EI and soft skills across organizations. Rather than replacing human-centered competencies, AI and digital platforms can enhance their development.

Applications include:

- AI-driven simulations: Virtual reality (VR) and AI tools simulate emotionally complex scenarios—such as handling a frustrated customer or negotiating with a difficult colleague—allowing employees to practice and receive feedback in safe environments.
- Gamification: Interactive games that reward empathy, collaboration, and adaptability can make training engaging and scalable. For instance, healthcare organizations have used VR empathy simulations to help doctors experience life from a patient's perspective.

- Analytics: HR analytics tools track soft skills development, linking employee performance data with outcomes such as customer satisfaction, employee engagement, and retention.

    Case Example – Accenture: Accenture uses AI-driven platforms to provide real-time feedback on communication and collaboration during training sessions, accelerating the development of interpersonal competencies.

    Case Example – Walmart: Walmart employs VR simulations to train employees in customer interaction and conflict resolution, reporting significant improvements in employee confidence and service delivery.

Technology also enables remote and hybrid learning, crucial in the post-pandemic workplace. Digital platforms allow geographically dispersed employees to access training and coaching, ensuring that EI and soft skills development remain integral regardless of location.

8.5 Future-Focused HR Strategy: Preparing for 2035

Looking ahead, organizations must anticipate how EI and soft skills will evolve in the next decade. Several trends will shape HR strategies:

- AI and Automation: As routine tasks become automated, the uniquely human skills of empathy, creativity, and collaboration will define competitive advantage (McKinsey, 2021).
- Hybrid and Remote Work: EI is critical for virtual leadership, as managers must build trust and cohesion without physical proximity.
- Generational Shifts: Gen Z employees, who now represent a growing share of the workforce, place high value on emotional authenticity, inclusion, and continuous feedback. HR policies must adapt accordingly.
- Diversity, Equity, and Inclusion (DEI): Soft skills are vital for inclusive leadership. Leaders must demonstrate cultural intelligence, empathy, and fairness to manage diverse teams effectively.
- Sustainability and CSR: Organizations that emphasize EI in leadership are better positioned to align with social responsibility and ethical values, which increasingly influence consumer and employee loyalty.

Future-ready organizations will not only invest in EI training but also embed it into strategic decision-making, ensuring that human-centered skills remain the cornerstone of organizational success in 2035 and beyond.

9: CONCLUSION

The service economy has significantly changed in recent decades due to fast technological progress, globalization, and shifting consumer expectations. In this context, the conventional emphasis on procedural efficiency, operational knowledge, and technical proficiency, while still significant, has been deficient. Organizations today must be adaptable, emotionally aware, and skilled in interpersonal interactions. Employees have evolved from just completing tasks to becoming key players in enhancing customer satisfaction, driving innovation, and shaping organizational culture. As a result, emotional intelligence and soft skills have become essential strategic assets that influence both personal and organizational success.

Emotional intelligence—defined as the capacity to notice, comprehend, control, and affect emotions in oneself and others—lays the groundwork for effective professional relationships. Soft skills, including communication, conflict resolution, empathy, adaptability, teamwork, and problem-solving, transform foundational abilities into practical competencies that enhance collaboration and strengthen organizational unity. EI and soft skills create the foundation for resilient, adaptive, and human-centered organizations. In fields like healthcare, education, hospitality, and customer service, where human interaction is essential, these skills are especially important. Evidence from these sectors shows that teams and leaders with strong emotional intelligence and soft skills achieve better results, both in performance metrics and in employee satisfaction and client engagement.

Leadership clearly demonstrates the strategic importance of these skills. Leaders who possess high emotional intelligence can build trust, manage conflicts within organizations, and create spaces that encourage creativity and teamwork. Soft skills like effective communication, active listening, and constructive feedback enhance emotional intelligence by enabling leaders to turn their emotional awareness into positive, actionable influence. This boosts employee engagement, lowers turnover, and reinforces organizational commitment. In healthcare, leaders with emotional intelligence enhance patient care results and promote staff well-being. In hospitality, staff skilled in empathy and communication achieve greater guest satisfaction and repeat business, demonstrating the economic importance of soft skills in addition to their human benefits.

Integrating emotional intelligence and soft skills into organizational practices, despite clear benefits, poses specific challenges. A major obstacle is assessment: technical skills can be quantified through tests, but measuring emotional intelligence and soft skills is inherently challenging. Self-report surveys, behavioral assessments, and 360-degree feedback provide insights but are frequently constrained by subjectivity, cultural bias, or social desirability effects. Organizations with strict hierarchies or conventional operational models may be reluctant to prioritize competencies viewed as “soft” or intangible. This resistance may appear as few training opportunities, little acknowledgment of interpersonal successes, or an excessive focus on technical results. The implementation process is complicated by cultural differences, as emotional expressions, communication styles, and interpersonal expectations differ widely across various regions and social contexts. Successful integration of emotional intelligence and soft skills demands tailored, context-aware approaches that honor cultural diversity and advance universal human-centered values.

Organizations need to take a strategic and systematic approach to tackle these challenges. Incorporating emotional intelligence and soft skills into recruitment, training, performance evaluations, and leadership development is crucial. Recruitment should extend beyond qualifications and experience to evaluate candidates' interpersonal skills using structured behavioral interviews, situational judgment tests, and simulation exercises. Training programs should go beyond theory to incorporate hands-on learning, role-playing, mentoring, and reflection, allowing employees to internalize and effectively apply their skills. Additionally, reward systems and recognition programs must be created to support behaviors that reflect emotional intelligence and strong interpersonal skills. Incorporating these skills into the core of the organization improves short-term performance and fosters long-term adaptability and resilience.

The emergence of hybrid work models, artificial intelligence integration, and cross-cultural collaboration underscores the growing relevance of emotional intelligence and soft skills. Remote and hybrid environments limit face-to-face interactions, making empathy, clear communication, and emotional regulation more critical than ever. AI-driven tools, while enhancing efficiency, cannot replicate the nuanced judgment, ethical decision-making, or relational understanding that humans bring to service delivery. Cross-cultural teams, increasingly common in multinational organizations, demand high levels of cultural intelligence, adaptability, and emotional awareness to navigate diverse norms and expectations effectively. In all these scenarios, EI and soft skills function as the glue that binds technology, process, and people into coherent, high-performing systems.

Looking forward, future research should focus on developing integrative models that explicitly link emotional intelligence and soft skills to evolving organizational trends and technological innovations. Studies exploring the longitudinal impact of these competencies on employee performance, retention, and organizational adaptability would provide valuable insights for HR practitioners. Furthermore, research examining how emotional intelligence interacts with AI-driven decision-making, digital communication, and remote collaboration can inform the development of training programs and organizational strategies that are both modern and human-centered.

Human resource practitioners must recognize that emotional intelligence and soft skills are essential, not optional. They need to be integrated into the organization's structures, policies, and culture. This entails fostering settings that promote ongoing growth, endorse emotionally aware leadership, and appreciate the importance of relational skills. Successful organizations tend to show greater resilience during disruptions, increased employee satisfaction and engagement, and improved customer relationships. These competencies change organizations from efficient machines into dynamic communities that can achieve operational and human-centered objectives.

In conclusion, the modern service economy requires a paradigm shift in how organizations conceptualize workforce capabilities. Technical skills alone are insufficient; success depends on the ability to navigate complex interpersonal dynamics, manage emotions constructively, and engage authentically with colleagues, clients, and stakeholders. Emotional intelligence and soft skills, far from being ancillary, are strategic drivers of performance, engagement, and organizational sustainability. While challenges in assessment, cultural adaptation, and organizational acceptance remain, the potential benefits are profound. By integrating these competencies into every facet of organizational practice, businesses can cultivate environments that are not only efficient but profoundly human-centered—ensuring long-term competitiveness, innovation, and societal contribution. In an era where change is constant and human connection remains paramount, emotional intelligence and soft skills are, unequivocally, the competencies that define success in the modern service economy.

REFERENCES

Andrews, J., & Higson, H. (2008). Graduate Employability, "Soft Skills" versus "Hard" Business Knowledge: A European Study. *Higher Education in Europe, 33*(4), 411–422. DOI: 10.1080/03797720802522627

Bar-On, R. (1997). The emotional quotient inventory (EQ-i) A test of emotional intelligence. Toronto Multi-Health Systems. - References - Scientific Research Publishing. Www.scirp.org. https://www.scirp.org/reference/referencespapers?referenceid=768114

Barling, J., Slater, F., & Kelloway, E. K. (2000). Transformational leadership and emotional intelligence: An exploratory study. *Leadership and Organization Development Journal, 21*(3), 157–161. DOI: 10.1108/01437730010325040

Boyatzis, R. E., Smith, M. L., & Blaize, N. (2006). Developing sustainable leaders through coaching and compassion. *Academy of Management Learning & Education, 5*(1), 8–24. DOI: 10.5465/amle.2006.20388381

Brackett, M. A., & Rivers, S. E. (2014). Transforming students' lives with social and emotional learning. *Journal of Psychology in Africa, 24*(2), 101–104. DOI: 10.1080/14330237.2014.903072

Carmeli, A. (2003). The relationship between emotional intelligence and work attitudes, behavior and outcomes: An examination among senior managers. *Journal of Managerial Psychology, 18*(8), 788–813. DOI: 10.1108/02683940310511881

Chamorro-Premuzic, T., Akhtar, R., & DAnnunzio, P. (2019). The Future of Work AI in Recruitment and Selection. Psychology Today. - References - Scientific Research Publishing. (2019). Scirp.org. https://www.scirp.org/reference/referencespapers?referenceid=3928131

Cherniss, C., & Goleman, D. (Eds.). (2001). *The emotionally intelligent workplace: How to select for, measure, and improve emotional intelligence in individuals, groups, and organizations*. Jossey-Bass.

Codier, E., Codier, D. D., & Marszalek, J. (2019). Emotional intelligence, nursing practice, and patient outcomes: A systematic review. *Nursing Outlook, 67*(2), 142–151. DOI: 10.1016/j.outlook.2018.08.005

Codier, E., Freel, M., Kamikawa, C., & Morrison, P. (2019). Emotional intelligence and patient outcomes: A systematic review and critique of the literature. *The Journal of Nursing Administration, 49*(2), 89–94. DOI: 10.1097/NNA.0000000000000713

Côté, S., & Miners, C. T. H. (2006). Emotional intelligence, cognitive intelligence, and job performance. *Administrative Science Quarterly, 51*(1), 1–28. DOI: 10.2189/asqu.51.1.1

Edmondson, A. (1999). Psychological safety and learning behavior in work teams. *Administrative Science Quarterly, 44*(2), 350–383. DOI: 10.2307/2666999

Ennis, G. (2011). Emotional intelligence and occupational stress: Examining relationships in a professional context. *The International Journal of Organizational Analysis, 19*(4), 390–405. DOI: 10.1108/19348831111173431

Gallup (2019). Global emotions report 2019. Gallup. https://www.gallup.com/analytics/248909/gallup-global-emotions-report.aspx

Goleman, D. (1995). *Emotional intelligence: Why it can matter more than IQ*. Bantam Books.

Goleman, D., Boyatzis, R., & McKee, A. (2013). Primal leadership: Unleashing the power of emotional intelligence (10th anniversary ed.). Harvard Business Review Press.

Grandey, A. A. (2000). Emotion regulation in the workplace: A new way to conceptualize emotional labor. *Journal of Occupational Health Psychology, 5*(1), 95–110. DOI: 10.1037/1076-8998.5.1.95 PMID: 10658889

Gunkel, M. (2016). *Cultural values, emotional intelligence, and conflict handling styles*. ScienceDirect. Retrieved from https://www.sciencedirect.com/science/article/pii/S1090951616300074

Health Education England. (2017). Framework 15: Developing the healthcare workforce. https://www.hee.nhs.uk

Hochschild, A. R. (1983). *The managed heart: Commercialization of human feeling*. University of California Press.

Hofstede, G. (1980). Culture and Organizations. *International Studies of Management & Organization, 10*(4), 15–41. DOI: 10.1080/00208825.1980.11656300

Hofstede, G., Hofstede, G. J., & Minkov, M. (2010). *Cultures and organizations: Software of the mind* (3rd ed.). McGraw-Hill.

House, R. J. (2004) Culture, Leadership, and Organizations The Globe Study of 62 Societies. Sage, Thousand Oaks. - References - Scientific Research Publishing. Www.scirp.org. https://www.scirp.org/reference/ReferencesPapers?ReferenceID=2010743

Hülsheger, U. R., & Schewe, A. F. (2011). On the costs and benefits of emotional labor: A meta-analysis of three decades of research. *Journal of Occupational Health Psychology, 16*(3), 361–389. DOI: 10.1037/a0022876 PMID: 21728441

Joseph, D. L., & Newman, D. A. (2010). Emotional intelligence: An Integrative Meta-Analysis and Cascading Model. *The Journal of Applied Psychology, 95*(1), 54–78. DOI: 10.1037/a0017286 PMID: 20085406

Kim, H. J., Oh, H., & Lee, S. (2019). The effect of emotional intelligence on service performance and customer satisfaction in the hospitality industry. *International Journal of Hospitality Management, 78*, 93–102. DOI: 10.1016/j.ijhm.2018.10.009

Kotsou, I., Nelis, D., Grégoire, J., & Mikolajczak, M. (2019). Emotional plasticity: Conditions and effects of improving emotional competence in adulthood. *The Journal of Applied Psychology, 104*(8), 1027–1045. DOI: 10.1037/apl0000391 PMID: 21443316

Levinson, W., Roter, D. L., Mullooly, J. P., Dull, V. T., & Frankel, R. M. (1997). Physician–patient communication: The relationship with malpractice claims among primary care physicians and surgeons. *Journal of the American Medical Association, 277*(7), 553–559. DOI: 10.1001/jama.1997.03540310051034 PMID: 9032162

Lievens, F., & Sackett, P. R. (2012). The validity of interpersonal skills assessment via situational judgment tests for predicting job performance in healthcare settings. *The Journal of Applied Psychology, 97*(2), 360–372. DOI: 10.1037/a0025741 PMID: 21842974

London, M., & Smither, J. W. (2002). Feedback orientation, feedback culture, and the longitudinal performance management process. *Human Resource Management Review, 12*(1), 81–100. DOI: 10.1016/S1053-4822(01)00043-2

Lopes, P. N., Salovey, P., Côté, S., Beers, M., & Petty, R. E. (2006). Emotion regulation abilities and the quality of social interaction. *Emotion (Washington, D.C.), 6*(1), 113–118. DOI: 10.1037/1528-3542.5.1.113 PMID: 15755224

Matsumoto, D., & Hwang, H. C. (2019). Cultural influences on emotional expression and regulation. In D. Matsumoto & H. C. Hwang (Eds.), Handbook of culture and emotion (2nd ed., pp. 3–24). Cambridge University Press.

Mayer, J. D., Roberts, R. D., & Barsade, S. G. (2008). Human Abilities Emotional Intelligence. The Annual Review of Psychology, 59, 507-536. - References - Scientific Research Publishing. (2015). Scirp.org. https://www.scirp.org/reference/referencespapers?referenceid=1536420

McKinsey & Company. (2021). Defining the skills citizens will need in the future world of work. https://www.mckinsey.com/industries/public-sector/our-insights/defining-the-skills-citizens-will-need-in-the-future-world-of-work

Meijerink, J., & Keegan, A. (2019). Conceptualizing human resource management in the gig economy: Toward a platform ecosystem perspective. *Journal of Managerial Psychology*, *34*(4), 214–232. DOI: 10.1108/JMP-07-2018-0277

O'Boyle, E. H., Humphrey, R. H., Pollack, J. M., Hawver, T. H., & Story, P. A. (2011). The relation between emotional intelligence and job performance: A meta-analysis. *Personality and Individual Differences*, *51*(5), 507–516. DOI: 10.1016/j.paid.2011.06.003

OECD. (2019). Education at a Glance 2019. OECD. https://www.oecd.org/en/publications/education-at-a-glance-2019_f8d7880d-en.html

Pulakos, E. D., Arad, S., Donovan, M. A., & Plamondon, K. E. (2000). Adaptability in the workplace: Development of a taxonomy of adaptive performance. *The Journal of Applied Psychology*, *85*(4), 612–624. DOI: 10.1037/0021-9010.85.4.612 PMID: 10948805

Robles, M. M. (2012). Executive perceptions of the top 10 soft skills needed in today's workplace. *Business Communication Quarterly*, *75*(4), 453–465. DOI: 10.1177/1080569912460400

Rozell, E. J., Pettijohn, C. E., & Parker, R. S. (2006). Emotional intelligence and dispositional affectivity as predictors of performance in salespeople. *Journal of Marketing Theory and Practice*, *14*(2), 115–124. DOI: 10.2753/MTP1069-6679140203

Sahlberg, P. (2011). *Finnish lessons: What can the world learn from educational change in Finland?* Teachers College Press.

Salas, E., Sims, D. E., & Burke, C. S. (2005). Is there a "big five" in teamwork? *Small Group Research*, *36*(5), 555–599. DOI: 10.1177/1046496405277134

Salovey, P., & Mayer, J. D. (1990). Emotional Intelligence. Imagination, Cognition and Personality, 9(3), 185–211. Sagepub. https://doi.org/DOI: 10.2190/DUGG-P24E-52WK-6CDG

Shaffer, M. A., Kraimer, M. L., Chen, Y.-P., & Bolino, M. C. (2012). Choices, challenges, and career consequences of global work experiences: A review and future agenda. *Journal of Management*, *38*(4), 1282–1327. DOI: 10.1177/0149206312441834

Shanafelt, T. D., Ripp, J., & Trockel, M. (2020). Understanding and addressing sources of anxiety among health care professionals during the COVID-19 pandemic. *Journal of the American Medical Association, 323*(21), 2133–2134. DOI: 10.1001/jama.2020.5893 PMID: 32259193

Slaski, M., & Cartwright, S. (2002). Health, performance and emotional intelligence: An exploratory study of retail managers. *Stress and Health, 18*(2), 63–68. DOI: 10.1002/smi.926

TalentSmart. (2019). Emotional intelligence 2.0: Annual emotional intelligence report. Retrieved from https://www.talentsmarteq.com

UNESCO. (2017). Education for Sustainable Development Goals Learning Objectives. UNESCO. - References - Scientific Research Publishing. (2017). Scirp.org. https://www.scirp.org/reference/referencespapers?referenceid=3510556

van Zyl, C. J., & Stander, M. W. (2014). The psychometric properties of the Emotional Quotient Inventory (EQ-i 2.0) in a South African context. *SA Journal of Industrial Psychology, 40*(1), 1–12. DOI: 10.4102/sajip.v40i1.1192

World Bank. (2023). Annual Report. Www.worldbank.org. https://thedocs.worldbank.org/en/doc/e0f016c369ef94f87dec9bcb22a80dc7-0330212023/original/Annual-Report-2023.pdf

World Economic Forum. (2020). The future of jobs report 2020. https://www.weforum.org/publications/the-future-of-jobs-report-2020

Zapf, D. (2002). Emotion work and psychological well-being: A review of the literature and some conceptual considerations. *Human Resource Management Review, 12*(2), 237–268. DOI: 10.1016/S1053-4822(02)00048-7

Chapter 8
Emotional Intelligence of Gig Employees:
Enhancing Work-Life Balance for Sustainable Productivity

Geetha Manoharan
http://orcid.org/0000-0002-8644-8871
SR University, India

Sanjeev Kumar
http://orcid.org/0000-0002-7375-7341
Lovely Professional University, India

El Sayed Mahmoud
http://orcid.org/0009-0007-4848-6643
City University, Ajman, UAE

ABSTRACT

This work examines how emotional intelligence (EI) supports gig economy workers in managing the unique challenges of their work, such as unpredictable schedules, job insecurity, and mental health risks. By enhancing emotional awareness and regulation, gig workers can better cope with stress and anxiety, enabling them to maintain a healthier work-life balance despite the flexible yet unstable nature of gig work. The chapter highlights that developing EI helps improve psychological well-being, resilience, and time management, which in turn supports sustained productivity and job satisfaction. It also discusses the importance of integrating emotional intelligence training and social support mechanisms to foster sustainable work practices and overall mental health among gig employees. The chapter emphasizes that enhancing EI is not only an individual responsibility but also requires

DOI: 10.4018/979-8-3373-6395-0.ch008

organizational support, such as training in collaboration, relationship building, and conflict resolution, especially as gig workers often join short-term teams with limited onboarding.

INTRODUCTION

The global economy is shifting toward gig work (Fisher & Cassady, 2019). Different challenges and opportunities arise for individual and organizational well-being. This paradigm shift necessitates reassessing employment frameworks, notably psychological capital needed to negotiate its uncertainties and demands (Joshi et al., 2024). Worker lifestyle, mental health, fair treatment, and well-being are concerns in the gig economy (Choudhary & Shireshi, 2022). Emotional intelligence, a non-cognitive skill, helps gig workers balance work and life and be productive. Gig employment is dangerous and without benefits, thus people must be adaptable (Parigi & Ma, 2016). This chapter suggests that gig economy workers with strong emotional intelligence might better manage their emotions and relationships for personal and professional success (Gómez et al., 2021). This chapter will also discuss how emotionally smart gig workers may utilize self-awareness and emotional regulation to manage unexpected cash sources and task adjustments, reducing stress and enhancing job satisfaction. Empathy and social skills may increase client interactions and collaboration in decentralized gigs, making work more durable and pleasant (Kuo et al., 2025). Policymakers and platforms may promote gig workers' emotional intelligence to minimize economic inequality and boost worker well-being (Hwang, 2024). This chapter will use models to discuss the benefits of emotional intelligence for gig workers.It will also show how identifying and controlling emotions and understanding and influencing others are crucial for reducing burnout and establishing resilience without organizational assistance (Fragkaki et al., 2024). Since gig workers must self-manage and adapt in challenging settings, they need emotional intelligence (Carminati, 2021). This method will allow a rigorous study of how emotional intelligence might benefit the gig economy. Emotional intelligence increases gig workers' work-life balance and productivity (Hsieh et al., 2023). Without job security or benefits, resourcefulness and self-management are crucial (Pande, 2024). The Rajasthan Platform Based Gig Workers Act, 2023, reclassifies gig workers and grants essential rights, supplementing emotional intelligence with institutional assistance (Rane, 2024). This legal reassessment implies that gig workers need comprehensive and integrated laws to categorize them and give them essential rights for decent living (Rane, 2024). Such legislation is needed to eliminate the labour code "blind spot" that denies gig workers minimum compensation, health insurance, and retirement (Rane, 2024).Strong legal frameworks that adapt to changing work are needed in the gig economy due to its precarious working conditions and lack of benefits (Montgomery & Baglioni, 2020) (Rane, 2024). While legislative reforms are needed, gig workers' emotional intelligence helps them navigate precarity and build autonomy and resilience.The gig economy's legal and social impacts on labor laws and worker protections require a greater knowledge of this shifting employment landscape (Hwang, 2024). Gig workers' various motives for self-employment and important issues, such as unequal access to benefits and legal protections, were emphasized in the research (Hwang, 2024 Whether they are independent contractors or employees affects their rights and social protections (Katiyatiya & Lubisi, 2024). Poor work-life balance is linked to reduced job satisfaction, psychological well-being, quality of life, and mental health issues such burnout and depression (Jalil et al., 2023) Pace & Sciotto, 2021. Work-life balance boosts creativity, mental health, and job engagement (Malik, 2023). Our gig economy has unique difficulties and possibilities, so work-life balance and happiness must be carefully explored. This study examines emotional intelligence attributes that substantially impact gig workers' work-life balance and productivity (Malik, 2023). For this, the study will address three essential questions:Gig workers' work-life balance depends on emotional intelligence - self-awareness, self-regulation, motivation, empathy, and social skills. Can emotional intelligence treatments improve gig economy workers' work-life balance and productivity? 2023 (Malik). Alameedine et al. 2023. How does gig economy technology and organization affect work-life balance, emotional intelligence, and productivity? When paired with emotional intelligence, gig work's autonomy, flexibility, and performance-based remuneration boost productivity and well-being (Koubova & Buchko, 2013).

Background of the Gig Economy

The "on-demand" or "sharing economy," or gig economy, has transformed several sectors and labour markets worldwide (Hwang, 2024). Technical advances, notably the widespread use of digital platforms that connect workers directly with customers, have driven this economic paradigm of short-term, flexible, and task-based labour (Oman et al., 2025).Disaggregating conventional employment structures into discrete jobs creates a flexible workforce that can quickly adjust to market changes (Koutsimpogiorgos et al., 2020) (Huang et al., 2020). As of 2020, 36% of the U.S. workforce was contingent or alternative, a major shift from full-time employment (Song, 2024). The gig economy brings both potential and problems, requiring a re-evaluation of labour laws and social safeguards to suit these workers' particular needs (Smedley & Rayment, 2019). Though the technical platforms allowing gig work are new, its core traits, such as unpredictable scheduling and piecework remuneration, resemble precarious labour and require a sophisticated legislative response (Stewart & Stanford, 2017). Job security and benefits are often denied gigging workers, despite their ostensible autonomy (Zietlow, 2020). Many workers assume a disproportionate amount of risk, especially during economic downturns and demand variations (Adams-Prassl et al., 2018).Algorithmic management systems in the gig economy pose ethical issues about worker monitoring, control, and discrimination, which can damage worker autonomy and well-being (Félix et al., 2023) (Tan et al., 2021).The gig economy, which accounts for nearly 30% of India's non-agricultural working force and 1.25% of its GDP (Sachdeva, 2024), illustrates this transformational transition. Asfahani et al. (2023) predict that the Saudi gig economy would be worth USD 2.7 trillion by 2025, proving its global economic significance.This globalisation highlights the need of understanding gig labour, especially in developing countries where it is a vital source of income during high unemployment and underemployment (Cieslik et al., 2021). Millions of gig economy employment is being generated in India, altering urban environments and linking workers with customers and clients across industries (Ramachandran & Kulandai, 2024). However, fast expansion typically comes before proper legal frameworks and social safety nets, leaving gig workers susceptible to abuse and economic instability.

Emotional Intelligence in the Workplace

This section discusses emotional intelligence and its growing importance in modern organisational paradigms, notably in improving individual and group performance (Midlage, 2025). Beyond cognitive talents, it includes the ability to identify, analyse, and control one's own emotions and those of others (Ashkanasy & Daus, 2002). Emotional Intelligence, also known as Emotional Quotient, is becoming a more important factor in professional success than intellectual intelligence (Salovey & Mayer, 1990). This enhanced view of intelligence shows how good emotion management and interpersonal skills increase professional cooperation, decision-making, and well-being (Fernandez, 2007). Research consistently shows that high emotional intelligence improves resilience, stress management, and leadership, improving personal well-being and organisational efficacy (Salovey & Mayer, 1990). In an age of automation and artificial intelligence, human-centric skills like empathy, collaboration, and adaptive problem-solving are becoming essential for complex work environments (Salovey & Mayer, 1990). Emotional intelligence - self-awareness, self-regulation, motivation, empathy, and social skills - is essential for individual well-being, corporate culture, and managerial communication (Prokhorova et al., 2020). Bar-On believes emotional intelligence is essential for human resource management, while Anand and UdayaSuritan say it helps managers understand and meet others' needs (Prado & Torres, 2019).The complex ability to sense, integrate, and control emotions is essential for leadership and team effectiveness (Koutsioumpa, 2023). A nuanced understanding of emotional states helps people navigate complex social dynamics, resolve conflicts constructively, and build strong professional relationships, which boosts productivity and job satisfaction in the gig economy (J & Soubramanian, 2024). Emotional intelligence is now recognized as an organizational asset, informing human resource strategies and leadership development (Coronado-Maldonado & Benítez-Márquez, 2023) (Ugoani, 2021). Developing emotional intelligence in a workforce may also improve adaptability, which is crucial in the gig economy's uncertainty and frequent shifts (Dhiman, 2017).Emotional intelligence facilitates gig people regulate to activity insecurity and flip stressors into possibilities for growth and resilience. Goleman defines emotional intelligence as the skills that allow humans to motivate themselves, conquer limitations, manipulate impulses and dissatisfaction, manage their mindsets, and save you suffering from impairing their ability to assume, empathize, and be optimistic (Suleman et al., 2019).

Work-Life Balance and Sustainable Productivity

The relationship between work-existence balance and productiveness is critical, particularly inside the gig economy, when professional and private limitations are blurred. This phase discusses how precise work-existence integration improves gig workers' well-being, productiveness, and monetary output. Effectively dealing with private and professional obligations reduces burnout, boosts activity pleasure, and improves work best and amount. This collectively useful interplay emphasizes the want for holistic organizational and character measures to maintain monetary achievement. Gig workers, who lack set up advantages and apparent differences, ought to self-control paintings-lifestyles obstacles for professional longevity and intellectual well-being. A good paintings-existence stability reduces psychological pain and improves cognitive feature, which improves project-oriented job overall performance (Rodrigues et al., 2024). This stability facilitates human beings' cognizance and be innovative, which reinforces productivity and sustains engagement even without ordinary organisational help (Petriglieri et al., 2018). A healthful work-existence stability can improve willpower and durability in gig economic system jobs (Bello et al., 2024), making proactive steps to preserve and recruit people crucial. Healthy paintings-lifestyles balance boosts undertaking pride, engagement, and professional willpower, motivating and boosting productivity (Bello et al., 2024). Groups that prioritize and facilitate work-lifestyles stability for his or her personnel, inclusive of gig people, have lower turnover prices and better employee morale, which improves overall performance and place of business lifestyle (Burton, 2012) (Bello et al., 2024).

SUPPORTING LITERATURE REVIEW

The following literature evaluation seriously synthesizes extant studies regarding the gig economic system, emotional intelligence, paintings-life balance, and sustainable productiveness, setting up a foundational understanding for the subsequent assessment. It delineates the conceptual frameworks and empirical findings that underpin the interconnections among those constructs, elucidating the right demanding conditions and opportunities furnished thru the evolving nature of labour (Mamatha, 2024). This section will have a examine how the growing prevalence of a ways-flung gig paintings, characterised thru its flexibility and shortage of conventional employment benefits, necessitates a re-assessment of set up paintings-lifestyles paradigms (wood et al., 2018). It will moreover delve into the consequences of algorithmic control and virtual systems on worker autonomy and nicely-being internal this context (wooden et al., 2018). furthermore, the evaluation will scrutinize the moral dimensions of human's analytics and emotional AI in monitoring and influencing gig worker behaviour, thinking about each their potential blessings and inherent risks (Tursunbayeva et al., 2021) (Chavan et al., 2025) (Wu, 2024). It is going to additionally explore the mental agreement acquainted in gig employment, contrasting it with conventional employment models and assessing its effect on employee loyalty and engagement (Hsieh et al., 2023) (Heeks, 2017). Moreover, the literature assessment will become aware of theoretical gaps regarding the software of emotional intelligence theories to the unique context of precarious gig paintings, approximately mitigating the stressors associated with unpredictable income and task insecurity (Wiener et al., 2021). Subsequently, it is going to address the essential for more nuanced theoretical models that account for the multidimensional nature of work-existence integration within the gig economic gadget, moving beyond traditional paintings-lifestyles stability frameworks. The assessment will further keep in mind how the informal monetary gadget, a high-quality context for a splendid deal gig paintings in low and middle-earnings nations, affects the dynamics of labour best and employee safety (Cieslik et al., 2021). This comprehensive synthesis pursuits to establish a sturdy theoretical foundation for understanding the complicated interaction among character emotional competencies and systemic elements in shaping the critiques of gig human beings, mainly inside the global South in which virtual exertions systems are an increasing number of commonplaces as an economic improvement method (Graham et al., 2017) (Palhad et al., 2023).

Emotional Intelligence Theories and Models

After comprehending the gig monetary device, this component examines emotional intelligence's theoretical foundations and essential models to analyse its importance in modern-day employment. Emotional intelligence is the popularity, data, use, and control of one's personal and others' emotions, which is important for navigating gig paintings's often ambiguous social and expert interactions. Salovey and Mayer and Goleman's functionality-based and blended models provide viewpoints on how emotional skills seem and impact adaptive conduct in dynamic paintings situations. Potential version treats emotional intelligence as a natural intelligence like cognitive intelligence, observable thru average overall performance-based totally completely exams (Iliceto & Fino, 2017). Mixed models, which integrate emotional talents with personality characteristics and social competences, offer a extra practical know-how of emotional intelligence in carried out conditions (Skrzypczyńska, 2020). The Salovey and Mayer model divides cognitive processing of emotional facts into four domains: sensing feelings, allowing cognition with emotions, comprehending feelings, and controlling emotions (Mayer et al., 2016) (Lubis et al., 2023). Emotionally wise people can better regulate to environmental demands through processing and the usage of emotional enters (Salovey & Mayer, 1990) (Mayer et al., 2016).

Emotional Intelligence and Work-Life Balance

This section critically examines the complicated link between emotional intelligence and paintings-existence stability, particularly within the gig financial system. It will discover how emotionally sensible behaviours and abilities can help gig people cope with the stressors of precarious employment, such as unpredictable income, abnormal schedules, and blurred expert and personal limitations, improving their properly-being and productivity (Hersing, 2017). It is going to have a look at how outstanding emotional intelligence frameworks' emotional self-regulation, empathy, and social talent help this populace control paintings-lifestyles interference and improve paintings-lifestyles (Abraham, 2004). Additionally, it is going to examine how emotional intelligence can construct resilience and adaptability, which can be important for paintings-existence stability in a hastily converting hard work market. A gig employee's capacity to monitor and differentiate moods outcomes their capability to expand and keep properly work-life obstacles (Cihan & Dılekmen, 2024). To reduce the mental toll of the gig economy and enhance private and expert results, this information is critical (Ishii & Horikawa, 2019).

Work-Life Balance and Productivity Nexus

Paintings-existence stability affects gig people' manufacturing, first-rate, and sustainability. Concord among work and life improves nicely-being, cognitive feature, engagement, and burnout, that are crucial to productivity inside the absence of conventional employment arrangements. An imbalance can reduce attention, tension, and motivation, decrease productiveness and possibly lead to job loss (Briner, 2000). This shows that gig economic system production and innovation are pushed by using work-lifestyles balance strategies. Growing answers to decorate gig humans' non-public and expert well-being requires information this courting (Kumar, 2024). Work-existence balance techniques enhance employee fitness and productiveness, making them essential in the gig monetary machine (Marecki, 2024). Offices that provide flexible paintings arrangements, telecommuting, and wellbeing programs file higher employee engagement, lower burnout, and a higher reputation, which in a roundabout way boosts productivity in an interdependent ecosystem (Bello et al., 2024).

Sustainability in the Context of Gig Work

This phase defines and explores sustainability in the context of gig employment, going beyond environmental interpretations to encompass the toughness, viability, and typical nicely-being of the freelance workforce. This involves assessing gig people' financial, social, and psychological resilience and the economic and moral results of these converting exertions paradigm on society (discipline & Chan, 2018). It will attention on how the gig financial system, while flexible, often hinders career increase and financial balance, traumatic a rethinking of sustainable work fashions (Kattaa & Byrne, 2018). We will additionally study how platform layout, regulatory frameworks, and person organisation influence gig work's viability and equity. This re-evaluation examines how sturdy institutional frameworks, and supportive organizational regulations can reduce precarity and create a greater sustainable gig worker's place of job, which include occupational damage safety and social safety nets (Ran & Zhao, 2023). Issues can be made on the gig version's long-term impact on installed challenge structures, social protection structures, and the tough paintings marketplace. This segment seeks to fully explain gig artwork sustainability and its significance to worker welfare and the labour environment. For gig people' contemporary and destiny well-being and economic stability, laws and practices want to take a complete method to sustainability.

Theoretical Framework on Emotional Intelligence as a Mediator

This segment will delineate the theoretical underpinnings of emotional intelligence and suggest its function as a vital mediator inside the courting the various intrinsic characteristics of gig paintings and the fulfilment of labour-lifestyles balance and sustainable productiveness. Especially, it will discover how numerous sides of emotional intelligence, which encompass self-recognition, self-regulation, motivation, empathy, and social competencies, allow gig workers to navigate the inherent uncertainties and needs in their flexible painting's preparations (Lei & Kaplan, 2023). This includes expertise how emotionally clever gig humans can proactively manage their schedules, negotiate patron expectations, and mitigate stressors, thereby remodelling capacity paintings-life conflicts into opportunities for boom and improved nicely-being. Moreover, emotional intelligence enables the improvement of robust coping mechanisms and fosters adaptive responses to the abnormal profit's streams and shortage of conventional benefits frequently associated with gig employment, thereby bolstering mental resilience and promoting sustainable engagement (Jibunoh et al., 2025). This mediatory position suggests that cultivating emotional intelligence amongst gig personnel can be a pivotal method for enhancing their capability to achieve equilibrium between professional demands and personal existence, in the end principal to greater regular and higher-first-rate output (Imteyaz et al., 2024).

Work-Life Balance as an Outcome

This phase will characteristic work-existence balance no longer without a doubt as a suitable nation however as a measurable very last result, deeply stimulated through the gig employee's emotional intelligence and the traits in their paintings environment (Joshi et al., 2024). It will have a look at several indicators of labour-existence balance, which includes perceived manipulate over artwork hours, integration of personal and expert spheres, and pleasure with popular lifestyles exceptional, demonstrating how those metrics characteristic tangible reflections of a gig worker's capability to efficiently manage the needs in their expert and private lives. Furthermore, this phase will talk how a better diploma of emotional intelligence can empower gig personnel to strategically allocate their time and energy, set suitable barriers, and proactively are attempting to find assist systems, all of which might be important for accomplishing and preserving maximum efficient paintings-existence equilibrium. This perspective emphasizes that artwork-lifestyles balance is not always really a loss of battle however an active, dynamic machine of harmonizing various existence roles, particularly critical in the context of the often-unstructured gig financial system (Abraham, 2000). This section will also find out the demanding situations inherent in engaging in paintings-lifestyles stability in the gig economic device, which incorporates the blurred lines amongst artwork and personal life, the stress to be constantly to be had, and the ability for social isolation (Fisher & Cassady, 2019) (Parigi & Ma, 2016). Therefore, the functionality to interact in effective emotional tough work - dealing with and displaying appropriate feelings - will become paramount for gig people to mitigate those worrying situations and hold expert efficacy without compromising personal nicely-being (Kuo et al., 2025).

Sustainable Productivity as the Goal

This phase defines sustainable productiveness as a multifaceted objective, encompassing no longer best the everyday transport of exceptional records artwork but moreover the long-term capability for sustained output without compromising the employee's physical, highbrow, or emotional fitness. It posits that this form of productivity is intrinsically related to a healthful work-existence stability, facilitated via using the apt application of emotional intelligence, as opposed to maximizing output at the cost of properly-being ("The significance of Taking a destroy," 2018). It elaborates on how emotional intelligence, by way of using fostering self-cognizance and self-law, enables gig humans to apprehend their limits, prevent burnout, and preserve an efficient tempo over prolonged intervals, thereby ensuring the toughness of their careers in the gig economic device. This angle underscores that proper productivity inside the gig monetary system is not completely about quantity but approximately the ability to continually produce the best work without succumbing to exhaustion, that is a common issue among gig people (Kuo et al., 2025) (Gómez et al., 2021). Furthermore, it highlights how emotional intelligence contributes to adaptability and resilience, allowing gig employees to regulate to fluctuating needs and keep their output first-class even amidst uncertain running conditions (Niere et al., 2023).

Model of Emotional Intelligence, Work-Life Balance, and Sustainable Productivity

This model integrates the ones theoretical constructs, providing a cyclical courting wherein emotional intelligence mediates the route to greater tremendous work-lifestyles balance, which in turn fosters sustainable productiveness. This framework posits that gig employees who show off higher degrees of emotional intelligence are higher geared up to navigate the complexities in their unbiased roles, fundamental to an extra harmonious integration of their expert and private lives, which ultimately interprets into sustained, satisfactory pleasant of professional output. This model further suggests that sustainable productiveness, through selling a feel of accomplishment and financial stability, can reciprocally help emotional nicely-being and because of this make contributions to a terrific greater strong artwork-existence balance (Proto, 2016). This dynamic interaction underscores the crucial function of emotional intelligence as a foundational functionality for gig employees looking for to thrive in the best labour panorama, emphasizing its capability to transform precarious work proper right into a source of private success and enduring expert fulfilment. This conceptual framework therefore offers a robust basis for empirical research into the unique mechanisms via which emotional intelligence affects the work-existence balance and productivity effects of gig employees. in addition, it highlights the potential for targeted interventions and training applications aimed toward improving emotional intelligence to seriously improve the overall nicely-being and economic stability of this burgeoning team of workers.

Methodology utilised

The gig economic gadget model changed into assessed for emotional intelligence, artwork-lifestyles balance, and productiveness. Gig humans' relationships and lifestyles will be surveyed quantitatively and qualitatively (Choudhary & Shireshi, 2022). Huge gig employee productivity, paintings-existence stability, and emotional intelligence might be tested psychometrically. A portion of survey respondents will attend semi-structured interviews to evaluate gig economy work-life balance and productivity (Hwang, 2024). Rich context and statistical generalizability characterize complex interactions. This convergent parallel mixed methods study will analyse quantitative and qualitative data to understand the issue.This method works well for studying the complicated relationship between emotional intelligence, work-life balance, and sustained productivity in the gig economy, where views vary. Quantitative cross-sectional research will examine gig workers' emotional intelligence, work-life balance, and productivity. The qualitative phase of interpretive phenomenology will reveal gig workers' work-life balance views and how emotional intelligence affects adaptation (Wong & Chan, 2021).In 2025, gig worker platforms and professional networks will distribute quantitative online surveys to expand and reflect the sample (Winkler-Titus et al., 2025). Population, emotional intelligence, work-life balance, and verified self-reported productivity are measured (Khan, 2022).Data validity increases with online anonymity as respondents are honest. To comprehend survey participants' qualitative perspectives, Li et al. (2023) will conduct semi-structured interviews. Interviews will examine gig workers' time, stress, and professional-personal boundaries (Mäntymäki et al., 2019). Opening-ended gig economy emotional labour interviews reveal surprising themes (Hoffmann, 2007).Qualitative samples will capture gig labour sector inequalities and demographic factors including gender, class, and caste, which greatly affect gig economy experiences (Gupta, 2020). This inclusive method is essential since gig workers' employment quality and well-being differ (Hsieh et al., 2023).As work-life balance and emotional labour are sensitive topics; data will examine participant well-being and researcher emotional effect. Lit may conceal relationships by accounting for gig job kind, gig economy length, and social support network access.500 quantitative survey responses plus 20-30 in-depth qualitative interviews with gig workers across platforms and sectors will provide statistical power and rich theme saturation (Brauchli et al., 2015). Gig worker forums, social media, and platform-specific marketing will post a survey link, followed by targeted qualitative interviewee contact based on survey findings and demographic diversity (Hwang, 2024). This complete collection will include trip-hailing, delivery, freelance creative labor, gig economy involvement, and experience (Radhakrishnan & Roy, 2023). Participants must work six months for useful work-life views. Traditional labour will be replaced by gig workers. Careful measure selection will ensure study reliability and validity. Time allocation, contentment, and perceived stress assess work-life balance, whereas the popular self-report exam measures emotional intelligence.Since gig worker productivity is subjective, task completion rates and output efficiency will be used.Open-ended qualitative interview questions can assist identify gig economy emotional regulation issues and enablers like platform algorithms and client interactions. Since emotional intelligence, work-life balance, and productivity are linked, this complete approach will help us comprehend the gig economy (Cram et al., 2022).

Data Analysis Techniques

Descriptive statistics will summarize demographics and key variables, followed by inferential statistical analyses, such as multiple regressions, to examine emotional intelligence, work-life balance, and productivity, controlling for relevant covariates. Hierarchical regression analysis will examine how emotional intelligence moderates the link between job demands and work-life balance and has a direct impact on productivity. To get a deep insight of gig workers' lives, thematic analysis will be used to find patterns, themes, and nuanced viewpoints in interview transcripts.By combining quantitative generalizability with qualitative depth, this mixed-methods technique will triangulate data and strengthen the study's conclusions. Integration will improve statistical correlation interpretation and reveal the processes and contextual elements affecting these linkages in the dynamic gig economy environment. With the aid of trying out complicated theoretical fashions with structural equation modelling, direct and oblique effects on latent dimensions like emotional intelligence and sustained productiveness may be examined (Nabila et al., 2019).

DISCUSSION

Greater emotionally smart gig workers have higher work-life stability, suggesting that they are better capable of deal with gig work's demands and versatility (Johnson, 2004). People with higher emotional control and empathy seem to better stability non-public and expert existence, improving nicely-being (Sari et al., 2022). Preliminary analyses display that gig people with high emotional competencies have better self-said performance and task of entirety fees, helping in advance research on emotional intelligence and task effects (Wong & regulation, 2017) (Silva & Coelho, 2018). This phase synthesizes quantitative statistics and interprets them considering emotional intelligence, gig paintings, and paintings-life integration studies. It will critically examine how emotional intelligence characteristics (self-awareness, self-regulation, social skills, empathy, and motivation) specifically affect this workforce's well-being and performance, acknowledging both verified and surprising discoveries. These results will also be used to gig platforms, politicians, and gig workers to promote a more emotionally aware and sustainable gig economy. The study's limitations will be acknowledged, and further research will be suggested to better understand emotional dynamics in contingent labor's changing landscape. Considering their varied effects on self-regulation and stress management in the flexible yet demanding gig environment, trait- and ability-based emotional intelligence models should be distinguished (Salovey & Mayer, 1990).The chapter will discuss how gig work's autonomy, precariousness, and emotional intelligence affect job satisfaction, burnout, and productivity (Montgomery & Baglioni, 2020) (Lee, 2017) (Chen et al., 2024). It will examine how gig workers' emotional experiences and management tactics are affected by gig economy ethics, notably worker status and perks (Tan et al., 2021) (Pande, 2024). Critically analyze how emotional intelligence might reduce the psychological stress gig workers face without traditional job benefits and social security (Rane, 2024).The increasing use of artificial intelligence in the workplace needs a study of how emotional intelligence improves employee well-being and mitigates risks, particularly in gig employment (Soulami et al., 2024). Understanding how generative AI tools affect work dynamics, job satisfaction, and mental health is crucial given their widespread application in professional fields, particularly the gig economy (Lozie et al., 2024).

Interpretation of Findings

The quantitative data on emotional intelligence and gig economy ideas will be examined to demonstrate their value for productivity and work-life balance. Examining gig workers' emotional regulation mechanisms to manage independent contracting constraints will reveal how adaptive emotional responses improve resilience and reduce burnout (Ashkanasy & Daus, 2002). The investigation will also explore how emotional intelligence regulates gig work's unpredictability and employment stability, impacting career continuity and engagement. Emotionally savvy behaviours reduce well-being risks and boost job satisfaction amid gig work's unpredictable scheduling and piecework pay (Stewart & Stanford, 2017). The study will evaluate how emotionally aware gig workers combine work and life despite schedule changes, enhancing life happiness and productivity. AI systems with emotional intelligence may alter gig workers' struggles and opportunities (Narimisaei et al., 2024).AI enhances workplaces, however psychological, social, and administrative difficulties may affect employee well-being, satisfaction, and performance (Kim et al., 2025). AI can improve productivity but potentially threaten workers' competence, autonomy, and relatedness, generating stress and employment instability (Hermann et al., 2025).The rising knowledge of AI in the workplace might contribute to emotional tiredness, notably via serial employment uncertainty and work interference with family, therefore businesses must address these issues (Zheng & Zhang, 2025). Gig workers' unstable working situations intensify AI integration's psychological consequences, requiring a greater look at how emotional intelligence might defend against these developing pressures (Jeong et al., 2024). Gig workers adapt to AI-driven task allocation and performance monitoring with emotional intelligence (Kim & Kim, 2024).

Emotional Intelligence and Work-Life Balance in Gig Workers

Emotional intelligence lets gig workers combine work and life, unlike typical jobs. Gig workers struggle to combine work and life, but emotional intelligence - self-awareness, self-regulation, empathy, and social skills - helps. Matching fluctuating professional responsibilities with wise emotional regulation limits spill over into personal time and protects mental health. Emotional intelligence helps gig workers establish limitations to better their personal life and professional performance. Understanding and controlling emotions helps gig workers avoid emotional weariness and maintain a healthy work rhythm (Salovey & Mayer, 1990). The gig economy requires proactive emotional management because there are no schedules or supervisors to minimize overwork and offer restorative pauses. Emotional intelligence and an internal locus of control allow gig workers to choose a work structure that matches their values and goals, providing them more freedom than in traditional jobs. People can prioritize life enjoyment above money since they can avoid commitments that impair their time or well-being (Koubova & Buchko, 2013). Emotionally savvy gig workers may also create strong social networks and seek aid, which enhances work-life integration and lowers independent contracting isolation (Aljarboa et al., 2022).

Work-Life Balance and Sustainable Productivity Outcomes

This part will study how work-life balance affects gig economy productivity. This entails studying how emotional intelligence-facilitated boundary control and time allocation improve interest, strain, and gig people' productivity and performance (Huang et al., 2020). Sustained productiveness increases task happiness and profession longevity, demonstrating the symbiotic hyperlink among private nicely-being and expert efficacy on this changing place of job. Very good paintings-existence stability reduces burnout, a not unusual hassle in excessive-autonomy, high-call for workplaces, assuring gig employees' lengthy-term fulfilment (Bello et al., 2024). This equilibrium between expert exertion and personal recuperation promotes innovation and creativity by permitting intellectual rejuvenation and the improvement of diverse views that can improve problem-fixing in specialised tasks (Petriglieri et al., 2018). To secure future engagements and be aggressive in a converting marketplace, gig employees should be capable of attain this balance and convey best quality offerings (Oman et al., 2025). Strategic work-existence stability also enables gig workers refresh their abilities and adapt to new era, improving their prolonged-time period employability and making the gig frame of workers extra flexible and adaptable. Supplying paintings-existence stability to gig employees facilitates corporations recruit and maintain pinnacle skills, developing a strong and proficient contractor pool (Bello et al., 2024). This underscores the strategic critical for systems to put into effect policies and assets that actively promote artwork-life integration for his or her independent contractors, going beyond transactional relationships to foster true well-being and sustained engagement (Bello et al., 2024) (Ferreira & Gomes, 2023). Each gig worker improves their pleasant of lifestyles, whilst systems growth carrier delivery and reduce turnover. Paintings-life stability impacts interest satisfaction, mental fitness, and first-rate of existence (Jalil et al., 2023). It includes allocating time, strength, and interest between professional and personal spheres such that neither negatively influences the other that is critical for happiness and decreased stress (Malik, 2023).

Theoretical Implications and limitations

Destiny investigations must consequently prioritize longitudinal research that track gig people' reviews over the years, contemplating an extra nuanced know-how of how work-existence balance evolves amidst fluctuating demand and private circumstances. This method should higher seize the dynamic interaction between outside monetary pressures and individual coping mechanisms. Similarly, research need to also discover the efficacy of platform-furnished interventions and assist mechanisms in improving emotional intelligence and fostering sustainable paintings-lifestyles stability among numerous gig employee populations, considering nearby and cultural variations (Doorn et al., 2022). Additionally, comparative research for the duration of extraordinary regulatory environments must dispose of darkness from excellent practices for integrating gig employees into broader social protection frameworks, making sure their well-being and productivity (Katiyatiya & Lubisi, 2024) (Rane, 2024). Moreover, interdisciplinary research combining insights from psychology, economics, and sociology should provide a holistic angle on the gig monetary gadget's effect on man or woman well-being and societal structures. Eventually, advanced statistical modelling, which encompass gadget studying techniques, can be employed to analyse massive datasets from gig systems, identifying predictive elements for burnout and maximum suitable artwork-life integration. This may allow the development of extra personalised interventions and coverage suggestions to precise gig artwork contexts and employee demographics. Such granular evaluation would possibly bypass beyond generalized assumptions to provide actionable insights for platforms, policymakers, and gig employees themselves, fostering an extra sustainable and equitable destiny for this evolving section of the exertions pressure. This deep dive into the nuanced dynamics of emotional intelligence and artwork-lifestyles stability within the gig economy well-known shows important pathways for fostering a resilient and green workforce.

Future Research Directions

For this reason, longitudinal studies of gig personnel' research are needed to higher understand how paintings-life balance adjustments with call for and personal circumstances. This approach might higher replicate the dynamic relationship amongst financial stresses and coping techniques. This research can also look at how platform-provided treatments and manual mechanisms beautify emotional intelligence and work-life stability amongst numerous gig people, considering nearby and cultural variations (Doorn et al., 2022). Comparisons of regulatory settings may display quality practises for integrating gig people into social safety frameworks to ensure their nicely-being and productivity (Katiyatiya & Lubisi, 2024) (Rane, 2024). Intellectual, economic, and sociological observe at the gig monetary system's consequences on people and society can also provide a greater entire image. Sooner or later, advanced statistical modelling, inclusive of system learning, might use gig platform datasets to uncover burnout predictors and ultimate paintings-lifestyles integration. Extra personalized interventions and policy proposals focused to gig work conditions and worker demographics would be feasible. Such complete studies would move past extensive assumptions to provide structures, politicians, and gig employees practical records, making this developing hard work force extra sustainable and equitable. This deep dive into gig financial system emotional intelligence and paintings-life balance offers key avenues for developing a resilient and effective team of workers.

CONCLUSION

Gig people' precise dreams require a multifaceted technique, in conjunction with strong help networks and personalised techniques to promote well-being and lengthy-time period commitment. In this moving tough work marketplace, systems, governments, and gig people should collaborate to cost emotional intelligence for character properly-being and productivity. The gig economic system has grown due to generation and hard work marketplace adjustments, thus its effects on employee properly-being and society should be understood (Palhad et al., 2023). Algorithmic control is green but opaque and can impede people' autonomy and mental safety (Félix et al., 2023). Moral platforms address trust, justice, equality, privacy, and transparency to lessen virtual exertions risks and enhance administrative centre fairness (Dedema & Rosenbaum, 2024). Digital value networks in the Global South exploit people with unpaid labour and social issues that demand robust regulatory frameworks (Nwachukwu et al., 2023). This ethical design tackles these issues. These frameworks must improve gig workers' rights; collectively negotiate to solve precarious working conditions and income inequality, and guarantee social security (Rane, 2024). Such policies must balance innovation and worker protection (Rane, 2024) (Graham et al., 2017).To guarantee technology benefits everyone, a global discourse on digital gig economy fair labour norms is essential (Heeks, 2017). Platform labour regulations should adhere to constitutional concepts such as human dignity and social justice to balance power imbalances and ensure technology benefits mankind (Ződi & Török, 2021).

Emotional intelligence modulates the relationship between gig work demands and work-life balance, supporting its role in lowering burnout and boosting job satisfaction. Self-awareness and self-regulation assist gig workers manage uncertainty and irregular work patterns, while empathy and social skills reduce conflict with clients and platforms (Cameron, 2024). Emotional competence helps gig workers cope with stress and boosts production (Joshi et al., 2024). The inconsistent income, lack of benefits, and social isolation of gig employment may aggravate stress and unhappiness if one lacks emotional intelligence (Fisher & Cassady, 2019). Europe and North America worry about job instability, whereas sub-Saharan Africa sees the gig economy as a source of money and opportunities (Cieslik et al., 2021).Policy should address gig economy regional issues and possibilities culturally (Heeks, 2017).Research should also research how culturally diverse emotional intelligence training programs might assist gig workers globally achieve work-life balance and productivity. The socio-economic factors that drive gig labour acceptance and the adaptive strategies people take to succeed are crucial. To predict burnout and enhance work-life integration, gig platform information might be analysed using machine learning and sophisticated data analytics. Individualized gig worker therapy and coaching would foster proactive well-being.

This part will teach gig workers and their employers how to improve emotional intelligence and work-life balance. Gig workers need self-awareness to detect emotional triggers and self-regulation abilities to manage stress and attention through shifting demands. Conversation and consumer empathy minimize war and enhance expert pride (Mamatha, 2024). Groups should invest in new emotional nicely-being structures and rules like sincere remarks and intellectual fitness services. To assist gig employees, control their schedules and decorate their careers, firms may also provide bendy running situations and talent improvement (Parigi & Ma, 2016). These thoughts emphasize a symbiotic dating among the gig economy's economic needs and its employees' properly-being, encouraging mutual information and proactive help to increase productivity and fine of existence. Gamifying structures can also increase engagement and praise task of entirety instantly, lowering alienation and motivating employees (Oprescu et al., 2014). In addition, superior AI and machine learning algorithms can predict employee weariness and provide timely and customized help (Gabriel & Aguinis, 2021). Predictive analytics with real-time performance assessments and self-reported well-being indicators might automate personalised break, skill-building, and mental health care suggestions (Jangid, 2024).

The gig economy must rethink employment paradigms to preserve worker well-being and provide fair opportunities for sustainable livelihoods (Choudhary & Shireshi, 2022).Since emotional skills are as vital as technical skills in contingent labour; this re-evaluation must prioritize emotional intelligence frameworks in platform design and worker support systems. An integrated strategy that balances economic efficiency and worker psychological and social well-being is stressed. To justify their widespread adoption, future research should quantify the gig economy's EI training programs' ROI.To determine how EI treatments effect worker retention, productivity, stress, and satisfaction, longitudinal research are needed (Bondanini et al., 2020) (Hwang, 2024).Emotional Intelligence and Artificial Intelligence may work together to improve gig workers' performance and well-being: EI is improved by AI-driven analytics (Dwivedi, 2025).Empathetic algorithms can evaluate worker emotions and provide personalised feedback to better emotional management and communication (Velagaleti, 2024). Innovative affective computing may evaluate micro emotional signs and offer proactive stress-reduction or resilience-boosting therapies in tough work settings (Mantello & Ho, 2023

REFERENCES

Abraham, R. (2000). The Role of Job Control as a Moderator of Emotional Dissonance and Emotional Intelligence–Outcome Relationships. *The Journal of Psychology*, *134*(2), 169–184. DOI: 10.1080/00223980009600860 PMID: 10766109

Abraham, R. (2004). Emotional Competence as Antecedent to Performance: A Contingency Framework. *Genetic, Social, and General Psychology Monographs*, *130*(2), 117–145. DOI: 10.3200/MONO.130.2.117-145 PMID: 15605972

Adams-Prassl, A., Freedman, J., & Adams-Prassl, J. (2018). Rethinking legal taxonomies for the gig economy. *Oxford Review of Economic Policy*, *34*(3), 475–494. DOI: 10.1093/oxrep/gry006

Aljarboa, B. E., An, E. P., Dator, W. L., Alshammari, S. A., Mostoles, R., Uy, M. M., Alrashidi, N., Alreshidi, M. S., Mina, E., & Gonzales, A. (2022). Resilience and Emotional Intelligence of Staff Nurses during the COVID-19 Pandemic. *Health Care*, *10*(11), 2120. DOI: 10.3390/healthcare10112120 PMID: 36360460

Asfahani, A. M., Alsobahi, G., & Dahlan, D. A. (2023). Navigating the Saudi Gig Economy: The Role of Human Resource Practices in Enhancing Job Satisfaction and Career Sustainability. *Sustainability (Basel)*, *15*(23), 16406. DOI: 10.3390/su152316406

Ashkanasy, N. M., & Daus, C. S. (2002). Emotion in the workplace: The new challenge for managers. *The Academy of Management Perspectives*, *16*(1), 76–86. DOI: 10.5465/ame.2002.6640191

Bello, B. G., Tula, S. T., Omotoye, G. B., Kess-Momoh, A. J., & Daraojimba, A. I.Binaebi Gloria BelloSunday Tubokirifuruar TulaGaniyu Bolawale OmotoyeAzeez Jason Kess-MomohAndrew Ifesinachi Daraojimba. (2024). Work-life balance and its impact in modern organizations: An HR review. *World Journal of Advanced Research and Reviews*, *21*(1), 1162–1173. DOI: 10.30574/wjarr.2024.21.1.0106

Bondanini, G., Giorgi, G., Ariza-Montes, A., Vega-Muñoz, A., & Andreucci-Annunziata, P. (2020). Technostress Dark Side of Technology in the Workplace: A Scientometric Analysis [Review of Technostress Dark Side of Technology in the Workplace: A Scientometric Analysis]. International Journal of Environmental Research and Public Health, 17(21), 8013. Multidisciplinary Digital Publishing Institute. DOI: 10.3390/ijerph17218013

Brauchli, R., Jenny, G. J., Füllemann, D., & Bauer, G. F. (2015). Towards a Job Demands-Resources Health Model: Empirical Testing with Generalizable Indicators of Job Demands, Job Resources, and Comprehensive Health Outcomes. *BioMed Research International*, *1*, 1–12. Advance online publication. DOI: 10.1155/2015/959621 PMID: 26557718

Briner, R. B. (2000). Relationships between Work Environments, Psychological Environments and Psychological Well-being [Review of Relationships between Work Environments, Psychological Environments and Psychological Well-being]. Occupational Medicine, 50(5), 299. Oxford University Press. DOI: 10.1093/occmed/50.5.299

Burton, S. L. (2012, April 2). How We Attain and Sustain Work-life Balance? All Days. DOI: 10.2118/152830-MS

Cameron, L. (2024). The Making of the "Good Bad" Job: How Algorithmic Management Manufactures Consent Through Constant and Confined Choices. *Administrative Science Quarterly*, *69*(2), 458–514. DOI: 10.1177/00018392241236163

Carminati, L. (2021). Emotions, Emotion Management and Emotional Intelligence in the Workplace: Healthcare Professionals' Experience in Emotionally-Charged Situations. *Frontiers in Sociology*, *6*, 640384. Advance online publication. DOI: 10.3389/fsoc.2021.640384 PMID: 33889607

Chavan, V., Cenaj, A., Shen, S., Bar, A., Binwani, S., Del Becaro, T., Funk, M., Greschner, L., Hung, R., Klein, S., Kleiner, R., Krause, S., Olbrych, S., Parmar, V., Sarafraz, J., Soroko, D., Don, D. W., Zhou, C., Vu, H. T. D., & Fresquet, X. (2025). Feeling Machines: Ethics, Culture, and the Rise of Emotional AI. DOI: 10.48550/ARXIV.2506.12437

Chen, Y., Huang, Z.-L., & Chu, H.-C. (2024). Relationships between emotional labor, job burnout, and emotional intelligence: an analysis combining meta-analysis and structural equation modeling [Review of Relationships between emotional labor, job burnout, and emotional intelligence: an analysis combining meta-analysis and structural equation modeling]. BMC Psychology, 12(1). BioMed Central. DOI: 10.1186/s40359-024-02167-w

Choudhary, V., & Shireshi, S. S. (2022). Analysing the Gig Economy in India and Exploring Various Effective Regulatory Methods to Improve the Plight of the Workers. *Journal of Asian and African Studies*, *57*(7), 1343–1356. DOI: 10.1177/00219096221082581

Cieslik, K., Banya, R., & Vira, B. (2021). Offline contexts of online jobs: Platform drivers, decent work, and informality in Lagos, Nigeria. *Development Policy Review, 40*(4), e12595. Advance online publication. DOI: 10.1111/dpr.12595

Cihan, M. Ö., & Dılekmen, M. (2024). Emotional intelligence training for pre-service primary school teachers: A mixed methods research. *Frontiers in Psychology, 15*, 1326082. Advance online publication. DOI: 10.3389/fpsyg.2024.1326082 PMID: 38979067

Coronado-Maldonado, I., & Benítez-Márquez, M. D. (2023). Emotional intelligence, leadership, and work teams: A hybrid literature review [Review of Emotional intelligence, leadership, and work teams: A hybrid literature review]. Heliyon, 9(10). Elsevier BV. DOI: 10.1016/j.heliyon.2023.e20356

Cram, W. A., Wiener, M., Tarafdar, M., & Benlian, A. (2022). Examining the Impact of Algorithmic Control on Uber Drivers' Technostress. *Journal of Management Information Systems, 39*(2), 426–453. DOI: 10.1080/07421222.2022.2063556

Dedema, M., & Rosenbaum, H. (2024). Socio-technical issues in the platform-mediated gig economy: A systematic literature review: An Annual Review of Information Science and Technology (ARIST) paper. *Journal of the Association for Information Science and Technology, 75*(3), 344–374. DOI: 10.1002/asi.24868

Dhiman, S. (2017). Emotional & Multiple Intelligences: 10 Different Ways of Being Smart. In Palgrave Macmillan US eBooks (p. 97). Palgrave Macmillan. DOI: 10.1057/978-1-137-55571-7_5

Dwivedi, D. (2025). Emotional Intelligence and Artificial Intelligence Integration Strategies for Leadership Excellence. *Advances in Research, 26*(1), 84–94. DOI: 10.9734/air/2025/v26i11235

Félix, B., Dourado, D., & Nossa, V. (2023). Algorithmic management, preferences for autonomy/security and gig-workers' wellbeing: A matter of fit? *Frontiers in Psychology, 14*, 1088183. Advance online publication. DOI: 10.3389/fpsyg.2023.1088183 PMID: 36910791

Fernandez, C. S. P. (2007). Emotional Intelligence in the Workplace. *Journal of Public Health Management and Practice, 13*(1), 80–82. DOI: 10.1097/00124784-200701000-00013 PMID: 17149104

Ferreira, P., & Gomes, S. (2023). Work–Life Balance and Work from Home Experience: Perceived Organizational Support and Resilience of European Workers during COVID-19. *Administrative Sciences, 13*(6), 153. DOI: 10.3390/admsci13060153

Fisher, S. L., & Cassady, E. A. (2019). Use of Relational eHRM Tools in Gig Worker Platforms. In *Advanced series in management* (p. 81). Emerald Publishing Limited. DOI: 10.1108/S1877-636120190000023007

Fragkaki, M., Kavga, A., Kelesi-Stavropoulou, M., & Fasoi, G. (2024). Emotional Intelligence of Primary Health Care Nurses: A Longitudinal Randomized Clinical Trial. *The Open Public Health Journal*, *17*(1), e18749445329730. Advance online publication. DOI: 10.2174/0118749445329730240729162817

Gabriel, K. P., & Aguinis, H. (2021). How to prevent and combat employee burnout and create healthier workplaces during crises and beyond. *Business Horizons*, *65*(2), 183–192. DOI: 10.1016/j.bushor.2021.02.037

Gómez, M. S., Sadovyy, M., & Bresó, E. (2021). Health-Care Professionals Amid the COVID-19 Pandemic: How Emotional Intelligence May Enhance Work Performance Traversing the Mediating Role of Work Engagement. *Journal of Clinical Medicine*, *10*(18), 4077. DOI: 10.3390/jcm10184077 PMID: 34575186

Graham, M., Hjorth, I., & Lehdonvirta, V. (2017). Digital labour and development: Impacts of global digital labour platforms and the gig economy on worker livelihoods. *Transfer: European Review of Labour and Research*, *23*(2), 135–162. DOI: 10.1177/1024258916687250 PMID: 28781494

Gupta, S. (2020).. . *Gendered Gigs.*, *1*, 1–10. Advance online publication. DOI: 10.1145/3392561.3394635

Heeks, R. (2017). Decent Work and the Digital Gig Economy: A Developing Country Perspective on Employment Impacts and Standards in Online Outsourcing, Crowdwork, Etc. SSRN Electronic Journal. https://doi.org/DOI: 10.2139/ssrn.3431033

Hermann, E., Puntoni, S., & Morewedge, C. K. (2025). GenAI and the psychology of work [Review of GenAI and the psychology of work]. Trends in Cognitive Sciences. Elsevier BV. DOI: 10.1016/j.tics.2025.04.009

Hersing, W. S. (2017). Managing cognitive bias in safety decision making: Application of emotional intelligence competencies. *The Journal of Space Safety Engineering*, *4*(3-4), 124–128. DOI: 10.1016/j.jsse.2017.10.001

Hoffmann, E. A. (2007). Open-Ended Interviews, Power, and Emotional Labor. *Journal of Contemporary Ethnography*, *36*(3), 318–346. DOI: 10.1177/0891241606293134

Hsieh, J., Adisa, O., Bafna, S., & Zhu, H. (2023). Designing Individualized Policy and Technology Interventions to Improve Gig Work Conditions. In *Proceedings of the 2nd Annual Meeting of the Symposium on Human-Computer Interaction for Work (CHIWORK '23). Association for Computing Machinery, New York, NY, USA*, Article 12, 1–9. Advance online publication. DOI: 10.1145/3596671.3598576

Hsieh, J., Karger, M., Zagal, L., & Zhu, H. (2023). Co-Designing Alternatives for the Future of Gig Worker Well-Being. In *Proceedings of the 2nd Annual Meeting of the Symposium on Human-Computer Interaction for Work (CHIWORK '23). Association for Computing Machinery, New York, NY, USA*, 664–687. Advance online publication. DOI: 10.1145/3563657.3595982

Huang, N., Burtch, G., Hong, Y., & Pavlou, P. A. (2020). Unemployment and Worker Participation in the Gig Economy: Evidence from an Online Labor Market. *Information Systems Research, 31*(2), 431–448. DOI: 10.1287/isre.2019.0896

Hwang, J. (2024a). The GIG economy and its effects on the labor market. *International Journal of Science and Research Archive, 13*(1), 3394–3404. DOI: 10.30574/ijsra.2024.13.1.1231

Hwang, J. (2024b). The GIG economy and its implications for labor laws and worker protections. *International Journal of Science and Research Archive, 13*(1), 3405–3416. DOI: 10.30574/ijsra.2024.13.1.1714

Iliceto, P., & Fino, E. (2017). The Italian version of the Wong-Law Emotional Intelligence Scale (WLEIS-I): A second-order factor analysis. *Personality and Individual Differences, 116*, 274–280. DOI: 10.1016/j.paid.2017.05.006

Imteyaz, K., Flores-Saviaga, C., & Savage, S. (2024). GigSense: An LLM-Infused Tool forWorkers' Collective Intelligence. arXiv (Cornell University). https://doi.org//arxiv.2405.02528DOI: 10.48550

Ishii, S., & Horikawa, E. (2019). The Emotional Intelligence of Japanese Mental Health Nurses. *Frontiers in Psychology, 10*, 2004. Advance online publication. DOI: 10.3389/fpsyg.2019.02004 PMID: 31543853

Merlin, J. I., & Soubramanian, P. (2024). From self-awareness to social savvy: how intrapersonal skills shape interpersonal competence in university students. *Frontiers in Psychology*, 15. DOI: 10.3389/fpsyg.2024.1469746

Jalil, N. I. A., Tan, S. A., Ibharim, N. S., Musa, A. Z., Ang, S. H., & Mangundjaya, W. L. (2023). The Relationship between Job Insecurity and Psychological Well-Being among Malaysian Precarious Workers: Work–Life Balance as a Mediator. *International Journal of Environmental Research and Public Health, 20*(3), 2758. DOI: 10.3390/ijerph20032758 PMID: 36768122

Jangid, A. (2024). AI and employee wellbeing: how artificial intelligence can monitor and improve mental health in the workplace. *International Journal of Advanced Research, 12*(10), 743–764. DOI: 10.21474/IJAR01/19693

Jeong, J., Kim, B., & Lee, J. (2024). Navigating AI transitions: How coaching leadership buffers against job stress and protects employee physical health. *Frontiers in Public Health, 12*, 1343932. Advance online publication. DOI: 10.3389/fpubh.2024.1343932 PMID: 38601504

Jibunoh, J., Ezichi, O., Okpanachi, V., Amaechi, C., Awosan, W., Tchoumo, P., & Sanusi, J. (2025). Impact of Remote Work Dynamics on Mental Health and Productivity. *Open Journal of Depression, 14*(1), 13–27. DOI: 10.4236/ojd.2025.141002

Johnson, H.-A. M. (2004). The Story Behind Service With A Smile: The Effects of Emotional Labor on Job Satisfaction, Emotional Exhaustion, and Affective Well-Being. http://usf.sobek.ufl.edu/content/SF/S0/02/49/82/00001/E14-SFE0000287.pdf

Joshi, A., Jain, S., & Gupta, P. K. (2024). Challenges and impact of the gig economy. *Deleted Journal, 2*(2), 96. DOI: 10.62617/se.v2i2.96

Katiyatiya, L. M., & Lubisi, N. (2024). The current social protection discourse, gig economy within the advent of COVID-19: Some emerging legal arguments. *Labor History, 1*. Advance online publication. DOI: 10.1080/0023656X.2024.2340610

Kattaa, M., & Byrne, M. (2018). Quality of work for Syrian refugees in Jordan. *Forced Migration Review, 58*, 45. https://doaj.org/article/602d90f04a9d4023852fa574b024522d

Khan, R. B. F. (2022). Mediation Role of Work Flexibility on the Linking of Work Family Conflict and Job Satisfaction. *Jurnal Bisnis Dan Manajemen, 9*(1), 87–93. DOI: 10.26905/jbm.v9i1.7627

Kim, B., & Kim, M. (2024). How artificial intelligence-induced job insecurity shapes knowledge dynamics: The mitigating role of artificial intelligence self-efficacy. *Journal of Innovation & Knowledge, 9*(4), 100590. DOI: 10.1016/j.jik.2024.100590

Kim, B., Kim, M.-J., & Lee, J. (2025). The dark side of artificial intelligence adoption: Linking artificial intelligence adoption to employee depression via psychological safety and ethical leadership. *Humanities & Social Sciences Communications*, *12*(1), 704. Advance online publication. DOI: 10.1057/s41599-025-05040-2

Koubova, V., & Buchko, A. A. (2013). Life-work balance. *Management Research Review*, *36*(7), 700–719. DOI: 10.1108/MRR-05-2012-0115

Koutsimpogiorgos, N., van Slageren, J., Herrmann, A., & Frenken, K. (2020). Conceptualizing the Gig Economy and Its Regulatory Problems. *Policy and Internet*, *12*(4), 525–545. DOI: 10.1002/poi3.237

Koutsioumpa, E. (2023). Contribution of Emotional Intelligence to Efficient Leadership. A Narrative Review [Review of Contribution of Emotional Intelligence to Efficient Leadership. A Narrative Review]. *Technium Social Sciences Journal*, *48*, 204–216. DOI: 10.47577/tssj.v48i1.9529

Kumar, D. (2024). The Impact of Remote Work on Employee Engagement and Productivity. *International Journal for Multidisciplinary Research*, *6*(6), 34103. Advance online publication. DOI: 10.36948/ijfmr.2024.v06i06.34103

Kuo, T.-S., Chu, L., Shih, C., Li, Y., & Kao, P.-L. (2025). Emotional labor, job satisfaction, and retention among home care workers in Taiwan: A comprehensive analysis. *Frontiers in Psychology*, *16*, 1545955. Advance online publication. DOI: 10.3389/fpsyg.2025.1545955 PMID: 40231001

Lee, H. J. (2017). How emotional intelligence relates to job satisfaction and burnout in public service jobs. *International Review of Administrative Sciences*, *84*(4), 729–745. DOI: 10.1177/0020852316670489

Lei, X., & Kaplan, S. A. (2023). The real-time and carry-over effects of injustice on performance and service quality in a ridesharing driver scenario. *Current Psychology (New Brunswick, N.J.)*, *42*(36), 32157–32178. DOI: 10.1007/s12144-022-04215-3 PMID: 36684460

Li, J., Cao, H., Lin, L., Hou, Y., Zhu, R., & Ali, A. E. (2023). User Experience Design Professionals' Perceptions of Generative Artificial Intelligence. arXiv (Cornell University). https://doi.org//arxiv.2309.15237DOI: 10.48550

Lozie, D. R., Omasa, R., Hesami, S., Zaman, S. M. H., Kajbaf, M., & Malik, A. (2024). Examining the impact of generative artificial intelligence on work dynamics. *Human Resources Management and Services*, *6*(2), 3420. DOI: 10.18282/hrms.v6i2.3420

Lubis, A. Y., Tjahjono, H. K., & Wahyuningsih, R. (2023). Literature review of the connection between emotional intelligence and employee performance in organizations. *Multidisciplinary Reviews*, *6*(4), 2023048. DOI: 10.31893/multirev.2023048

Malik, N. (2023). Organizations Should Maintain Employee's Work-Life Balance. *Journal of Economics Finance and Management Studies*, *6*(8). Advance online publication. DOI: 10.47191/jefms/v6-i8-29

Mamatha, C. N. (2024). A Study on Workplace Flexibility and Job Quality in the Gig Economy: Perspective from Workers and Employers. *International Journal of Research Publication and Reviews*, *5*(9), 3028–3038. DOI: 10.55248/gengpi.5.0924.2666

Mantello, P., & Ho, T. M. (2023). Emotional AI and the future of wellbeing in the post-pandemic workplace. *AI & Society*, *39*(4), 1883–1889. DOI: 10.1007/s00146-023-01639-8 PMID: 36776535

Mäntymäki, M., Baiyere, A., & Islam, A. K. M. N. (2019). Digital platforms and the changing nature of physical work: Insights from ride-hailing. *International Journal of Information Management*, *49*, 452–460. DOI: 10.1016/j.ijinfomgt.2019.08.007

Marecki, Ł. J. (2024). Impact of work-life balance on employee productivity and well-being. *Journal of Management and Financial Sciences*, *50*(50). Advance online publication. DOI: 10.33119/JMFS.2023.50.9

Mayer, J. D., Caruso, D. R., & Salovey, P. (2016). The Ability Model of Emotional Intelligence: Principles and Updates. *Emotion Review*, *8*(4), 290–300. DOI: 10.1177/1754073916639667

Midlage, L. (2025). Emotional Intelligence in the Workplace. *Enhancing Team Dynamics.*, *4*(1), 17–22. DOI: 10.59298/RIJCIAM/2025/411722

Montgomery, T., & Baglioni, S. (2020). Defining the gig economy: Platform capitalism and the reinvention of precarious work. *The International Journal of Sociology and Social Policy*, *41*(9/10), 1012–1025. DOI: 10.1108/IJSSP-08-2020-0400

Nabila, A., Pratiwi, R., & Usman, O. (2019). Effect of Work Experience, Age of Employee, Training, Emotional Intelligence, of Work Productivity. SSRN Electronic Journal. DOI: 10.2139/ssrn.3313230

Narimisaei, J., Naeim, M., Imannezhad, S., Samian, P., & Sobhani, M. (2024). Exploring emotional intelligence in artificial intelligence systems: a comprehensive analysis of emotion recognition and response mechanisms [Review of Exploring emotional intelligence in artificial intelligence systems: a comprehensive analysis of emotion recognition and response mechanisms]. Annals of Medicine and Surgery, 86(8), 4657. Wolters Kluwer. DOI: 10.1097/MS9.0000000000002315

Niere, M. I. E., Mecon, , Narsico, L. O., & Narsico, P. G. (2023). Workplace Stressors, Employee Welfare, and Productivity. *International Journal of Multidisciplinary Applied Business and Education Research*, *4*(12), 4379–4389. DOI: 10.11594/ijmaber.04.12.18

Nwachukwu, N. M., Roberts, J. S., & Montoya, L. N. (2023). The Glamorisation of Unpaid Labour: AI and its Influencers. arXiv (Cornell University). https://doi.org//arxiv.2308.02399DOI: 10.48550

Oman, Z. U., Bhati, K., & Ahmed, A. (2025). The rise of the gig economy in India: Market domination and the need to regulate the future of work. *World Journal of Advanced Research and Reviews*, *25*(3), 1790–1798. DOI: 10.30574/wjarr.2025.25.3.0935

Oprescu, F., Jones, C., & Katsikitis, M. (2014). I PLAY AT WORK—Ten principles for transforming work processes through gamification. *Frontiers in Psychology*, *5*. Advance online publication. DOI: 10.3389/fpsyg.2014.00014 PMID: 24523704

Pace, F., & Sciotto, G. (2021). Gender Differences in the Relationship between Work–Life Balance, Career Opportunities and General Health Perception. *Sustainability (Basel)*, *14*(1), 357. DOI: 10.3390/su14010357

Palhad, S., Onwubu, S. C., Singh, R. P., Thakur, R., Thakur, S., & Mkhize, G. (2023). The Benefits and Challenges of the Gig Economy: Perspective of Gig Workers and Small Medium and Micro Enterprises (SMMEs) in South Africa. *African Journal of Inter/Multidisciplinary Studies,* *5*(1), 1. DOI: 10.51415/ajims.v5i1.1051

Pande, N. (2024). What Are The Economic Implications Of The Rise Of The Gig Economy On Employment Stability And Benefits? *IOSR Journal of Business and Management*, *26*(10), 1. DOI: 10.9790/487X-2610070113

Parigi, P., & Ma, X. (2016). The gig economy. *XRDS Crossroads The ACM Magazine for Students*, *23*(2), 38–41. DOI: 10.1145/3013496

Petriglieri, G., Ashford, S. J., & Wrzesniewski, A. (2018). Agony and Ecstasy in the Gig Economy: Cultivating Holding Environments for Precarious and Personalized Work Identities. *Administrative Science Quarterly*, *64*(1), 124–170. DOI: 10.1177/0001839218759646

Prado, J. C. A., & Torres, R. A. Z. (2019). Validation of the Wong and Law Emotional Intelligence Scale for Chilean managers. *Suma Psicologica*, *26*(2), 110–118. Advance online publication. DOI: 10.14349/sumapsi.2019.v26.n2.7

Prokhorova, M. P., Лебедева, T. E., Shkunova, A. A., Sineva, N. L., & Казначеева, C. H. (2020). Emotional Intelligence as a Factor of Corporate Culture. DOI: 10.2991/assehr.k.200723.058

Proto, E. (2016). Are happy workers more productive? *IZA World of Labor: Evidence-Based Policy Making*. Advance online publication. DOI: 10.15185/izawol.315

Radhakrishnan, A., & Roy, N. S. (2023). Gig Economy Workers' Livelihood: A Qualitative Study of Ride-Hailing Platforms in Bangalore City, India. *Artha Vijnana*. Advance online publication. DOI: 10.21648/OPST6018

Ramachandran, M., & Kulandai, A. (2024). Gig Workers: A Paradigm Shift in the Indian Workforce—A Bibliometric Analysis and Future Directions. *Metamorphosis*. Advance online publication. DOI: 10.1177/09726225241257731

Ran, X., & Zhao, Y. (2023). Behind the flexibility: Insufficient occupational injury protection of gig workers in China. *Frontiers in Public Health*, *11*, 1117180. Advance online publication. DOI: 10.3389/fpubh.2023.1117180 PMID: 37139392

Rane, V. (2024). Platform-based Gig Workers: a Blind Spot in the Indian Labour Laws. SSRN Electronic Journal.DOI: 10.2139/ssrn.4821229

Rodrigues, R., Teixeira, N., & Costa, B. V. (2024). The Impact of Perceived Leadership Effectiveness and Emotional Intelligence on Employee Satisfaction in the Workplace. *Merits*, *4*(4), 490–501. DOI: 10.3390/merits4040035

Sachdeva, T. (2024). The Gig Economy in India: Unpacking the Economic and Social Implications. *International Journal for Research Publication and Seminars*, *15*(3), 166–176. DOI: 10.36676/jrps.v15.i3.1465

Salovey, P., & Mayer, J. D. (1990). Emotional Intelligence. *Imagination, Cognition and Personality*, *9*(3), 185–211. DOI: 10.2190/DUGG-P24E-52WK-6CDG

Sari, Y. N., Amin, S., & Kurniawan, D. (2022). Mediating effect of positive emotions on work-life balance and employee performance. *BISMA Jurnal Bisnis Dan Manajemen*, *16*(1), 20. DOI: 10.19184/bisma.v16i1.28234

Silva, D., & Coelho, A. (2018). The impact of emotional intelligence on creativity, the mediating role of worker attitudes and the moderating effects of individual success. *Journal of Management & Organization*, *25*(2), 284–302. DOI: 10.1017/jmo.2018.60

Skrzypczyńska, K. (2020). Significance of emotional intelligence in leadership. *Journal of Positive Management*, *9*(4), 66. DOI: 10.12775/JPM.2018.155

Smedley, D., & Rayment, A. (2019). Changes in employment law: Mitigating the gig economy. *Nursing and Residential Care*, *21*(6), 345–348. DOI: 10.12968/nrec.2019.21.6.345

Song, Y. (2024). Impact of Technological Advancements on Work and Employment Patterns. *Journal of Advanced Sociology*, *5*(1), 63–76. DOI: 10.47941/jas.1856

Soulami, M., Benchekroun, S., & Galiulina, A. (2024). Exploring how AI adoption in the workplace affects employees: a bibliometric and systematic review [Review of Exploring how AI adoption in the workplace affects employees: a bibliometric and systematic review]. Frontiers in Artificial Intelligence, 7. Frontiers Media. DOI: 10.3389/frai.2024.1473872

Stewart, A., & Stanford, J. (2017). Regulating work in the gig economy: What are the options? *Economic and Labour Relations Review*, *28*(3), 420–437. DOI: 10.1177/1035304617722461

Suleman, Q., Hussain, I., Syed, M. A., Parveen, R., Lodhi, I. S., & Mahmood, Z. (2019). Association between emotional intelligence and academic success among undergraduates: A cross-sectional study in KUST, Pakistan. *PLoS One*, *14*(7), e0219468. Advance online publication. DOI: 10.1371/journal.pone.0219468 PMID: 31291333

Tan, Z. M., Aggarwal, N., Cowls, J., Morley, J., Taddeo, M., & Floridi, L. (2021). The ethical debate about the gig economy: A review and critical analysis [Review of The ethical debate about the gig economy: A review and critical analysis]. Technology in Society, 65, 101594. Elsevier BV. DOI: 10.1016/j.techsoc.2021.101594

Tursunbayeva, A., Pagliari, C., Lauro, S. D., & Antonelli, G. (2021). The ethics of people analytics: Risks, opportunities and recommendations. *Personnel Review*, *51*(3), 900–921. DOI: 10.1108/PR-12-2019-0680

Ugoani, J. (2021). Emotional Intelligence and its Impact on Effective Human Resource Management. *International Journal of Economics and Financial Research*, *71*(71), 5–13. DOI: 10.32861/ijefr.71.5.13

van Doorn, N., Ferrari, F., & Graham, M. (2022). Migration and Migrant Labour in the Gig Economy: An Intervention. *Work, Employment and Society, 37*(4), 1099–1111. DOI: 10.1177/09500170221096581 PMID: 37588943

Velagaleti, S. B. (2024). Empathetic Algorithms: The Role of AI in Understanding and Enhancing Human Emotional Intelligence. *Deleted Journal, 20*(3s), 2051–2060. DOI: 10.52783/jes.1806

Wiener, M., Cram, W. A., & Benlian, A. (2021). Algorithmic control and gig workers: A legitimacy perspective of Uber drivers. *European Journal of Information Systems, 32*(3), 485–507. DOI: 10.1080/0960085X.2021.1977729

Winkler-Titus, N., Gerber, C., & Ngalo, V. (2025). Well-being of remote workers: Work characteristics and challenges. *SA Journal of Human Resource Management, 23*. Advance online publication. DOI: 10.4102/sajhrm.v23i0.2876

Wong, C., & Law, K. S. (2017). The effects of leader and follower emotional intelligence on performance and attitude: An exploratory study. In *Routledge eBooks* (p. 97). Informa. DOI: 10.4324/9781315250601-10

Wong, K. P., & Chan, A. H. S. (2021). Exploration of the Socioecological Determinants of Hong Kong Workers' Work-Life Balance: A Grounded Theory Model. *International Journal of Environmental Research and Public Health, 18*(20), 10732. DOI: 10.3390/ijerph182010732 PMID: 34682475

Wood, A. J., Graham, M., Lehdonvirta, V., & Hjorth, I. (2018). Good Gig, Bad Gig: Autonomy and Algorithmic Control in the Global Gig Economy. *Work, Employment and Society, 33*(1), 56–75. DOI: 10.1177/0950017018785616 PMID: 30886460

Wu, J. (2024). Social and ethical impact of emotional AI advancement: The rise of pseudo-intimacy relationships and challenges in human interactions. *Frontiers in Psychology, 15*, 1410462. Advance online publication. DOI: 10.3389/fpsyg.2024.1410462 PMID: 39564589

Zheng, J., & Zhang, T. (2025). Association Between AI Awareness and Emotional Exhaustion: The Serial Mediation of Job Insecurity and Work Interference with Family. *Behavioral Sciences (Basel, Switzerland), 15*(4), 401. DOI: 10.3390/bs15040401 PMID: 40282023

Zietlow, R. E. (2020). The New Peonage: Liberty and Precarity for Workers in the Gig Economy. SSRN Electronic Journal. DOI: 10.2139/ssrn.3641677

Ződi, Z., & Török, B. (2021). Constitutional Values in the Gig-Economy? Why Labor Law Fails at Platform Work, and What Can We Do about It? *Societies (Basel, Switzerland), 11*(3), 86. DOI: 10.3390/soc11030086

Chapter 9

Employee Engagement, Emotional Intelligence, and Well-Being as Strategic Drivers in the Modern Service Economy

Jamal Dadios Magantor
http://orcid.org/0009-0003-3575-5147
Bath Spa University Academic Centre, UAE

Varinder Singh Rana
http://orcid.org/0009-0008-8562-8265
College of Business, City University, Ajman, UAE

Aisha Khan
http://orcid.org/0009-0009-7679-3661
International American University, RAK, UAE

ABSTRACT

Today's service economy is founded upon innovation, adaptability, and human interaction. However, workers within the service sector suffer from hybrid work stress, burnout, and high employee turnover. It is argued in this chapter that employee engagement, emotional intelligence (EI), and wellness represent competence needs for organizations to thrive. Organizational psychology concepts, HR strategy concepts, and concepts from positive psychology are discussed to highlight how leaders with knowledge of EI can construct resilience and exemplary service. Also outlined is how HR can integrate these concepts into talent management and planning in var-

DOI: 10.4018/979-8-3373-6395-0.ch009

ious sectors such as teaching, healthcare, hospitality, and financial sectors. Using theory, application, and research, the chapter provides HR practitioners practical tools. The message is simple: investment in employee engagement and wellness not only creates happier employees, it creates competitive strength that translates to loyal customers and profitable return.

THE HUMAN IMPERATIVE IN A STRAINED SERVICE ECONOMY

For a long time, we've measured the success of the service economy with spreadsheets and charts—tracking productivity, efficiency, and growth. But this focus on numbers misses the human story unfolding just beneath the surface. A serious human capital crisis is brewing. The very people who make this economy work, from the nurse at the bedside to the financial advisor building trust, are stretched to their breaking point. This isn't something we can ignore. It's a signal that we need a major strategic shift, moving away from a narrow obsession with productivity toward a more holistic focus on human sustainability.

A serious human capital crisis is unfolding in the service economy, requiring organizations to shift from a narrow focus on productivity toward a broader commitment to human sustainability. A recent report revealed that 82% of the global workforce feels at risk of burnout, a condition associated with emotional exhaustion, cynicism, and reduced professional efficacy (Forbes, 2025). Burnout is also contributing to disengagement. Gallup reported that U.S. employee engagement fell to a 10-year low, with only 31% of employees engaged and 17% actively disengaged (Gallup, 2025). This translates to approximately 8 million fewer engaged workers in the United States compared to the 2020 peak (Gallup, 2025). Disengagement also carries significant organizational costs. Mercer reported an average voluntary turnover rate of 13.0% in the U.S. workforce (Mercer, 2025), while replacing an employee may cost organizations up to $15,000 in recruitment, training, and lost productivity (Forbes, 2025).

So, this brings us to the core argument of this chapter: Employee Engagement, Emotional Intelligence (EI), and Well-being aren't just nice-to-have HR programs. They are fundamental strategic assets that are crucial for managing risk, building resilience, and driving performance that lasts. Simply put, ignoring the human element is a recipe for decline. In the pages that follow, we'll break down these ideas, give them a solid theoretical footing, and then explore how they work in the real world across different service industries. We'll look at how HR can shift from just putting out fires to proactively building a culture where people can thrive. And finally, we'll introduce an integrated model—the Engaged-Intelligent-Well (EIW) framework—to help leaders build organizations that are not just productive, but are truly great places to work. Organizations are actively exploring evidence-based strategies to mitigate employee burnout and improve mental health outcomes (Spring Health, 2025).

CONCEPTUAL FOUNDATIONS: THE PILLARS OF A THRIVING WORKFORCE

So, how do we build a workplace where people actually want to be, a place that's both resilient and high-performing? It all starts with understanding a few big ideas about what makes people tick at work. Three concepts are the real cornerstones: Employee Engagement, Emotional Intelligence, and Well-being. People often talk about them separately, but their real magic happens when they work together. This section will give a quick rundown of each one, setting the stage for how we can strategically combine them.

Employee Engagement: From Personal Investment to Organizational Reciprocity

The concept of employee engagement was first introduced by William Kahn (1990), who defined personal engagement as the harnessing of organizational members' selves to their work roles, allowing individuals to express themselves physically, cognitively, and emotionally during role performance (Kahn, 1990). Kahn identified three psychological conditions necessary for engagement: meaningfulness, safety, and availability. These conditions determine whether individuals are willing and able to fully invest themselves in their work.

Kahn pinpointed three psychological conditions that make it possible for us to fully invest ourselves. Think of it like a three-legged stool:

- **Meaningfulness:** Do I feel like my work is worth it? Does it matter? This is the "why" that makes the effort feel like a good investment.
- **Safety:** Can I be my real self here without worrying about negative fallout? This is about feeling that the environment is supportive and that I can trust my colleagues and leaders.
- **Availability:** Do I actually have the resources—physical, emotional, and mental—to engage? This acknowledges that even in the best job, if you're drained by other things, you just can't show up 100%.

Building on this foundation, Alan Saks (2006) applied Social Exchange Theory to explain employee engagement, suggesting that employees reciprocate organizational support through increased engagement (Saks, 2006). Saks further distinguished between job engagement, which relates to one's specific tasks, and organizational engagement, which reflects an employee's connection to the organization as a whole.

Emotional Intelligence: The Competency That Defines Modern Leadership

Emotional intelligence (EI) was first conceptualized by Peter Salovey and John D. Mayer (1990) as the ability to perceive, understand, and regulate emotions in oneself and others (Salovey & Mayer, 1990). Later, Daniel Goleman (1995) popularized the concept, arguing that emotional intelligence is a stronger predictor of workplace success than traditional cognitive intelligence (Goleman, 1995).

Goleman (1995) further identified four key domains of emotional intelligence: self-awareness, self-management, social awareness, and relationship management, which collectively contribute to effective leadership and interpersonal functioning **(Goleman, 1995)**.

Daniel Goleman made the idea famous, arguing that at work, EI is a much better predictor of who will succeed than traditional smarts like IQ. In fact, his research suggested that for jobs at every level, EI is twice as important as IQ (Goleman, 1995) . His popular framework breaks EI down into four main areas:

- **Self-Awareness:** Knowing your own emotions, strengths, and weaknesses, and how they affect other people.
- **Self-Management:** Being able to control your impulses, manage your moods, and think before you act.
- **Social Awareness:** This includes empathy—the ability to understand where other people are coming from emotionally and treat them accordingly.
- **Relationship Management:** Being good at building relationships, creating networks, and finding common ground with others.

In the service world, EI isn't a nice-to-have; it's the basic operating system for good leadership and customer service. A leader with high EI is much better at creating that psychological safety that Kahn talked about. They can sense the mood of their team, offer support when it's needed, and handle conflicts in a way that builds trust, creating an environment where people feel safe and valued.

Well-being at Work: The Science of Flourishing

The concept of well-being is grounded in positive psychology, particularly the work of Martin Seligman (2011), who introduced the PERMA model of flourishing (Seligman, 2011). The model consists of five elements: Positive Emotion, Engagement, Relationships, Meaning, and Accomplishment, which together define a holistic framework for human well-being.

PERMA stands for five core elements of a fulfilling life:

- **P - Positive Emotion:** Feeling good things like joy, hope, and gratitude. It's about fostering an optimistic mindset.
- **E - Engagement:** Getting so absorbed in what you're doing that you lose track of time—that "flow" state. This connects right back to Kahn's idea of engagement.
- **R - Relationships:** Having real, positive connections with other people. We're social creatures, and this is fundamental to us.
- **M - Meaning:** Feeling like you're part of something bigger than yourself. This gives us a sense of purpose.
- **A - Accomplishment:** The drive to achieve things, master skills, and feel competent.

For a company, the PERMA model is an incredibly practical tool. It's a blueprint for creating a workplace where people can genuinely flourish. Instead of just trying to reduce stress, a PERMA-based strategy asks better questions: How can we make jobs more engaging? How can we help people build stronger relationships at work? How do we connect the daily grind to a bigger mission? When companies start doing this, they move beyond just preventing burnout and start building the psychological strength that fuels creativity, resilience, and great performance over the long haul.

The PERMA framework provides organizations with a practical model for fostering not only employee satisfaction but also long-term psychological flourishing (Seligman, 2011).

The Strategic HR Mandate: From Theory to Institutional Practice

Okay, so we have the theories. We understand the importance of engagement, emotional intelligence, and well-being. Now what? Ideas are great, but they're pretty useless until they're woven into the fabric of an organization. This is where the modern Human Resources function has to step up. HR needs to be more than just an administrative or compliance department; it needs to become the architect of a human-centric culture, systematically embedding these principles into how the company actually operates.

HR as the Architect of a Human-Centric Culture

The biggest change needed is a shift in mindset. A big one. HR leaders have to champion the idea that investing in people isn't just a cost—it's the single most important driver of long-term success. This means walking into the C-suite with data that connects people-focused metrics to the bottom line.

Research has consistently demonstrated that highly engaged employees contribute to improved organizational performance. Business units with higher levels of employee engagement show greater profitability, productivity, and customer satisfaction, alongside lower turnover and absenteeism (Gallup, n.d.).

Figure 1. Strategic HR leaders use data to connect employee well-being initiatives to key business performance indicators

Institutionalizing EI and Engagement Across the Talent Lifecycle

A great culture isn't built with posters on the wall. It's built through the day-to-day processes and systems that people experience. HR's job is to weave the threads of EI and engagement into every single stage of an employee's journey with the company.

- **Talent Acquisition:** It starts before day one. Job descriptions shouldn't just be a list of technical skills; they should shout about the company's commitment to a supportive culture. Interviews, especially for leaders, can be designed to look for emotional intelligence, ensuring new hires will add to the culture, not detract from it.
- **Onboarding:** The first 90 days are everything. Onboarding has to be more than just paperwork and an IT password. It's the prime opportunity to immerse new hires in a culture of psychological safety and respect, which is a direct precursor to engagement (Kahn, 1990).
- **Leadership Development:** This is probably the most important lever HR can pull. Managers account for approximately 70% of the variance in employee engagement, highlighting the critical role of leadership in shaping workplace experiences (Gallup, n.d.)HR can build leadership programs that are all about developing emotional intelligence. This means training on how to listen, give good feedback, handle conflict, and build psychological safety. Tools such as the Bar-On Emotional Quotient Inventory (EQ-i) provide structured assessments to support leadership development in emotional intelligence (Bar-On, 1997).
- **Performance Management:** Let's be honest, the old-school annual review often creates more anxiety than anything else. A modern approach turns performance management into an ongoing conversation about growth, strengths, and goals. It becomes a tool to help people get better, not just a judgment.
- **Succession Planning:** By finding and nurturing future leaders who are strong in emotional intelligence, HR makes sure that the positive culture will outlast the current leadership team.

Connecting Human Capital to Business Outcomes with Data

To keep its seat at the strategic table, HR has to show that its work is making a tangible difference. This means getting smart with analytics, moving beyond just tracking activities (like how many people attended a training) to tracking outcomes (like whether turnover went down in teams with EI-trained managers).

A continuous listening strategy, using things like quick pulse surveys, is key to getting a real-time read on the employee experience. But collecting the data is only the first step. The most important part is closing the loop. Research indicates that organizations that actively share employee feedback and involve staff in action planning demonstrate significantly higher engagement levels, with increases of up to 23% compared to organizations that fail to close the feedback loop (Press Ganey, 2024). This creates a powerful cycle: people feel heard, they see real change, and they become more engaged, which leads to better business results. The data is clear: as engagement drops, turnover skyrockets, which is a direct hit to the bottom line.

By mastering this cycle of listening, analyzing, acting, and measuring, HR proves its value as a strategic partner. It takes the big ideas of engagement, EI, and well-being and turns them into something that is measurable, manageable, and absolutely essential to the company's success.

Sector-Specific Deep Dive: Engagement, EI, and Well-being in Action

The big ideas of engagement, emotional intelligence, and well-being are universal, sure. But they aren't one-size-fits-all. How you apply them has to be tailored to the specific pressures and realities of each industry. So, let's get real and take a closer look at four major service sectors—hospitality, healthcare, education, and finance—to see what challenges they're facing and how a focus on people can make a real difference.

HOSPITALITY & TOURISM: MANAGING EMOTIONAL LABOR AND THE GUEST EXPERIENCE

Challenges

Hospitality is, at its heart, a people business. The quality of a guest's experience depends almost completely on the quality of the human interactions they have. But this industry is under a ton of pressure. It's famous for its incredibly high turnover rates; the U.S. Retail and Wholesale industry, which is a decent comparison, has the highest turnover of any sector at a jaw-dropping 26.7% (Mercer, 2025) . Frontline workers have to perform a huge amount of "emotional labor"—constantly managing their own feelings to seem positive and welcoming, no matter how a guest is behaving. Add in long hours and often low pay, and you've got a perfect recipe for burnout and disengagement (Hospitality Insights by EHL, 2024).

Analysis & Strategic Application

In the world of hospitality, the line connecting employee happiness to business success is incredibly short and direct. It's simple: a miserable, checked-out employee can't create a genuinely wonderful guest experience . So, investing in your people is a direct investment in your brand. Here, Emotional Intelligence isn't a soft skill; it's a survival skill. Staff who are trained in EI are better at handling the stress of emotional labor (self-regulation), figuring out what guests need before they even ask (empathy), and calming down tough situations (relationship management). And using Seligman's PERMA model can be a powerful antidote to the industry's grind. Building positive peer **Relationships** can create a buffer against stress, while connecting daily chores to the **Meaning** of creating amazing experiences can turn a job into a craft.

Figure 2. A highly engaged and diverse hospitality team is the foundation of superior guest experiences

Case Vignette: The Engaged Hotelier

Consider the story of a boutique hotel chain that was struggling with high turnover and so-so service scores. They decided to tackle the problem head-on with an engagement strategy based on the idea of reciprocity: if we treat our people well, they'll treat our guests well. First, they ditched the old "employee of the month" plaque and launched a digital platform where anyone—peers or managers—could give points and badges for specific actions that lived up to the company's values, like "Problem Solver" or "Guest Hero." This gave people immediate, meaningful praise . At the same time, they trained their managers to build high-quality, trust-based relationships with every single person on their team, instead of treating them like interchangeable parts. The result? Within 18 months, staff turnover dropped by 30%, and their guest satisfaction scores jumped 15 points. It was a clear return on their investment in people (HubEngage, n.d.).

HEALTHCARE: COMBATING BURNOUT AND FOSTERING PATIENT-CENTERED CARE

Challenges

The healthcare industry is in a full-blown crisis. After years of systemic pressure, made so much worse by the pandemic, the sector is drowning in burnout, compassion fatigue, and a massive retention problem. In 2023, an incredible one out of every five healthcare workers quit their job, and that number was even higher—one in four—for those with less than two years on the job . Nurses, who are the absolute backbone of the system, are still the least engaged group. And what's really scary is that engagement among leaders has also been falling for three years, which means the very people who are supposed to fix the problem are also burning out. In healthcare, disengagement isn't just a business problem—it's a threat to public health (Vantage Circle, 2025).

Analysis & Strategic Application

The link between a healthcare worker's engagement and a patient's outcome is powerful and, frankly, a little terrifying. A major study by the UK's National Health Service found a direct correlation: higher staff engagement was linked to lower patient mortality rates (Press Ganey, 2024). Healthcare pros with high emotional intelligence are simply better at delivering true patient-centered care. They have the empathy and communication skills to build trust, which can improve how well patients stick to their treatments. Studies have confirmed that higher EI in clinicians is tied to better doctor-patient relationships and lower rates of burnout (Fletcher et al., 2007). Using the PERMA model here can be a lifesaver. Helping people find **Meaning** in their work, building supportive peer **Relationships** to fight isolation, and creating chances for professional **Accomplishment** can all help build a psychological shield against the incredible demands of the job (Press Ganey, 2024).

Figure 3. The immense physical and emotional toll on healthcare workers underscores the urgent need for well-being and engagement strategies

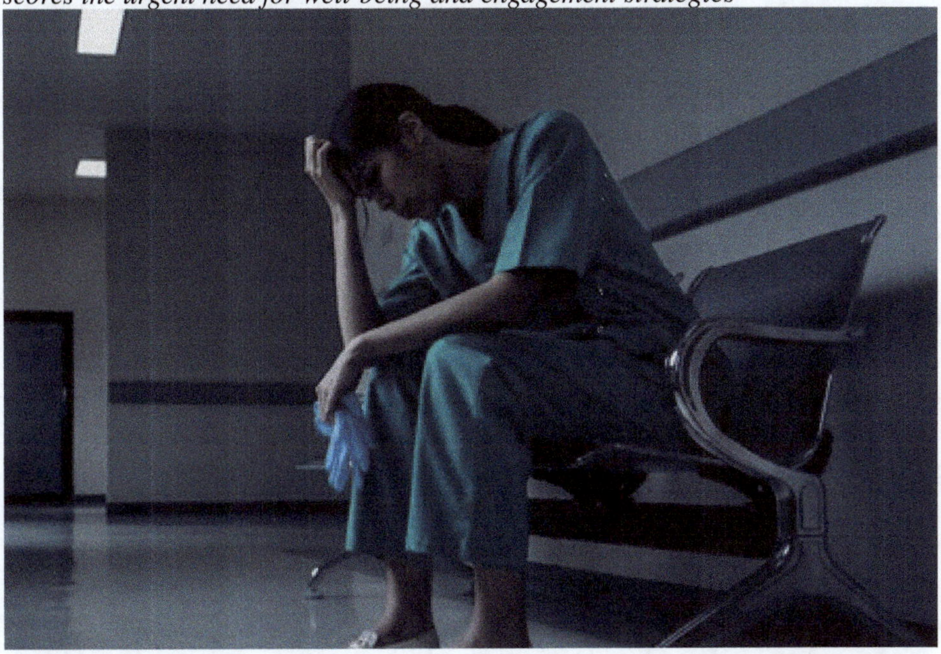

Case Vignette: The Resilient Hospital System

Picture a large hospital system that saw a tiny, fragile uptick in employee engagement after the pandemic (from a 4.02 to a 4.04 out of 5). They wanted to build on that flicker of hope. They realized that a huge source of stress was that people were afraid to speak up, so they launched a big initiative focused on psychological safety and leader support. Instead of just issuing orders from the top, they empowered frontline teams to identify their own problems and work through them in structured, facilitated sessions . This gave people a voice and a sense of control. The hospital also invested a lot in training managers to be more supportive and to create a sense of belonging on their teams. A year later, the units that had been part of these initiatives reported much lower burnout rates and a 15% drop in the number of employees who said they were planning to leave. It was proof that empowering people is a powerful way to improve both retention and well-being (Fletcher et al., 2007).

EDUCATION: ADDRESSING FACULTY WELL-BEING TO ENHANCE STUDENT SUCCESS

Challenges

The education world, from elementary schools to universities, is dealing with a massive well-being problem. A 2024 report actually ranked education dead last among all industries for employee well-being, with especially bad scores for work-life balance and psychological safety (The Educator, 2024). In higher ed, voluntary turnover for staff hit a record high of 14.3% in the 2022-23 school year. And a full third of all higher ed employees say they're likely to start looking for a new job (The Educator, 2024). This isn't just an HR problem. When faculty and staff are burnt out, it directly impacts the quality of the learning environment, which in turn affects student engagement and success. The education sector has been identified as having the lowest employee well-being across industries . Institutional efforts to promote wellness cultures in higher education have been increasingly emphasized in recent literature (Higher Ed Today, 2024).

Analysis & Strategic Application

The well-being of an educator is directly tied to the well-being of their students. It's a simple truth. A stressed-out, disengaged professor can't create the kind of supportive, inspiring classroom that students need to do their best work. This makes emotional intelligence in academic leaders incredibly important for creating departmental cultures that are collaborative and supportive, not toxic and cutthroat. The CUPA-HR survey gives us a clear path forward: the top reasons people are leaving are pay, a desire for remote work, and a need for more flexibility. Universities need to wake up and realize that a rigid, one-size-fits-all approach to work isn't working. The data even shows that women and employees of color are much more likely to prefer hybrid or remote work. So, addressing these needs isn't just about retaining talent; it's also an issue of equity.

A significant gap exists between the work arrangements higher education employees prefer and their current reality. Data source: CUPA-HR.

Case Vignette: The University of Well-being

A mid-sized university, seeing its turnover rates climb and its climate survey results tank, decided to do something about it. They launched a big "Wellness Culture" initiative. They started from the premise that faculty and staff are the first line of support for students, so they offered Mental Health First Aid training to everyone to help them spot and respond to signs of distress in both students and colleagues . The university's teaching center even created a toolkit for professors to weave short, simple wellness practices like mindfulness into their classes. But the most critical change was that the administration finally rethought its rigid on-site work policy and allowed departments to create more flexible, hybrid schedules. A year later, a follow-up survey showed a 10% jump in job satisfaction, a drop in turnover, and students were even saying that their classes felt more supportive and less stressful.

FINANCIAL SERVICES: NAVIGATING STRESS, DIGITALIZATION, AND PSYCHOLOGICAL SAFETY

Challenges

The financial services industry is a pressure cooker. You've got the stress of market swings, intense competition, and constant regulatory oversight. On top of all that, you have the disruption of digitalization and a huge fight over return-to-office mandates. A 2023 Deloitte survey found a major disconnect: while a lot of firms are demanding people be in the office three or four days a week, only 18% of employees actually want that. The risk of people leaving is real—66% of hybrid workers said they'd probably quit if they were forced back to the office full-time (Deloitte, 2023). And there's another hidden stressor: personal financial anxiety. A 2024 study found that almost half of all American workers, even those in high-paying jobs, are regularly running out of money before their next pay check arrives (Instant, 2024). A mismatch exists between employer expectations and employee preferences, with many organizations requiring office attendance despite employee resistance.

Figure 4. The high-pressure environment of financial services makes stress management and psychological safety critical for employee well-being

Analysis & Strategic Application

In an industry like finance, psychological safety—that feeling that you can speak up without being punished—isn't just a "nice-to-have." It's a business necessity. When risk management and ethical behavior are everything, you absolutely need employees to feel safe enough to voice concerns, question bad ideas, and admit mistakes. Emotionally intelligent leadership is the only way to create this kind of safety. Leaders who can practice empathy and manage their own reactions are less likely to shoot the messenger and more likely to foster open dialogue. On top of that, firms are starting to realize that their employees' own financial well-being is a huge, and often ignored, part of their overall well-being. Being stressed about money is a major distraction that hurts focus and productivity. So, offering proactive financial wellness programs isn't just a nice perk; it's a smart way to reduce employee anxiety and improve performance.

Case Vignette: The Financially Healthy Firm

PayPal offers a fantastic example of a company that took its employees' financial health seriously. They did an internal study and found something disturbing: even though they paid competitive wages, almost two-thirds of their hourly workers were running out of money between paychecks . They recognized this as a fundamental roadblock to both engagement and well-being. So, they launched a major program. They didn't just raise wages; they also lowered the cost of healthcare and made every single employee a shareholder. And, crucially, they gave everyone access to financial education and counseling. This holistic approach, which directly addresses the "Availability" condition for engagement, dramatically reduced financial stress. In turn, it boosted loyalty, engagement, and productivity, setting a whole new standard for what it means to be a responsible employer in the financial sector. This case illustrates a holistic approach to employee financial well-being (Financial Health Network, n.d.).

AN INTEGRATED FRAMEWORK AND FUTURE DIRECTIONS

So, let's tie all this together. We've seen that employee engagement, emotional intelligence, and well-being aren't just separate buzzwords. They're deeply connected, and they all work together to drive success. But to actually use these ideas, leaders need a simple, cohesive way to think about them. This section offers a model for doing just that—the Engaged-Intelligent-Well (EIW) Strategic HR Model—and talks about what it means for leaders and for future research.

The Engaged-Intelligent-Well (EIW) Strategic HR Model

The EIW model isn't just a diagram; it's a story about cause and effect. It shows how smart HR and leadership actions, rooted in emotional intelligence and a real commitment to well-being, create the right conditions for people to become highly engaged. That engagement then leads to better service and performance that can last. It's a virtuous cycle.

The EIW Strategic HR Model

- **Strategic Inputs (The Levers):** This is where HR and leaders take action. These are the levers you can pull.
    - o **EI-Based Leadership:** Hiring, training, and promoting leaders who are emotionally intelligent.
    - o **PERMA-Informed Job & Work Design:** Designing jobs to be meaningful and give people autonomy; creating fair recognition systems.
    - o **Supportive Policies:** Offering real flexibility, good well-being programs (mental, physical, and financial), and fair pay.

- **Psychological Mediators (The Conditions):** These actions don't magically create engagement. They create the right internal feelings for employees, the conditions that Kahn identified.
    - **Meaningfulness:** People see how their work fits into a bigger picture.
    - **Psychological Safety:** People feel trusted, respected, and safe to be themselves.
    - **Availability:** People have the energy and resources they need to do their best work.
- **Core Outcome (The State):** When those conditions are met, you get the prize.
    - **High Employee Engagement:** People willingly pour their energy, focus, and passion into their jobs.
- **Strategic Impact (The Results):** This high level of engagement then produces the business results every company wants.
    - **Enhanced Service Excellence:** Engaged people deliver great customer service. Period.
    - **Organizational Resilience:** A healthy, engaged workforce can handle change and bounce back from setbacks.
    - **Sustainable Business Performance:** You see it in lower turnover, higher profits, and more innovation.

This model changes the whole conversation. It shows that things like wellness programs and flexible work aren't just "perks." They are strategic moves to create the psychological safety and availability that people need to engage. It makes it clear that leadership training isn't "soft stuff"; it's the main way you build a meaningful and safe workplace.

Implications for Leaders and a Call for Interdisciplinary Research

For any leader, from the C-suite to the front line, this model has big implications. It means we have to stop seeing employees as resources to be managed and start seeing them as partners to be enabled. It means treating well-being as a leading indicator of future success, not just a side project or a benefit. This takes courage. It takes the courage to invest in people for the long term, even when there's short-term financial pressure, and the courage to trust people with the flexibility they need to do their best work.

The complexity here also screams for more integrated research. The walls that often separate fields like organizational psychology, HR, counseling, and even finance need to come down. We need to see more research that:

- **Is Longitudinal:** Studies that follow organizations over time to prove the causal links in the EIW model.
- **Is Cross-Cultural:** Research that explores how these ideas play out in different cultures, so global companies can adapt their strategies.
- **Examines Technology's Role:** Studies that look at how AI and automation can be used to help people, not replace them—for instance, by automating boring tasks to free people up for more meaningful, creative work.

So, what's the bottom line? The burnout, disengagement, and turnover we're seeing everywhere aren't just a temporary slump. They're symptoms of an old way of thinking that valued short-term productivity over long-term human sustainability. The way forward is to recognize that a company's greatest competitive advantage is a workforce that is not just productive, but engaged; not just skilled, but emotionally intelligent; and not just showing up, but truly flourishing. That's the future of work.

REFERENCES

Bar-On, R. (1997). *The Bar-On Emotional Quotient Inventory (EQ-i): Technical manual*. Multi-Health Systems.

CUPA-HR. (2023, September). *The CUPA-HR 2023 Higher Education Employee Retention Survey*. Retrieved from https://www.cupahr.org/resource/higher-ed-employee-retention-survey-findings-september-2023/

Deloitte. (2023, August 1). *Cultivating employee engagement in financial services*. Retrieved from https://www.deloitte.com/us/en/insights/industry/financial-services/improve-employee-engagement.html

Financial Health Network. (n.d.). PayPal case study. https://finhealthnetwork.org/employer-finhealth-toolkit/identify-solutions/paypal-case-study/

Fletcher, I., Leadbetter, P., Curran, A., & O'Sullivan, H. (2007). Emotional intelligence and patient-centred care. *Medical Education*, *41*(3), 213–214.

Forbes. (2025, March 17). *Employee Burnout: The Hidden Threat Costing Companies Millions*. Retrieved from https://www.forbes.com/sites/julianhayesii/2025/03/17/employee-burnout-the-hidden-threat-costing-companies-millions/

Gallup. (2025, January 13). *U.S. Employee Engagement Sinks to 10-Year Low*. Retrieved from https://www.gallup.com/workplace/654911/employee-engagement-sinks-year-low.aspx

Gallup. (n.d.). *How to Improve Employee Engagement in the Workplace*. Retrieved from https://www.gallup.com/workplace/285674/improve-employee-engagement-workplace.aspx

Goleman, D. (1995). *Emotional intelligence*. Bantam Books.

Higher Ed Today. (2024, May 13). *Creating and Sustaining Wellness Cultures for Faculty, Staff, and Students*. Retrieved from https://www.higheredtoday.org/2024/05/13/wellness-cultures-for-student-success/

Hospitality Insights by EHL. (2024, February 15). *Employee engagement: The method behind hospitality success*. Retrieved from https://hospitalityinsights.ehl.edu/employee-engagement-method-hospitality-success

HubEngage. (n.d.). *Hospitality Employee Engagement Case Studies*. Retrieved from https://www.hubengage.com/hospitality-employee-engagement/

Instant. (2024, September 3). *Actionable Insights from the 2024 Wages & Wellbeing Study*. Retrieved from https://www.instant.co/insights-from-the-2024-wages-wellbeing-study/

Kahn, W. A. (1990). Psychological conditions of personal engagement and disengagement at work. *Academy of Management Journal, 33*(4), 692–724. DOI: 10.2307/256287

Mercer. (2025, August). *Results of the 2025 US Turnover Surveys*. Retrieved from https://www.imercer.com/articleinsights/workforce-turnover-trends

Press Ganey. (2024, July 17). *Employee engagement in 2024: Trends, challenges, and opportunities*. Retrieved from https://info.pressganey.com/press-ganey-blog-healthcare-experience-insights/employee-engagement-in-2024-trends

Saks, A. M. (2006). Antecedents and consequences of employee engagement. *Journal of Managerial Psychology, 21*(7), 600–619. DOI: 10.1108/02683940610690169

Salovey, P., & Mayer, J. D. (1990). Emotional intelligence. *Imagination, Cognition and Personality, 9*(3), 185–211. DOI: 10.2190/DUGG-P24E-52WK-6CDG

Seligman, M. E. P. (2011). *Flourish: A visionary new understanding of happiness and well-being*. Free Press.

Spring Health. (2025, April 11). *How HR Leaders Can Tackle Employee Burnout*. Retrieved from https://www.springhealth.com/blog/how-hr-leaders-can-tackle-employee-burnout

The Educator. (2024, August 21). *Education Sector Ranks Lowest for Employee Wellbeing, Great Place To Work® Report Reveals*. Retrieved from https://the-educator.org/education-sector-ranks-lowest-for-employee-wellbeing-great-place-to-work-report-reveals/

Vantage Circle. (2025, March 25). *Employee Engagement in Healthcare: Trends, Challenges, and Strategies*. Retrieved from https://www.vantagecircle.com/en/blog/employee-engagement-in-healthcare-industry/

Chapter 10
Employee Retention in the Tunisian Private Sector: The Case of Two Companies

Achouak Chouchane
http://orcid.org/0009-0004-3300-753X
University of Sfax, Tunisia

Rim Maalej
Faculty of Economics and Management of Sfax, Tunisia

ABSTRACT

This study examines the critical challenge of employee retention in the Tunisian private sector through an in-depth analysis of two leading companies: SOPAL and SOTIM. The qualitative research conducted reveals that employee retention depends on several interdependent factors, including work environment, compensation, leadership, and career advancement opportunities. Our findings demonstrate that Tunisian companies face specific challenges related to their socio-economic context, requiring tailored strategies. The study identifies concrete approaches to improve retention, such as developing a positive work environment, equitable reward systems, and continuous training programs. This research provides business leaders and HR professionals with practical insights to develop effective retention policies, thereby contributing to organizational stability and sustainable success for Tunisian companies. The lessons learned from this study can be applied to other similar contexts in emerging countries.

DOI: 10.4018/979-8-3373-6395-0.ch010

INTRODUCTION

The success and survival of organizations depend on the performance and satisfaction of their employees. They must meet their expectations to retain their talents (Mir & Mufeed, 2016). Thus, employee retention is an essential tool for providing the organization with a sustainable competitive advantage. The latter is a process that encourages staff to remain in the organization for a long period (Roy,2018).

According to Haider et al.(2015), it is essential to retain talented employees to achieve individual and organizational objectives. Indeed, retaining employees is important for preserving the development and growth of organizations (Vasanthan et al., 2025).

Employees ensure the fulfillment of customer expectations by providing them with high-quality service and offering a high level of production. Furthermore, retaining employees in their positions protects the company from a negative impact on the turnover rate, which is associated with direct and indirect costs. These costs are generally related to the process of recruiting and onboarding new employees (Dugovicova, 2019).

However, employee retention is a significant problem encountered by all organizations, particularly in the Tunisian private sector. Although Tunisian employees prefer the public sector to the private sector – noting that the state encourages the increase of Tunisian employment in the private sector by granting them subsidies – they prioritize security as well as favorable and advantageous working conditions in the public sector, such as shorter working hours, high salaries, and longer annual leave, rather than working a six-day week with a lower salary.

Thus, the situation in the Tunisian private sector raises a very important question: why does the Tunisian private sector not retain its employees, despite all the efforts made by the State? This research examines the factors that increase employee retention in the Tunisian private sector, particularly in two Tunisian companies: SOPAL "Societe de Production d'Articles en Laiton" and SOTIM "Société Tunisienne Industrielle de Mousse".

Other studies show that employees leave their organizations due to dissatisfaction and the absence of a favorable social climate, which leads to decreased productivity, lower employee morale, increased employee absenteeism, and increased staff turnover (Nwabuzor, 2018).

Many works on employee retention have been published in the United States. The lack of this type of research in Africa and particularly in Tunisia reinforces the need to conduct studies on this subject. Hence the objective of this research is to study this theme within the SOPAL and SOTIM companies. Furthermore, there are important factors such as, for example, work climate, compensation and reward, leadership, social benefits, etc., which play a fundamental role in employee retention. It is a subject that is not always studied in depth in the Tunisian private sector. In this sense, what are the key factors that contribute to employee retention in the Tunisian private sector?

1.- LITERATURE REVIEW

Employee retention is becoming one of the most important challenges companies face today (Pregnolato et al., 2017). It is considered a problem due to the lack of talents as well as the costs incurred by the organization in terms of money, time, and effort required to recruit and train replacements (Alhmoud & Rjoub, 2019).

1.1. Retention Factors

Several studies have identified many factors that can contribute to employee retention. According to Korantwi-Barimah (2017), leadership, career, the organization's vision and mission, a favorable work climate, and cooperation are factors that influence employee retention. Another study by Kadiresan et al. (2016) supports that the effectiveness of these elements, notably work climate, employee social benefits, training and development, are important for employee retention.

Consequently, several studies have analyzed this subject as well as the factors affecting employee retention to develop sustainable solutions and identify why employee retention is so difficult.

In this study, we focused on the following four retention factors: work climate, compensation and rewards, leadership, and career development.

1.1.1. Work Climate

The work climate is part of employee engagement at work. It includes relationships with managers and colleagues, organizational culture, as well as personal development (Poh, 2017). This also refers to the atmosphere of an organization where employees perform their tasks. Thus, organizations that succeed in providing a favorable work environment are able to improve their employees' motivation and engagement, which ultimately leads to positive outcomes (Hanaysha,2016).

George (2015) argued that an appropriate work climate, when it includes a pleasant work experience, adequate resources, and a certain degree of flexibility, is favorable for employee retention.

Note that the work climate can vary from one company to another. For example, industrial companies need a climate where workers have the opportunity to use all their capacities; while commercial companies that deal directly with customers should follow a psychological dimension to interact and understand their customers in a meaningful way (Umamaheswari & Krishnan,2016).

According to Kundu and Lata (2017), a favorable work climate motivates the employee to stay in the same organization long-term. It fosters good relationships with managers, interactions among themselves, and organizational support. Researchers have confirmed that a favorable organizational culture modifies employee behavior to adapt to their organization's culture, which, in turn, improves employee retention.

Lei et al. (2018) established that a friendly and stress-free work climate, building relationships among colleagues, and encouraging open communication are essential factors for job satisfaction, which also improve staff retention.

Furthermore, such a climate implies a degree of autonomy and empowerment that can be recognized by employees. It also includes work support and the presence of stimulating challenges. In this case, employees feel recognized, and by supporting their skills development, you allow them to be happy atwork.

Today, talent retention has become more crucial. Companies promote the empowerment and autonomy of workers, their emotional commitment to the company, their capacity for renewal, and their fit with the modification and permanent deployment of their skills.

1.1.2. Compensation and Reward

Compensation is a financial payment made to a person in exchange for their efforts and results, for example, for a job position(Sharew,2018).

However, compensation can go beyond salary to include all resources available to employers to attract, motivate, and retain employees. These resources cover all forms of exchange of money, services, and benefits(Breashy,2016).

As for reward, it is something the organization provides to employees in response to their contributions and performance. A reward can be intrinsic or extrinsic. It can take the form of cash, such as bonuses, or recognition, such as certificates.

Compensation and reward play a primordial role in attracting and retaining talented employees, particularly those with better skills and exceptional performance.

Several studies have proven that satisfaction regarding compensation is an integral part of employee retention. According to Haider et al. (2015), compensation is the essential factor that shows the employee's commitment and intention, and it is the reason why the individual remains in that organization. They also explain that with growing competition between companies, it becomes crucial to retain the most competent workers to ensure the sustainability of the organization.

To retain employees, one of the solutions is to offer them higher salaries. This approach is corroborated by the work of Turnea (2018), according to whom it is impossible to rely solely on non-financial practices (such as recognition or career development) to retain talent; the granting of attractive financial rewards therefore remains essential.

Compensation and reward represent one of the important elements that influence staff turnover. When individuals receive insufficient financial rewards and low salaries, they consider that participation is perceived as a burden; and consequently, they tend to leave companies. On the other hand, they argued that good pay could be an important determinant of job satisfaction, which pushes the employee to achieve higher productivity within the organization (Al Mamun &Nazmul, 2017).

Finally, compensation remains a more important element in overall employee retention than personal growth (Parveen et al., 2017).

1.1.3. Leadership

Leadership is a relationship through which a person influences the behavior of other people. It is a process that motivates and supports others to work enthusiastically towards achieving their goals. Thus, leadership is a human factor that connects employees to each other and encourages them to achieve these goals (Wakabi,2016).

Numerous studies highlight the essential role of leadership in maintaining employee retention. Covella et al. (2017) proved that leaders could retain a more experienced employee and decrease turnover intention by maintaining good relationships with them. They must also involve the employee in feedback and focus on the fit between their skills and abilities and the task requirements.

Sharew (2018) supported this idea and adds that employees and leaders should consider task design, how they distribute work, delegation, and autonomy. They can thus develop and provide recommendations that recognize their contributions.

When the leader supports open communication and maintains strong relationships with their employees, the latter will be more involved in the organization. Furthermore, employees' turnover intentions are likely to be low, and they will not seek other new job opportunities (Jwu etal.,2018).

Therefore, leadership represents an important factor for employee retention, for which a better leader must understand the importance of a balanced life between professional and private life to retain their employees long-term (for example, flexible working hours, remote work, etc.). The human side of leadership is one of the most important elements that determine the success or failure of employee retention.

Furthermore, the study by Batool et al. (2018) highlights the determining impact of leadership styles on employee retention. The authors emphasize the need to motivate and support employees, as well as to involve them in decisions. They conclude that workers need trustworthy leaders who know how to appreciate and recognize their value. They know themselves well, accept themselves, and are honest with themselves. They are in tune with their employees' values.

1.1.4. Career Development

Career development is considered the acquisition of new skills and the use of different learning methods that is profitable for the employee as well as for the organization (Aguenza & Som, 2018).

In other words, career development is a method that helps the organization maximize the productivity of its human resources and achieve its objectives by ensuring the best fit between people and jobs (Mckay, 2019). Therefore, the company must focus on how its employees manage their careers. It will implement devices that offer a structure allowing employees to progress in the career path they have chosen (Mckay, 2019). They describe career development as continuous learning and development activities aimed at acquiring transversal skills, related to employment and career. It represents one of the main keys to achieving employee loyalty and sustaining the company's activity.

The literature review revealed varied results concerning the significant importance of career development on employee retention. The study by Saleem et al. (2018) looked into the necessity for organizations to increase their staff retention capabilities and minimize brain drain by identifying the factors affecting this retention. This study revealed that opportunities for career growth are one of the most determining factors for employee retention.

Fletcher et al. (2018) argued that training and development encourage the employee to stay and not leave, particularly by increasing the pleasant effect on work that triggers motivation processes. Thus, training has become a fundamental part of the employee's life. It ensures continuity in the professional lives of employees who wish to achieve career advancement.

On the other hand, Umamaheswari and Krishnan (2016) revealed that it is not only career development that can retain employees, but organizations must consider the expectations of their workers by changing, for example, their function as an essential determinant of motivation.

Logically, companies must encourage employees by ensuring career progression, a good work climate, improved compensation, etc.

2.- RESEARCH METHODOLOGY

In order to carry out this survey concerning the retention of employees, we have chosen to use a qualitative approach with the help of a semi-structured interview guide. This last is considered to be “A technique intended to collect, in the perspective of their analysis, discursive data reflecting notably the conscious or unconscious mental universe of individuals" (Thiétart et al., 1999, pp.422-448).

Thus, we need to know information on the importance of the retention of employees. According to Bühlmann and Tettamanti (2007) stipulate that in qualitative research, researchers are concerned with mechanisms or phenomena still little studied through surveys of a more exploratory character, with a strong emphasis on description, a focus on the understanding of phenomena and the development of theories aiming to understand in the most complete way possible the data collected.

Within the framework of this research, we opt for an exploratory approach which is judged the most appropriate, since it has for object to ensure the emergence of new theories as well as the identification of new concepts or of new explanatory variables in domains where knowledge is still little developed (Thiétart et al.1999).

In this research, the retention of employees is a notion little studied in the Tunisian context as well theoretically as empirically, it suffers from a lack of conceptualization and from an absence of theoretical models.

Our objective being the exploration and the understanding of the retention within the companies from a case study. Thus, this study was carried out in two companies "SOPAL" and "SOTIM" to have more information relevant and reliable and a better communication.

Concerning the selection of the sample of this research, the question of the number of interviews to retain is a complex problem. In order to solve the problem of the size of the sample, the literature highlights two principles namely the replication (Yin, 1990) and the saturation (Glaser & Strauss, 1967). According to this last, the adequate size of a sample is that which ensures a theoretical saturation. When the researcher stops at a certain number of interviews at which he does not find additional information to enrich the theory, hence the researcher considers phenomena already noted, at this level the saturation is reached.

According to Yin (1990), the adequate size of a sample is that which is based on the logic of replication following the degree of certainty. When there does not appear any new output after an analysis of the data to validate the theory, at this level the replication is completed. Hence, the researcher must add research interviews and proceed to successive replications to reach the saturation.

Starting from these two cases, the researcher must make his own approximation as to the theoretical saturation or as to the replication. Within the framework of this research, we have followed the recommendations proposed by Eisenhardt (1989) who has warned to include a number of interviews between four and ten to do a rigorous research and validate a theory.

With regard to what precedes, we have allowed to foresee a number of eight face-to-face interviews. This has allowed us to meet the number of people necessary for this survey which lasts two successive days for each company. It was indeed more interesting to do interviews more or less long, in order to collect a number of responses larger on the same subjects and to have a little of freedom to express one's opinion. Thus, we have chosen executives and employees who are heterogeneous (by taking into account women and men occupying very different functions). Moreover, we have also taken care to choose people belonging to different generations (generation 1: from 25 to 45 and generation 2: from 45 to 60).

3.- PRESENTATION OF THE SELECTED CASES

In order to well understand the composition of this research work, we are going now to present it in the form of a summary table, specifying the characteristics of each employee questioned. For the sake of anonymity, we only stipulate the first names of the employees.

Table 1. Profile of interviewees from SOPAL and SOTIM companies

Company SOTIM	Seniority	Age	Sex	Position / Role	Interview duration
Interviewee Name: Ms. Fadwa	5 years	36	Female	FemaleManager of quality and production management	45mn
Interviewee Name:Mr. Salmen	4 years	44	Male	Commercial director	30mn
Interviewee Name: Mr. Slim	8 years	46	Male	HR director	1h:30mn
Interviewee Name: Mr. Yassine	18 years	40	Male	Production director	30mn
Company SOPAL	**Seniority**	**Age**	**Sex**	**Position / Role**	**Interview duration**
Interviewee Name: Mr. Nizar	12 years	55	Male	Manager Product Quality and Metrology Laboratory	30mn
Interviewee Name: Mr. Said	3 years	25	Male	HR development	1heure
Interviewee Name: Ms. Fatma	6 years	32	Female	Commercial assistant: delivery display of client	30mn
Interviewee Name: Ms. Hela	2 years	33	Female	Commercial assistant: delivery	30mn

The objective is to profit from each response given by each person, and to see if certain responses converge according to the age of the person, of their status in the company, of their seniority. In order to apprehend the functioning, the attitudes of the employees questioned and their expectations, we are going in this part to briefly present the size and the sector of activity of two companies "SOPAL" and "SOTIM" that we have selected in our city located in Sfax (it is the second large city in Tunisia and quite recognized for a vast industrial zone) in which we have carried out our interview. The choice of the first company SOPAL, which is created in 1981, is very famous on the national and international scale. Currently, it has become a leader in Tunisia in the manufacturing and the distribution of products in the sectors of sanitary equipment, of water connection and of Gas connection. Its growth has been returned by a continuous improvement on the quality and permanent innovation of the products and at the service of the consumer.

Also, it is benefited by a total integration of its process. Its technical design office is characterized by a better equipment, more efficient in design and in development. SOPAL "Société de Production d'articles en Laiton" is an industrial company (where it belongs to the very competitive sector) which brings together several trades for example: 14 hot stamping, gravity foundry, pressure injection, digital command machining, robotic polishing and surface treatment (nickel plating/chromium plating) totally automated. It employs 1000 employees. It is a leader on the Tunisian market. It occupies a very strong competitive position. Today SOPAL bases its strategy of growth on the international scale on the development of a brand policy, in Tunisia, in the Arab Maghreb Union and in West Africa.

The choice of the second company SOTIM "Societe Nouvelle Industrie De Mousse et De Matelas Ressorts" is very reputed in the region of Sfax. It is Created in 1968. SOTIM is an industrial unit operating in the sector of chemistry and it is specialized in the production of foam and in the manufacturing of spring mattresses. Since this date, the company is characterized by a good situation of development thanks to the professionalism and to the know-how of the managers. The manufacturing of spring mattresses is the specialty of SOTIM since 1981, it continues to be it currently and in the future, since it has decided to widen its range to better adapt to each requirement of the client. It has begun to develop on the international markets. It employs currently 330 people of which 25 senior executives and 20 senior technicians. The good quality of the components, the sophisticated technologies of realization and the precision of the finishes make the CONFORTEX mattresses a support of rest comfortable and durable in time. Today, the new SOTIM uses more artificial intelligence on the three production workshops.

4.- ANALYSIS AND DISCUSSIONS OF THE SELECTED RESPONSES

4.1. Analysis of the selected responses

All along the elaboration of the interview guide, we have made the choice to ask open questions in order to leave a partial freedom of expression relatively wide to the employees that we have questioned.

This interview guide deals with the retention of employees. The goal of this part is to understand the structure of the interview guide and the expected responses through each question asked. To study in a more clear and more precise way the content of the interview guide, we are going to present this one in the form of a table (see Appendix).

Table 2. Case of the SOTIM company

	MS. Fadwa	Mr Salmen	Mr Slim	Mr Yassine
The benefits you currently receive contribute to your retention	"Cooperation is an encouraging factor to continue working here. Consequently, it is interesting to work in a group because work on the spring mattress production line always depends on this cooperation."	"A good work atmosphere, effective information sharing, and active listening among colleagues: I have found at SOTIM a relationship of trust with my manager, who grants me significant autonomy in decision-making, except in entirely exceptional cases."	"The main mission of my position as Human Resources Director (HRD) is to create a good work atmosphere, while demonstrating sociability and understanding. Teamwork offers several advantages at SOTIM: skill improvement, facilitation of information sharing and exchange, increased work efficiency, and better organization. "Furthermore, strong communication has been established between us, the managers, and our leadership. Seniority plays a determining role in this dynamic."	"When I express interest in a training course, the company is quick to offer it to me. As Mr. Yassine explains, teamwork is essential for progress, particularly in spring mattress manufacturing where assembly line work requires genuine cooperation among employees. The main advantage that motivates me to stay lies in the total delegation of responsibilities." "Mr. Yassine states that he is very satisfied with his position within the company. He maintains particularly cordial relations with the owner and benefits from specific advantages compared to other managers, such as a company car, trips, among others."

continued on following page

Table 2. Continued

	MS. Fadwa	Mr Salmen	Mr Slim	Mr Yassine
"Reasons for staying with or leaving the company"	"I am staying in my current position at SOTIM primarily because the team is exceptional. Indeed, I feel fully satisfied with the harmony and excellent work atmosphere that prevails within my department."	"The significant leeway in terms of autonomy and responsibility granted by management constitutes the main reason for my attachment to this company. This is actually what motivated me to return after an absence of fifteen years. The manager granted me real freedom of action coupled with a system of self-control and self-evaluation."	"Within SOTIM, I consider myself fully satisfied with my position due to the excellent working conditions. I have never considered leaving the company or even changing positions. This stability can be explained in particular by my prior experience in 2003 at a confectionery belonging to the same owner. Unlike the latter, SOTIM benefits from a particularly positive and stimulating work atmosphere."	"According to him, the leader plays a determining role in employee retention. Thanks to these particular efforts, Mr. Yassine benefits from specific advantages compared to other managers. He is, in fact, one of the few managers who has never left SOTIM. Mr. Yassine states that he has no intention of leaving, especially since he has been able to observe the paths of two colleagues who had left the company before eventually returning to it."
"Are you looking for better offers from other companies?"	"Currently, I consider myself fully satisfied with my working conditions, particularly the participative spirit established with management. This relationship of trust and this involvement in decisions allow me to thrive professionally within SOTIM."	"If I were to consider new opportunities, it would be to create my own project. I am not looking for offers from other companies."	"I did indeed work at a confectionery belonging to the same owner as SOTIM in 2003. However, I left that company due to less advantageous working conditions."	"In my opinion, no other company offers a more attractive package than SOTIM. The only situation that could make me leave would be to start my own business."

Table 3. Case of the SOPAL Company

	Mr Nizar	*Mr Said*	*Ms. Fatma*	*Ms. Héla*
The benefits you currently receive contribute to your retention	"Our company offers advantages in terms of training and prioritizes teamwork through a participative and collegial style with my collaborators. Concretely, employees benefit from autonomy and full empowerment in their daily tasks, while being partially integrated into the final decision-making process. I cannot make any decision without first consulting my colleagues. They enjoy effective communication with genuine information sharing (which contributes to their well-being) in a non-centralized environment."	"Training holds a central position within SOPAL, as evidenced by our 'profailing' program. Our company distinguishes itself through its respect for fundamental values: discipline, sharing of ideas, creativity, continuous learning, and decision-making autonomy - all while maintaining respect for the hierarchy. Regarding the work climate, managers' offices remain permanently open to facilitate mutual assistance, which promotes smooth communication between different departments. This approach generates optimal responsiveness. Individual work has no place here: we systematically prioritize team synergy, idea exchange, and a resolutely participative approach. These elements constitute the distinctive organizational culture of SOPAL."	"Management demonstrates active listening and encourages me by regularly adopting my proposals. It gives me the opportunity to develop my ideas by offering me suitable training at any time. These training sessions have a significant impact on employees' mindset. Personally, they contribute to my psychological well-being at work. Our commercial department systematically organizes three annual training sessions, and the company always remains open to any additional justified request."	"A strong relationship of solidarity exists with my commercial manager, fostering a non-centralized mode of operation. During holiday periods, we cover for each other, thus avoiding any excessive accumulation of work. Our missions being interdependent, this organization allows us to adopt a collaborative work style marked by: Smooth communication; Effective information sharing; Autonomy in decision-making. Our manager demonstrates a flexible approach. Of course, for particularly sensitive matters, we systematically consult him."

continued on following page

Table 3. Continued

	Mr Nizar	*Mr Said*	*Ms. Fatma*	*Ms. Héla*
Reasons for staying with or leaving the company	"The presence of an extremely favorable social climate is a decisive reason for me to stay with the company. Our work environment is characterized by a complete absence of humiliation between the owner and collaborators. Several concrete elements form the basis of this exceptional relationship: mutual respect even in case of errors, friendly relations, a positive atmosphere, and constant encouragement. Particularly noteworthy, our owner maintains genuine closeness with employees, sharing not only our professional concerns but also certain aspects of our personal lives. This human involvement represents a key motivational factor and perfectly meets our professional and human expectations."	"Mr. Saïd affirms his attachment to SOPAL due to the special efforts made by the company. Several elements contribute to this loyalty: the allocation of bonuses for new ideas proposed, significant involvement in the decision-making process, as well as a rewarding work environment marked by regular encouragement. The company also distinguishes itself by organizing unique events: celebrations of global holidays, conventions in partner hotels, distribution of tickets for festivals or shows, invitations of renowned artists, and organization of excursions. Particular attention is even given to employees' families, with the exceptional possibility of welcoming their children to the workplace."	Ms. Fatma acknowledges having seriously considered switching to an international company in the medical sector, motivated by salary stagnation at SOPAL (after six years with the company). However, two decisive factors ultimately made her stay: 1. The exceptional quality of the work environment and professional relationships; 2. The incompatibility of the new position's requirements (particularly frequent travel) with her family obligations, especially caring for her two young daughters. This dilemma perfectly illustrates the complex balance between professional and personal motivations in career decisions." **1.**	"Ms. Héla rules out any possibility of leaving SOPAL, as her previous four-year experience as commercial and marketing manager in another company was marked by difficult working conditions: frequent travel, excessive pressure, rigid hierarchical relationships, poor social climate, lack of recognition, and above all, a glaring gap between the contributions required and the compensation offered. The decision to leave that previous job became inevitable when she reached a professional impasse, noting the complete absence of reward for her efforts. This contrasting experience explains her current attachment to SOPAL where she finally finds a balanced professional environment."

continued on following page

Table 3. Continued

	Mr Nizar	*Mr Said*	*Ms. Fatma*	*Ms. Héla*
"Are you looking for better offers from other companies?"	"I declare myself fully satisfied with the working conditions and atmosphere within our company, particularly when compared to those offered by similar companies in our region."	"I consider myself fully satisfied with this company. In Sfax, it is rare to find companies offering such working conditions and benefits."	"Ms. Fatma is actively considering exploring other professional opportunities: 'If I were single, I wouldn't hesitate to change jobs, as the compensation offered in the international medical sector is significantly more attractive. Furthermore, being still young, I want to try my luck elsewhere, despite the benefits offered by our management such as hotel conventions, access to fairs and festivals. However, these benefits remain marginal for us compared to the executives and managers who receive significantly higher salaries.'"	"Currently, I am not considering seeking other professional opportunities, particularly after having experienced a previous difficult situation. Ms. Héla emphasizes that the positive social climate and quality of internal communication represent major assets, reflecting both special efforts by management and distinctive benefits offered by the owner to retain talent. She expresses strong satisfaction with these specific characteristics that distinguish SOPAL."

4.2. Discussion of Results

This research studies the factors of employee retention in the Tunisian private sector. The main motivation of this study is to help companies find solutions for employee retention (to keep them for longer periods). In the Tunisian private sector, the employee turnover rate is high, which constitutes a major challenge for many private companies.

At this level, we discuss this research work accompanied by other research found by some researchers.

According to Earle (2003), a good climate in companies represents an essential factor for retaining and motivating employees, meaning that if a company provides a satisfying work climate for their employees, they are more likely to stay in this company for a longer period. They will thus be more creative and more productive.

Compensation and reward provide a good feeling of belonging, which can lead to employee retention. This survey goes in the same direction as the research of George (2015) who argued that better compensation, presence of bonuses, and agreement of social benefits etc., are favorable for employee retention. For this, employees are likely to stay with their company if they have a positive perception towards the work environment.

Also, better rewards could be an important factor for keeping employees motivated. The opinions of the interviewees and especially in the SOPAL company converge with the idea that private sector employees place great value on the rewards granted to them by their employers. Consequently, companies should grant their employees reward programs, recognition, and more engagement at their work level which allows employees to develop their careers which makes them more motivated and more productive.

According to Leslie et al. (2016), compensation can be one of the main ways to motivate and retain employees because it encourages them to stay in position longer and leads to their satisfaction and engagement at work.

Let us not forget that the valorization of efforts, encouragement, compliments have a reward effect on employee retention, which positively influences the execution of tasks at work with more efficiency.

Moreover, this survey also confirms the results of Sharew (2018), Covella et al. (2017) and Batool et al. (2018). They emphasize the importance of the role of leaders who involve the employee in decision-making to make them more creative and more productive. According to the viewpoints of the interviewees from both companies, the leader can intervene on the degree of autonomy granted to the employee. They direct and animate work groups by encouraging them to create new production methods. They also establish excellent interpersonal relationships with them. Thus, they are particularly interested in the retention and skills of employees.

Leadership plays a crucial role at the level of employee retention. Good leadership contributes to creating a good work climate where employees feel engaged and involved which increases productivity. They must mobilize and empower each employee, know how to delegate, practice active listening, offer a good atmosphere, motivate their team and each time provide continuous training. In this framework, Tunisian private sector employees (SOPAL and SOTIM) prefer a company that offers them continuous training to improve their competence and their career development.

In this case, these two Tunisian private companies can collect the viewpoints of their employees in the form of a questionnaire regarding their training needs based on the problems encountered in their professional life. For execution, they can begin a distribution of individual questionnaires. This step is indispensable because it allows the collection of essential information for the development of training plans that are in adequacy with their real needs. This phase also allows having a database on which the company develops training activities that will respond to its real needs and those of its employees and that will bring it concrete and brief results.

Finally, training allows the employees of SOPAL and SOTIM to acquire a strong personality allowing them to access a high social level, and an appreciable place as well as their continuity in the professional life of the organization.

5. RECOMMENDATION

According to the responses retained in this research, it is recommended that company leaders ensure that their employees are well compensated in a fair manner which increases motivation and performance (Dixon, 2016).

Indeed, Joubert et al (2017) found that employees who are well compensated lead to better productivity. To satisfy employees, it is also suggested that companies must offer equal rewards between different levels of employees which will improve employee retention.

Also, the work climate plays an essential role in this study. Mondal and Saha (2017) proved that unfavorable work conditions bother or disturb employees which would cause stress also conflicts which reduces employee satisfaction.

Even, the lack of useful communication, mutual trust, mutual aid within work and the absence of opportunities to collectively solve problems constitute obstacles to employee retention.

Thus, the creation of a good work atmosphere should be one of the priorities of leaders to maintain employee retention. To guarantee the continuity and success of employee talent retention, companies need individual and collective participation to improve their competence as well as to highlight the professionalism of employees.

Working in a community leads to communication that helps to build and install an atmosphere of intersubjectivity and a mutual agreement.

Let us add further, it is recommended that employers must pay particular attention to leadership styles that serve to engage and satisfy employees. The emphasis should not be placed only on compensation, promotion and work conditions but also on the manner in which leadership is exercised because employees find it comfortable to work with good leadership as indicated by the interviewees of SOPAL and SOTIM.

The leader of a Tunisian company whether private or public must always adopt a different style that applies to the retention of employee talents. They must play a central and essential role in the development of their employees' skills.

They must be more democratic, collegial and more open. They must know how to direct and animate employees by encouraging them to create new production methods. They must motivate employees by ensuring a deployment of their continuous training.

The director must, in fact, communicate with their employees where mutual understanding is mandatory. They must converse, bring ideas closer, put in community knowledge with their employees of different functions and grant themselves information on common goals and on the way to achieve them. When employees clearly express their viewpoints and their directors are more open and more attentive, communication would be more effective. The latter would help to apprehend the reaction of a member facing a requested work, to limit the difficulties they may encounter and, subsequently, find suitable resources. Moreover, good communication between the leader and the employees can reduce oppositions and can help find solutions in a constructive manner, which would fully contribute to organizational performance.

Good leadership is a process that encourages staff members to stay in an organization. Let us add further that trust plays an important role at the level of employee retention. The study of Papa et al. (2018) shows that retention promotes trust and engagement among employees. Indeed, it is essential to include trust in employee responsibility. The interpersonal relationship maintained by the director with their employees is one of the means that can contribute largely to the success of organizational performance. Trust would thus be associated with better communication. For example, at the evaluation level, open communication between the director and their employees would allow solving problems and cleaning up the organizational climate; which would strongly contribute to employee retention and to the organizational performance of the company.

On the other hand, companies that implement a flexible work schedule attract more employees compared to other companies that have a rigid work schedule. Consequently, it is advised that leaders must practice a strategy that offers flexible work schedules to retain employees. Companies that seek to recruit qualified and competent employees must offer work-life balance opportunities in order to keep them (Kumari, 2005).

It is essential for an organization to understand the challenges that affect professional life, particularly those encountered by women. Indeed, these challenges can influence their job satisfaction, their performance and their motivation to fully engage in the organization. This understanding is all the more crucial as an increasing number of women are present today in the labor market.

According to Haider et al (2016), work-life balance is an essential element on employee engagement towards the organization, job satisfaction, retention and family situation. An imbalance between work life and private life leads to a decrease in productivity, stress, job dissatisfaction and conflict between employees.

According to Umamaheswari and Krishnan (2016), the existence of flexible work practices helps the employee to find a balance between work life and personal life which can lead to an improvement in retention, a reduction in absenteeism and an increase in staff engagement and productivity. Companies can offer different benefits such as childcare alternatives, flexible work schedules and shared responsibilities, etc (Lee, 2019). These elements contribute to creating a favorable work environment, to avoiding turnover intentions and to bringing a sustainable competitive advantage for their organizations (Towns, 2019).

A final recommendation is to continue research in the field of work-life balance to identify the reason or reasons that explain why women are more affected than men. Employee retention and work-life balance are research that could be studied in the future. Consequently, organizations must pay more attention to work-life balance and develop strategies that correspond to their needs in order to retain these talented employees.

CONCLUSION

Employee retention is essential for all organizations and it is often considered a better strategy to gain a competitive advantage. It is necessary to achieve success, consistency and effectiveness of organizations (Khandelwal & Shekhawat, 2018).

Thus, a high retention rate has several positive impacts on the organization. It results in employees having the loyalty necessary to manage a company which requires less time and resources to train new employees (Hoffman, 2018). Retaining employees is important in terms of long-term success for organizations (Dugovicova, 2019).

Following the integration of artificial intelligence, employee retention is an essential tool to keep an organization on the right track.

The integration of technology, by offering more flexibility, has become an essential tool for companies seeking to retain their talents in a highly competitive context.

Let us not hide that this study presents two limits, it does not guarantee that it includes all factors affecting employee retention. Thus, it is suggested that for future researchers to add other influencing factors. Moreover, this study is limited to the incorporation of respondents from only the private sector in Tunisia.

Moreover, this exploratory study can give other future research paths. The first future path is the implementation of a continuous learning and training system, which provides the required skills to employees, ensuring that the leaders of the organization use an effective leadership style and they focus on the development of their employees' skills. The last suggestion is to measure employee appreciation at the level of compensation and reward systems in order to ensure that companies provide an adequate system.

REFERENCES

Aguenza, B. B., & Som, A. P. M. (2018). Motivational factors of employee retention and engagement in organizations. *International Journal of Advances in Management and Economics*, *1*(6), 88–95.

Al Mamun, C. A., & Nazmul, H. M. (2017). Factors affecting employee turnover and sound retention strategies in business organization: A conceptual view. *Problems and Perspectives in Management*, *15*(1), 63–71.

Alhmoud, A., & Rjoub, H. (2019). Total rewards and employee retention in a Middle Eastern context. *SAGE Open*, *9*(2). DOI: 10.1177/2158244019840118

Batool, T., Sehar, S., Qasim, A. P., Afzal, M., & Gilani, S. A. (2018). The influence of supportive nursing leadership for retention of staff nurses in private hospital of Lahore. *Annals of Punjab Medical College*, *12*(4), 272–275.

Breashy, A. E. (2016). *Total compensation vs. total rewards: The difference*. LinkedIn. Retrieved October 26, 2016, from https://www.linkedin.com/pulse/total-compensation-vs-rewards-difference-ali-el-breashy-assoc-cipd

Bühlmann, F., & Tettamanti, M. (2007). Le statut de l'approche qualitative dans des projets de recherche interdisciplinaires. *Recherches Qualitatives*, *3*, 191–213.

Covella, G., McCarthy, V., Kaifi, B., & Cocoran, D. (2017). Leadership's role in employee retention. *Business Management Dynamics*, *7*(5), 1–15.

Dixon, S. A. (2016). *Retention of information technology employees* (Publication No. 10246165) [Doctoral dissertation, University of Phoenix]. ProQuest Dissertations and Theses Global.

Dugovicova, J. (2019). *Impact of employee motivation on employee retention rates* (Publication No. 13812916) [Doctoral dissertation, Webster University]. ProQuest Dissertations and Theses Global.

Earle, H. A. (2003). Building a workplace of choice: Using the work environment to attract and retain top talent. *Journal of Facilities Management*, *2*(3), 244–257. DOI: 10.1108/14725960310807944

Eisenhardt, K. M. (1989). Building theories from case study research. *Academy of Management Review*, *14*(4), 532–550. DOI: 10.5465/amr.1989.4308385

Fletcher, L., Alfes, K., & Robinson, D. (2018). The relationship between perceived training and development and employee retention: The mediating role of work attitudes. *The International Journal of Human Resource Management*, *29*(18), 2701–2728. DOI: 10.1080/09585192.2016.1262888

George, C. (2015). Retaining professional workers: What makes them stay? *Employee Relations*, *37*(1), 102–121. DOI: 10.1108/ER-07-2014-0073

Glaser, B. G., & Strauss, A. L. (1967). *The discovery of grounded theory: Strategies for qualitative research*. Sociology Press.

Haider, M., Aamir, A., Hamid, A. B. A., & Akhtar, C. S. (2016). Work-life balance, job satisfaction and nurses retention: Moderating role of work volition. *International Journal of Business Excellence*, *10*(4), 488–501. DOI: 10.1504/IJBEX.2016.078730

Haider, M., Rasli, A., Akhtar, C. S., Yusoff, R. B. M., Malik, O. M., Aamir, A., & Tariq, F. (2015). The impact of human resource practices on employee retention in the telecom sector. *International Journal of Economics and Financial Issues*, *5*(1S), 63–69.

Hanaysha, J. (2016). Testing the effects of employee engagement, work environment, and organizational learning on organizational commitment. *Procedia-Social and Behavioral Sciences*, *229*, 289–297. DOI: 10.1016/j.sbspro.2016.07.139

Hoffman, B. (2018, November 16). *The importance of employee retention–The key to a successful business*. HR Technologist. Retrieved from https://www.hrtechnologist.com/articles/employee-engagement/the-importance-of-employee-retention-the-key-to-a-successful-business/

Joubert, P., Madau, D., & Grobler, B. (2017). Employee retention and talent management at a sugar mill in South Africa. *Problems and Perspectives in Management*, *15*(3), 306–315. DOI: 10.21511/ppm.15(3).2017.06

Jwu, S. C., Zaiton, H., Abdullah, S. M., & Kasa, M. E. (2018). The relationship between employee attitude towards training and employee retention in telecommunication. *Journal of Cognitive Sciences and Human Development*, *4*(1), 1–14. DOI: 10.33736/jcshd.852.2018

Kadiresan, V., Kamil, N. M., Mazlan, M. R. M., Musah, M. B., & Selamat, M. H. (2016). The influence of human resource practices on employee retention: A case study. *International Journal of Human Resources Studies*, *6*(3), 122–148. DOI: 10.5296/ijhrs.v6i3.10112

Khandelwal, A., & Shekhawat, N. (2018). Role of talent retention in reducing employee turnover. *Journal of Modern Management & Entrepreneurship (JMME)*, *8*(1), 1–5.

Korantwi-Barimah, J. S. (2017). Factors influencing the retention of academic staff in a Ghanaian technical university. *Human Resource Management Research*, *7*(3), 111–119. DOI: 10.5923/j.hrmr.20170703.01

Kumari, N. (2005). *Factors influencing the retention of employees in the IT services industry in Bengaluru* [Doctoral dissertation, University of Jharkhand]. Retrieved from https://www.iujharkhand.edu.in/Nancy-Kumari-Thesis.pdf

Kundu, S. C., & Lata, K. (2017). Effects of supportive work environment on employee retention: Mediating role of organizational engagement. *International Journal of Organizational Analysis*, *25*(4), 703–722. DOI: 10.1108/IJOA-07-2016-1049

Lee, L. C. (2019). *Strategies for increasing healthcare employees' retention* (Publication No. 27544502) [Doctoral dissertation, Walden University]. ProQuest Dissertations and Theses Global.

Lei, K. Y., Basit, A., & Hassan, Z. (2018). The impact of talent management on job satisfaction: A study among the employees of a travel agency in Malaysia. *Indonesian Journal of Applied Business and Economic Research*, *1*(1), 1–19.

Leslie, B., Anderson, C., Horman, J., King, J., & Overly, A. (2016). Generation Z perceptions of a positive workplace environment. *Employee Responsibilities and Rights Journal*, *33*(1), 1–17. DOI: 10.1007/s10672-015-9275-4

McKay, D. (2019). *What is career development? This is how to progress in your job*. Cleverism. Retrieved September 23, 2019, from https://www.cleverism.com/what-is-career-development/

Mir, A. A., & Mufeed, U. (2016). Employee retention–A key tool for achieving competitive advantage. *International Journal of Engineering and Management Research (IJEMR)*, *6*(6), 334–337.

Mondal, A., & Saha, B. (2017). Job satisfaction of secondary school teachers in relation to personality and emotional intelligence. *American Journal of Educational Research*, *5*(10), 1097–1101. DOI: 10.12691/education-5-10-11

Nwabuzor, N. (2018). *Exploring employee retention strategies in the US hotel industry* (Publication No. 10826121) [Doctoral dissertation, Walden University]. ProQuest Dissertations and Theses Global.

Papa, A., Dezi, L., Gregori, G. L., Mueller, J., & Miglietta, N. (2018). Improving innovation performance through knowledge acquisition: The moderating role of employee retention and human resource management practices. *Journal of Knowledge Management*, *22*(8), 1671–1692. DOI: 10.1108/JKM-09-2017-0411

Parveen, M., Maimani, K., & Kassim, N. M. (2017). Quality of work life: The determinants of job satisfaction and job retention among RNs and OHPs. *International Journal for Quality Research*, *11*(1), 173–194. DOI: 10.18421/IJQR11.01-10

Poh, M. (2017). *5 characteristics of a positive work environment*. Hongkiat. Retrieved November 18, 2017, from https://www.hongkiat.com/blog/positive-working-environment/

Pregnolato, M., Bussin, M. H., & Schlechter, A. F. (2017). Total rewards that retain: A study of demographic preferences. *SA Journal of Human Resource Management*, *15*(1), 1–10. DOI: 10.4102/sajhrm.v15i0.901

Roy, B. (2018). Factors determining employee retention: A study in banks. *International Journal of Management Studies*, *5*(2), 101–108. DOI: 10.18843/ijms/v5i2(11)/13

Saleem, A., Khan, R. A., & Manzoor, A. (2018). Determinants of project team retention in private consultancies of Pakistan. *Global Management Journal for Academic & Corporate Studies*, *8*(2), 150–161.

Sharew, A. (2018). *Assessment of employee retention practices in Development Bank of Ethiopia* [Master's thesis, St. Mary's University]. Institutional Repository.

Thiétart, R. A., Florence, A. P., Angot, J., Baumard, P. H., & Blanc, A. (1999). *Méthodes de recherche en management*. Dunod.

Towns, A. (2019). *Effective strategies to increase employee retention in higher education institutions* (Publication No. 27544502) [Doctoral dissertation, Walden University]. ScholarWorks.

Turnea, E. S. (2018). Attraction and retention of the employees: A study based on multinationals from Romania. *Procedia-Social and Behavioral Sciences*, *238*, 73–80. DOI: 10.1016/j.sbspro.2018.03.010

Umamaheswari, S., & Krishnan, J. (2016). Work force retention: Role of work environment, organization commitment, supervisor support and training & development in ceramic sanitary ware industries in India. *Journal of Industrial Engineering and Management (JIEM)*, *9*(3), 612–633. DOI: 10.3926/jiem.1915

Vasanthan, R., Babu, M. R. N., Dzuvichu, K., Chong, S. T., Rana, V. S., & Singh, A. (2025). Bridging social norms theory and community mobilization: Pathways for overcoming gender stereotypes in women's economic empowerment programs. *Enterprise Development & Microfinance, 35*(1), 159–176. ISSN: 1755-1978 (Print), 1755-1986 (Online)

Wakabi, B. M. (2016). Leadership style and staff retention in organisations. *International Journal of Science and Research*, *5*(1), 412–416.

Yin, R. K. (1990). *Case study research: Design and methods* (5th ed.). Sage Publications.

APPENDIX

Table 4. Interview Guide

Preambule: **"We thank you for your collaboration in this interview. Our research is part of an academic study. We guarantee the confidentiality of our discussions. We would like you to first tell us about your role within the company, and then your opinion on employee retention in Tunisian companies. We are following an interview guide, but we can address other points if necessary. Please feel free to share all your spontaneous thoughts."»**	
Theme	**Employee Retention**
1. Benefits and Retention	- Do you consider that the current benefits provided by the company contribute to retaining you?
2. Reasons for Leaving or Staying	– In your opinion, what are the main factors that would encourage an employee to stay in this company or, conversely, to leave it?
3. Active Job Searching	-- Are you currently considering looking for professional opportunities in other companies? If yes, why? – Have you ever been tempted by external job offers? What elements would make the difference for you?

Chapter 11
Human Capital Development in the Modern Service Sector:
A Faith-Inspired Strategic Approach From Islam

Naseem Akhter
http://orcid.org/0009-0002-7504-1715
Shaheed Benazir Bhutto Women University, Peshawar, Pakistan

ABSTRACT

In this chapter, the author investigates the future of Islamic ethical and strategic thinking to contribute to the agreeable amounts of human-capital formation in the new service economy. Following the current digital change in the service sector, including innovation as well as digitisation, there is a necessity to formalise a strategic human resource management (SHRM) based on three fundamental principles: ethical values, egalitarian values, and people values. The chapter argues that Islamic directives which emphasise trust (Amanah), justice (Adl), consultation (Shura) and social responsibility are a potent capital formation factor among human beings. Using the provisions of the Holy Quran, the hadith and current case studies in Muslim majorities, the chapter has introduced a faith-grounded approach in which the Islamic teachings are incorporated with evidence-based human resources in its practices. Moreover, the chapter depicts the ways in which Islamic views can be aligned with modern SHRM goals to achieve organisational sustainability, increase leadership ethics, safeguard employee welfare, and improve organisational foresight as a whole.

DOI: 10.4018/979-8-3373-6395-0.ch011

INTRODUCTION

The growth of human capital has been central to the transformation as well as the continuity of the modern service-based economies. Service-based economies, contrary to traditional industrial models that mainly depend on a material-driven system, gain their competitive power through less tangible materials like skills, knowledge and values that are instilled in individuals (Becker, 1993). The latest educational literature invariably suggests that the organisation of the workforce should be contextualised in ethical and value-based paradigms, and hence productivity development should be congruent with the other social and moral aims in the society (Sen, 1999).

Islam is a religion-spiritual construct which regulates complete personal maturation by ensuring that there exists a balance of tension between profane competence and ethical duty. The importance of talent development is supported by three fundamentals like *amanah* (faithfulness),*ihsan* (excellence in worship) and *ukhuwwah* (brotherhood). In addition, there is a promotion of values such as justice, cooperation and civic excellence (Ali, 2010). The paradigm is known to not only increase the effectiveness of the professionals, but also improve social welfare through the creation of care-oriented, responsible environments of service.

Another approach to methodology would be to redefine the concept of human-capital development under the Islamic paradigm and specifically in the light of the growing service sector. The reconceptualization, by restoring the connection between economic action and moral requirements, is a solution to the challenges of the present period, i.e., alienation, consumerism, and inequality. As a result, it will ease strategic human-capital investment which is in line with Islamic logic.

As a result of this fact, the question will be how such a moral investment is forced to increase productivity, but also safeguard human dignity in the established industry of service.

THE REVOLUTION OF THE SERVICE ECONOMY

Digital Transformation

The service industry is undergoing digital transformation at an increasing pace and requires the implementation of the latest technologies, including artificial intelligence, data analytics, and virtual meeting software, such as Zoom. This makes it necessary for organisations to develop human capital that can navigate these technological advancements without compromising the human aspects of service excellence.

In the modern service economy, emotional intelligence, empathy, and interpersonal competencies are playing an increasingly important role. In the sphere of human capital development, there is an immediate necessity to focus on the breeding of those indeterminate and, nevertheless, imperative abilities, which imply high-quality service delivery.

Service organisations are forced to maintain innovativeness in their business processes, interaction with customers, and business models. At that, the human capital practices ought to contribute to the establishment of the culture of innovation, flexibility, and entrepreneurship among the employees.

These is with the converging trends, there is an irony that genuine human resource management solutions are required of an ethical nature and that are both holistic in nature to meet the needs of performance compared to the competence of meeting human dignity requirements. The Islamic values offer a strong course of taking care of such issues; the Islamic philosophical beliefs that apply to them are based on compulsory jurisprudence, following which the success of organisations can be achieved over a period of fourteen centuries.

CHAPTER OBJECTIVES

Examine Core Components

The aim is to examine the internal constituents of human capital formation in the service sector, establish the critical presence of competencies, structures, and strategic requirements of organisations that are competitive in intention to refine competitiveness and advancement.

Embolden Islamic Principles

This will entail the examination of some of the crucial Islamic principles in application to strategic Hr services, recruitment, motivation, and performance management and employee welfare, thus illustrating their applicability today.

Become compatible with Faith and Practice

The objective will be to combine the Islamic teachings and evidence-based concepts of SHRM to develop frameworks which can support the development of ethical, inclusive and purpose-focused cultures in the workplace.

Suggest a Religious-Based System.

This involves the creation of an overall HR model usable within the service-oriented sectors of society, specifically in Muslim majority or Islamic-oriented cultures, and with lucrative implementation guidelines.

Provide Case-Based Insights

It aims to explore the practical implementation of the strategies of Islamic HR regulation to service organisations, to investigate their outcomes, effective practices, and implementation issues.

Assess moral Investments

It seeks to determine the nature of the innovation, staff retention and organisational vigour in contemporary service settings due to Islamic ethics.

RESEARCH GAP

Academic Literature Gaps

Although there has been a considerable amount of research on strategic human resource management and there is increased interest in the field of Islamic management studies, there are still major gaps in the literature. Existing frameworks of strategic human resource management have largely been shaped by Western perspectives and often overlook the role of culturally embedded ethical systems in enhancing organisational efficiency (Ali, 2010; Beekun & Badawi, 2005).

There remains a significant gap in the literature concerning the integration of Islamic principles with modern service-based human resource strategies. Service industries, in particular, are underrepresented, with much of the existing Islamic management research primarily focused on banking and finance (Beekun & Badawi, 2005). Moreover, the available literature has often treated Islamic values as peripheral rather than integral components of strategic human resource development.

Globalisation of business operations necessitates a general urgency for culturally responsive HR models that are capable of working well across different religious and cultural settings. The chapter fills these gaps, as it gives the systematic incorporation of Islamic norms with the contemporary SHRM practices, specifically adapted to the distinctive needs and challenges in the service economy.

LITERATURE REVIEW

Classical Islamic Sources

The Holy Quran and Hadith literature provide comprehensive guidance on work relations, workers' rights, and organisational management. The Holy Quran emphasises personal responsibility and merit-based effort, stating that "there is nothing for a person except what they strive for" (Qur'an 53:39).

Islamic Management Today

Contemporary perspectives on Islamic organisational behaviour emphasise the importance of values-based leadership and stakeholder-oriented decision-making. These approaches highlight that Islamic ethical principles can enhance organisational performance while maintaining strong moral standards (Ali, 2010; Beekun & Badawi, 2005).

Service Application

Empirical evidence from Muslim-majority contexts suggests that Islamic human-resource practices can be effectively applied across diverse service sectors, including healthcare, education, and hospitality. These practices have demonstrated adaptability and relevance in different organisational settings, indicating their broader applicability within the service economy (Ali, 2010).

Service Economy SHRM in the Literature

Paradigms of Service Excellence.

Contemporary strategic human resource management emphasises service innovation, employee capabilities, and customer-centric approaches to enhance organisational performance (Zeithaml et al., 2020). Strategies for developing human capital must align workforce capabilities with these service imperatives.

Online Transformation Influence

Research on digital transformation highlights that effective service transformation relies on the continuous development and enhancement of human capabilities (Vial, 2021). Organisations must therefore balance the adoption of automation with ongoing investment in employee skills to ensure adaptability, innovation, and sustainable performance.

Employee Well-being Focus

Contemporary strategic human resource management increasingly recognises the relationship between employee well-being and performance in service settings (Wright & Cropanzano, 1998). A holistic approach to human development, which considers both personal and professional well-being, contributes to improved organisational outcomes.

Sustainability Integration

Environmental and social sustainability are increasingly integrated into human resource strategies in service organisations (Jackson et al., 2019). This trend aligns with Islamic values of stewardship and social responsibility, emphasising ethical responsibility and long-term organisational sustainability.

Recent academic discussions have expanded the understanding of human capital practices in service economies, particularly in the context of digital transformation and evolving governance frameworks. Evidence suggests that value-based leadership is associated with higher levels of employee engagement and organisational commitment. Ethical human resource practices are also linked to increased employee trust and reduced turnover intentions. Comparative perspectives indicate that both religious and secular ethical frameworks offer important insights into employee well-being, creating opportunities for integrating Islamic ethical principles into global human resource management discourse. Furthermore, the growing use of artificial intelligence in recruitment and performance management raises critical concerns related to privacy, fairness, and transparency, highlighting the need for robust ethical governance. Taken together, these developments suggest that Islamic ethical frameworks can contribute meaningfully to contemporary strategic human resource management, particularly in technologically advanced, diverse, and sustainability-oriented organisational environments.

RESEARCH METHODOLOGY

This chapter adopts an interdisciplinary research approach that integrates classical Islamic knowledge with contemporary research methodologies. This integrative strategy enhances the reliability of the study and supports the development of faith-informed human resource practices relevant to modern service organisations. The study begins with a systematic literature review of peer-reviewed research in human resource management, Islamic management, organisational psychology, and service-sector studies, incorporating both recent contributions and foundational works.

In parallel, the research examines primary Islamic sources, including the Holy Quran, authenticated Hadith collections, and classical jurisprudential texts, to identify principles related to labour relations, workplace behaviour, and organisational leadership. These sources are analysed to extract ethical and managerial themes relevant to strategic human resource management.

A thematic content analysis is employed to identify recurring patterns across the data, supported by qualitative coding techniques to enhance methodological clarity and reduce interpretive bias. Additionally, the chapter includes a multi-case study analysis of service-sector organisations in Muslim-majority contexts that have implemented Islamic-oriented human resource practices. These cases provide practical insights into implementation strategies, challenges, and observable outcomes. Together, these methodological components create a comprehensive framework that combines doctrinal analysis, empirical observation, and contemporary human resource research.

STRATEGIC HUMAN CAPITAL DEVELOPMENT

Human Capital definition in Services

Human capital in the service economy refers to the knowledge, skills, competencies, and attributes that enable individuals and organisations to deliver high-quality customer experiences, foster innovation, and sustain growth. Unlike manufacturing-based sectors, service-oriented human capital is characterised by its intangible nature, strong interpersonal interactions, and direct engagement with customers (Becker, 2020).

Strategic SHRM

Strategic human capital development involves the systematic acquisition, development, and retention of talent in alignment with organisational goals and market demands. It focuses on enhancing competencies, optimising performance, and creating sustainable competitive advantage through people-centred strategies.

The idiosyncratic properties of the service sector, such as the absence of spatial, time, or physical separation of production and consumption, the intangibility of results, and a high degree of contact with customers, dictate specialised requirements in developing human capital, which promote emotional intelligence, flexibility, and lifelong learning.

SERVICE SECTOR STRATEGIC HRM CHALLENGES

Service organisations face the challenge of attracting, developing, and retaining employees who possess both technical expertise and strong interpersonal skills required for service excellence. This challenge is further intensified by rapid technological advancements, which require continuous upskilling and reskilling to adapt to the evolving nature of operations (Cappelli & Tavis, 2021).

Service occupations often involve significant emotional labour, particularly in frontline roles, which can place both psychological and physical demands on employees. Organisations seeking sustainable performance must therefore balance workforce well-being with operational efficiency. Creating supportive work environments that promote innovation while safeguarding employees' mental and physical health is essential (Bakker & Demerouti, 2020).

Developing organisational cultures that foster continuous innovation while maintaining high-quality service delivery remains a persistent challenge for service organisations. Human resource practices must therefore promote creativity, effective risk management, and reliability to sustain operational efficiency and enhance customer satisfaction (Anderson et al., 2019).

The digital transformation of service organisations has significantly reshaped recruitment, training, and performance management practices. Technologies such as artificial intelligence (AI), predictive HR analytics, and digital learning platforms are increasingly integrated into human resource functions. While these tools enhance efficiency and scalability, they also raise important ethical concerns related to bias, data privacy, and transparency. Responsible digital HR practices can be guided by Islamic ethical principles such as *amanah* (trust), *adl* (justice), and *ihsan* (excellence). Organisations must ensure that algorithmic decisions are regularly evaluated for fairness and that data governance policies protect employee dignity and privacy. Integrating ethical oversight into digital HR systems enables organisations to align technological innovation with organisational values and human dignity.

ISLAMIC ETHICAL FOUNDATIONS IN HRM

Ihsan (Excellence)

Ihsan promotes continuous improvement and high performance, encouraging individuals to perform their duties with excellence and a strong sense of accountability before Allah (SWT).

Taqwa (God-consciousness)

Taqwa guides ethical decision-making by fostering a deep sense of responsibility, integrity, and accountability in workplace behaviour.

Amanah (Trust)

Amanah represents trustworthiness and responsibility, fostering a culture of reliability, accountability, and mutual respect within organisations.

'Adl (Justice)

Adl emphasises fairness and equity in all organisational practices, including recruitment, compensation, and performance management, ensuring that employees are treated justly.

Shura (Consultation)

Shura encourages participatory decision-making, enhancing collaboration, shared responsibility, and collective ownership in organisational processes.

These values, *amanah, adl, ihsan, and shura,* closely align with key theoretical frameworks in human resource management. The Resource-Based View identifies human resources as a source of competitive advantage, while Islamic ethical principles reinforce this perspective by emphasising trust, justice, and collective responsibility in developing employee competencies (Beekun & Badawi, 2005). Similarly, Human Capital Theory highlights the importance of knowledge and skill development, which is also strongly encouraged in Islamic teachings as a contribution to individual and societal well-being (Ali, 2010). Together, these perspectives extend traditional HR theories beyond efficiency to incorporate equity, empathy, and sustainable, value-oriented practices in strategic human resource management.

EMPLOYEE RIGHTS IN AN ISLAMIC FRAMEWORK

Basic Trade Union Rights

Islamic teachings outline a comprehensive set of employee rights, including fair wages, safe working conditions, the protection of human dignity, and safeguards against exploitation. The Prophet Muhammad (peace be upon him) emphasised the importance of timely and fair compensation, stating that a worker should be paid before their sweat dries (Ibn Majah). Employers are therefore encouraged to uphold dignity and fairness in all labour relations, fostering ethical organisational practices that minimise exploitation.

Equality, Non-Discrimination and Gender Inclusion

The Holy Quran emphasises equality and non-discrimination, stating that human dignity is not determined by race, ethnicity, or social status, but by moral character and piety (Qur'an 49:13). In organisational contexts, this principle supports merit-based and equitable human resource practices, where competence and ethical conduct guide decision-making. Gender inclusion is a key dimension of this framework, as Islamic teachings promote justice, respect, and equal access to opportunities, thereby supporting inclusive workplace environments. Practices such as transparent promotion systems, flexible working arrangements, and leadership development opportunities for both men and women contribute to building trust and employee satisfaction (Metcalfe, 2011). Collectively, these principles foster a culture of inclusiveness, fairness, and respect for all employees.

Work-Life Balance

Islam promotes a balanced approach to life that integrates spiritual, personal, and professional responsibilities. Work is regarded as a form of worship when performed ethically and without neglecting family or religious obligations. Such balance supports employee well-being, enhances productivity, and contributes to holistic human development within organisations.

Rights to Professional Development

Islam places strong emphasis on lifelong learning and encourages individuals to continuously seek knowledge as part of personal and professional development. This principle establishes both a right and a responsibility for employees to engage in ongoing skill development. Organisations that invest in professional training and development initiatives contribute to both individual growth and improved organisational performance.

Islamic Management Leadership values

Islamic leadership emphasises moral responsibility, justice, consultation (*shura*), compassion (*rahma)*, and integrity. Leaders are expected to act ethically and engage in participatory decision-making, fostering organisational cultures based on trust, engagement, and sustainability. These values should be reflected in recruitment and performance appraisal systems, with a focus on competence, ethical conduct, continuous improvement (*ihsan*), and trustworthiness (*amanah).*

EMPLOYEE ENGAGEMENT AND MOTIVATION FROM QUR'ANIC TEACHINGS

Pay Systems/compensation Policies/rewards

Compensation and reward systems in organisations extend beyond financial calculations to reflect underlying ethical values and principles. In Islamic thought, compensation is considered a moral responsibility grounded in justice, fairness, and accountability. Employers are therefore encouraged to design reward systems that are equitable and aligned with employees' contributions, ensuring that wages are fair and delivered promptly. Such practices reinforce employee dignity and promote trust, motivation, and organisational commitment.

Equity and transparency are fundamental principles of compensation in Islamic organisational contexts. The concept of justice (*adl*) is emphasised in the Holy Quran as a core ethical principle guiding human interactions (Qur'an 16:90). In practice, organisations can uphold this principle by implementing transparent pay structures, clearly defined promotion criteria, and non-discriminatory compensation policies. Such measures enhance trust between employees and management, reduce perceptions of bias, and ensure that organisational practices align with principles of fairness, accountability, and ethical responsibility.

In addition to financial compensation, non-financial rewards play an important role in enhancing employee motivation and satisfaction. These include recognition, opportunities for career advancement, meaningful work, and a supportive organisational environment. Such intrinsic rewards reflect Islamic values that emphasise human dignity, respect, and professional development. By encouraging cooperation, teamwork, and mutual respect, organisations can foster a sense of collective responsibility and commitment among employees, grounded in the principles of *ihsan* (excellence) and *amanah* (trust).

Islamic compensation philosophy also emphasises social responsibility, recognising employees not only as contributors to organisational performance but also as members of the wider community. Organisations can integrate these values by supporting charitable initiatives, encouraging voluntary contributions, and aligning reward systems with broader social welfare objectives. These practices reflect the Islamic principle of stewardship (*khilafah*) and the responsibility to utilise resources for the benefit of society. Such an approach strengthens organisational commitment, enhances employee motivation, and promotes a sense of shared purpose between individuals and the wider community.

Summing up, the process of the reward systems and the compensation philosophy Snabk presented by Muslims offer an umbrella of approaches that include financial justice, non-financial recognition, transparency, and social responsibility. The modern model of compensation is supported by the pillars of equity, empathy, and human dignity, where performance recognition and the inclusion of social welfare are also other elements of developing an engaged workforce. Through the incorporation of reward practices into contemporary human-resource technologies, organisations would be in a position to alter reward mechanisms into moral and ethical bases that would inspire employees and establish sustainable organisational cultures based on justice and benevolence (Ahmad and Owoyemi, 2021).

CASE STUDY: ISLAMIC BANKING SERVICES IN MALAYSIA

Introduction and Adoption

The Malaysian Islamic banking industry presents a sound platform on which the adoption of faith-based human resource practices in service-oriented companies draws. Large organisations, including Bank Islam Malaysia Berhad (BIMB), have adopted Islamic philosophy in every aspect of HR management; thus, developing unique organisational cultures that meet both the financial goals and social needs requirements (Rahman and Hassan, 2020). Such a combination of *Shariah*-compliant values about HR practices has catapulted such institutions not only to be installed as financial giants but also to be their role models of being ethical actors in the international banking environment.

The promotion of Islamic HR practices in Malaysia has been done in an organized and non-exclusive way. It started with a comprehensive stakeholder consultation, as this would mean that not only the employees but also the customers would understand the logic behind the organisational transformation. Extensive training programmes were then given to HR professionals to make them knowledgeable and skilled in incorporating Islamic principles in recruitment, appraisal and rewards regimes. Leadership commitment became one of the most crucial issues because the image of making Islamic values part of the corporate culture was constantly established by top management. Through explanation of purposes and seamless integration of new ones into the establishment of the current policy frameworks, employees adjusted to the changes without impairing the operational performance (Rahman and Hassan, 2020).

Key Outcomes

These transformations have produced some quantifiable as well as observable results. The reports of organisations like BIMB revealed that faith-based HR practices have increased staff retention by 15 percentage points compared to many traditional banks, and this goes to show that faith-based HR practices serve to promote higher employee commitment and satisfaction. Also, the rates of customer satisfaction were notably elevated, and the surveys revealed an increase that stemmed from providing value-based services preceding the presence of trust, compassion, and moral responsibility towards customers (Ahmad and Owoyemi, 2021). These results also show that the incorporation of Islamic values in HR systems has advantages to internal and external stakeholders.

Best Practices

The experience of the Malaysians managed to generate a number of best-practice models. This advancement was made possible with the creation of intensive ethics-training programmes which added to the increase of technical skills, moral and spiritual growth. Profit-sharing plans designed in conformity with the economic codes of Islam gave the employees financial incentives but nurtured the societal sense of community in the success of the organisation. Besides, the inclusivity and increased respect towards employee welfare were strengthened by the provision of prayer facilities and the possibility to adjust work schedules and allowances so that they could be able to celebrate their religiously associated holidays (Hassan and Ahmad, 2019). These practices enable the conversion of the Islamic values into realistic and practical, employee-oriented steps.

The effects of the Malaysian Islamic banking market prove that faith-based HR strategies can be effective and beneficial to service-oriented business functioning in a competitive market situation. The achievement of such structures as successful as the institutions like the BIMB can highlight the value of commitment by leadership, stringent implementation strategies and permanence of alignment with HR programmes and professional moral and ethical practices. The identified positive outcomes such as a rise in employee satisfaction, employee retention, employee enrichment, and better organisational culture can be used as the testament to the idea of how Islamic HR management can overcome the challenges that the creation of the sustainable and goal-driven based organisations have to work with and, therefore, can be viewed as the viable model in other industries and areas, in which the needs of the business and the demands inherent in the ethical or religious standards needed to be balanced.

INFORMATION: CASE STUDY: UAE HEALTHCARE.

The United Arab Emirates health industry is synonymous with the effective application of Islamic principles with international practices in the provision of health care. Extensive human-resources research involving studies on the entire approach within organisations like the Dubai Health Authority has been designed that serve to support Islamic values and, at the same time, meet the requirements of both international healthcare system regulations and Islamic accreditation requirements.

2018: Framework Development

The equitable focus on flawless religious validity and operational competence within the sphere of medicine was developed as a result of the collaborative partnership between religious scholars, medical specialists, and human-resources professionals, thus complementing the elaborate development of a scientifically supported Islamic health human-resources system.

2019: Pilot Implementation

Its first application involved three large hospitals and primarily sub-areas like recruitment practice, the programme of staff development and patient-care procedures based on Islamic ethics and medical best practice.

2020: Expansion and Refinement

The systematic roll-out featured continuous enhancement to systems throughout the examination, including feedback systems, where medical professionals and patients worked side by side to optimise implementation plans and eliminate new arising complexity.

2021-2026: Initiated Excellence

Ongoing efforts have demonstrated quantifiable positive results in employee contentment, patient outcomes and organisationa2018: Framework Development

The authors wrote the structure in such strictness so that it could meet the demands of sticking to the assent of religion, coupled with the incorporation of bottom-up practicability in the context of medicine. This was done with simultaneous bargaining between the religious scholars, clinicians and human resource experts, in the process offering incessant chances to clarify the holism of an Islamic human-asset well-being framework that is construct-based.

2019: Pilot Implementation

The first implementation involved three major hospitals, though the primary focus was carried at sub-domains like recruitment procedures, professional development programmes, and patient-care procedures in conformity with Islamic ethics and best medical practices supported by evidence.

2020: Expansion and Refinement

Later stages of the implementation included massive improvements to all processes. The clinicians and patients worked together on feedback and attempted to streamline their implementation plans by attempting to reduce the arising complexities.

2021-2026: Initiated Excellence

The accumulated efforts resulted in the achievement of the substantively positive outcomes that may be noted in the context of increased staff satisfaction levels and clinical performance, as well as organisational efficiency. These successes aid in adherence to the international healthcare standards. Performance, not to mention compliance with global healthcare standards.

CASE STUDY: PAKISTANI EDUCATION SERVICES

Transformational Leadership Model.

The most effective Islamic universities in Pakistan have sought new faculty and staff development strategies, which have improved the values of the Islamic leadership and incorporated them into current standards of educational quality. It is important to note that such institutions like the International Islamic University in Islamabad or the Aga Khan University are good examples of holistic solutions (Salleh & Ibrahim, 2021).

The schemes that these universities have formulated do not just feature the teaching patterns but the making of teachers to be sound moral examples, and hence producing the kind of differentiating professionals who are educationally competent and whose sole desire is moral uprightness. This multilateral mindset recognises the various roles that teachers can participate in the lives of the students and also in society.

Impact Dakota Incorporated

In this respect, the above novelties in student-centred educational services have produced tremendous results in organisational performance and sustainability. Retention of faculty has been seen to be over 90Percent, satisfaction rates are invariably in the top quartile as well and the graduates show professional competence together with moral reasoning.

Beyond Borders Hospitality Services of Saudi Arabia CASE Study. Intervention of Strategies of Strategy in Some Cultures.

Hospitality services in Saudi Arabia have largely succeeded in integrating Islamic values and international service quality to provide an experience that underscores identity with a blend of uniformity of cultural aspects with global luxury benchmarks, as well as global service management.

STAFF DEVELOPMENT PROGRAMS

Enhanced education includes agility, hospitality, cultural competency and Islamic ethics that help the members of staff conduct themselves with other international clientele without compromising on authenticity and personal integrity.

High Service Framework

Combining Islamic hospitality values (*karam*) with modern practices of guest-relationship-management creates unique experiences and makes Saudi hospitality stand out among international players in the hospitality industry.

The hypothesis that faith-based human resource practices have no adverse effects on service excellence but, in fact, can positively affect excellence by helping to create competitive configurations based on authentic cultural differences and stronger employee connectivity is supported by empirical evidence.

Empirical Evidence and Metrics

The effectiveness of ethically-based human resource systems in service organizations is gaining favorable support from the available empirical research. Based on the evidence presented in the Malaysian healthcare industry, the HR practices based on values contribute to teamwork, burnout reduction, and increased employee satisfaction (Yahya and Faiz, 2020).

Research in the hospitality industry of the United Arab Emirates has shown that the paradigm of trust-based leadership considerably increases the quality of the services and customer satisfaction (Al-Suwaidi and Barakat, 2021).

These empirical results show that the HR policies that are inspired by Islamic principles do not only have normative value but can also have some empirical links with quantifiable performance changes.

LESSON GRIDS CASE-STUDY LESSONS

Commitment as a Leader

Effective implementations were also based on strong leadership involvement and their obvious modelling of Islamic values. Leaders of organisations that encouraged wholesale change and excellence, which prevailed, were those leaders who practised true excellence in management values.

Stakeholder Engagement

Effective organisations took resources and time to involve every organisational stakeholder, such as employees, customers, suppliers and the general community, to aid learning and assist in the execution of the Islamic HR structure.

Continuous Process Renewal

Successful organisations had a culture of constant improvement, a habit of regularly measuring results, integrating feedback, and streamlining their Islamic HR to maximise efficiency and respond to arising issues.

Integration, Not Addition

The best implementations realised assimilation of Islamic ideals in the prevailing systems instead of introducing unique aspects of Islam. This system's view was holistic and ensured that conflicting or competing systems would not be developed.

STRATEGIC FAITH-BASED HR MODEL: BOTTOM, ABOVE

The concept of human resource management (HRM) is one of the most crucial procedures which conditions the development of organisational culture and performance, especially in service-focused businesses where human capital is one of the primary determining factors. The Strategic Faith-Based HR Model is envisioned as a model which aims to harmonise Islamic ethical principles and values with modern HRM practices in societies where Muslims represent the majority, and Islam embodies a powerful impact. This construct not only identifies the spiritual aspect of the work environment but also deliberates the commercial needs, including competitiveness, productivity, and sustainability, which allows organisations the spillover effect to ensure success in both the moral and commercial realms (Hassan and Ahmad, 2019).

The model is in support of total incorporation and not partial incorporation of Muslim practices. Because of this, the instillation of ethical principles should be wholesale throughout all HR practices-recruitment, training, compensation, appraisal and employee relations, as opposed to piecemeal applications. At this, flexibility is also listed among the core values, as one understands that different domains and cultures require customised applications. This consistency and flexibility allow organisations to maintain Islamic values and to be highly efficient and competitive in the global arena (Rahman and Hassan, 2020).

Plan and Implementation Process

The first part of implementing the Strategic Faith-Based HR Model is assessment and preparation. To determine the suitability of the existing practices using Islamic values and the gaps, organisations should identify gaps by carrying out cultural audits, leadership capability audits, and stakeholder audits. These formulations of diagnoses give a stable change base based on existing realities and organisational robustness (Al-Buraey, 2021).

After assessment, there is the vision and strategy development of entities. A vision which incorporates Islamic ideals: *adl (justice), amanah (trust), and ihsan* (excellence) and corporate goals is developed by the collaborative effort of leaders. Such values are operationalised into strategic plans and broken into actionable roadmaps with milestones, performance measures and the allocation of resources. Organisational alignment requires essential leadership buy-in and talkative consistency (Hassan and Ahmad, 2019).

The next stage entails an organized planning and harmonization of human resources policies, procedures and technological structures so as to integrate Islamic values into the organization. Recruitment procedures are guided by the ethics and right conduct, equitable appraisal systems and transparency developed by the strong reward system. This is achieved through complete integration that goes beyond the departmental separation of HR systems and other activities along with operational areas, contributing to ethical compliance and better efficiency in operations (Rahman and Hassan, 2020).

Change management and implementation needs to be carried out in bits. A facilitated transition can overcome resistance through the deployment of on-the-job training programs, a premeditated strategy of communication, as well as by involving the appropriate stakeholders. Employees require a rational-emotive way of change and hence making modelling and commitment essential factors; otherwise, the lack of either can cause failures in implementation (Al-Buraey, 2021).

Last but not least, sustained sustainability would be ensured by staying current with the models and constantly making them better and better. The business and ethical performance are measured through measurement systems, balanced scorecards. It is also dynamic and receptive to changing conditions, with frequent reviews and a feedback loop to ensure organizations maximize systems that would allow them to deal with emerging challenges (Hassan and Ahmad, 2019).

CONCEPTUAL MODEL EXPLANATION

The conceptual framework was formulated in the current chapter and this explains how the Islamic ethical principles affect the human-resource functions and thus the effect on the organisational performance. Recruitment, training, performance management and employee well-being are based on ethical principles such as, *Amanah and Adl.* Therefore, the effects of such human-resource practices are based on the outcomes such as engagement, trust, and quality service delivery among the employees. With the statement of these interrelations, the chapter proves its point and shows that Islamic ethics can be successfully used as a strategic resource to build efficient and sustainable human-capital systems.

CROSS-CULTURAL AND GLOBALIZATION CHALLENGES

The organisations in the service sector are becoming more and more a part of multicultural settings, which require HR structures that not only practice the straightforward moral principles, but also consider cultural diversity. The moral foundation that can be used to provide ethical decision-making in intercultural contexts is provided by Islamic principles, which are basically based on justice, respect and consultation (Abbasi et al., 2010). However, multinational environments require the consideration of the heterogeneous legal frameworks, employment practices, and labour rights. According to cross-cultural studies, ethical principles need to be aligned with international standards, otherwise conflict will be inevitable, as well as to guarantee equity (Robertson and Fadil, 1999). A cross-cultural approach clarifies how the Islamic HR models can be modified and retain their fundamental ethical commitments.

IMPLEMENTATION AND PRACTICAL CHALLENGES

Nevertheless, faith-based human resource systems face very serious challenges in their application in the real world despite their strengths. Such barriers encompass poor perception among the managers, organisational resistance to change, training inconsistencies and a basic conflict between the profit-oriented goals and ethical obligations (Hashim, 2009). In addition, it is challenging to integrate participatory processes, including meaningful consultation or ethical audits, in many organizations (Hassan, 2016). To overcome these limitations, it is essential to conduct the capacity building systematically, develop strong communication policies and align organisational values with the normal course of HR activities. It is imperative to identify these obstacles to increase the sustainability of ethical HRM models in the long term.

CONCLUSION

Transformative Potential of Islamic HR

The benefits of the Islamic HR organisational structure resonate with the international sustainability actions, especially the United Nations Sustainable Development Goals (SDGs). The Islamic values on equal pay and equitable labour rights are a direct furtherance of SDG 8 (Decent Work and Economic Growth), thus creating inclusive development and alleviating poverty (Ahmad and Owoyemi, 2021).

The first dimension also focuses on longitudinal learning, reflecting SDG 4 (Quality Education), as it suggests investing in constant skill enhancement. This commitment to equal opportunity is in line with SDG 5 (Gender Equality), which positively influences culturally sensitive methods of the workplace. Additionally, accountability in ensuring transparency, proper corporate governance, and consultations appeals to SDG 16 (Peace, Justice, and Strong Institutions) hence improving trust in the stakeholders (Rahman & Hassan, 2020).

Strategic Recommendations and Future Directions

Companies with an ingrained religious HR system exhibit strengths of flexibility and perseverance even in a highly turbulent environment. This makes them prepared to cope with uncertainty coupled with ethical decision-making to mutually consult (*shura*) and to think long-term. The spiritual aspect at the workplace creates intrinsic motivation, which helps to continue commitment in challenging times (Al-Buraey, 2021).

The Islamic assumptions of HR do not oppress or inhibit innovation; on the contrary, it assists in creative thinking based on psychological safety, anticipatory cognition and ceaseless improvement in the principle of *ihrsan*. Evaluative cultures, which are built on responsibility, can be achieved by offering moral grounds on which employees are enabled to be innovative (Hassan and Ahmad, 2019).

The functioning of Islamic ethical principles in the context of the hybrid and remote work-place is a subject of future research, as digital communication channels and dynamic work schedules are altering the traditional HR framework. More academic research is needed to explain the way AI-driven HR solutions can be adjusted to match faith-based principles, especially in the fields of recruitment screening and performance appraisal (Brougham and Haar, 2018). The empirical research that explores the show economy, cross-cultural team processes, and the relative well-being of the Muslim and non-Muslim contexts would make Islamic HRM frameworks more practical (Rana et al., 2021).

Implementation Hurdles and Problems

Although there are inherent strengths of a Strategic Faith-Based HR Model, its practices are challenged by significant challenges when attempting its implementation. When dealing with a diverse workforce with African Muslims and non-Muslims, cultural sensitivity and inclusion should be considered. Islam as an underlying ethic must agree with universal principles such as fairness, dignity, and honesty to be inclusive of everyone and respect all human beings (Rahman and Hassan, 2020).

Another important factor is regulatory compliance. Organisations need to ensure that the practices of HR are aligned with both the domestic and international legislations of labour and international labour standards, and yet utilise the faith-based aspects, which are aware of the religious facets. Law should be applied properly to avoid unintentional bias and maintain fairness (Ahmad and Owoyemi, 2021).

The third challenge is performance measurement. There is usually less focus on moral and spiritual outcomes; powerful appraisal programs are stressed, which will record such variables as employee engagement, ethical behaviour, social efficacy, profitability, and efficiency (Hassan and Ahmad, 2019).

Implementing change management requires that it be recognised as complex. Changing organisational culture requires taking into consideration both the emotional and the structural aspects. Leaders should be facilitative, resource-endowed endowed and developmentally engaged. It should encourage shared change and not top-down mandates, and there should be more understanding (Almeshtig-, Healey, 2014).

Potential Islamic HR Revolution

So much transformational gap is provided by the Strategic Faith-Based HR Model to businesses in the Muslim-majority and Islamically oriented cultures. When the managerial governance integrates the Islamic ethics into the contemporary HR practices, organisations will be in a position to attain a better level of employee performance, ethical behaviour, customer loyalty and sustainability levels over the long term. The results of the empirical research in Malaysia, the UAE, Pakistan, and Saudi Arabia show that these frameworks make them viable as well as render global competitiveness and cultural authenticity (Rahman & Hassan, 2020).

Website Strategy and Vision

The competent growth of HR professionals is a necessity. They should educate practitioners about the existing strategic HRM and relevant Islamic concepts the regulations of control over work. Integrated training programmes make it possible to realise faith-based HR systems which allow designing and implementing such initiatives (Hassan and Ahmad, 2019).

A longitudinal study should take centre stage in elucidating the future role of Islamic HR practice and in coming up with practical elements of measurement. The use of evidence-based models makes the implementation better (Ahmad and Owoyemi, 2021).

There should be increased governmental policy and regulatory enabling in Muslim majority countries. Nationally recommended guidelines, tax concessions, and trail-blazing organisations can be used to promote a wide uptake. Their approach to national competitiveness is through the institutionalisation of values-based HR, which can be supported by enacting policies (Al-Buraey, 2021).

International cooperation is also encouraged, since organisations are able to use success stories in a variety of setups. Knowledge dissemination elevates the completeness of Islamic HR models and enhances compliance with the Islamic compliance and ethical codes, plus the IMF business-ethics toolbox to support the relevance in the universal markets (Rahman and Hassan, 2020).

REFERENCES

Abbasi, A. S., Rehman, K., & Bibi, A. (2010). Islamic leadership model: An accountability perspective. *World Applied Sciences Journal*, *9*(3), 230–238.

Al-Buraey, M. A. (2021). Organizational resilience through Islamic values: Conceptual framework and empirical evidence. *Journal of Islamic Business and Management*, *11*(2), 134–156.

Ali, A. J. (2010). *Islamic perspectives on management and organization*. Edward Elgar Publishing., DOI: 10.4337/9781849805506

Anderson, N., Potočnik, K., & Zhou, J. (2019). Innovation and creativity in organizations: A state-of-the-science review. *Journal of Management*, *40*(5), 1297–1333. DOI: 10.1177/0149206314527128

Bakker, A. B., & Demerouti, E. (2020). Job demands–resources theory: Taking stock and looking forward. *Journal of Occupational Health Psychology*, *25*(6), 1–15. DOI: 10.1037/ocp0000179 PMID: 27732008

Becker, G. S. (1993). *Human capital: A theoretical and empirical analysis* (3rd ed.). University of Chicago Press. DOI: 10.7208/chicago/9780226041223.001.0001

Beekun, R. I., & Badawi, J. A. (2005). *Leadership: An Islamic perspective*. Amana Publications.

Brougham, D., & Haar, J. (2018). Smart technology, artificial intelligence, robotics, and algorithms in the workplace: HRM implications. *International Journal of Human Resource Management*, *29*(5), 1053–1078. DOI: 10.1080/09585192.2016.1277576

Cappelli, P., & Tavis, A. (2021). The performance management revolution. *Harvard Business Review*, *99*(3), 58–67. https://hbr.org/2021/03/the-performance-management-revolution

Hashim, J. (2009). Islamic revival in human resource management practices among selected Islamic organisations in Malaysia. *International Journal of Islamic and Middle Eastern Finance and Management*, *2*(3), 251–267. DOI: 10.1108/17538390910986362

Hassan, A. (2016). Islamic ethical practices and corporate performance: Challenges in implementation. *Journal of Islamic Management Studies*, *4*(1), 55–72.

Hassan, A., & Ahmad, F. (2019). Leadership effectiveness in Islamic organizations: An empirical study. *International Journal of Management Studies*, *26*(2), 67–84.

Jackson, S. E., Renwick, D. W. S., Jabbour, C. J. C., & Muller-Camen, M. (2019). State-of-the-art and future directions for green human resource management. *German Journal of Human Resource Management, 25*(2), 99–116. DOI: 10.1177/2397002219831001

Metcalfe, B. D. (2011). Women, empowerment and development in Arab Gulf states: A critical appraisal. *Gender in Management, 26*(3), 189–205. DOI: 10.1108/17542411111130988

Rahman, A. A., & Hassan, M. K. (2020). Faith-based human resource practices in Islamic banking: Evidence from Malaysia. *International Journal of Islamic and Middle Eastern Finance and Management, 13*(4), 655–673. DOI: 10.1108/IMEFM-01-2019-0008

Robertson, C. J., & Fadil, P. A. (1999). Ethical decision making in multinational organizations: A comparison of global values. *Journal of Business Ethics, 19*(4), 385–392. DOI: 10.1023/A:1005742016867

Salleh, M. J., & Ibrahim, N. A. (2021). Educational leadership through Islamic principles: Pakistani university case studies. *Educational Management International, 15*(4), 112–128.

Sen, A. (1999). *Development as freedom*. Alfred A. Knopf.

Vial, G. (2021). Understanding digital transformation: A review and research agenda. *The Journal of Strategic Information Systems, 28*(2), 118–144. DOI: 10.1016/j.jsis.2019.01.003

Wright, T. A., & Cropanzano, R. (1998). Psychological well-being and job satisfaction as predictors of job performance. *Journal of Occupational Health Psychology, 5*(1), 84–94. DOI: 10.1037/1076-8998.5.1.84 PMID: 10658888

Yahya, K. K., & Faiz, W. M. (2020). Value-driven HR practices and employee outcomes in Malaysian healthcare organisations. *Asia Pacific Journal of Human Resources, 58*(4), 565–583. DOI: 10.1111/1744-7941.12245

Zeithaml, V. A., Bitner, M. J., & Gremler, D. D. (2020). *Services marketing: Integrating customer focus across the firm* (8th ed.). McGraw-Hill Education.

Compilation of References

Abbasi, A. S., Rehman, K., & Bibi, A. (2010). Islamic leadership model: An accountability perspective. *World Applied Sciences Journal*, *9*(3), 230–238.

Abdullah, Z., Ahsan, N., & Alam, S. S. (2013). The effect of human capital and knowledge management on organizational performance. *Proceedings of the International Conference on Social Science Research.*

Abraham, R. (2000). The Role of Job Control as a Moderator of Emotional Dissonance and Emotional Intelligence–Outcome Relationships. *The Journal of Psychology*, *134*(2), 169–184. DOI: 10.1080/00223980009600860 PMID: 10766109

Abraham, R. (2004). Emotional Competence as Antecedent to Performance: A Contingency Framework. *Genetic, Social, and General Psychology Monographs*, *130*(2), 117–145. DOI: 10.3200/MONO.130.2.117-145 PMID: 15605972

Adams-Prassl, A., Freedman, J., & Adams-Prassl, J. (2018). Rethinking legal taxonomies for the gig economy. *Oxford Review of Economic Policy*, *34*(3), 475–494. DOI: 10.1093/oxrep/gry006

Adeleye, I. (2011). Theorising human resource management in Africa: Beyond cultural relativism. *African Journal of Business Management*, *5*(6), 2028–2029.

Aguenza, B. B., & Som, A. P. M. (2018). Motivational factors of employee retention and engagement in organizations. *International Journal of Advances in Management and Economics*, *1*(6), 88–95.

Akwei, C., & Nwachukwu, C. (2023). An exploration of contextual factors affecting the nexus of competitive strategy and human resource management practices in Nigeria's emerging economy context. *International Journal of Human Resource Management*, *34*(16), 3079–3122. DOI: 10.1080/09585192.2022.2104128

Al Helou, E. (2024). Egypt's currency crisis threatens Red Sea projects. *Economy Middle East*. https://economymiddleeast.com/news/egypt-currency-red-sea/

Al Jazeera Staff. (2023). Mourning and worrying about the future in rural Egypt. *Al Jazeera*. https://www.aljazeera.com/features/2023/12/14/mourning-and-worrying-about-the-future-in-rural-egypt

Al Mamun, C. A., & Nazmul, H. M. (2017). Factors affecting employee turnover and sound retention strategies in business organization: A conceptual view. *Problems and Perspectives in Management*, *15*(1), 63–71.

Al-Buraey, M. A. (2021). Organizational resilience through Islamic values: Conceptual framework and empirical evidence. *Journal of Islamic Business and Management, 11*(2), 134–156.

Alhmoud, A., & Rjoub, H. (2019). Total rewards and employee retention in a Middle Eastern context. *SAGE Open*, *9*(2). DOI: 10.1177/2158244019840118

Ali, A. J. (2010). *Islamic perspectives on management and organization*. Edward Elgar Publishing., DOI: 10.4337/9781849805506

Aljarboa, B. E., An, E. P., Dator, W. L., Alshammari, S. A., Mostoles, R., Uy, M. M., Alrashidi, N., Alreshidi, M. S., Mina, E., & Gonzales, A. (2022). Resilience and Emotional Intelligence of Staff Nurses during the COVID-19 Pandemic. *Health Care*, *10*(11), 2120. DOI: 10.3390/healthcare10112120 PMID: 36360460

Alshemmari, J. M. H. J., & Al Monawer, F. H. (2024). Analyzing the relationship between workplace diversity and innovation and its influence on organizational performance. *Journal of System and Management Sciences*, *14*(1), 471–489. https://doi.org/10.33168/JSMS.2024.0127

Amirkhanyan, H., Krawczyk, M. W., & Wilamowski, M. (2021). Gender inequality and national gender gaps in overconfidence. *PLoS One*, *16*(4), e0249459. https://doi.org/10.1371/journal.pone.0249459

Ananthi, P., Ramya, T. E., & Janani, R. (2023, June). Ensemble based intrusion detection system for IoT device. In *2023 International Conference on Sustainable Computing and Smart Systems (ICSCSS)* (pp. 1073-1078). IEEE. DOI: 10.1109/ICSCSS57650.2023.10169426

Anderson, N., Potočnik, K., & Zhou, J. (2019). Innovation and creativity in organizations: A state-of-the-science review. *Journal of Management*, *40*(5), 1297–1333. DOI: 10.1177/0149206314527128

Andrews, J., & Higson, H. (2008). Graduate Employability, “Soft Skills” versus “Hard” Business Knowledge: A European Study. *Higher Education in Europe*, *33*(4), 411–422. DOI: 10.1080/03797720802522627

Arnett, J. J. (2002). The psychology of globalization. American psychologist, 57(10). *The American Psychologist, 57*(10), 774–783. DOI: 10.1037/0003-066X.57.10.774 PMID: 12369500

Arslan, A., Kamara, S., Golgeci, I., & Tarba, S. Y. (2022). Civil society organisations' management dynamics and social value creation in the post-conflict volatile contexts pre and during COVID-19. *The International Journal of Organizational Analysis, 30*(7), 20–33. DOI: 10.1108/IJOA-01-2021-2573

Asfahani, A. M., Alsobahi, G., & Dahlan, D. A. (2023). Navigating the Saudi Gig Economy: The Role of Human Resource Practices in Enhancing Job Satisfaction and Career Sustainability. *Sustainability (Basel), 15*(23), 16406. DOI: 10.3390/su152316406

Ashkanasy, N. M., & Daus, C. S. (2002). Emotion in the workplace: The new challenge for managers. *The Academy of Management Perspectives, 16*(1), 76–86. DOI: 10.5465/ame.2002.6640191

Atiku, S. O., Omisore, B. O., & Akinyemi, A. I. (2024). Leadership commitment and employee engagement in diversity and inclusion initiatives. *International Journal of Organizational Leadership, 13*(1), 45–60.

Bach, S. A., & Milman, A. (1996). A novel technique for reviewing a hospitality management curriculum. *Hospitality & Tourism Educator, 8*(1), 37–40. DOI: 10.1080/23298758.1996.10685709

Bailenson, J. N. (2021). Nonverbal overload: A theoretical argument for the causes of Zoom fatigue. *Technology, Mind, and Behavior, 2*(1), 1–6. DOI: 10.1037/tmb0000030

Baker, S., Bloom, N., & Davis, S. (2016). Measuring economic policy uncertainty. *The Quarterly Journal of Economics, 131*(4), 1593–1636. DOI: 10.1093/qje/qjw024

Bakker, A. B., & Demerouti, E. (2017). Job demands–resources theory: Taking stock and looking forward. *Journal of Occupational Health Psychology, 22*(3), 273–285. DOI: 10.1037/ocp0000056 PMID: 27732008

Bakker, A. B., Tims, M., & Derks, D. (2012). Proactive personality and job performance: The role of job crafting and work engagement. *Human Relations, 65*(10), 1359–1378. DOI: 10.1177/0018726712453471

Bandura, A. (1991). Social cognitive theory of self-regulation. *Organizational Behavior and Human Decision Processes, 50*(2), 248–287. DOI: 10.1016/0749-5978(91)90022-L

Bardoel, E. A., Pettit, T. M., De Cieri, H., & McMillan, L. (2014). Employee resilience: An emerging challenge for HRM. *Asia Pacific Journal of Human Resources, 52*(3), 279–297. DOI: 10.1111/1744-7941.12033

Barling, J., Slater, F., & Kelloway, E. K. (2000). Transformational leadership and emotional intelligence: An exploratory study. *Leadership and Organization Development Journal, 21*(3), 157–161. DOI: 10.1108/01437730010325040

Barney, J. (1991). Firm resources and sustained competitive advantage. *Journal of Management, 17*(1), 99–120. DOI: 10.1177/014920639101700108

Barney, J. B., & Wright, P. M. (1998). On becoming a strategic partner: The role of human resources in gaining competitive advantage. *Human Resource Management, 37*(1), 31–46. DOI: 10.1002/(SICI)1099-050X(199821)37:1<31::AID-HRM4>3.0.CO;2-W

Bar-On, R. (1997). The emotional quotient inventory (EQ-i) A test of emotional intelligence. Toronto Multi-Health Systems. - References - Scientific Research Publishing. Www.scirp.org. https://www.scirp.org/reference/referencespapers?referenceid=768114

Bar-On, R. (1997). *The Bar-On Emotional Quotient Inventory (EQ-i): Technical manual.* Multi-Health Systems.

Barroso Castro, C. M., Martín Armario, E., & Martín Ruiz, D. (2004). The influence of employee organizational citizenship behavior on customer loyalty. *International Journal of Service Industry Management, 15*(1), 27–53. DOI: 10.1108/09564230410523321

Batool, T., Sehar, S., Qasim, A. P., Afzal, M., & Gilani, S. A. (2018). The influence of supportive nursing leadership for retention of staff nurses in private hospital of Lahore. *Annals of Punjab Medical College*, *12*(4), 272–275.

Baum, T., Mooney, S. K., Robinson, R. N., & Solnet, D. (2020). COVID-19's impact on the hospitality workforce–new crisis or amplification of the norm? *International Journal of Contemporary Hospitality Management, 32*(9), 2813–2829. DOI: 10.1108/IJCHM-04-2020-0314

Becker, G. S. (1993). *Human capital: A theoretical and empirical analysis* (3rd ed.). University of Chicago Press. DOI: 10.7208/chicago/9780226041223.001.0001

Beekun, R. I., & Badawi, J. A. (2005). *Leadership: An Islamic perspective*. Amana Publications.

Bello, B. G., Tula, S. T., Omotoye, G. B., Kess-Momoh, A. J., & Daraojimba, A. I.Binaebi Gloria BelloSunday Tubokirifuruar TulaGaniyu Bolawale OmotoyeAzeez Jason Kess-MomohAndrew Ifesinachi Daraojimba. (2024). Work-life balance and its impact in modern organizations: An HR review. *World Journal of Advanced Research and Reviews, 21*(1), 1162–1173. DOI: 10.30574/wjarr.2024.21.1.0106

Bellou, V. (2009). Profiling the desirable psychological contract for different groups of employees: Evidence from Greece. *International Journal of Human Resource Management, 20*(4), 810–830. DOI: 10.1080/09585190902770711

Bennell, P., & Akyeampong, K. (2007). *Teacher motivation in Sub-Saharan Africa and South Asia. Educational Papers, 71*. Department for International Development.

Blau, P. M. (1964). Exchange and power in social life. *Trans-Action.*

Bondanini, G., Giorgi, G., Ariza-Montes, A., Vega-Muñoz, A., & Andreucci-Annunziata, P. (2020). Technostress Dark Side of Technology in the Workplace: A Scientometric Analysis [Review of Technostress Dark Side of Technology in the Workplace: A Scientometric Analysis]. International Journal of Environmental Research and Public Health, 17(21), 8013. Multidisciplinary Digital Publishing Institute. DOI: 10.3390/ijerph17218013

Bowen, D. E., & Ostroff, C. (2004). Understanding HRM–firm performance linkages: The role of the 'strength' of the HRM system. *Academy of Management Review, 29*(2), 203–221. DOI: 10.5465/amr.2004.12736076

Boyatzis, R. E., Smith, M. L., & Blaize, N. (2006). Developing sustainable leaders through coaching and compassion. *Academy of Management Learning & Education, 5*(1), 8–24. DOI: 10.5465/amle.2006.20388381

Brackett, M. A., & Rivers, S. E. (2014). Transforming students' lives with social and emotional learning. *Journal of Psychology in Africa, 24*(2), 101–104. DOI: 10.1080/14330237.2014.903072

Branicki, L., Steyer, V., & Sullivan-Taylor, B. (2019). Why resilience managers aren't resilient, and what human resource management can do about it. *International Journal of Human Resource Management, 30*(8), 1261–1286. DOI: 10.1080/09585192.2016.1244104

Brauchli, R., Jenny, G. J., Füllemann, D., & Bauer, G. F. (2015). Towards a Job Demands-Resources Health Model: Empirical Testing with Generalizable Indicators of Job Demands, Job Resources, and Comprehensive Health Outcomes. *BioMed Research International, 1*, 1–12. Advance online publication. DOI: 10.1155/2015/959621 PMID: 26557718

Breashy, A. E. (2016). *Total compensation vs. total rewards: The difference.* LinkedIn. Retrieved October 26, 2016, from https://www.linkedin.com/pulse/total-compensation-vs-rewards-difference-ali-el-breashy-assoc-cipd

Breevaart, K., Bakker, A. B., Hetland, J., Demerouti, E., Olsen, O. K., & Espevik, R. (2014). Daily transactional and transformational leadership and daily employee engagement. *Journal of Occupational and Organizational Psychology*, *87*(1), 138–157. DOI: 10.1111/joop.12041

Briner, R. B. (2000). Relationships between Work Environments, Psychological Environments and Psychological Well-being [Review of Relationships between Work Environments, Psychological Environments and Psychological Well-being]. Occupational Medicine, 50(5), 299. Oxford University Press. DOI: 10.1093/occmed/50.5.299

Britt, T. W., Shen, W., Sinclair, R. R., Grossman, M. R., & Klieger, D. M. (2016). How much do we really know about employee resilience? *Industrial and Organizational Psychology: Perspectives on Science and Practice*, *9*(2), 378–404. DOI: 10.1017/iop.2015.107

Brodkin, E. Z. (2011). Policy work: Street-level organizations under new managerialism. *Journal of Public Administration: Research and Theory*, *21*(2, Supplement 2), 253–277. DOI: 10.1093/jopart/muq093

Brogaard, J., & Detzel, A. (2015). The asset-pricing implications of government economic policy uncertainty. *Management Science*, *61*(1), 3–18. DOI: 10.1287/mnsc.2014.2044

Brotheridge, C. M., & Grandey, A. A. (2002). Emotional labor and burnout: Comparing two perspectives of "people work.". *Journal of Vocational Behavior*, *60*(1), 17–39. DOI: 10.1006/jvbe.2001.1815

Brougham, D., & Haar, J. (2018). Smart technology, artificial intelligence, robotics, and algorithms in the workplace: HRM implications. *International Journal of Human Resource Management*, *29*(5), 1053–1078. DOI: 10.1080/09585192.2016.1277576

Brunetto, Y., Xerri, M., & Farr-Wharton, B. (2022). Doing better with less: Do behavioural capabilities affect street-level bureaucrats' ability to deliver public value? *Public Management Review*, *26*(5), 1136–1155. DOI: 10.1080/14719037.2022.2133159

Bühlmann, F., & Tettamanti, M. (2007). Le statut de l'approche qualitative dans des projets de recherche interdisciplinaires. *Recherches Qualitatives*, *3*, 191–213.

Burton, S. L. (2012, April 2). How We Attain and Sustain Work-life Balance? All Days. DOI: 10.2118/152830-MS

Cadmus, E. (2006). Succession planning: Multilevel organizational strategies for the new workforce. *The Journal of Nursing Administration*, *36*(6), 298–303. DOI: 10.1097/00005110-200606000-00004 PMID: 16766908

Cameron, L. (2024). The Making of the "Good Bad" Job: How Algorithmic Management Manufactures Consent Through Constant and Confined Choices. *Administrative Science Quarterly*, *69*(2), 458–514. DOI: 10.1177/00018392241236163

Cappelli, P., & Tavis, A. (2021). The performance management revolution. *Harvard Business Review*, *99*(3), 58–67. https://hbr.org/2021/03/the-performance-management-revolution

Carmeli, A. (2003). The relationship between emotional intelligence and work attitudes, behavior and outcomes: An examination among senior managers. *Journal of Managerial Psychology*, *18*(8), 788–813. DOI: 10.1108/02683940310511881

Carminati, L. (2021). Emotions, Emotion Management and Emotional Intelligence in the Workplace: Healthcare Professionals' Experience in Emotionally-Charged Situations. *Frontiers in Sociology*, *6*, 640384. Advance online publication. DOI: 10.3389/fsoc.2021.640384 PMID: 33889607

Carver, C. S., & Scheier, M. F. (2016). *Perspectives on personality* (8th ed.). Pearson.

Chamorro-Premuzic, T., Akhtar, R., & DAnnunzio, P. (2019). The Future of Work AI in Recruitment and Selection. Psychology Today. - References - Scientific Research Publishing. (2019). Scirp.org. https://www.scirp.org/reference/referencespapers?referenceid=3928131

Chang, S., Gong, Y., Way, S. A., & Jia, L. (2013). Flexibility-oriented HRM systems, absorptive capacity, and market responsiveness and firm innovativeness. *Journal of Management*, *39*(7), 1924–1951. DOI: 10.1177/0149206312466145

Chartered Institute of Personnel and Development. (2017). *Strategic human resource management* (CIPD Factsheet). CIPD. https://www.cipd.co.uk/knowledge/strategy/hr/strategic-hrm-factsheet#6744

Chathoth, P., Altinay, L., Harrington, R. J., Okumus, F., & Chan, E. S. (2016). Co-production versus co-creation: A process based continuum in the hotel service context. *International Journal of Hospitality Management*, *32*, 11–20. DOI: 10.1016/j.ijhm.2012.03.009

Chaudhry, S., & Sharma, D. (2017). Workforce diversity and employee performance: A study of organizational effectiveness. *International Journal of Human Resource Studies*, *7*(3), 45–58.

Chavan, V., Cenaj, A., Shen, S., Bar, A., Binwani, S., Del Becaro, T., Funk, M., Greschner, L., Hung, R., Klein, S., Kleiner, R., Krause, S., Olbrych, S., Parmar, V., Sarafraz, J., Soroko, D., Don, D. W., Zhou, C., Vu, H. T. D., & Fresquet, X. (2025). Feeling Machines: Ethics, Culture, and the Rise of Emotional AI. DOI: 10.48550/ARXIV.2506.12437

Chen, Y., Huang, Z.-L., & Chu, H.-C. (2024). Relationships between emotional labor, job burnout, and emotional intelligence: an analysis combining meta-analysis and structural equation modeling [Review of Relationships between emotional labor, job burnout, and emotional intelligence: an analysis combining meta-analysis and structural equation modeling]. BMC Psychology, 12(1). BioMed Central. DOI: 10.1186/s40359-024-02167-w

Chen, H., Chen, R., Bernard, S., & Rahman, I. (2019). US hotel industry revenue: An ARDL bounds testing approach. *International Journal of Contemporary Hospitality Management*, *31*(4), 1720–1743. DOI: 10.1108/IJCHM-01-2018-0031

Cherniss, C., & Goleman, D. (Eds.). (2001). *The emotionally intelligent workplace: How to select for, measure, and improve emotional intelligence in individuals, groups, and organizations*. Jossey-Bass.

Choudhary, V., & Shireshi, S. S. (2022). Analysing the Gig Economy in India and Exploring Various Effective Regulatory Methods to Improve the Plight of the Workers. *Journal of Asian and African Studies*, *57*(7), 1343–1356. DOI: 10.1177/00219096221082581

Cieslik, K., Banya, R., & Vira, B. (2021). Offline contexts of online jobs: Platform drivers, decent work, and informality in Lagos, Nigeria. *Development Policy Review*, *40*(4), e12595. Advance online publication. DOI: 10.1111/dpr.12595

Cihan, M. Ö., & Dılekmen, M. (2024). Emotional intelligence training for pre-service primary school teachers: A mixed methods research. *Frontiers in Psychology*, *15*, 1326082. Advance online publication. DOI: 10.3389/fpsyg.2024.1326082 PMID: 38979067

Codier, E., Codier, D. D., & Marszalek, J. (2019). Emotional intelligence, nursing practice, and patient outcomes: A systematic review. *Nursing Outlook*, *67*(2), 142–151. DOI: 10.1016/j.outlook.2018.08.005

Codier, E., Freel, M., Kamikawa, C., & Morrison, P. (2019). Emotional intelligence and patient outcomes: A systematic review and critique of the literature. *The Journal of Nursing Administration*, *49*(2), 89–94. DOI: 10.1097/NNA.0000000000000713

Coffie, R. B., Odikro, D., & Turkson, J. K. (2022). A thematic approach to succession planning, leadership continuity, and organizational growth: Spotlight on chief executive officers in Ghanaian industry. *African Journal of Applied Research*, *8*(2), 83–100. DOI: 10.26437/ajar.31.10.2022.06

Collings, D., & Mellahi, K. (2009). Strategic talent management: A review and research agenda. *Human Resource Management Review*, *19*(4), 304–313. DOI: 10.1016/j.hrmr.2009.04.001

Collins, C. J. (2021). Expanding the resource-based view model of strategic human resource management. *International Journal of Human Resource Management*, *32*(2), 331–358. DOI: 10.1080/09585192.2019.1711442

Combs, J., Liu, Y., Hall, A., & Ketchen, D. (2006). How much do high-performance work practices matter? A meta-analysis of their effects on organizational performance. *Personnel Psychology*, *59*(3), 501–528. DOI: 10.1111/j.1744-6570.2006.00045.x

Cooke, F. L., Cooper, B., Bartram, T., Wang, J., & Mei, H. (2019). Mapping the relationships between high-performance work systems, employee resilience and engagement: A study of the banking industry in China. *International Journal of Human Resource Management*, *30*(8), 1239–1260. DOI: 10.1080/09585192.2015.1137618

Cooke, F. L., Xiao, Q., & Xiao, M. (2021). Extending the frontier of research on (strategic) human resource management in China: A review of David Lepak and colleagues' influence and future research direction. *International Journal of Human Resource Management*, *32*(1), 183–224. DOI: 10.1080/09585192.2020.1803949

Cooper, C. L., Liu, Y., & Tarba, S. Y. (2014). Resilience, HRM practices and impact on organizational performance and employee well-being. *International Journal of Human Resource Management*, *25*(17), 2466–2471. DOI: 10.1080/09585192.2014.926688

Coronado-Maldonado, I., & Benítez-Márquez, M. D. (2023). Emotional intelligence, leadership, and work teams: A hybrid literature review [Review of Emotional intelligence, leadership, and work teams: A hybrid literature review]. Heliyon, 9(10). Elsevier BV. DOI: 10.1016/j.heliyon.2023.e20356

Côté, S., & Miners, C. T. H. (2006). Emotional intelligence, cognitive intelligence, and job performance. *Administrative Science Quarterly*, *51*(1), 1–28. DOI: 10.2189/asqu.51.1.1

Coutu, D. L. (2002). How resilience works. *Harvard Business Review*, *80*(5), 46–56.

Covella, G., McCarthy, V., Kaifi, B., & Cocoran, D. (2017). Leadership's role in employee retention. *Business Management Dynamics*, *7*(5), 1–15.

Cram, W. A., Wiener, M., Tarafdar, M., & Benlian, A. (2022). Examining the Impact of Algorithmic Control on Uber Drivers' Technostress. *Journal of Management Information Systems*, *39*(2), 426–453. DOI: 10.1080/07421222.2022.2063556

CUPA-HR. (2023, September). *The CUPA-HR 2023 Higher Education Employee Retention Survey*. Retrieved from https://www.cupahr.org/resource/higher-ed-employee-retention-survey-findings-september-2023/

Deci, E. L., & Ryan, R. M. (2000). The "what" and "why" of goal pursuits: Human needs and the self-determination of behavior. *Psychological Inquiry*, *11*(4), 227–268. DOI: 10.1207/S15327965PLI1104_01

Dedema, M., & Rosenbaum, H. (2024). Socio-technical issues in the platform-mediated gig economy: A systematic literature review: An Annual Review of Information Science and Technology (ARIST) paper. *Journal of the Association for Information Science and Technology*, *75*(3), 344–374. DOI: 10.1002/asi.24868

Delery, J. E., & Doty, D. H. (1996). Modes of theorizing in strategic human resource management: Tests of universalistic, contingency, and configurational performance predictions. *Academy of Management Journal*, *39*(4), 802–835. DOI: 10.2307/256713

Delery, J. E., & Roumpi, D. (2017). Strategic human resource management, human capital and competitive advantage: Is the field going in circles? *Human Resource Management Journal*, *27*(1), 1–21. DOI: 10.1111/1748-8583.12137

Delery, J., & Gupta, N. (2016). Human resource management practices and organizational effectiveness: Internal fit matters. *Journal of Organizational Effectiveness: People and Performance*, *3*(2), 139–163. DOI: 10.1108/JOEPP-03-2016-0028

Dello Russo, S., Mascia, D., & Morandi, F. (2018). Individual perceptions of HR practices, HRM strength and appropriateness of care: A meso, multilevel approach. *International Journal of Human Resource Management*, *29*(2), 286–310. DOI: 10.1080/09585192.2016.1165276

Deloitte. (2023, August 1). *Cultivating employee engagement in financial services*. Retrieved from https://www.deloitte.com/us/en/insights/industry/financial-services/improve-employee-engagement.html

Devaux, P. (2023). *Egypt: Buying time*. BNP Paribas Economic Research. https://economic-research.bnpparibas.com/html/en-US/Egypt-Buyingtime-4/14/2023,48481

Dhiman, S. (2017). Emotional & Multiple Intelligences: 10 Different Ways of Being Smart. In Palgrave Macmillan US eBooks (p. 97). Palgrave Macmillan. DOI: 10.1057/978-1-137-55571-7_5

Dibben, P., Brewster, C., Brookes, M., Cunha, R., Webster, E., & Wood, G. (2017). Institutional legacies and HRM: Similarities and differences in HRM practices in Portugal and Mozambique. *International Journal of Human Resource Management*, *28*(18), 2519–2537. DOI: 10.1080/09585192.2016.1164225

DiMaggio, P. J., & Powell, W. W. (1991). The iron cage revisited: Institutional isomorphism and collective rationality in organizational fields. In Powell, W. W., & DiMaggio, P. J. (Eds.), *The new institutionalism in organizational analysis* (pp. 195–200). University of Chicago Press.

Dixon, S. A. (2016). *Retention of information technology employees* (Publication No. 10246165) [Doctoral dissertation, University of Phoenix]. ProQuest Dissertations and Theses Global.

Dugovicova, J. (2019). *Impact of employee motivation on employee retention rates* (Publication No. 13812916) [Doctoral dissertation, Webster University]. ProQuest Dissertations and Theses Global.

Dweck, C. S. (2006). *Mindset: The new psychology of success*. Random House.

Dwivedi, D. (2025). Emotional Intelligence and Artificial Intelligence Integration Strategies for Leadership Excellence. *Advances in Research*, *26*(1), 84–94. DOI: 10.9734/air/2025/v26i11235

Earle, H. A. (2003). Building a workplace of choice: Using the work environment to attract and retain top talent. *Journal of Facilities Management*, *2*(3), 244–257. DOI: 10.1108/14725960310807944

Edmondson, A. (1999). Psychological safety and learning behavior in work teams. *Administrative Science Quarterly*, *44*(2), 350–383. DOI: 10.2307/2666999

Eisenhardt, K. M. (1989). Building theories from case study research. *Academy of Management Review*, *14*(4), 532–550. DOI: 10.5465/amr.1989.4308385

Ellickson, M., & Logsdon, K. (2002). Determinants of job satisfaction of municipal government employees. *Public Personnel Management*, *31*(3), 343–358. DOI: 10.1177/009102600203100307

Ennis, G. (2011). Emotional intelligence and occupational stress: Examining relationships in a professional context. *The International Journal of Organizational Analysis*, *19*(4), 390–405. DOI: 10.1108/19348831111173431

Ererdi, C., Nurgabdeshov, A., Kozhakhmet, S., Rofcanin, Y., & Demirbag, M. (2022). International HRM in the context of uncertainty and crisis: A systematic review of literature (2000–2018). *International Journal of Human Resource Management, 33*(12), 2503–2540. DOI: 10.1080/09585192.2020.1863247

Español, M. (2023, June). Egypt remittances plunge amid economic uncertainty. *Al-Monitor*. https://www.al-monitor.com/originals/2023/06/egypt-remittances-plunge-amid-economic-uncertainty

Farooq, O., Jabbouri, I., & Naili, M. (2024). The nexus between economic policy uncertainty and access to finance: A study of developing countries. *International Journal of Managerial Finance, 20*(1), 222–246. DOI: 10.1108/IJMF-11-2022-0507

Farr-Wharton, B., Brunetto, Y., Wankhade, P., Saccon, C., & Xerri, M. (2021). Comparing the impact of authentic leadership on Italian and UK police officers' discretionary power, well-being and commitment. *Policing, 44*(5), 741–755. DOI: 10.1108/PIJPSM-09-2020-0156

Félix, B., Dourado, D., & Nossa, V. (2023). Algorithmic management, preferences for autonomy/security and gig-workers' wellbeing: A matter of fit? *Frontiers in Psychology, 14*, 1088183. Advance online publication. DOI: 10.3389/fpsyg.2023.1088183 PMID: 36910791

Feng, X., Lo, Y. L., & Chan, K. C. (2019). Impact of economic policy uncertainty on cash holdings: Firm-level evidence from an emerging market. *Asia-Pacific Journal of Accounting & Economics, 29*(2), 1–23. DOI: 10.1080/16081625.2019.1694954

Feng, Y. (2001). Political freedom, political instability, and policy uncertainty: A study of political institutions and private investment in developing countries. *International Studies Quarterly, 45*(2), 271–294. DOI: 10.1111/0020-8833.00191

Fernandez, C. S. P. (2007). Emotional Intelligence in the Workplace. *Journal of Public Health Management and Practice, 13*(1), 80–82. DOI: 10.1097/00124784-200701000-00013 PMID: 17149104

Ferrary, M. (2015). Investing in transferable strategic human capital through alliances in the luxury hotel industry. *Journal of Knowledge Management, 19*(5), 1006–1023. DOI: 10.1108/JKM-01-2015-0045

Ferreira, P., & Gomes, S. (2023). Work–Life Balance and Work from Home Experience: Perceived Organizational Support and Resilience of European Workers during COVID-19. *Administrative Sciences, 13*(6), 153. DOI: 10.3390/admsci13060153

Financial Health Network. (n.d.). PayPal case study. https://finhealthnetwork.org/employer-finhealth-toolkit/identify-solutions/paypal-case-study/

Fisher, S. L., & Cassady, E. A. (2019). Use of Relational eHRM Tools in Gig Worker Platforms. In *Advanced series in management* (p. 81). Emerald Publishing Limited. DOI: 10.1108/S1877-636120190000023007

Fitriani, N., & Sudiarditha, I. K. R. (2024). Uncovering Research Clusters in Job Satisfaction and Organizational Commitment: A VOSviewer Approach. *International Journal of Research and Review*, *11*(6), 536–545. DOI: 10.52403/ijrr.20240659

Fletcher, L., Alfes, K., & Robinson, D. (2018). The relationship between perceived training and development and employee retention: The mediating role of work attitudes. *The International Journal of Human Resource Management*, *29*(18), 2701–2728. DOI: 10.1080/09585192.2016.1262888

Fletcher, I., Leadbetter, P., Curran, A., & O'Sullivan, H. (2007). Emotional intelligence and patient-centred care. *Medical Education*, *41*(3), 213–214.

Flynn, A. (2022, November 14). Floating the pound: Currency devaluation in Egypt. *The American University in Cairo*. https://www.aucegypt.edu/news/floating-pound-currencydevaluation-egypt

Folkman, S., & Moskowitz, J. T. (2000). Positive affect and the other side of coping. *The American Psychologist*, *55*(6), 647–654. DOI: 10.1037/0003-066X.55.6.647 PMID: 10892207

Forbes. (2025, March 17). *Employee Burnout: The Hidden Threat Costing Companies Millions*. Retrieved from https://www.forbes.com/sites/julianhayesii/2025/03/17/employee-burnout-the-hidden-threat-costing-companies-millions/

Fragkaki, M., Kavga, A., Kelesi-Stavropoulou, M., & Fasoi, G. (2024). Emotional Intelligence of Primary Health Care Nurses: A Longitudinal Randomized Clinical Trial. *The Open Public Health Journal*, *17*(1), e18749445329730. Advance online publication. DOI: 10.2174/0118749445329730240729162817

Frankl, V. E. (2017). *Man's search for meaning*. Beacon Press.

Frasier, N. (2019). Preparing nurse managers for authentic leadership: A pilot leadership development program. *The Journal of Nursing Administration*, *49*(2), 79–85. DOI: 10.1097/NNA.0000000000000714 PMID: 30664579

Frenzel, A. C. (2014). Teacher emotions. In Linnenbrink-Garcia, E. A., & Pekrun, R. (Eds.), *International handbook of emotions in education* (pp. 494–519). Routledge.

Fulmer, R. M., & Conger, J. A. (2004). Developing Leaders With 2020 Vision. *Financial Executive*, *20*(5).

Gabriel, K. P., & Aguinis, H. (2021). How to prevent and combat employee burnout and create healthier workplaces during crises and beyond. *Business Horizons*, *65*(2), 183–192. DOI: 10.1016/j.bushor.2021.02.037

Gallardo, E. S.-C.-G., Sánchez-Cañizares, S.-M., López-Guzmán, T., & Margarida Nascimento Jesus, M. (2010). Employee satisfaction in the Iberian hotel industry: The case of Andalusia (Spain) and the Algarve (Portugal). *International Journal of Contemporary Hospitality Management*, *22*(3), 321–334. DOI: 10.1108/09596111011035936

Gallup (2019). Global emotions report 2019. Gallup. https://www.gallup.com/analytics/248909/gallup-global-emotions-report.aspx

Gallup. (2025, January 13). *U.S. Employee Engagement Sinks to 10-Year Low*. Retrieved from https://www.gallup.com/workplace/654911/employee-engagement-sinks-year-low.aspx

Gallup. (n.d.). *How to Improve Employee Engagement in the Workplace*. Retrieved from https://www.gallup.com/workplace/285674/improve-employee-engagement-workplace.aspx

Gannon, J. M., Roper, A., & Doherty, L. (2015). Strategic human resource management: Insights from the international hotel industry. *International Journal of Hospitality Management*, *47*, 65–75. DOI: 10.1016/j.ijhm.2015.03.003

Garcia, M. B., Revano, T. F., & Contreras, G. S. (2019). Microlearning as a learning tool for hospitality training. *Journal of Human Resources in Hospitality & Tourism*, *18*(4), 516–533.

Garcia, R., & Lee, C. (2022). Beyond automation: The role of emotional intelligence in the digitalized hospitality sector. *Journal of Hospitality and Tourism Technology*, *13*(1), 45–62.

George, C. (2015). Retaining professional workers: What makes them stay? *Employee Relations*, *37*(1), 102–121. DOI: 10.1108/ER-07-2014-0073

Ghlichlee, B., & Goodarzi, A. (2023). Strategic human resource practices and new product development performance: The mediating role of intellectual capital. *Journal of Intellectual Capital*, *24*(3), 730–756. DOI: 10.1108/JIC-11-2020-0360

Ghoneim, E. (2023). [Article in Arabic]. *Veto Gate*. https://www.vetogate.com/4818653

Gioia, D. A., & Chittipeddi, K. (2017). Sensemaking and sensegiving in strategic change initiation. *Strategic Management Journal*, *12*(6), 433–448. DOI: 10.1002/smj.4250120604

Gioia, D. A., Corley, K. G., & Hamilton, A. L. (2013). Seeking qualitative rigor in inductive research: Notes on the Gioia methodology. *Organizational Research Methods, 16*(1), 15–31. DOI: 10.1177/1094428112452151

Gittell, J. H., Cameron, K., Lim, S., & Rivas, V. (2006). Relationships, layoffs, and organizational resilience: Airline industry responses to September 11. *The Journal of Applied Behavioral Science, 42*(3), 300–329. DOI: 10.1177/0021886306286466

Glaser, B. G., & Strauss, A. L. (1967). *The discovery of grounded theory: Strategies for qualitative research.* Sociology Press.

Gok, G. O., & Gok, M. S. (2016). Emerging economies: Comparative analysis of MIST and IBSA. *Eurasian Journal of Soil Science, 4*(2), 1–13. DOI: 10.15604/ejss.2016.04.02.001

Goleman, D., Boyatzis, R., & McKee, A. (2013). Primal leadership: Unleashing the power of emotional intelligence (10th anniversary ed.). Harvard Business Review Press.

Goleman, D. (1995). *Emotional intelligence.* Bantam Books.

Goleman, D. (1995). *Emotional intelligence: Why it can matter more than IQ.* Bantam Books.

Gölgeci, I., Arslan, A., Dikova, D., & Gligor, D. M. (2020). Resilient agility in volatile economies: Institutional and organizational antecedents. *Journal of Organizational Change Management, 33*(1), 100–113. DOI: 10.1108/JOCM-02-2019-0033

Gómez, M. S., Sadovyy, M., & Bresó, E. (2021). Health-Care Professionals Amid the COVID-19 Pandemic: How Emotional Intelligence May Enhance Work Performance Traversing the Mediating Role of Work Engagement. *Journal of Clinical Medicine, 10*(18), 4077. DOI: 10.3390/jcm10184077 PMID: 34575186

Gouldner, A. W. (1960). The norm of reciprocity: A preliminary statement. *American Sociological Review, 25*(2), 161–178. DOI: 10.2307/2092623

Graham, M., Hjorth, I., & Lehdonvirta, V. (2017). Digital labour and development: Impacts of global digital labour platforms and the gig economy on worker livelihoods. *Transfer: European Review of Labour and Research, 23*(2), 135–162. DOI: 10.1177/1024258916687250 PMID: 28781494

Grandey, A. A. (2000). Emotion regulation in the workplace: A new way to conceptualize emotional labor. *Journal of Occupational Health Psychology, 5*(1), 95–110. DOI: 10.1037/1076-8998.5.1.95 PMID: 10658889

Grandey, A. A., Diefendorff, J. M., & Rupp, D. E. (2013). *Emotional labor in the 21st century*. Routledge. DOI: 10.4324/9780203100851

Grandey, A. A., & Melloy, R. C. (2017). The state of the heart: Emotional labor as emotion regulation reviewed and revised. *Journal of Occupational Health Psychology*, *22*(3), 407–422. DOI: 10.1037/ocp0000067 PMID: 28150996

Gross, J. J. (2015). Emotion regulation: Current status and future prospects. *Psychological Inquiry*, *26*(1), 1–26. DOI: 10.1080/1047840X.2014.940781

Groves, K. S. (2007). Integrating leadership development and succession planning best practices. *Journal of Management Development*, *26*(3), 239–260. DOI: 10.1108/02621710710732146

Guest, G., Bunce, A., & Johnson, L. (2006). How many interviews are enough? An experiment with data saturation and variability. *Field Methods*, *18*(1), 59–82. DOI: 10.1177/1525822X05279903

Gunkel, M. (2016). *Cultural values, emotional intelligence, and conflict handling styles*. ScienceDirect. Retrieved from https://www.sciencedirect.com/science/article/pii/S1090951616300074

Guo, Y., Chen, X., & Zhang, L. (2023). Leadership commitment and inclusive workplace culture: Implications for diversity management. *Journal of Organizational Behavior*, *44*(2), 210–225.

Gupta, S. (2020).. . *Gendered Gigs.*, *1*, 1–10. Advance online publication. DOI: 10.1145/3392561.3394635

Gursoy, D., & Chi, C. G. (2020). Effects of COVID-19 pandemic on hospitality industry: A review of the current situations and a research agenda. *Journal of Hospitality Marketing & Management*, *29*(5), 527–529. DOI: 10.1080/19368623.2020.1788231

Gursoy, D., Chi, O. H., Lu, L., & Nunkoo, R. (2019). Consumers' acceptance of artificially intelligent (AI) device use in service delivery. *International Journal of Information Management*, *49*, 157–169. DOI: 10.1016/j.ijinfomgt.2019.03.008

Haddock-Millar, J., Sanyal, C., & Müller-Camen, M. (2016). Green human resource management: A comparative qualitative case study of a United States multinational corporation. *International Journal of Human Resource Management*, *27*(2), 192–211. DOI: 10.1080/09585192.2015.1052087

Hagen, B., Zucchella, A., & Ghauri, P. N. (2018). From fragile to agile: Marketing as a key driver of entrepreneurial internationalization. *International Marketing Review*, *36*(2), 260–288. DOI: 10.1108/IMR-01-2018-0023

Haider, M., Aamir, A., Hamid, A. B. A., & Akhtar, C. S. (2016). Work-life balance, job satisfaction and nurses retention: Moderating role of work volition. *International Journal of Business Excellence*, *10*(4), 488–501. DOI: 10.1504/IJBEX.2016.078730

Haider, M., Rasli, A., Akhtar, C. S., Yusoff, R. B. M., Malik, O. M., Aamir, A., & Tariq, F. (2015). The impact of human resource practices on employee retention in the telecom sector. *International Journal of Economics and Financial Issues*, *5*(1S), 63–69.

Hanaysha, J. (2016). Testing the effects of employee engagement, work environment, and organizational learning on organizational commitment. *Procedia-Social and Behavioral Sciences*, *229*, 289–297. DOI: 10.1016/j.sbspro.2016.07.139

Haque, A., & Khan, S. I. (2023). Promoting meaningfulness in work for higher job satisfaction: Will intent to quit make trouble for business managers? *Journal of Organizational Effectiveness: People and Performance*, *10*(3), 455–476. DOI: 10.1108/JOEPP-02-2022-0020

Hashim, J. (2009). Islamic revival in human resource management practices among selected Islamic organisations in Malaysia. *International Journal of Islamic and Middle Eastern Finance and Management*, *2*(3), 251–267. DOI: 10.1108/17538390910986362

Hassan, A. (2016). Islamic ethical practices and corporate performance: Challenges in implementation. *Journal of Islamic Management Studies*, *4*(1), 55–72.

Hassan, A., & Ahmad, F. (2019). Leadership effectiveness in Islamic organizations: An empirical study. *International Journal of Management Studies*, *26*(2), 67–84.

Health Education England. (2017). Framework 15: Developing the healthcare workforce. https://www.hee.nhs.uk

Heeks, R. (2017). Decent Work and the Digital Gig Economy: A Developing Country Perspective on Employment Impacts and Standards in Online Outsourcing, Crowdwork, Etc. SSRN Electronic Journal. https://doi.org/DOI: 10.2139/ssrn.3431033

Hermann, E., Puntoni, S., & Morewedge, C. K. (2025). GenAI and the psychology of work [Review of GenAI and the psychology of work]. Trends in Cognitive Sciences. Elsevier BV. DOI: 10.1016/j.tics.2025.04.009

Hersing, W. S. (2017). Managing cognitive bias in safety decision making: Application of emotional intelligence competencies. *The Journal of Space Safety Engineering*, *4*(3-4), 124–128. DOI: 10.1016/j.jsse.2017.10.001

Higher Ed Today. (2024, May 13). *Creating and Sustaining Wellness Cultures for Faculty, Staff, and Students*. Retrieved from https://www.higheredtoday.org/2024/05/13/wellness-cultures-for-student-success/

Hochschild, A. R. (1983). *The managed heart: Commercialization of human feeling*. University of California Press.

Hoffman, B. (2018, November 16). *The importance of employee retention–The key to a successful business*. HR Technologist. Retrieved from https://www.hrtechnologist.com/articles/employee-engagement/the-importance-of-employee-retention-the-key-to-a-successful-business/

Hoffmann, E. A. (2007). Open-Ended Interviews, Power, and Emotional Labor. *Journal of Contemporary Ethnography*, *36*(3), 318–346. DOI: 10.1177/0891241606293134

Hofstede, G. (1980). Culture and Organizations. *International Studies of Management & Organization*, *10*(4), 15–41. DOI: 10.1080/00208825.1980.11656300

Hofstede, G., Hofstede, G. J., & Minkov, M. (2010). *Cultures and organizations: Software of the mind* (3rd ed.). McGraw-Hill.

Hoque, K. (2013). *Human resource management in the hotel industry: Strategy, innovation and performance*. Routledge., DOI: 10.4324/9780203020869

Hospitality Insights by EHL. (2024, February 15). *Employee engagement: The method behind hospitality success*. Retrieved from https://hospitalityinsights.ehl.edu/employee-engagement-method-hospitality-success

House, R. J. (2004) Culture, Leadership, and Organizations The Globe Study of 62 Societies. Sage, Thousand Oaks. - References - Scientific Research Publishing. Www.scirp.org. https://www.scirp.org/reference/ReferencesPapers?ReferenceID=2010743

Howie, L. (2007). The terrorism threat and managing workplaces. *Disaster Prevention and Management*, *16*(1), 70–78. DOI: 10.1108/09653560710729820

Hsieh, J., Adisa, O., Bafna, S., & Zhu, H. (2023). Designing Individualized Policy and Technology Interventions to Improve Gig Work Conditions. In *Proceedings of the 2nd Annual Meeting of the Symposium on Human-Computer Interaction for Work (CHIWORK '23). Association for Computing Machinery, New York, NY, USA*, Article 12, 1–9. Advance online publication. DOI: 10.1145/3596671.3598576

Hsieh, J., Karger, M., Zagal, L., & Zhu, H. (2023). Co-Designing Alternatives for the Future of Gig Worker Well-Being. In *Proceedings of the 2nd Annual Meeting of the Symposium on Human-Computer Interaction for Work (CHIWORK '23). Association for Computing Machinery, New York, NY, USA*, 664–687. Advance online publication. DOI: 10.1145/3563657.3595982

Huang, N., Burtch, G., Hong, Y., & Pavlou, P. A. (2020). Unemployment and Worker Participation in the Gig Economy: Evidence from an Online Labor Market. *Information Systems Research, 31*(2), 431–448. DOI: 10.1287/isre.2019.0896

HubEngage. (n.d.). *Hospitality Employee Engagement Case Studies*. Retrieved from https://www.hubengage.com/hospitality-employee-engagement/

Hülsheger, U. R., & Schewe, A. F. (2011). On the costs and benefits of emotional labor: A meta-analysis of three decades of research. *Journal of Occupational Health Psychology, 16*(3), 361–389. DOI: 10.1037/a0022876 PMID: 21728441

Hwang, J. (2024a). The GIG economy and its effects on the labor market. *International Journal of Science and Research Archive, 13*(1), 3394–3404. DOI: 10.30574/ijsra.2024.13.1.1231

Hwang, J. (2024b). The GIG economy and its implications for labor laws and worker protections. *International Journal of Science and Research Archive, 13*(1), 3405–3416. DOI: 10.30574/ijsra.2024.13.1.1714

Iliceto, P., & Fino, E. (2017). The Italian version of the Wong-Law Emotional Intelligence Scale (WLEIS-I): A second-order factor analysis. *Personality and Individual Differences, 116*, 274–280. DOI: 10.1016/j.paid.2017.05.006

Imteyaz, K., Flores-Saviaga, C., & Savage, S. (2024). GigSense: An LLM-Infused Tool forWorkers' Collective Intelligence. arXiv (Cornell University). https://doi.org//arxiv.2405.02528DOI: 10.48550

Inegbedion, H., Sunday, E., Asaleye, A., Lawal, A., & Adebanji, A. (2020). Managing diversity for organizational efficiency. *SAGE Open, 10*(1), 1–10. DOI: 10.1177/2158244019900173

Ingale, A. (2024). Succession Planning And Leadership Development Are Important In Creating A Talent Pipeline Within Human Resource Management. Available at *SSRN* 5031223.

Instant. (2024, September 3). *Actionable Insights from the 2024 Wages & Wellbeing Study*. Retrieved from https://www.instant.co/insights-from-the-2024-wages-wellbeing-study/

International Labour Organization. (2021). *A literature review of diversity and inclusion in the workplace*. ILO.

Ishii, S., & Horikawa, E. (2019). The Emotional Intelligence of Japanese Mental Health Nurses. *Frontiers in Psychology*, *10*, 2004. Advance online publication. DOI: 10.3389/fpsyg.2019.02004 PMID: 31543853

Ivanov, S., & Webster, C. (2019). Conceptual framework of the use of robots, artificial intelligence and service automation in travel, tourism, and hospitality companies. In S. Ivanov & C. Webster (Eds.), *Robots, Artificial Intelligence, and Service Automation in Travel, Tourism and Hospitality*. Emerald Publishing Limited. DOI: 10.1108/978-1-78756-687-320191001

Ivanov, S., Gretzel, U., Berezina, K., Sigala, M., & Webster, C. (2023). Progress on robotics in hospitality and tourism: A review of the literature. *Journal of Hospitality and Tourism Technology*, *14*(2), 145–183.

Ivanov, S., Webster, C., & Stoilova, E. (2020). The impact of automation and AI on the hospitality workforce. In *Robots, artificial intelligence, and service automation in travel, tourism and hospitality*. Emerald Publishing Limited.

Jackson, S. E., Renwick, D. W. S., Jabbour, C. J. C., & Muller-Camen, M. (2019). State-of-the-art and future directions for green human resource management. *German Journal of Human Resource Management*, *25*(2), 99–116. DOI: 10.1177/2397002219831001

Jackson, S. E., & Schuler, R. S. (1995). Understanding human resource management in the context of organizations and their environment. *Annual Review of Psychology*, *46*(1), 237–264. DOI: 10.1146/annurev.ps.46.020195.001321

Jackson, S. E., Schuler, R. S., & Jiang, K. (2014). An aspirational framework for strategic human resource management. *The Academy of Management Annals*, *8*(1), 1–56. DOI: 10.5465/19416520.2014.872335

Jakhete, M., Shende, P., Patil, P. A., Rana, V. S., & Raina, A. (2025). Synthesizing best practice frameworks for results measurement in multi-stakeholder social entrepreneurship initiatives. *Enterprise Development & Microfinance*, *35*(1), 140–158.

Jalil, N. I. A., Tan, S. A., Ibharim, N. S., Musa, A. Z., Ang, S. H., & Mangundjaya, W. L. (2023). The Relationship between Job Insecurity and Psychological Well-Being among Malaysian Precarious Workers: Work–Life Balance as a Mediator. *International Journal of Environmental Research and Public Health*, *20*(3), 2758. DOI: 10.3390/ijerph20032758 PMID: 36768122

Jangid, A. (2024). AI and employee wellbeing: how artificial intelligence can monitor and improve mental health in the workplace. *International Journal of Advanced Research, 12*(10), 743–764. DOI: 10.21474/IJAR01/19693

Jennings, P. A., & Greenberg, M. T. (2009). The prosocial classroom: Teacher social and emotional competence in relation to student and classroom outcomes. *Review of Educational Research, 79*(1), 491–525. DOI: 10.3102/0034654308325693

Jeong, J., Kim, B., & Lee, J. (2024). Navigating AI transitions: How coaching leadership buffers against job stress and protects employee physical health. *Frontiers in Public Health, 12*, 1343932. Advance online publication. DOI: 10.3389/fpubh.2024.1343932 PMID: 38601504

Jiang, K., Lepak, D. P., Hu, J., & Baer, J. C. (2012). How does human resource management influence organizational outcomes? A meta-analytic investigation of mediating mechanisms. *Academy of Management Journal, 55*(6), 1264–1294. DOI: 10.5465/amj.2011.0088

Jiang, K., & Messersmith, J. (2018). On the shoulders of giants: A meta-review of strategic human resource management. *International Journal of Human Resource Management, 29*(1), 6–33. DOI: 10.1080/09585192.2017.1384930

Jibunoh, J., Ezichi, O., Okpanachi, V., Amaechi, C., Awosan, W., Tchoumo, P., & Sanusi, J. (2025). Impact of Remote Work Dynamics on Mental Health and Productivity. *Open Journal of Depression, 14*(1), 13–27. DOI: 10.4236/ojd.2025.141002

Johnson, H.-A. M. (2004). The Story Behind Service With A Smile: The Effects of Emotional Labor on Job Satisfaction, Emotional Exhaustion, and Affective Well-Being. http://usf.sobek.ufl.edu/content/SF/S0/02/49/82/00001/E14-SFE0000287.pdf

Joseph, D. L., & Newman, D. A. (2010). Emotional intelligence: An Integrative Meta-Analysis and Cascading Model. *The Journal of Applied Psychology, 95*(1), 54–78. DOI: 10.1037/a0017286 PMID: 20085406

Joshi, A., Jain, S., & Gupta, P. K. (2024). Challenges and impact of the gig economy. *Deleted Journal, 2*(2), 96. DOI: 10.62617/se.v2i2.96

Joubert, P., Madau, D., & Grobler, B. (2017). Employee retention and talent management at a sugar mill in South Africa. *Problems and Perspectives in Management*, *15*(3), 306–315. DOI: 10.21511/ppm.15(3).2017.06

Jwu, S. C., Zaiton, H., Abdullah, S. M., & Kasa, M. E. (2018). The relationship between employee attitude towards training and employee retention in telecommunication. *Journal of Cognitive Sciences and Human Development*, *4*(1), 1–14. DOI: 10.33736/jcshd.852.2018

Kabalina, V., Zelenova, O., & Reshetnikova, K. (2019). Contemporary human resource management practices in Russia: Flexibility under uncertainty. *International Studies of Management & Organization*, *49*(4), 422–440. DOI: 10.1080/00208825.2019.1646490

Kadiresan, V., Kamil, N. M., Mazlan, M. R. M., Musah, M. B., & Selamat, M. H. (2016). The influence of human resource practices on employee retention: A case study. *International Journal of Human Resources Studies*, *6*(3), 122–148. DOI: 10.5296/ijhrs.v6i3.10112

Kahn, W. A. (1990). Psychological conditions of personal engagement and disengagement at work. *Academy of Management Journal*, *33*(4), 692–724. DOI: 10.2307/256287

Kandampully, J., Zhang, T., & Bilgihan, A. (2018). Customer loyalty: A review and future directions with a special focus on the hospitality industry. *International Journal of Contemporary Hospitality Management*, *30*(4), 2194–2214.

Kandampully, J., Zhang, T., & Bilgihan, A. (2021). Emotional intelligence: The essential ingredient for success in the hospitality industry. *Journal of Hospitality and Tourism Insights*, *4*(4), 400–416.

Karatepe, O. M., & Olugbade, O. A. (2016). The mediating role of work engagement in the relationship between high-performance work practices and job outcomes of employees in Nigeria. *International Journal of Contemporary Hospitality Management*, *28*(10), 2350–2371. DOI: 10.1108/IJCHM-03-2015-0145

Karim, J., & Weisz, R. (2021). Emotional intelligence as a moderator of stressor–strain relationships: A study of managers in a developing country. *Journal of Managerial Psychology*, *36*(3), 234–247.

Katiyatiya, L. M., & Lubisi, N. (2024). The current social protection discourse, gig economy within the advent of COVID-19: Some emerging legal arguments. *Labor History*, *1*. Advance online publication. DOI: 10.1080/0023656X.2024.2340610

Katou, A. A. (2013). The link between HR practices, psychological contract fulfilment, and organisational performance in Greece: An economic crisis perspective. *Journal of Industrial Engineering and Management*, *6*(2), 568–594. DOI: 10.3926/jiem.501

Kattaa, M., & Byrne, M. (2018). Quality of work for Syrian refugees in Jordan. *Forced Migration Review*, *58*, 45. https://doaj.org/article/602d90f04a9d4023852fa574b024522d

Kernbach, S., & Schutte, N. S. (2005). The impact of service provider emotional intelligence on customer satisfaction. *Journal of Services Marketing, 19*(7), 438–444. DOI: 10.1108/08876040510625945

Khandelwal, A., & Shekhawat, N. (2018). Role of talent retention in reducing employee turnover. *Journal of Modern Management & Entrepreneurship (JMME)*, *8*(1), 1–5.

Khan, R. B. F. (2022). Mediation Role of Work Flexibility on the Linking of Work Family Conflict and Job Satisfaction. *Jurnal Bisnis Dan Manajemen, 9*(1), 87–93. DOI: 10.26905/jbm.v9i1.7627

Kim, B., & Kim, M. (2024). How artificial intelligence-induced job insecurity shapes knowledge dynamics: The mitigating role of artificial intelligence self-efficacy. *Journal of Innovation & Knowledge, 9*(4), 100590. DOI: 10.1016/j.jik.2024.100590

Kim, B., Kim, M.-J., & Lee, J. (2025). The dark side of artificial intelligence adoption: Linking artificial intelligence adoption to employee depression via psychological safety and ethical leadership. *Humanities & Social Sciences Communications, 12*(1), 704. Advance online publication. DOI: 10.1057/s41599-025-05040-2

Kim, H. J., Oh, H., & Lee, S. (2019). The effect of emotional intelligence on service performance and customer satisfaction in the hospitality industry. *International Journal of Hospitality Management, 78*, 93–102. DOI: 10.1016/j.ijhm.2018.10.009

Kim, J. (2016). Private tutoring and emotional labor in South Korea. *Asia Pacific Journal of Education, 36*(4), 552–568.

Kim, M., Kim, J., & Wong, A. K. F. (2021). The impact of artificial intelligence and emotional intelligence on customer satisfaction in the hotel industry. *Journal of Hospitality Marketing & Management, 30*(6), 677–702.

Kim, S., & Wright, P. M. (2011). Putting strategic human resource management in context: A contextualized model of high commitment work systems and its implications in China. *Management and Organization Review, 7*(1), 153–174. DOI: 10.1111/j.1740-8784.2010.00185.x

Kim, T., Yoo, J. J. E., & Lee, G. (2012). Emotional intelligence and emotional labor acting strategies among frontline hotel employees. *International Journal of Contemporary Hospitality Management, 24*(7), 1029–1046. DOI: 10.1108/09596111211258900

King, D. D., Newman, A., & Luthans, F. (2016). Not if, but when we need resilience in the workplace. *Journal of Organizational Behavior, 37*(5), 782–786. DOI: 10.1002/job.2063

King, K. A. (2017). The talent climate: Creating an organisational context supportive of sustainable talent development through implementation of a strong talent system. *Journal of Organizational Effectiveness: People and Performance*, *4*(4), 298–314. DOI: 10.1108/JOEPP-03-2017-0023

Kinman, G., & Wray, S. (2018). Presenteeism in academic employees: Examining the role of work-related stressors. *Higher Education Research & Development*, *37*(3), 518–531.

Klusmann, U., Richter, D., & Lüdtke, O. (2016). Teachers' emotional exhaustion is negatively related to students' achievement: Evidence from a large-scale assessment study. *Journal of Educational Psychology*, *108*(8), 1193–1203. DOI: 10.1037/edu0000125

Korantwi-Barimah, J. S. (2017). Factors influencing the retention of academic staff in a Ghanaian technical university. *Human Resource Management Research*, *7*(3), 111–119. DOI: 10.5923/j.hrmr.20170703.01

Kosasih, F. G., Yohana, C., & Handaru, A. W. (2024). Job Satisfaction and Organizational Commitments: A Meta-Analysis. *EARTH SCIENCES AND HUMAN CONSTRUCTIONS*, *4*, 43–50. DOI: 10.37394/232024.2024.4.5

Kotsou, I., Mikolajczak, M., Heeren, A., Grégoire, J., & Leys, C. (2019). Improving emotional intelligence: A systematic review of existing work and future challenges. *Emotion Review*, *11*(2), 151–165. DOI: 10.1177/1754073917735902

Kotsou, I., Nelis, D., Grégoire, J., & Mikolajczak, M. (2019). Emotional plasticity: Conditions and effects of improving emotional competence in adulthood. *The Journal of Applied Psychology*, *104*(8), 1027–1045. DOI: 10.1037/apl0000391 PMID: 21443316

Koubova, V., & Buchko, A. A. (2013). Life-work balance. *Management Research Review*, *36*(7), 700–719. DOI: 10.1108/MRR-05-2012-0115

Koutsimpogiorgos, N., van Slageren, J., Herrmann, A., & Frenken, K. (2020). Conceptualizing the Gig Economy and Its Regulatory Problems. *Policy and Internet*, *12*(4), 525–545. DOI: 10.1002/poi3.237

Koutsioumpa, E. (2023). Contribution of Emotional Intelligence to Efficient Leadership. A Narrative Review [Review of Contribution of Emotional Intelligence to Efficient Leadership. A Narrative Review]. *Technium Social Sciences Journal*, *48*, 204–216. DOI: 10.47577/tssj.v48i1.9529

Krasnik, M. S., Verma, R., & Andersson, T. D. (2021). Employee well-being and burnout in the hospitality industry: A systematic review. *International Journal of Hospitality Management, 94*, 102824.

Kumar, D. (2024). The Impact of Remote Work on Employee Engagement and Productivity. *International Journal for Multidisciplinary Research, 6*(6), 34103. Advance online publication. DOI: 10.36948/ijfmr.2024.v06i06.34103

Kumari, N. (2005). *Factors influencing the retention of employees in the IT services industry in Bengaluru* [Doctoral dissertation, University of Jharkhand]. Retrieved from https://www.iujharkhand.edu.in/Nancy-Kumari-Thesis.pdf

Kundu, S. C., & Lata, K. (2017). Effects of supportive work environment on employee retention: Mediating role of organizational engagement. *International Journal of Organizational Analysis*, *25*(4), 703–722. DOI: 10.1108/IJOA-07-2016-1049

Kuntz, J. R., Näswall, K., & Malinen, S. (2016). Resilient employees in resilient organizations: Flourishing beyond adversity. *Industrial and Organizational Psychology: Perspectives on Science and Practice, 9*(2), 456–462. DOI: 10.1017/iop.2016.39

Kuo, T.-S., Chu, L., Shih, C., Li, Y., & Kao, P.-L. (2025). Emotional labor, job satisfaction, and retention among home care workers in Taiwan: A comprehensive analysis. *Frontiers in Psychology, 16*, 1545955. Advance online publication. DOI: 10.3389/fpsyg.2025.1545955 PMID: 40231001

Kur, E., & Bunning, R. (2002). Assuring corporate leadership for the future. *Journal of Management Development, 21*(10), 761–779. DOI: 10.1108/02621710210448039

Kwong, C., Demirbag, M., Wood, G., & Cooke, F. L. (2021). Human resource management in the context of high uncertainties. *International Journal of Human Resource Management, 32*(17), 3569–3599. DOI: 10.1080/09585192.2021.1966203

Lado, A. A., & Wilson, M. C. (1994). Human resource systems and sustained competitive advantage: A competency-based perspective. *Academy of Management Review, 19*(4), 699–727. DOI: 10.2307/258742

Lakshman, C., Wang, L., Adhikari, A., & Cheng, G. (2022). Flexibility-oriented HRM practices and innovation: Evidence from China and India. *International Journal of Human Resource Management, 33*(12), 2473–2502. DOI: 10.1080/09585192.2020.1861057

Lakshmi, M. V. (2024). A study on strategic succession planning ensuring a pipeline of future leaders in workfreaks corporate services pvt ltd. *International Scientific Journal of Engineering and Management, 03*(05), 1–9. DOI: 10.55041/ISJEM01790

Larivière, B., Bowen, D. A., Andreassen, T. W., Kunz, W., Sirianni, N. J., Voss, C., Wünderlich, N. V., & De Keyser, A. (2017). Service Encounter 2.0: An investigation into the roles of technology, employees and customers. *Journal of Business Research, 79*, 238–246. DOI: 10.1016/j.jbusres.2017.03.008

Larsson, A. S., Martin, R., & Edwards, M. R. (2022). Insider econometrics meets people analytics and strategic human resource management. *International Journal of Human Resource Management, 33*(12), 2373–2419. DOI: 10.1080/09585192.2020.1847166

Lee, L. C. (2019). *Strategies for increasing healthcare employees' retention* (Publication No. 27544502) [Doctoral dissertation, Walden University]. ProQuest Dissertations and Theses Global.

Lee, H. J. (2017). How emotional intelligence relates to job satisfaction and burnout in public service jobs. *International Review of Administrative Sciences, 84*(4), 729–745. DOI: 10.1177/0020852316670489

Lee, J. H., Mustapha, A., & Hwang, J. (2019). Enhancing ethnic restaurant visits and reducing risk perception: The effect of information and protection motivation. *Journal of Hospitality and Tourism Insights, 2*(4), 341–357. DOI: 10.1108/JHTI-10-2018-0068

Lei, K. Y., Basit, A., & Hassan, Z. (2018). The impact of talent management on job satisfaction: A study among the employees of a travel agency in Malaysia. *Indonesian Journal of Applied Business and Economic Research*, *1*(1), 1–19.

Leithwood, K., Sun, J., & Pollock, K. (2020). *How school leaders contribute to student success: The four paths framework.* Springer.

Lei, X., & Kaplan, S. A. (2023). The real-time and carry-over effects of injustice on performance and service quality in a ridesharing driver scenario. *Current Psychology (New Brunswick, N.J.), 42*(36), 32157–32178. DOI: 10.1007/s12144-022-04215-3 PMID: 36684460

Lepak, D. P., & Shaw, J. D. (2008). Strategic HRM in North America: Looking to the future. *International Journal of Human Resource Management, 19*(8), 1486–1499. DOI: 10.1080/09585190802200272

Leslie, B., Anderson, C., Horman, J., King, J., & Overly, A. (2016). Generation Z perceptions of a positive workplace environment. *Employee Responsibilities and Rights Journal*, *33*(1), 1–17. DOI: 10.1007/s10672-015-9275-4

Leuhery, F. (2024). Leadership and diversity inclusion practices in modern organizations. *Journal of Human Resource and Sustainability Studies, 12*(1), 55–70.

Levinson, W., Roter, D. L., Mullooly, J. P., Dull, V. T., & Frankel, R. M. (1997). Physician–patient communication: The relationship with malpractice claims among primary care physicians and surgeons. *Journal of the American Medical Association, 277*(7), 553–559. DOI: 10.1001/jama.1997.03540310051034 PMID: 9032162

Lievens, F., & Sackett, P. R. (2012). The validity of interpersonal skills assessment via situational judgment tests for predicting job performance in healthcare settings. *The Journal of Applied Psychology, 97*(2), 360–372. DOI: 10.1037/a0025741 PMID: 21842974

Li, J., Bonn, M. A., & Ye, B. H. (2021). The effect of emotional intelligence on turnover intention in the hospitality industry: The mediating role of job satisfaction. *International Journal of Contemporary Hospitality Management, 33*(4), 1259–1278.

Lipsky, M. (1980). *Street-level bureaucracy: Dilemmas of the individual in public services*. Russell Sage Foundation.

Liu, B. T. (2008). Public service motivation and job satisfaction in chaina: An investigation of generalisability and instrumentality. *International Journal of Manpower, 29*(8). Advance online publication. DOI: 10.1108/01437720810919297

Li, X., Qin, X., Jiang, K., Zhang, S., & Gao, F. Y. (2015). Human resource practices and firm performance in China: The moderating roles of regional human capital quality and firm innovation strategy. *Management and Organization Review, 11*(2), 237–261. DOI: 10.1017/mor.2015.12

London, M., & Smither, J. W. (2002). Feedback orientation, feedback culture, and the longitudinal performance management process. *Human Resource Management Review, 12*(1), 81–100. DOI: 10.1016/S1053-4822(01)00043-2

Lopes, P. N., Salovey, P., Côté, S., Beers, M., & Petty, R. E. (2006). Emotion regulation abilities and the quality of social interaction. *Emotion (Washington, D.C.), 6*(1), 113–118. DOI: 10.1037/1528-3542.5.1.113 PMID: 15755224

Lozie, D. R., Omasa, R., Hesami, S., Zaman, S. M. H., Kajbaf, M., & Malik, A. (2024). Examining the impact of generative artificial intelligence on work dynamics. *Human Resources Management and Services, 6*(2), 3420. DOI: 10.18282/hrms.v6i2.3420

Lubis, A. Y., Tjahjono, H. K., & Wahyuningsih, R. (2023). Literature review of the connection between emotional intelligence and employee performance in organizations. *Multidisciplinary Reviews, 6*(4), 2023048. DOI: 10.31893/multirev.2023048

Lu, H. W., While, A. E., & Louise Barriball, K. (2005). Job satisfaction among nurses: A literature review. *International Journal of Nursing Studies, 42*(2), 211–227. DOI: 10.1016/j.ijnurstu.2004.09.003 PMID: 15680619

Machado, L. A. N., & de Castro, D. F. L., Junior. (2019). Strategic human resources management and hotel performance. *European Journal of Tourism, Hospitality and Recreation, 9*(2), 117–130. https://tmstudies.net/index.php/ectms/article/view/1065

Machado, C., & de Castro, P. J.Junior. (2019). Strategic human resource management and hotel performance: A systematic literature review. *Journal of Human Resources in Hospitality & Tourism, 18*(4), 434–460.

Madera, J. M., Dawson, M., & Guchait, P. (2017). The role of HR in promoting ethical leadership and psychological safety in the hospitality industry. *Cornell Hospitality Quarterly, 58*(3), 239–249.

Madera, J. M., Dawson, M., Guchait, P., & Belarmino, A. M. (2017). Strategic human resources management research in hospitality and tourism: A review of current literature and suggestions for the future. *International Journal of Contemporary Hospitality Management, 29*(1), 48–67. DOI: 10.1108/IJCHM-02-2016-0051

Majeed, S., Kim, W. G., & Kim, H. (2023). The role of emotional intelligence in frontline employees' customer-oriented behaviors. *Journal of Services Marketing, 37*(1), 78–92.

Malik, N. (2023). Organizations Should Maintain Employee's Work-Life Balance. *Journal of Economics Finance and Management Studies, 6*(8). Advance online publication. DOI: 10.47191/jefms/v6-i8-29

Mamatha, C. N. (2024). A Study on Workplace Flexibility and Job Quality in the Gig Economy: Perspective from Workers and Employers. *International Journal of Research Publication and Reviews, 5*(9), 3028–3038. DOI: 10.55248/gengpi.5.0924.2666

Mantello, P., & Ho, T. M. (2023). Emotional AI and the future of wellbeing in the post-pandemic workplace. *AI & Society, 39*(4), 1883–1889. DOI: 10.1007/s00146-023-01639-8 PMID: 36776535

Mäntymäki, M., Baiyere, A., & Islam, A. K. M. N. (2019). Digital platforms and the changing nature of physical work: Insights from ride-hailing. *International Journal of Information Management, 49*, 452–460. DOI: 10.1016/j.ijinfomgt.2019.08.007

Marecki, Ł. J. (2024). Impact of work-life balance on employee productivity and well-being. *Journal of Management and Financial Sciences, 50*(50). Advance online publication. DOI: 10.33119/JMFS.2023.50.9

Marginson, S. (2016). High participation systems of higher education. *The Journal of Higher Education*, *87*(2), 243–271. DOI: 10.1080/00221546.2016.11777401

Marler, J. H., & Boudreau, J. W. (2017). An evidence-based review of HR Analytics. *International Journal of Human Resource Management*, *28*(1), 3–26. DOI: 10.1080/09585192.2016.1244699

Martin, D. C. (2024). Building Organizational Readiness through Effective Succession Planning.

Maslow, A. H. (1943). A theory of human motivation. *Psychological Review*, *50*(4), 370–396. DOI: 10.1037/h0054346

Maslow, A. H. (1954). *Motivation and personality*. Harper & Row.

Masten, A. S. (2014). *Ordinary magic: Resilience in development*. Guilford Press.

Matsumoto, D., & Hwang, H. C. (2019). Cultural influences on emotional expression and regulation. In D. Matsumoto & H. C. Hwang (Eds.), Handbook of culture and emotion (2nd ed., pp. 3–24). Cambridge University Press.

Mayer, J. D., Roberts, R. D., & Barsade, S. G. (2008). Human Abilities Emotional Intelligence. The Annual Review of Psychology, 59, 507-536. - References - Scientific Research Publishing. (2015). Scirp.org. https://www.scirp.org/reference/referencespapers?referenceid=1536420

Mayer, J. D., Caruso, D. R., & Salovey, P. (2016). The Ability Model of Emotional Intelligence: Principles and Updates. *Emotion Review*, *8*(4), 290–300. DOI: 10.1177/1754073916639667

McKay, D. (2019). *What is career development? This is how to progress in your job*. Cleverism. Retrieved September 23, 2019, from https://www.cleverism.com/what-is-career-development/

McKinsey & Company. (2021). Defining the skills citizens will need in the future world of work. https://www.mckinsey.com/industries/public-sector/our-insights/defining-the-skills-citizens-will-need-in-the-future-world-of-work

Mehra, G. (1991). Mental Health as a moderator variable of intrinsic job satisfaction and occupational stress. *Psychological Studies*.

Meijerink, J., & Keegan, A. (2019). Conceptualizing human resource management in the gig economy: Toward a platform ecosystem perspective. *Journal of Managerial Psychology*, *34*(4), 214–232. DOI: 10.1108/JMP-07-2018-0277

Mercer. (2025, August). *Results of the 2025 US Turnover Surveys*. Retrieved from https://www.imercer.com/articleinsights/workforce-turnover-trends

Merlin, J. I., & Soubramanian, P. (2024). From self-awareness to social savvy: how intrapersonal skills shape interpersonal competence in university students. *Frontiers in Psychology*, 15. DOI: 10.3389/fpsyg.2024.1469746

Meseguer-Sánchez, V., Gálvez-Sánchez, F. J., López-Martínez, G., & Molina-Moreno, V. (2021). Corporate Social Responsibility and Sustainability: A Bibliometric Analysis of Their Interrelations. *Sustainability (Basel)*, *13*(4), 16–36. DOI: 10.3390/su13041636

Metcalfe, B. D. (2011). Women, empowerment and development in Arab Gulf states: A critical appraisal. *Gender in Management*, *26*(3), 189–205. DOI: 10.1108/17542411111130988

Miao, C., Humphrey, R. H., & Qian, S. (2022). A meta-analysis of emotional intelligence and work attitudes. *Journal of Occupational and Organizational Psychology*, *95*(1), 1–27.

Michaelson, R., & Farouk, M. (2023, May 8). Inflation, IMF austerity and grandiose military plans edge more Egyptians into poverty. *The Guardian*. https://www.theguardian.com/global-development/2023/may/08/inflation-imf-austerity-and-grandiose-military-plans-edge-more-egyptians-into-poverty

Midlage, L. (2025). Emotional Intelligence in the Workplace. *Enhancing Team Dynamics.*, *4*(1), 17–22. DOI: 10.59298/RIJCIAM/2025/411722

Miller, D. (1991). Stale in the saddle: CEO tenure and the match between organization and environment. *Management Science*, *37*(1), 34–52. DOI: 10.1287/mnsc.37.1.34

Mir, A. A., & Mufeed, U. (2016). Employee retention–A key tool for achieving competitive advantage. *International Journal of Engineering and Management Research (IJEMR)*, *6*(6), 334–337.

Mir, R. A., & Rastogi, E.R.A. (2025). Mitigating employee turnover in hospitality industry through emotional intelligence: Evidence from Kashmir India. *Geo Journal of Tourism and Geosites*, *58*(1), 250–270. DOI: 10.30892/gtg.58144-1429

Mohnblatt, D. (2023, January 16). Egyptian economy continues to deteriorate with future uncertain. *The Media Line*. https://themedialine.org/by-region/egyptian-economy-continues-todeteriorate-with-future-uncertain/

Mondal, A., & Saha, B. (2017). Job satisfaction of secondary school teachers in relation to personality and emotional intelligence. *American Journal of Educational Research*, *5*(10), 1097–1101. DOI: 10.12691/education-5-10-11

Montgomery, T., & Baglioni, S. (2020). Defining the gig economy: Platform capitalism and the reinvention of precarious work. *The International Journal of Sociology and Social Policy*, *41*(9/10), 1012–1025. DOI: 10.1108/IJSSP-08-2020-0400

Morris, S. N. (2023). Cultural diversity in the workplace and the role of management. *American Journal of Industrial and Business Management*, *13*(5), 380–393. DOI: 10.4236/ajibm.2023.135024

Mousa, M. (2024a). From announcing their pregnancy to returning to work: The experience of pregnant street-level bureaucrats in non-Western public contexts. *Public Integrity*, •••, 1–17. DOI: 10.1080/10999922.2024.2304763

Mousa, M. (2024b). What determines the engagement of nurses in organizational learning post Covid-19? The role of street-level bureaucracy and Florence Nightingale theories. *Public Integrity*, •••, 1–16. DOI: 10.1080/10999922.2024.2348902

Mousa, M. (2025). Gig work, management education and changes in working conditions: A qualitative study. *Industrial and Commercial Training*, *57*(1), 82–98. DOI: 10.1108/ICT-07-2024-0066

Mousa, M., & Abdelgaffar, H. (2023). Career shock of hotel employees and their individual resilience: An exploratory study. *Consumer Behavior in Tourism and Hospitality*, *18*(2), 228–240. DOI: 10.1108/CBTH-06-2022-0134

Mousa, M., Avolio, B., & Pahlevan Sharif, S. (2023b). Emancipation and street-level bureaucracy in non-western contexts: The representation of neurodiverse individuals in public sector organizations. *Public Integrity*, *26*(4), 439–454. DOI: 10.1080/10999922.2023.2247867

Mousa, M., & Samara, G. (2022). Mental health of business academics within the COVID-19 era: Can meaningful work help? A qualitative study. *Employee Relations*, *44*(4), 764–784. DOI: 10.1108/ER-04-2021-0170

Mousa, M., Tarba, S., Arslan, A., & Cooper, C. (2023a). When extreme work becomes the norm: An exploration of coping strategies of public sector nurses. *Public Management Review*, *27*(1), 297–316. DOI: 10.1080/14719037.2023.2246493

Murphy, C., Klotz, A. C., & Kreiner, G. E. (2017). Blue skies and black boxes: The promise (and practice) of grounded theory in human resource management research. *Human Resource Management Review*, *27*(2), 291–305. DOI: 10.1016/j.hrmr.2016.08.006

Nabila, A., Pratiwi, R., & Usman, O. (2019). Effect of Work Experience, Age of Employee, Training, Emotional Intelligence, of Work Productivity. SSRN Electronic Journal. DOI: 10.2139/ssrn.3313230

Narimisaei, J., Naeim, M., Imannezhad, S., Samian, P., & Sobhani, M. (2024). Exploring emotional intelligence in artificial intelligence systems: a comprehensive analysis of emotion recognition and response mechanisms [Review of Exploring emotional intelligence in artificial intelligence systems: a comprehensive analysis of emotion recognition and response mechanisms]. Annals of Medicine and Surgery, 86(8), 4657. Wolters Kluwer. DOI: 10.1097/MS9.0000000000002315

Niere, M. I. E., Mecon, , Narsico, L. O., & Narsico, P. G. (2023). Workplace Stressors, Employee Welfare, and Productivity. *International Journal of Multidisciplinary Applied Business and Education Research*, *4*(12), 4379–4389. DOI: 10.11594/ijmaber.04.12.18

Nieves, J., & Quintana, A. (2018). Human resource practices and innovation in the hotel industry: The mediating role of human capital. *Tourism and Hospitality Research*, *18*(1), 72–83. DOI: 10.1177/1467358415624137

Noddings, N. (2013). *Caring: A relational approach to ethics and moral education* (2nd ed.). University of California Press.

Nwabuzor, N. (2018). *Exploring employee retention strategies in the US hotel industry* (Publication No. 10826121) [Doctoral dissertation, Walden University]. ProQuest Dissertations and Theses Global.

O'Boyle, E. H., Humphrey, R. H., Pollack, J. M., Hawver, T. H., & Story, P. A. (2011). The relation between emotional intelligence and job performance: A meta-analysis. *Personality and Individual Differences*, *51*(5), 507–516. DOI: 10.1016/j.paid.2011.06.003

OECD. (2019). Education at a Glance 2019. OECD. https://www.oecd.org/en/publications/education-at-a-glance-2019_f8d7880d-en.html

Ogunyomi, P., & Bruning, N. S. (2016). Human resource management and organizational performance of small and medium sized enterprises (SMEs) in Nigeria. *International Journal of Human Resource Management*, *27*(6), 612–634. DOI: 10.1080/09585192.2015.1033640

Okpilike, M. E. (2012). The place of social interaction in the Nigerian school system: Implications for school life. *Developing Countries Journal*, *2*(10), 132–142.

Oman, Z. U., Bhati, K., & Ahmed, A. (2025). The rise of the gig economy in India: Market domination and the need to regulate the future of work. *World Journal of Advanced Research and Reviews*, *25*(3), 1790–1798. DOI: 10.30574/wjarr.2025.25.3.0935

Oprescu, F., Jones, C., & Katsikitis, M. (2014). I PLAY AT WORK—Ten principles for transforming work processes through gamification. *Frontiers in Psychology*, *5*. Advance online publication. DOI: 10.3389/fpsyg.2014.00014 PMID: 24523704

Organisation for Economic Co-operation and Development. (2022). *OECD services trade restrictiveness index*. OECD Publishing.

Ozdemir, O., Han, W., & Dalbor, M. (2022). Economic policy uncertainty and hotel occupancy: The mediating effect of consumer sentiment. *Journal of Hospitality and Tourism Insights*, *5*(2), 253–273. DOI: 10.1108/JHTI-08-2020-0149

Paauwe, J. (2009). HRM and performance: Achievements, methodological issues and prospects. *Journal of Management Studies*, *46*(1), 129–142. DOI: 10.1111/j.1467-6486.2008.00809.x

Paauwe, J., Wright, P., & Guest, D. (2013). HRM and performance: What do we know and where should we go? In Paauwe, J., Wright, P., & Guest, D. (Eds.), *Human resource management and performance: Achievements and challenges* (pp. 1–15). Wiley.

Pace, F., & Sciotto, G. (2021). Gender Differences in the Relationship between Work–Life Balance, Career Opportunities and General Health Perception. *Sustainability (Basel)*, *14*(1), 357. DOI: 10.3390/su14010357

Palhad, S., Onwubu, S. C., Singh, R. P., Thakur, R., Thakur, S., & Mkhize, G. (2023). The Benefits and Challenges of the Gig Economy: Perspective of Gig Workers and Small Medium and Micro Enterprises (SMMEs) in South Africa. *African Journal of Inter/Multidisciplinary Studies*, *5*(1), 1. DOI: 10.51415/ajims.v5i1.1051

Panadero, E. (2017). A review of self-regulated learning: Six models and four directions for research. *Frontiers in Psychology*, *8*, 422. Advance online publication. DOI: 10.3389/fpsyg.2017.00422 PMID: 28503157

Pande, N. (2024). What Are The Economic Implications Of The Rise Of The Gig Economy On Employment Stability And Benefits? *IOSR Journal of Business and Management*, *26*(10), 1. DOI: 10.9790/487X-2610070113

Pandit, D., Joshi, M. P., Sahay, A., & Gupta, R. K. (2018). Disruptive innovation and dynamic capabilities in emerging economies: Evidence from the Indian automotive sector. *Technological Forecasting and Social Change*, *129*, 323–329. DOI: 10.1016/j.techfore.2017.09.035

Papa, A., Dezi, L., Gregori, G. L., Mueller, J., & Miglietta, N. (2018). Improving innovation performance through knowledge acquisition: The moderating role of employee retention and human resource management practices. *Journal of Knowledge Management*, *22*(8), 1671–1692. DOI: 10.1108/JKM-09-2017-0411

Parigi, P., & Ma, X. (2016). The gig economy. *XRDS Crossroads The ACM Magazine for Students*, *23*(2), 38–41. DOI: 10.1145/3013496

Parveen, M., Maimani, K., & Kassim, N. M. (2017). Quality of work life: The determinants of job satisfaction and job retention among RNs and OHPs. *International Journal for Quality Research*, *11*(1), 173–194. DOI: 10.18421/IJQR11.01-10

Payne, R. A., Hovarter, R., Howell, M., Draws, C., & Gieryn, D. (2018). Succession planning in public health: Addressing continuity, costs, and compliance. *Nurse Leader*, *16*(4), 253–256. DOI: 10.1016/j.mnl.2018.05.008

Pedersen, L. H., Andersen, L. B., & Thomsen, N. (2020). Motivated to act and take responsibility: Integrating insights from community psychology in PSM research. *Public Management Review*, *22*(7), 999–1023. DOI: 10.1080/14719037.2020.1740307

Petriglieri, G., Ashford, S. J., & Wrzesniewski, A. (2018). Agony and Ecstasy in the Gig Economy: Cultivating Holding Environments for Precarious and Personalized Work Identities. *Administrative Science Quarterly*, *64*(1), 124–170. DOI: 10.1177/0001839218759646

Pine, B. J., & Gilmore, J. H. (1998). Welcome to the experience economy. *Harvard Business Review*, *76*, 97–105. PMID: 10181589

Pintrich, P. R. (2000). The role of goal orientation in self-regulated learning. In Boekaerts, M., Pintrich, P. R., & Zeidner, M. (Eds.), *Handbook of self-regulation* (pp. 451–502). Academic Pres. DOI: 10.1016/B978-012109890-2/50043-3

Poh, M. (2017). *5 characteristics of a positive work environment*. Hongkiat. Retrieved November 18, 2017, from https://www.hongkiat.com/blog/positive-working-environment/

Pollard, T. M. (2001). Changes in mental well-being, blood pressure and total cholesterol levels during workplace reorganization: The impact of uncertainty. *Work and Stress*, *15*(1), 14–28. DOI: 10.1080/02678370110064609

Powell, W. W., & Snellman, K. (2004). The knowledge economy. *Annual Review of Sociology*, *30*(1), 199–220. DOI: 10.1146/annurev.soc.29.010202.100037

Prado, J. C. A., & Torres, R. A. Z. (2019). Validation of the Wong and Law Emotional Intelligence Scale for Chilean managers. *Suma Psicologica*, *26*(2), 110–118. Advance online publication. DOI: 10.14349/sumapsi.2019.v26.n2.7

Pregnolato, M., Bussin, M. H., & Schlechter, A. F. (2017). Total rewards that retain: A study of demographic preferences. *SA Journal of Human Resource Management*, *15*(1), 1–10. DOI: 10.4102/sajhrm.v15i0.901

Prendergast, C., & Topel, R. H. (1996). Favouritism in organizations. *Journal of Political Economy*, *104*(5), 958–978. DOI: 10.1086/262048

Prentice, C. (2020). Emotional intelligence and the hospitality workforce: A systematic review. *Anatolia*, *31*(2), 331–342.

Prentice, C., & Nguyen, M. (2021). The role of emotional intelligence in the service encounter: A systematic review. *Journal of Service Theory and Practice*, *31*(1), 1–24.

Press Ganey. (2024, July 17). *Employee engagement in 2024: Trends, challenges, and opportunities.* Retrieved from https://info.pressganey.com/press-ganey-blog-healthcare-experience-insights/employee-engagement-in-2024-trends

Prokhorova, M. P., Лебедева, Т. Е., Shkunova, A. A., Sineva, N. L., & Казначеева, С. Н. (2020). Emotional Intelligence as a Factor of Corporate Culture. DOI: 10.2991/assehr.k.200723.058

Proto, E. (2016). Are happy workers more productive? *IZA World of Labor: Evidence-Based Policy Making*. Advance online publication. DOI: 10.15185/izawol.315

Pulakos, E. D., Arad, S., Donovan, M. A., & Plamondon, K. E. (2000). Adaptability in the workplace: Development of a taxonomy of adaptive performance. *The Journal of Applied Psychology*, *85*(4), 612–624. DOI: 10.1037/0021-9010.85.4.612 PMID: 10948805

Radhakrishnan, A., & Roy, N. S. (2023). Gig Economy Workers' Livelihood: A Qualitative Study of Ride-Hailing Platforms in Bangalore City, India. *Artha Vijnana*. Advance online publication. DOI: 10.21648/OPST6018

Radhika, J., & Mahalakshmi, P. (2024). Diversity, equity, and inclusion practices and employee well-being. *International Journal of Management Research and Review*, *14*(2), 88–101.

Rafaqat, S., Rafaqat, S., Rafaqat, S., & Rafaqat, D. (2022). The impact of workforce diversity on organizational performance. *Journal of Economics and Behavioral Studies*, *14*(2), 39–50. DOI: 10.22610/jebs.v14i2(J).3301

Rahman, A. A., & Hassan, M. K. (2020). Faith-based human resource practices in Islamic banking: Evidence from Malaysia. *International Journal of Islamic and Middle Eastern Finance and Management*, *13*(4), 655–673. DOI: 10.1108/IMEFM-01-2019-0008

Raisch, S., & Krakowski, S. (2021). Artificial intelligence and management: The automation–augmentation paradox. *Academy of Management Review*, *46*(1), 192–210. DOI: 10.5465/amr.2018.0072

Ramachandran, M., & Kulandai, A. (2024). Gig Workers: A Paradigm Shift in the Indian Workforce—A Bibliometric Analysis and Future Directions. *Metamorphosis*. Advance online publication. DOI: 10.1177/09726225241257731

Ramya, M., Santhanakrishnan, C., Janani, M., & Poonkodi, S. (2026). A Comparative Analysis of Network Intrusion Detection Systems in Machine Learning and Deep Learning for Securing IoT devices. In *Improving Threat Detection, Network Security, and Incident Response With AI* (pp. 1-20). IGI Global Scientific Publishing.

Rane, V. (2024). Platform-based Gig Workers: a Blind Spot in the Indian Labour Laws. SSRN Electronic Journal.DOI: 10.2139/ssrn.4821229

Rane, D. (2011). Employee Job Satisfaction: An essence of organization. *HRM Review*, *11*(27), 10–16.

Ran, X., & Zhao, Y. (2023). Behind the flexibility: Insufficient occupational injury protection of gig workers in China. *Frontiers in Public Health*, *11*, 1117180. Advance online publication. DOI: 10.3389/fpubh.2023.1117180 PMID: 37139392

Reade, C. (2009). Human resource management implications of terrorist threats to firms in the supply chain. *International Journal of Physical Distribution & Logistics Management*, *39*(6), 469–485. DOI: 10.1108/09600030910985820

Reid, M. (2005). Applying succession management benefits for leadership continuity. [JBER]. *Journal of Business & Economics Research*, *3*(6). Advance online publication. DOI: 10.19030/jber.v3i6.2782

Ren, Y., Guo, Q., Zhu, H., & Ying, W. (2019). The effects of economic policy uncertainty on China's economy: Evidence from time-varying parameter FAVAR. *Applied Economics*, *52*(29), 1–19. DOI: 10.1080/00036846.2019.1707475

Reshma, J., & Velmurugan, G. (2024). Organisational and Job Satisfaction: A Decade of Research Trends, Systematic Mapping, and Bibliometric Analysis. *International Journal of Computational and Experimental Science and Engineering*, *11*(1). Advance online publication. DOI: 10.22399/ijcesen.741

Robertson, C. J., & Fadil, P. A. (1999). Ethical decision making in multinational organizations: A comparison of global values. *Journal of Business Ethics*, *19*(4), 385–392. DOI: 10.1023/A:1005742016867

Robles, M. M. (2012). Executive perceptions of the top 10 soft skills needed in today's workplace. *Business Communication Quarterly*, *75*(4), 453–465. DOI: 10.1177/1080569912460400

Rodrigues, R., Teixeira, N., & Costa, B. V. (2024). The Impact of Perceived Leadership Effectiveness and Emotional Intelligence on Employee Satisfaction in the Workplace. *Merits*, *4*(4), 490–501. DOI: 10.3390/merits4040035

Rodriguez-Keyes, E., Schneider, D., & Keenan, E. K. (2021). Emotional labor in online teaching: Faculty experiences during COVID-19. *Journal of Social Work Education*, *57*(Suppl. 1), 123–136.

Roeser, R. W., Skinner, E., Beers, J., & Jennings, P. A. (2013). Mindfulness training and teachers' professional development: An emerging area of research and practice. *Child Development Perspectives*, *6*(2), 167–173. DOI: 10.1111/j.1750-8606.2012.00238.x

Rosenzweig, E. Q., Chen, X. Y., Song, Y., Baldwin, A., Barger, M. M., Cotterell, M. E., Dees, J., Injaian, A. S., Weliweriya, N., Walker, J. R., Wiegert, C. C., & Lemons, P. P. (2024). Beyond STEM attrition: Changing career plans within STEM fields in college is associated with lower motivation, certainty, and satisfaction about one's career. *International Journal of STEM Education*, *11*(1), 15. DOI: 10.1186/s40594-024-00475-6

Rossidis, I., Belias, D., & Vasiliadis, L. (2021). Standardization vs. adaptation of HRM practices in the hospitality industry: A systematic literature review. *Tourism and Hospitality*, *2*(4), 365–379.

Rossidis, I., Belias, D., & Vasiliadis, L. (2021). Standardization vs. localization in HRM: A review of the literature in the hospitality context. *Journal of Tourism. Heritage & Services Marketing*, *7*(1), 3–10.

Rossidis, I., Belias, D., & Vasiliadis, L. (2021). Strategic human resource management in the international hospitality industry: An extensive literature review. In Kavoura, A., Kefallonitis, E., & Theodoridis, P. (Eds.), *Strategic innovative marketing and tourism* (pp. 173–182). Springer., DOI: 10.1007/978-3-030-72469-6_22

Roumpi, D. (2023). Rethinking the strategic management of human resources: Lessons learned from Covid-19 and the way forward in building resilience. *The International Journal of Organizational Analysis*, *31*(1), 215–231. DOI: 10.1108/IJOA-09-2021-2974

Roumpi, D., & Delery, J. E. (2019). Strategic HRM: Where do we go from here? In Wilkinson, A., Bacon, N., Lepak, D., & Snell, S. (Eds.), *The Sage handbook of human resource management* (pp. 423–438). Sage. DOI: 10.4135/9781529714852.n25

Roumpi, D., Magrizos, S., & Nicolopoulou, K. (2020). Virtuous circle: Human capital and human resource management in social enterprises. *Human Resource Management*, *59*(5), 401–421. DOI: 10.1002/hrm.22002

Roy, B. (2018). Factors determining employee retention: A study in banks. *International Journal of Management Studies*, *5*(2), 101–108. DOI: 10.18843/ijms/v5i2(11)/13

Rozell, E. J., Pettijohn, C. E., & Parker, R. S. (2006). Emotional intelligence and dispositional affectivity as predictors of performance in salespeople. *Journal of Marketing Theory and Practice*, *14*(2), 115–124. DOI: 10.2753/MTP1069-6679140203

Sachdeva, T. (2024). The Gig Economy in India: Unpacking the Economic and Social Implications. *International Journal for Research Publication and Seminars*, *15*(3), 166–176. DOI: 10.36676/jrps.v15.i3.1465

Sahinoz, S., & Cosar, E. E. (2018). Economic policy uncertainty and economic activity in Turkey. *Applied Economics Letters*, *25*(21), 1517–1520. DOI: 10.1080/13504851.2018.1430321

Sahlberg, P. (2011). *Finnish lessons: What can the world learn from educational change in Finland?* Teachers College Press.

Saks, A. M. (2006). Antecedents and consequences of employee engagement. *Journal of Managerial Psychology*, *21*(7), 600–619. DOI: 10.1108/02683940610690169

Salas, E., Sims, D. E., & Burke, C. S. (2005). Is there a "big five" in teamwork? *Small Group Research*, *36*(5), 555–599. DOI: 10.1177/1046496405277134

Saleem, A., Khan, R. A., & Manzoor, A. (2018). Determinants of project team retention in private consultancies of Pakistan. *Global Management Journal for Academic & Corporate Studies*, *8*(2), 150–161.

Salleh, M. J., & Ibrahim, N. A. (2021). Educational leadership through Islamic principles: Pakistani university case studies. *Educational Management International*, *15*(4), 112–128.

Salovey, P., & Mayer, J. D. (1990). Emotional Intelligence. Imagination, Cognition and Personality, 9(3), 185–211. Sagepub. https://doi.org/DOI: 10.2190/DUGG-P24E-52WK-6CDG

Salovey, P., & Grewal, D. (2020). The science of emotional intelligence. *Current Directions in Psychological Science*, *29*(6), 531–535.

Sari, Y. N., Amin, S., & Kurniawan, D. (2022). Mediating effect of positive emotions on work-life balance and employee performance. *BISMA Jurnal Bisnis Dan Manajemen*, *16*(1), 20. DOI: 10.19184/bisma.v16i1.28234

Saxena, A. (2014). Workforce diversity: A key to improve productivity. *Procedia Economics and Finance*, *11*, 76–85.

Schalk, R. (2004). Changes in the employment relationship across time. In Coyle-Shapiro, J., Shore, L. M., Taylor, S., & Tetrick, L. E. (Eds.), *The employment relationship: Examining psychological and contextual perspectives* (pp. 284–311). Oxford University Press. DOI: 10.1093/oso/9780199269136.003.0013

Schaufeli, W. B., & Bakker, A. B. (2004). Job demands, job resources, and their relationship with burnout and engagement: A multi-sample study. *Journal of Organizational Behavior*, *25*(3), 293–315. DOI: 10.1002/job.248

Schweitzer, K., & Graebe, J. (2024). Leadership Succession Planning for ANCC Accredited Providers in Nursing Continuing Professional Development. *Journal of Continuing Education in Nursing*, *55*(7), 321–325. DOI: 10.3928/00220124-20240610-02 PMID: 38959097

Seligman, M. E. P. (2011). *Flourish: A visionary new understanding of happiness and well-being*. Free Press.

Sen, A. (1999). *Development as freedom*. Alfred A. Knopf.

Shaffer, M. A., Kraimer, M. L., Chen, Y.-P., & Bolino, M. C. (2012). Choices, challenges, and career consequences of global work experiences: A review and future agenda. *Journal of Management*, *38*(4), 1282–1327. DOI: 10.1177/0149206312441834

Shanafelt, T. D., Ripp, J., & Trockel, M. (2020). Understanding and addressing sources of anxiety among health care professionals during the COVID-19 pandemic. *Journal of the American Medical Association, 323*(21), 2133–2134. DOI: 10.1001/jama.2020.5893 PMID: 32259193

Sharew, A. (2018). *Assessment of employee retention practices in Development Bank of Ethiopia* [Master's thesis, St. Mary's University]. Institutional Repository.

Sharma, A., Shin, H., Santa-María, M. J., & Nicolau, J. L. (2021). The role of emotional intelligence in the service recovery performance of hospitality employees. *International Journal of Hospitality Management, 94*, 102837.

Sharma, P., Kong, T. T. C., & Kingshott, R. P. (2021). Internal service quality as a driver of employee satisfaction, commitment and performance: Exploring the role of employee readiness for change. *Journal of Service Management, 32*(1), 118–140.

Shaw, J. D., Dineen, B. R., Fang, R., & Vellella, R. F. (2009). Employee–organization exchange relationships, HRM practices, and quit rates of good and poor performers. *Academy of Management Journal, 52*(5), 1016–1033. DOI: 10.5465/amj.2009.44635525

Siambi, J. K. (2022). Leadership succession planning and organization transition: A review of literature. International Journal of Managerial Studies and Research, 10(3), pp. (16-30).

Sikora, D. M., Thompson, K. W., Russell, Z. A., & Ferris, G. R. (2016). Reimagining overqualified human resources to promote organizational effectiveness and competitive advantage. *Journal of Organizational Effectiveness: People and Performance, 3*(1), 23–42. DOI: 10.1108/JOEPP-03-2015-0012

Silva, D., & Coelho, A. (2018). The impact of emotional intelligence on creativity, the mediating role of worker attitudes and the moderating effects of individual success. *Journal of Management & Organization, 25*(2), 284–302. DOI: 10.1017/jmo.2018.60

Singh, M. (1990). Job satisfication, Job involvement and Participation amongest different categories of bank employees. *Journal of the Indian Acedamy of applied. Psychology (Savannah, Ga.).*

Skrzypczyńska, K. (2020). Significance of emotional intelligence in leadership. *Journal of Positive Management, 9*(4), 66. DOI: 10.12775/JPM.2018.155

Slaski, M., & Cartwright, S. (2002). Health, performance and emotional intelligence: An exploratory study of retail managers. *Stress and Health, 18*(2), 63–68. DOI: 10.1002/smi.926

Smedley, D., & Rayment, A. (2019). Changes in employment law: Mitigating the gig economy. *Nursing and Residential Care*, *21*(6), 345–348. DOI: 10.12968/nrec.2019.21.6.345

Solis-Grant, M. J., Espinoza-Parcet, C., Sepulveda-Carrasco, C., Perez-Villalobos, C., Rodriguez-Nunez, I., Pincheira-Martinez, C., Gomez-Varela, J. P., & Aranguiz-Ibarra, D. (2022). Inclusion at universities: Psychometric properties of an inclusive management scale. *PLoS One*, *17*(1), e0262011. https://doi.org/10.1371/journal.pone.0262011

Song, Y. (2024). Impact of Technological Advancements on Work and Employment Patterns. *Journal of Advanced Sociology*, *5*(1), 63–76. DOI: 10.47941/jas.1856

Soulami, M., Benchekroun, S., & Galiulina, A. (2024). Exploring how AI adoption in the workplace affects employees: a bibliometric and systematic review [Review of Exploring how AI adoption in the workplace affects employees: a bibliometric and systematic review]. Frontiers in Artificial Intelligence, 7. Frontiers Media. DOI: 10.3389/frai.2024.1473872

Spector, P. E. (1997). *Job satisfaction: Application, assessment, causes, and consequences* (Vol. 3). Sage. DOI: 10.4135/9781452231549

Spreitzer, G. M., Cameron, L., & Garrett, L. (2017). Alternative work arrangements: Two images of the new world of work. *Annual Review of Organizational Psychology and Organizational Behavior*, *4*(1), 473–499. DOI: 10.1146/annurev-orgpsych-032516-113332

Spring Health. (2025, April 11). *How HR Leaders Can Tackle Employee Burnout*. Retrieved from https://www.springhealth.com/blog/how-hr-leaders-can-tackle-employee-burnout

Stewart, A., & Stanford, J. (2017). Regulating work in the gig economy: What are the options? *Economic and Labour Relations Review*, *28*(3), 420–437. DOI: 10.1177/1035304617722461

Storey, J., Ulrich, D., & Wright, P. M. (2019). *Strategic human resource management: A research overview*. Routledge. DOI: 10.4324/9780429490217

Suleman, Q., Hussain, I., Syed, M. A., Parveen, R., Lodhi, I. S., & Mahmood, Z. (2019). Association between emotional intelligence and academic success among undergraduates: A cross-sectional study in KUST, Pakistan. *PLoS One*, *14*(7), e0219468. Advance online publication. DOI: 10.1371/journal.pone.0219468 PMID: 31291333

Sun, L. Y., Aryee, S., & Law, K. S. (2007). High-performance human resource practices, citizenship behavior, and organizational performance: A relational perspective. *Academy of Management Journal, 50*(3), 558–577. DOI: 10.5465/amj.2007.25525821

TalentSmart. (2019). Emotional intelligence 2.0: Annual emotional intelligence report. Retrieved from https://www.talentsmarteq.com

Tambe, P., Cappelli, P., & Yakubovich, V. (2019). Artificial intelligence in human resources management: Challenges and a path forward. *California Management Review, 61*(4), 15–42. DOI: 10.1177/0008125619867910

Tan, Z. M., Aggarwal, N., Cowls, J., Morley, J., Taddeo, M., & Floridi, L. (2021). The ethical debate about the gig economy: A review and critical analysis [Review of The ethical debate about the gig economy: A review and critical analysis]. Technology in Society, 65, 101594. Elsevier BV. DOI: 10.1016/j.techsoc.2021.101594

Taxer, J. L., & Frenzel, A. C. (2015). Facets of teachers' emotional lives: A quantitative investigation of teachers' genuine, faked, and hidden emotions. *Teaching and Teacher Education, 49*, 78–88. DOI: 10.1016/j.tate.2015.03.003

The Educator. (2024, August 21). *Education Sector Ranks Lowest for Employee Wellbeing, Great Place To Work® Report Reveals*. Retrieved from https://the-educator.org/education-sector-ranks-lowest-for-employee-wellbeing-great-place-to-work-report-reveals/

The Statesman. (2023), available at: https://www.thestatesman.com/opinion/egypts-downturn-1503244320.html

Theurer, C. P., Tumasjan, A., Welpe, I. M., & Lievens, F. (2018). Employer branding: A brand equity-based literature review and research agenda. *International Journal of Management Reviews, 20*(1), 155–179. DOI: 10.1111/ijmr.12121

Thiétart, R. A., Florence, A. P., Angot, J., Baumard, P. H., & Blanc, A. (1999). *Méthodes de recherche en management*. Dunod.

Towns, A. (2019). *Effective strategies to increase employee retention in higher education institutions* (Publication No. 27544502) [Doctoral dissertation, Walden University]. ScholarWorks.

Trading economics (2023), available at: https://tradingeconomics.com/egypt/unemployment-rate

Tung, V. W. S., & Law, R. (2022). The potential for tourism and hospitality experience research using artificial intelligence. *Journal of Travel Research, 61*(4), 735–739.

Turhan, M. (2014). Organizational cronyism: A scale development and validation from the perspective of teachers. *Journal of Business Ethics, 123*(2), 295–308. DOI: 10.1007/s10551-013-1839-3

Turnea, E. S. (2018). Attraction and retention of the employees: A study based on multinationals from Romania. *Procedia-Social and Behavioral Sciences*, *238*, 73–80. DOI: 10.1016/j.sbspro.2018.03.010

Tursunbayeva, A., Pagliari, C., Lauro, S. D., & Antonelli, G. (2021). The ethics of people analytics: Risks, opportunities and recommendations. *Personnel Review, 51*(3), 900–921. DOI: 10.1108/PR-12-2019-0680

Tussyadiah, I. P. (2020). A review of research into automation in tourism: Launching the Annals of Tourism Research Curated Collection on Artificial Intelligence and Robotics in Tourism. *Annals of Tourism Research, 81*, 102883. DOI: 10.1016/j.annals.2020.102883

Ugoani, J. (2021). Emotional Intelligence and its Impact on Effective Human Resource Management. *International Journal of Economics and Financial Research, 71*(71), 5–13. DOI: 10.32861/ijefr.71.5.13

Ulrich, D., & Dulebohn, J. H. (2015). Are we there yet? What's next for HR? *Human Resource Management Review, 25*(2), 188–204. DOI: 10.1016/j.hrmr.2015.01.004

Umamaheswari, S., & Krishnan, J. (2016). Work force retention: Role of work environment, organization commitment, supervisor support and training & development in ceramic sanitary ware industries in India. *Journal of Industrial Engineering and Management (JIEM)*, *9*(3), 612–633. DOI: 10.3926/jiem.1915

UNCTAD. (2021). *World investment report 2021: Investing in sustainable recovery*. United Nations.

UNESCO. (2017). Education for Sustainable Development Goals Learning Objectives. UNESCO. - References - Scientific Research Publishing. (2017). Scirp.org. https://www.scirp.org/reference/referencespapers?referenceid=3510556

Utaminingsih, S., Hariyadi, A., & Sofiyati, D. (2024). Analysis of Learning Leadership Management Based on Soft Skill. *Uniglobal Journal of Social Sciences and Humanities, 3*(2), 18–25.

van Doorn, N., Ferrari, F., & Graham, M. (2022). Migration and Migrant Labour in the Gig Economy: An Intervention. *Work, Employment and Society, 37*(4), 1099–1111. DOI: 10.1177/09500170221096581 PMID: 37588943 van Zyl, C. J., & Stander, M. W. (2014). The psychometric properties of the Emotional Quotient Inventory (EQ-i 2.0) in a South African context. *SA Journal of Industrial Psychology*, *40*(1), 1–12. DOI: 10.4102/sajip.v40i1.1192

Vantage Circle. (2025, March 25). *Employee Engagement in Healthcare: Trends, Challenges, and Strategies*. Retrieved from https://www.vantagecircle.com/en/blog/employee-engagement-in-healthcare-industry/

Vasanthan, R., Babu, M. R. N., Dzuvichu, K., Chong, S. T., Rana, V. S., & Singh, A. (2025). Bridging social norms theory and community mobilization: Pathways for overcoming gender stereotypes in women's economic empowerment programs. *Enterprise Development & Microfinance, 35*(1), 159–176. ISSN: 1755-1978 (Print), 1755-1986 (Online)

Vasanthan, R., Nath Babu, M., Dzuvichu, K., & Chong, T. S., Singh Rana, V., & Singh, A. (2025). Bridging Social Norms Theory and Community Mobilization: Pathways for Overcoming Gender Stereotypes in Women's Economic Empowerment Programs. *Enterprise Development & Microfinance, 35*(1), 159–176. Retrieved from https://papjournals.com/index.php/edm/article/view/13

Vasanthan, R., Babu, M. N., Dzuvichu, K., Chong, T. S., Rana, V. S., & Singh, A. (2025). Bridging social norms theory and community mobilization: Pathways for overcoming gender stereotypes in women's economic empowerment programs. *Enterprise Development & Microfinance*, *35*(1), 159–176.

Velagaleti, S. B. (2024). Empathetic Algorithms: The Role of AI in Understanding and Enhancing Human Emotional Intelligence. *Deleted Journal*, *20*(3s), 2051–2060. DOI: 10.52783/jes.1806

Vial, G. (2021). Understanding digital transformation: A review and research agenda. *The Journal of Strategic Information Systems*, *28*(2), 118–144. DOI: 10.1016/j.jsis.2019.01.003

Wakabi, B. M. (2016). Leadership style and staff retention in organisations. *International Journal of Science and Research*, *5*(1), 412–416.

Wallo, A., & Coetzer, A. (2023). Understanding and conceptualising the daily work of human resource practitioners. *Journal of Organizational Effectiveness: People and Performance*, *10*(2), 180–198. DOI: 10.1108/JOEPP-01-2022-0013

Wang, D., Tsui, A. S., Zhang, Y., & Ma, L. (2003). Employment relationships and firm performance: Evidence from an emerging economy. *Journal of Organizational Behavior*, *24*(5), 511–535. DOI: 10.1002/job.213

Wiener, M., Cram, W. A., & Benlian, A. (2021). Algorithmic control and gig workers: A legitimacy perspective of Uber drivers. *European Journal of Information Systems*, *32*(3), 485–507. DOI: 10.1080/0960085X.2021.1977729

Williams, T. A., & Shepherd, D. A. (2016). Building resilience or providing sustenance: Different paths of emergent ventures in the aftermath of Haiti earthquake. *Academy of Management Journal*, *59*(6), 2069–2102. DOI: 10.5465/amj.2015.0682

Winkler-Titus, N., Gerber, C., & Ngalo, V. (2025). Well-being of remote workers: Work characteristics and challenges. *SA Journal of Human Resource Management*, *23*. Advance online publication. DOI: 10.4102/sajhrm.v23i0.2876

Wong, A. K. F., Kim, S., Kim, J., & Han, H. (2021). How the COVID-19 pandemic affected hotel employee stress: The moderating role of emotional intelligence. *International Journal of Hospitality Management*, *93*, 102798. DOI: 10.1016/j.ijhm.2020.102798 PMID: 36919180

Wong, C., & Law, K. S. (2017). The effects of leader and follower emotional intelligence on performance and attitude: An exploratory study. In *Routledge eBooks* (p. 97). Informa. DOI: 10.4324/9781315250601-10

Wong, K. P., & Chan, A. H. S. (2021). Exploration of the Socioecological Determinants of Hong Kong Workers' Work-Life Balance: A Grounded Theory Model. *International Journal of Environmental Research and Public Health*, *18*(20), 10732. DOI: 10.3390/ijerph182010732 PMID: 34682475

Wood, A. J., Graham, M., Lehdonvirta, V., & Hjorth, I. (2018). Good Gig, Bad Gig: Autonomy and Algorithmic Control in the Global Gig Economy. *Work, Employment and Society*, *33*(1), 56–75. DOI: 10.1177/0950017018785616 PMID: 30886460

World Bank. (2023). Annual Report. Www.worldbank.org. https://thedocs.worldbank.org/en/doc/e0f016c369ef94f87dec9bcb22a80dc7-0330212023/original/Annual-Report-2023.pdf

World Bank. (2023). https://documents.worldbank.org/en/publication/documents-reports/documentdetail/099624304122329292/idu07c72dd550d99104e560a5fd0e79e14053665

World Economic Forum. (2020). The future of jobs report 2020. https://www.weforum.org/publications/the-future-of-jobs-report-2020

World Economic Forum. (2020). *The future of jobs report 2020.* World Economic Forum.

World Health Organization. (n.d.). Mental health: Strengthening our response. World Health Organization. https://www.who.int/news-room/fact-sheets/detail/mental-health-strengthening-our-response

Wright, P. M., & Snell, S. A. (1998). Toward a unifying framework for exploring fit and flexibility in strategic human resource management. *Academy of Management Review*, *23*(4), 756–772. DOI: 10.2307/259061

Wright, P., & McMahan, G. (1992). Theoretical perspectives for strategic human resource management. *Journal of Management*, *18*(2), 295–322. DOI: 10.1177/014920639201800205

Wright, T. A., & Cropanzano, R. (1998). Psychological well-being and job satisfaction as predictors of job performance. *Journal of Occupational Health Psychology*, *5*(1), 84–94. DOI: 10.1037/1076-8998.5.1.84 PMID: 10658888

Wu, J. (2024). Social and ethical impact of emotional AI advancement: The rise of pseudo-intimacy relationships and challenges in human interactions. *Frontiers in Psychology*, *15*, 1410462. Advance online publication. DOI: 10.3389/fpsyg.2024.1410462 PMID: 39564589

Yadav, P. V., Kollimath, U. S., Chavan, T. V., Pisal, D. T., Giramkar, S. A., & Swamy, S. M. (2023), Impact of Artificial Intelligence (AI) in Talent Acquisition Process: A study with reference to IT Industry, *International Conference on Intelligent and Innovative Technologies in Computing, Electrical and Electronics (IITCEE)*, Bengaluru, India, 2023, pp. 885-889, DOI: 10.1109/IITCEE57236.2023.10090973

Yahya, K. K., & Faiz, W. M. (2020). Value-driven HR practices and employee outcomes in Malaysian healthcare organisations. *Asia Pacific Journal of Human Resources*, *58*(4), 565–583. DOI: 10.1111/1744-7941.12245

Yang, K., & Kassekert, A. (2010). Linking management reform with employee job satisfaction: Evidence from federal agencies. *Journal of Public Administration: Research and Theory*, *20*(2), 413–436. DOI: 10.1093/jopart/mup010

Yang, Y., & Konrad, A. M. (2011). Understanding diversity management practices: Implications of institutional theory and resource-based theory. *Group & Organization Management*, *36*(1), 6–38. DOI: 10.1177/1059601110390997

Yin, H., Huang, S., & Wang, W. (2019). Work environment characteristics and teacher well-being: The mediation of emotion regulation strategies. *International Journal of Environmental Research and Public Health*, *16*(23), 4717. DOI: 10.3390/ijerph16234717 PMID: 31779268

Yin, R. K. (1990). *Case study research: Design and methods* (5th ed.). Sage Publications.

Zafar, A., & Akhtar, G. K. H. (2020). Effect of succession planning on organizational growth. *Journal of Social Sciences and Humanities*, *59*(1), 21–33. DOI: 10.46568/jssh.v59i1.323

Zahoor, N., Roumpi, D., Tarba, S., Arslan, A., & Golgeci, I. (2024). The role of digitalization and inclusive climate in building a resilient workforce: An ability–motivation–opportunity approach. *Journal of Organizational Behavior*, *45*(9), 1431–1459. DOI: 10.1002/job.2800

Zapf, D. (2002). Emotion work and psychological well-being: A review of the literature and some conceptual considerations. *Human Resource Management Review*, *12*(2), 237–268. DOI: 10.1016/S1053-4822(02)00048-7

Zeithaml, V. A., Bitner, M. J., & Gremler, D. D. (2020). *Services marketing: Integrating customer focus across the firm* (8th ed.). McGraw-Hill.

Zhao, K., Hsieh, W., Faulkner, N., & Smith, L. (2025). Evidence-based diversity, equity, and inclusion frameworks in organizations. *Human Resource Development Review*, *24*(1), 15–31.

Zheng, J., & Zhang, T. (2025). Association Between AI Awareness and Emotional Exhaustion: The Serial Mediation of Job Insecurity and Work Interference with Family. *Behavioral Sciences (Basel, Switzerland)*, *15*(4), 401. DOI: 10.3390/bs15040401 PMID: 40282023

Zietlow, R. E. (2020). The New Peonage: Liberty and Precarity for Workers in the Gig Economy. SSRN Electronic Journal. DOI: 10.2139/ssrn.3641677

Zimmerman, B. J. (2002). Becoming a self-regulated learner: An overview. *Theory into Practice*, *41*(2), 64–70. DOI: 10.1207/s15430421tip4102_2

Zimmerman, B. J., & Moylan, A. R. (2009). Self-regulation: Where metacognition and motivation intersect. In Hacker, D. J., Dunlosky, J., & Graesser, A. C. (Eds.), *Handbook of metacognition in education* (pp. 299–315). Routledge.

Zimmerman, B. J., & Schunk, D. H. (2011). *Handbook of self-regulation of learning and performance*. Routledge.

Ződi, Z., & Török, B. (2021). Constitutional Values in the Gig-Economy? Why Labor Law Fails at Platform Work, and What Can We Do about It? *Societies (Basel, Switzerland)*, *11*(3), 86. DOI: 10.3390/soc11030086

About the Contributors

Varinder Singh Rana is a senior academic leader and internationally published researcher with over 24 years of experience in hospitality and tourism. He serves as Department Chair of Hospitality and Hotel Management and Deputy Director – Research at City University Ajman, UAE. He holds a PhD in Hospitality and has authored over 55 research publications and 15 academic books. His research focuses on sustainable tourism, hospitality technologies, green marketing, and AI applications in food and beverage systems. Dr. Rana holds multiple international patents and copyrights and has received numerous awards for research and innovation. He actively contributes as a keynote speaker, research supervisor, and academic resource person at global conferences and institutions.

Aisha Khan is an Assistant Professor at International American University, RAK, UAE. She holds a PhD in Sustainable HRM and has over five years of experience in teaching, research, and academic mentoring. Alongside her academic role, she has been working as an HR Consultant since 2019, supporting organizations in developing sustainable and strategic HR practices. Her research interests include sustainable HRM, strategic HRM, green leadership, emotional intelligence, and corporate governance. Dr. Khan has published in leading Scopus-, ABDC-, and ABS-indexed journals and actively presents her work at international conferences. She also contributes to the academic community as a session chair, moderator, and speaker at global conferences and webinars. Dr. Khan is committed to advancing sustainability and responsible management practices through research, teaching, and industry collaboration, aiming to create meaningful impact in both academia and professional practice.

***

Atanu Bhattacharya has Started the career in Front Office with Radisson Hotels in 2010 and served till the position of Lobby Manager. Joined the academics in 2014 and has been in association with some reputed colleges all over India such as Golden Regency Institute, AIMS College of Hotel Management, Regal College of Hotel Management & Tourism, Om Sterling Global University and is currently working as Head of the Department, Medhavi Skills University. He has 13 International Research Papers under his belt. He has also secured publishing authority for 6 Indian Patents under Intellectual Property Rights.

Arabela Briciu is Associate Professor at the Department of Social Sciences and Communication, Faculty of Sociology and Communication, Transilvania University of Braşov, Romania. She holds from 2016 a PhD in Mass Communication Studies Field of Research, from University of Bucharest, Faculty of Journalism and Communication. Her research interests are in the area of public and political discourse, social networks and organizational branding and identity. Her scientific activity produced in the last years was disseminated through several books and book chapters, more than 10 academic journal articles, more than 20 international and national conferences. She's also involved in two Erasmus + projects: ReNewEurope - Rediscovering „NewEurope" – On-Wheels summer school for Balkan/Central and Eastern Europe trans-border history and politics, (2020-1-PL01- KA203-081999) and IncEdu- Developing Inclusive Education for Students with Disabilities in Sri Lankan Universities (609871-EPP-1-2019-1-LK -EPPKA2-CBHE-JP). Her work focuses on discourse analysis, mainly qualitative research on the discursive interaction between media, public opinion and political agents. At the same time, she's been involved in publishing the results about promotion of cultural heritage and evaluation of mobile applications for cultural tourism.

Victor-Alexandru Briciu is Associate Professor at the Department of Social Sciences and Communication. He received his PhD in 2015 in Mass Communication Studies Field of Research, from University of Bucharest, Faculty of Journalism and Communication. His research and teaching interests are oriented towards communication, public relations campaigns and strategies, branding, online branding strategies and his scientific activity produced in the last years was disseminated through several books and book chapters, more than 10 academic journal articles, more than 25 international and national conferences. He's been involved in projects and grants investigating online place branding strategies and communication through Social Media.

Tanusree Chakraborty is a Ph. D in Applied Psychology from Calcutta University, MA (Applied Psychology) with Specialization in Organizational

Psychology, PGDHRM and MBA (HR), with 20 plus years of work experience. She has been associated with a number of B-Schools and Universities of repute in Kolkata, Madurai, Bangalore, and Chennai. Presently she is working with Administrative Staff College of India (ASCI), Hyderabad as a Faculty in the Centre for Management Studies. Having thoroughly good academic track record with university ranks, she is an Ex-research fellow of Indian Council of Medical Research. She has around 60 publications under her credit in reputed journals and books, among which Internet Research Journal, International Journal of Human Resource Management, International Journal of Productivity and Performance Management are great feathers in her cap. She has presented research papers in 80 plus international conferences of repute, where she has been awarded the Best Paper Award many times. She has conducted Management Development Programmes with the State Productivity Councils and National Productivity Councils. She has trained practicing managers of several Public and Private sector companies, in the areas of Behavioral Sciences and Human Resource Management. As a psychologist she has conducted Psychometric testing with 12,000 plus employees. As a trainer, she has trained 15,000 plus employees in her career. Companies where she has been a resource person include Indian Oil, BHEL, NHPC, NTPC, THDCIL, WBPDC, DVC, BPCL, DRDO, PFC, GAIL, ONGC, Exide Industries, NMDC, Power Grid Corp, Department of Science and Technology- GoI, National Institute of Communications Finance etc. Among the banks, she has associated herself as a trainer with State Bank of India, Canara Bank, Central Bank of India, Punjab National Bank, Axis Bank, etc. She has published books with the IGI Global Publishers, titled Appreciative Inquiry Approaches to Organizational Transformation, with Taylor and Francis, CRC Press, Human Resource Management in a Post-Epidemic Global Environment-Roles, Strategies, and Implementations, Agile Leadership for Industry 4.0 and Interdisciplinary Approaches in Management Education, Digitalization in Higher Education, Gender Equality in Modern Perspectives etc. A few more books are in the advanced stages of forthcoming publication. She has been a panel member in admission and recruitment processes, GDPIs conducted in academic institutes and corporate. Besides, she has also been a regular faculty for management institutes of repute including ASCI, teaching MBA and PGDM, where she has been a passionate teacher supporting students in academics and other institution building activities. She has been an active member in clubs and committees of the institutes she has worked for. She has been a reviewer and editor of reputed books and journals, and Editor-in Chief of the ASCI PGDM Chronicle- A Bi-annual Newsletter.

Denisa Gabor is a practitioner and an M.A. graduate of Transilvania University of Bra ov's Master's Program in Human Resources Management and Development. She also has a bachelor's degree from the same university. She is interested in the strategic evolution of human resources, particularly at the intersection of talent management, social media, and digital marketing. Her research explores how the ongoing digital transformation of the HR field creates new opportunities for employer branding and engaging the modern workforce.

Sanjit Cletus Gomes serves as the Dean of Studies at the International School of Hospitality Management (ISHM), Kolkata. With extensive academic and administrative experience, he plays a pivotal role in shaping the institution's academic framework, ensuring quality education, and fostering a culture of excellence.

Sowmya Kudanthai Ramalingam is a faculty with two decades of experience in teaching management subjects, research, publications, International and industrial relations. Currently holds the position of Professor in Management Studies, specializing in Human Resource Management and Organizational Behaviour at Vel Tech University in India. Presently tasked with overseeing International Relations within the School of Management. Additionally, Sowmya Kudanthai Ramalingam is a Research Fellow at INTI International University, Malaysia and International Advisory Board Member & Adjunct Researcher in Spectrum International university College, Malaysia. She has authored books, approximately 80 contributions in peer-reviewed national and international journals and proceedings that are indexed in Scopus. An active participant in more than 100 conferences, workshops, and seminars at both national and international levels. Her academic pursuits have taken her to the USA, Ethiopia, Nairobi, Egypt, Malaysia, Dubai, Sri Lanka, and Singapore for significant assignments. Sowmya Kudanthai Ramalingam is a Fellow of the World Business Institute, Australia, and has received several accolades, including the "Outstanding Faculty in Organization Behaviour" award in 2017, a national award for excellence in teaching and research in 2018, and the Indo-Thai academic award for "academic leadership" in 2019. She also possesses two years of overseas experience as an expatriate in Africa. She is open to extraordinary academic Opportunities, and Global Collaborations.

Sanjeev Kumar Is a Professor in Lovely Professional University Punjab India. He received Undergraduate in Hotel Management from Osmania University, Postgraduate in Tourism Management from Madurai Kamaraj University. He completed Doctor of Philosophy in Hospitality Management in 2019 from Amity University Jaipur India. His research areas lies in food Service Industry, his research focuses on Alcoholic beverages, Event management and Sustainable Management Practices, Metaverse, AI Machine Learning and Artificial Intelligence. He published more than 80 research papers, articles and chapters in Scopus Indexed, UGC

Approved and peer reviewed Journals and books. Dr. Sanjeev Kumar participated and acted as resource person in various National and International conferences, seminars, session chair, research workshops and industry talks and his work has been widely cited. Dr. Sanjeev also edited more than 20 books with various International Publishers such as IGI Global, Cambridge Scholars, Emerald, CABI, Bentham Science, Taylor & Francis. Dr Sanjeev is an active researcher and has published numerous research articles in prestigious National and International journals and books.

Rashmi Kumari received her B. Tech degree in Computer Science & Engineering from BIT Sindri, Dhanbad, India, in 2018 and MBA degree in Human Resource Management from BIT Mesra, Ranchi, India, in 2020. She is currently working toward the Ph.D. degree with Department of Management, Birla Institute of Technology Mesra, Ranchi, India. Her research interest includes Green Human Resource Management and Organisational Behaviour. She has authored or co-authored various research articles in prestigious journals, book chapters and conference proceedings.

Geetha Manoharan is currently working in Telangana as an Associate professor at SR University. She is the university-level PhD program coordinator and has also been given the additional responsibility of In Charge Director of Publications and Patents under the Research Division at SR University.

Manidipa Mukherjee is an Assistant Professor at the International School of Hospitality Management (ISHM), Kolkata. With academic expertise in Hospital Management, she actively mentors undergraduate and postgraduate students, bridging the gap between theoretical knowledge and industry practice.

Giselle P. Phillips is a higher education administrator, digital learning consultant, and academic with over a decade of experience at the University of the West Indies (UWI). She combines expertise in operational management, instructional design, and human resource development. As a senior administrator in the Office of the Campus Registrar, she oversees academic timetabling, staff supervision, and data-driven decision-making. Concurrently, as an Adjunct Lecturer and Course Developer, she designs and delivers postgraduate courses, integrates emerging technologies, and mentors research students. A PhD candidate in Human Resource Management, Giselle has presented internationally on emotional labour and organizational commitment and is a member of SHRM, ATD, and the International Academic Forum.

J. Shanthi Priya is a Ph.D. Research Scholar in the Department of Management at VelTech Rangarajan Dr.Sagunthala R&D Institute of Science and Techology. Shanthi Priya J. is an accomplished academic and educator in the field of Management, specializing in Finance and Human Resource Management. With a strong academic foundation and a passion for teaching, she has served as an Assistant Professor. Her involvement extends beyond teaching to participating in university-level, such as serving as Chief AUR for Anna University.

Varinder Singh Rana is Department Chair of Hospitality and Hotel Management and Deputy Director- Research at City University Ajman, Ajman, United Arab Emirates

Navneet Ranjan is the Head of Department – Hospitality & Tourism at Medhavi Skills University. He has been instrumental in developing industry-relevant curricula, mentoring students, and promoting experiential learning across academic programs. His research interests include vocational education models, competency-based training, and industry-academia collaboration. Navneet has led multiple initiatives that align academic learning with real-world applications in the hospitality sector. He is known for fostering innovation, enhancing student engagement, and building strong industry partnerships. This publication reflects his commitment to advancing research-driven education and professional excellence in hospitality and tourism.

S. Raja is an accomplished academic and researcher specializing in Human Resource and Marketing Management. He holds a PhD from Annamalai University and an MBA from Anna University. Currently serving as an Associate Professor and Research Supervisor at Vel Tech Rangarajan Dr. Sagunthala R&D Institute of Science and Technology in Chennai, Dr. Raja guides research scholars and contributes to curriculum development in Digital Marketing. With over 15 years of teaching experience, including his previous role as an Assistant Professor at SRM Valliammai Engineering College, Dr. Raja has made significant contributions as a research advisor, NPTEL coordinator, and project guide. He has authored seven books on management topics, published over 60 research articles, and presented papers at various national and international conferences'. Raja's research focuses on organizational climate, innovative work behaviour, and the impact of digital tools in management. His dedication to academic excellence has been recognised with multiple awards, including the Young Researcher Award.

S K Pooja is a very enthusiastic and determined PGDM student in the Administrative Staff College of India, specialising in Human Resources and Marketing. She is quite inclined towards People Management and has a goal of making a difference in the field with great strategies. She believes in the art of

People Management and is curious and passionate about research into developing Innovative HR Solutions, Talent Acquisition, and Employee Engagement. She is an analytical person and is great with people; therefore, she would be one emerging professional who can bring change to tomorrow's HR shape.

Timcy Sachdeva holds a doctorate degree in management, specializing in finance from Guru Gobind Singh Indraprastha University. With a teaching and research experience of 19 years, she has various publications in international journals, Scopus indexed and ABDC listed journals. Dr. Sachdeva has participated in many national and international conferences including IIMs, IIT and MDI and has chaired sessions in them as well. She is a sought-after trainer for financial econometrics and modeling and has conducted many FDPs for faculty and research scholars across India. She has also authored book on Fundamentals of Financial Modeling using Excel. Dr. Timcy Sachdeva is currently Associate Professor in Vivekananda Institute of Professional Studies-TC, affiliated to Guru Gobind Singh Indraprastha University.

V. S. Sharada is a Ph.D. scholar in the area of Organizational Behavior and Human Resource Management (OBHR) at the Indian Institute of Management Visakhapatnam (IIM-V), one of India's premier institutions. She holds a Post Graduate Diploma in Management (PGDM) from the prestigious Administrative Staff College of India (ASCI), Hyderabad, where she developed a strong foundation in research and academic inquiry. Sharada is a focused and passionate researcher, with a keen interest in human behavior, organizational culture, employee well-being, and the interplay of technology and human resource practices. Her scholarly pursuits are marked by an impressive track record: she has presented research papers at top-tier national and international conferences, including the Eastern Academy of Management (EAOM) 2025 and the Academy of Management (AOM) 2025 Annual Meetings—prestigious platforms known for thought leadership in management research. Her research contributions include several published book chapters across reputed international publishers, reflecting her commitment to advancing knowledge through rigorous academic writing. She has also undertaken research internships at leading institutions such as IIT Bombay, Goa Institute of Management (GIM), and NIT Silchar, where she honed her skills in empirical research, data analysis, and interdisciplinary exploration. Sharada brings a unique blend of analytical thinking and creative expression to her work. Trained in the classical Indian instrument Veena, she embodies the unity of art and science—an approach that enriches her research with depth, imagination, and holistic understanding. Her ability to merge logical reasoning with intuitive insight makes her a promising scholar poised to contribute meaningfully to academia and the field of organizational studies. With an unwavering dedication to academic excellence and a deep-seated curiosity for exploring human systems, Ms. Sharada stands out as a rising thought leader and an emerging researcher to watch in the OBHR domain.

Ridhima Sharma is an Associate Professor of Management at Vivekananda Institute of Professional Studies-Technical Campus. With a teaching and research experience of 14 years, she has contributed several articles to the journals of national & international repute and have presented papers in national and international conferences apart from authoring books. Her research interests include Customer Relationship Management, Sustainable consumer behavior, Mental Health, Artificial Intelligence. She is completed her Post Doc from Amity University, Dubai.

Amrik Singh is working with Lovely Professional University, Punjab, India. He is PhD in Hospitality Management from Kurukshetra University, India. His area of expertise in tourism and hospitality, human resource management, sustainability, waste management, green practices, restaurant and resort management. He has published more than 35 research papers including peer reviewed, ugc indexed and scopus indexed research articles and book chapters. He is associated as editorial board members and reviewers with reputed and scopus indexed journals.

Uday Pratap Singh is having twelve years of experience in hospitality with nine years of education and three years of experience in industry in front office. Currently working in Amity University Rajasthan as Assistant professor. Taking subjects of front office and tourism. Published research paper and patents in field of hospitality.

Koushik Vedula is currently pursuing a Post Graduate Diploma in Management (PGDM) at the Administrative Staff College of India (ASCI). His academic interests are centered around Finance and Human Resources (HR), with a strong focus on the synergy between Technology and Finance. Koushik is particularly passionate about exploring how technological advancements can revolutionize financial management and decision-making processes. He has actively participated in various projects and competitions in the fields of finance and management, aiming to contribute to research at the intersection of technology, finance, and organizational behavior.

Index

www.ingramcontent.com/pod-product-compliance
Lightning Source LLC
LaVergne TN
LVHW080902300926
849162LV00003B/515
* 9 7 9 8 3 3 7 3 6 3 9 5 0 *